LIB051005 R3/78

SIMON FRASER UNIVERS

SIMON Unler FRASER UNIVERSITY

Y0-BTB-764

REC'D APR

The social history of Canada

MICHAEL BLISS, GENERAL EDITOR

A history of farmers' movements

in Canada

LOUIS AUBREY WOOD

WITH AN INTRODUCTION BY FOSTER J. K. GRIEZIC

UNIVERSITY OF TORONTO PRESS
Toronto and Buffalo

© University of Toronto Press 1975

Toronto and Buffalo

Printed in Canada

ISBN (casebound) 0-8020-2079-8

ISBN (paperback) 0-8020-6193-1

Library of Congress Cataloging in Publication Data

Wood, Louis Aubrey, 1883-1955
  A history of farmers' movements in Canada

  (The Social history of Canada; 25 ISSN 0085-6207)
  Reprint of the 1924 ed. published by Ryerson Press, Toronto.
  Bibliography: p.
  1. Agricultural societies — Canada — History. 2. Agriculture and
  politics — Canada — History. 3. Patrons of Husbandry. 4. Agriculture,
  Cooperative — Canada — History. I. Title. II. Series: The Social
  history of Canada; 25.
  HD1486.C2W6 1975   338.1'06'271   73-91559
  ISBN 0-8020-2079-8

This book has been published with the assistance of a grant from the
Canada Council.

The original edition of this work was published in Toronto in 1924 by the
Ryerson Press.

An introduction

BY FOSTER J. K. GRIEZIC

A History of Farmers' Movements in Canada, still the best study of
the origins and early development of agrarian protest in Canada, was
not written by a career historian for an academic audience. Instead,
it was a history intended for both popular and scholarly readers,
written by a concerned intellectual whose chief previous publication
had dealt with seventeenth-century theology.

Louis Aubrey Lorne Wood, born 19 August 1883, was the only
son of George Wood, a businessman sales representative in London,
Ontario, and his wife Selina (Dobbin), a former school teacher. After
elementary and secondary schooling in London and one year at
Western University of Ontario (now the University of Western Ontario), he completed his studies at the University of Toronto, graduating with an Honours History Bachelor of Arts degree in 1904. At
Toronto he was influenced by professors George Wrong of the Department of History and James Mavor of the Department of Political
Economy.[1] Wood did well in history, but took time to develop his
competence in economics; he achieved a first class standing in his
final year after mediocre results the preceding two. Undecided about
a future career, but leaning towards theology, he took a Bachelor of
Divinity degree at Montreal Presbyterian College between 1904 and
1908, graduating as gold medalist and recipient of the McCorkill
travelling scholarship. He continued his formal education at the University of Heidelberg, again stressing theology, but also attending
courses in history, political science, international law, and economics. Wood received his doctorate *in Historia cum laude superato,
iura ,et honores* from Heidelberg in 1911; his dissertation was on
'The Form and Origin of Milton's Antitrinitarian Conception.'

Returning to Canada, Wood embarked on a varied teaching
career. He lectured in religious history at the fledgling Robertson
Presbyterian College at Edmonton in 1912-13. During his tenure
there, he married Dora Elson, daughter of Peter Elson, a prominent
farmer and MP who represented East Middlesex for the Conservatives
in the House of Commons from 1904 to 1913. Wood returned to
London in 1913, joined the Department of History at Western, and
was appointed Professor in 1917. He taught a wide range of histories
and also offered courses in the Department of Political Economy. By
1920 he had relinquished his teaching connection with the Department of History to concentrate on economics, offering courses on
socialism, labour, transportation, banking, and other topics. He

also assisted in the establishment of a Department of Business Administration.

In 1924, the year in which *A History of Farmers' Movements in Canada* was published, Wood accepted a position as assistant professor in the Department of Economics at the University of Oregon at Eugene, Oregon. There he taught introductory economics and specialized courses in labour relations. In 1928-9 he was Sterling Research Fellow at Yale and in 1933-4 was visiting Professor of Economics at the University of Chicago. In 1930 Wood was promoted to Associate Professor at Oregon and five years later, Professor. On his retirement in 1949 he was appointed Professor Emeritus, a position he held until his death in 1955. After settling in Oregon, Wood became an American citizen and was active in Democratic politics. During the 1930s he advised state and federal government agencies dealing with the problems of the depression.[2] In 1930 he was a member of Oregon's Committee on Unemployment and later was an adviser to the Industrial Accident Commission and a member of the Board of Directors of the National Institute of Immigrant Welfare. In 1938, he served as a research member of the Subcommittee on Seasonal Agricultural Labour under the auspices of the Pacific Coast Regional Committee of the Social Science Research Council. He supported Franklin D. Roosevelt's 'New Deal' policies and those of Roosevelt's successor, Harry S. Truman. Wood was nominated as the Democratic candidate, but was unsuccessful in the election for Congressman from Oregon's Fourth Congressional District in 1946, and in 1948 and 1950 tried but failed to receive the Democratic senatorial nomination.

Although he was not a prolific writer, Wood had gained early writing experience contributing to the 'Reporters' Folio' section of the *Presbyterian College Journal* in Montreal. His doctoral dissertation, a well argued piece of work, was published in booklet form in 1911. His first two books were in the Chronicles of Canada series, co-edited by his former history professor at Toronto, George M. Wrong. *The War Chief of the Six Nations: A Chronicle of Joseph Brant* xvi (Toronto 1914) and *The Red River Colony: A Chronicle of the Beginnings of Manitoba* xxi (Toronto 1915) are slim productions based on secondary material. *A History of Farmers' Movements in Canada,* easily his most important book, was followed by one other major study, *Union-Management Cooperation on the*

Railroads (New Haven, Conn. 1931) in the Yale Publications in Economics, Social Science, and Government series. The latter book is a somewhat uncritical study of the relationship between organized labour and management on the railroads, strongly endorsing co-operation and unjustifiably optimistic of the benefits produced by the system. Indeed, Wood's uncritical approach led him to ignore the significance of his conclusion that 'the companies receive more lucrative returns from practices of co-operation than do the [working] men' (p 235). According to Wood, improvement of the labourers' lot could be left safely to the caprice of management.

It is difficult to establish precisely when Wood became interested in the social, economic, and political manifestations of the farmers' movements in Canada. He had, of course, lived through the period of greatest agrarian dissatisfaction with the eastern, monopolistic domination of Canada's rapid economic expansion. He had no experience as a farmer, but the Grange and the Patrons of Industry were strong in the London region where he grew up in the last quarter of the nineteenth century. Furthermore, Wood's interest in reform is not surprising inasmuch as he exhibited a number of the characteristics of the social gospeller as described by Richard Allen in *The Social Passion: Religion and Social Reform in Canada 1914-1928* (Toronto 1971). He was a staunch Presbyterian; he attended the Presbyterian college when that denomination was reconsidering its role vis-à-vis the social and economic conditions of the period;[3] and he had married a devout Methodist, whose church officers also were re-evaluating the church's position on social reform. Between 1917 and 1920, when Wood's interests were turning from history to current economic issues, the agitation and discontent of organized farmers and organized labour were at their height. In 1920 Wood's courses on Canadian post-Confederation industrial development used such books as Edward Porritt's *Sixty Years of Protection in Canada* (Winnipeg 1913) and Gustavus Myers' *History of Canadian Wealth* (Chicago 1914).[4] In his combined course on labour conditions, socialism, and syndicalism one of the recommended texts was O.D. Skelton's *Socialism: A Critical Analysis* (Boston 1911). From 1922 to 1924 Wood offered a course in rural economics which included readings on rural land banks and credit, and direct legislation.

These courses coincided with Wood's interest in the farmers' movements. His reformism was evident in his advocacy of a minimum wage law for women and minors in Ontario, although this issue did not have the support of the United Farmers of Ontario. He seemed to believe in the validity of the farmers' grievances and was generally emphathetic to their cause. Wood, like other academics such as C.B. Sissons and James Mavor, was attracted to the reformism of the farmers' movements and their struggles to improve their position in Canadian society. This led to his researching and writing *A History of Farmers' Movements in Canada.*[5]

The book is an admirable and judicious detailed record of the means used by farmers between 1870 and 1924 to remedy the economic, social, and political injustices from which they suffered. They urged practical economic and political reforms — cheaper transportation, improved marketing practices, nationalization of public utilities, increased availability of farm credit, reform of government fiscal policy to cheapen the necessities of life, the introduction of participatory democracy, and other measures — as well as calling for a moral purification of business and government. Their methods of pursuing their aims shifted from diverse co-operative economic ventures to the political activity which produced the independent political action of the 1920s. Wood rightly emphasizes the importance in agrarian history of early organizations like the Grange, which originated from the indigenous desire to correct injustices to farmers and provided the foundation for subsequent expansion. Although he does not analyze the social composition of the early agrarian groups, Wood does demonstrate how the impetus for organization radiated from Protestant Anglo-Saxons of southwestern Ontario. This leadership shifted to the prairies in the early decades of the twentieth century. Indeed, the prairie leaders, many of whom were Ontario-born, provided considerable assistance in organizing the United Farmers of Ontario and the UF Co-op, an important point that Wood neglects. When former leaders such as John Kennedy and J.J. Morrison believed that the time was ripe to organize Quebec farmers, however, others such as T.A. Crerar demurred.[6] As a result they lost a valuable opportunity to make headway there, for, as Letourneau indicates, there was considerable agrarian discontent in Quebec,[7] a situation only incidently referred to by Wood.

Wood's study shows how complaints about urbanization and rural depopulation, stemming from inadequate consideration of agricultural needs, began to be voiced as early as the 1870s. The tariff, so vital to the industrial-manufacturing class, was always a focus of agrarian dissatisfaction. One of the significant themes of agrarian rhetoric was the myth, perpetrated by intellectuals and the upper classes, of the idyllic, sturdy, industrious, self-sufficient yeoman farmer, indispensable to the development of Canada.[8] Only gradually did farmers come to see themselves as an exploited, ill paid economic and social group, and even then they referred to themselves as a 'group' or 'class' interchangeably, eschewing, as does Wood himself, the use of the term in the Marxian sense. They turned to direct political action only when it seemed that working through the traditional parties did not allow for sufficient consideration of their problems or a realistic input into the decision-making process. Wood perhaps minimizes the importance of agrarian opposition to conscription and of the formation of the Union government as a turning point in the politicization of farmers.[9] He does, however, illustrate how rank and file farmers were ill used by leaders such as Caleb Mallory, who was willingly co-opted by the Liberal party to arrange various saw-offs in the federal election of 1896.[10] This pattern of collaboration was later followed by R.C. Henders, T.A. Crerar, Ontario Premier E.C. Drury, Progressive whip J. Fred Johnston, and Robert Forke.

A History of Farmers' Movements in Canada presents agrarian protest as an uneven development, but one generally moving forward in linear progress. By 1924, Wood concluded optimistically, farmers were near the summit of their achievement, with bright prospects for future gains. In fact, after 1924 the farmers' movements underwent complex changes which had only limited success in reforming Canadian society. In the 1920s political involvement, the most visible expression of farmer discontent, experienced a marked decline. Existing organizational structures were fractured, to be succeeded by new organizations tending towards redefined goals that were economically class-oriented. The depression of the 1930s inflicted heavy blows on the farmers, particularly in the grain-growing prairies, producing a resurgence of political and organizational activity. The farmers' political action through the CCF and, later, the NDP, was limited regionally and was necessarily in alliance with the industrial labouring class; farmers' organizations in the post-World War II years continued to be wracked by differences over objectives and methods, precluding the possibility of a united farmers' national front. Despite increased government participation in agriculture, the continuance of agrarian complaints and organizational activity indicated that farmers recognized the continuing need for constant articulation of their particular point of view.

The dissident Progressive party that arrived so dramatically on the Canadian political scene between 1918 and 1921 fragmented. The erosion, begun in the autumn of 1922, continued with the formation of the 'Ginger Group,' which objected to chairman Robert Forke's friendly relationship with Prime Minister King's Liberal administration. An attempt to reorganize and restructure the party in a conference at Regina, on 4-6 August 1925, failed. Former leader Crerar's proposed reorganization on national lines, eliminating contests with Liberal candidates and broadening the membership to include non-farmers, was received with suspicion and distrust by farmer political leaders; they interpreted the suggestion as not simply an attempt to establish a western party, but as another attempt to align them with the Liberals and undermine the farmers as an economic class.[11] The already notorious division between followers of Crerar and Henry Wise Wood was further accentuated. Progressive representation declined sharply in the 1925 and 1926 general elections, when there were returned twenty-four and twenty unhyphenated Progressives, respectively, almost all from the prairies. After the 1926 election, in which Crerar actively campaigned for the Liberals, Robert Forke was co-opted into the Liberal party as Minister of Immigration. Four years later Forke was appointed to the Senate, Crerar entered King's government as Minister of Railways and Canals, and Progressive representation dwindled in the federal election to a corporal's guard of twelve, which included nine United Farmers of Alberta, two Saskatchewan Progressives, and one United Farmers of Ontario representative. Popular support dropped from 23.1 per cent in 1921 to 3.2 per cent in 1930; no Progressive candidates were returned in 1935.[12]

The farmers' provincial political parties fared a little better than their national counterpart, but this success was restricted to the prairies. After their 1923 defeat in Ontario, UFO representation fell to six in 1930 and one sole survivor in 1937; in Quebec and the

Maritimes farmer members of the legislative assemblies had disappeared by 1925. In Saskatchewan during the early 1920s the Progressives were unable to break the hold of the Liberal government that was, in effect, a pseudo-farmers' government and was closely allied with the Saskatchewan Grain Growers' Association. By 1923 John Maharg, former Progressive MP and briefly a provincial cabinet minister in Premier Martin's Liberal administration, was leader of the small Progressive group that formed the official opposition. In 1929 the remnants of this group co-operated with the resurgent Conservative party to oust the Liberal machine. A provincial farmer government remained in office in Manitoba until 1936; they last contested a provincial election as United Farmers of Manitoba candidates in 1932; one year later they began their career of coalescing with the old-line parties. The United Farmers of Alberta continued in office until 1935, when the regime was toppled by a combination of factors. Scandal forced Premier J. Brownlee to resign, leaving his successor, R.D. Reid, vulnerable to the messianic appeal of Social Credit, which promised an end to the ravages of the depression and which reigned in Alberta until 1971.

Why did the farmers' political movements lose support? In the 1920s the inability to resolve conflicting views of organization, methods, and aims constantly wracked the movements. Manitoba Progressives flirted with and were finally won by the Liberals; Saskatchewan Progressives were alternately wooed and combatted by the two old parties; United Farmers of Ontario supporters returned to their former political affiliations, while only the United Farmers of Alberta remained an economic group movement. Furthermore, the organizational basis of the Progressives was decimated from 1923 to 1928. Membership in the farmers' organizations fell dramatically. The Canadian Council of Agriculture, 150,000 strong in 1921, had less than half that membership a year later. Provincial organizations experienced a similar dropping off:[13] UFO membership plunged from a high of 60,000 in 1921 to approximately 7,000 in 1923; the United Farmers' organizations of New Brunswick, Nova Scotia, British Columbia, and Quebec disapeared by 1925. Both the Canadian Countil of Agriculture, the farmers' national pseudo-political organization, and the United Farmers of Ontario withdrew from active politics in 1923. A year later the Saskatchewan Grain Growers' Association retired from politics, as did the United Farmers of Manitoba in 1928. The provincial organizations, suspicious of political opportunism, prohibited their executives from holding joint offices in political or other organizations.

The political movement and the existing organizations were undermined by the severe post-war agricultural depression from 1920 to 1925, which was particularly difficult on the prairies. This was evident in 1920 and 1921 when the price of wheat fell 50 per cent and livestock prices also dropped while the cost of living remained high, a trend which continued until agricultural prices began to improve in 1925.[14] During these years farm wholesale prices fell more than all wholesale prices. All the older farmers' organizations were adversely affected by the farmers' financial plight.

Farming also underwent a process of change in the 1920s. There was a shift towards large-scale operations that required more farm machinery. The number of farmers remained relatively stable but the number of owner-occupied farms declined and acreage was increased in an attempt to compensate for the drop in prices.[15] The seriousness of the farmers' situation was confirmed in the Report of the Select Committee of the House of Commons which investigated agricultural conditions in 1923, by the 1923 appointment of a federal royal commission to investigate the grain trade, and by the Progressives, who spearheaded attempts to break the international shipping combine that increased grain growers' marketing costs. And there were other indications of the farmers' weakened condition. Farmers' co-operatives in Nova Scotia and New Brunswick failed. Tight money, high interest rates, and bank and business failures led to demands for monetary and banking changes to assist farmers.[16] It may be, as Professor Lipset asserts, that Progressive support was 'more a product of immediate discontent than of long-term crisis' and that as conditions that spawned the movement were erased so too was the movement,[17] but the conditions did not disappear. Although the number of automobiles, trucks, and combines increased on the prairies in the late 1920s, a heavy burden of mortgage and credit debt went hand in hand with a slowed growth in farm investment.[18] Obviously for most farmers the twenties had not been 'roaring.' Farmers continued to seek ways to defend their position as independent owners against the concentration of power in the hands of the small class of Canadian capitalists.

Western farmers were urged to renew organizational activity, stressing self-help on economic class lines. The Farmers' Union, a militant, radical organization founded late in 1921 at Ituna, Saskatchewan, led the way. By 1926 it had absorbed the SGGA, and the United Farmers of Canada (Saskatchewan Section) was formed. The UFC consisted of approximately 20,000 members, slightly less than one-half of the membership of the SGGA at its height in 1921. The UFC's Manitoba branch was absorbed by the UFM in 1928; in Alberta it maintained friendly relations with the UFA, instead of organizing independently. In 1924 Quebec farmers formed a successor to the FUQ, L'Union Catholique des Cultivateurs, which also emphasized co-operative action.

Farmers' Union supporters were leaders in advocating economic improvement through producers' co-operatives, especially wheat pools, to counter the pressures of large-scale commercialized and mechanized agriculture. There was dissatisfaction with the profit motivation of the Saskatchewan Co-operative Elevator Company and the United Grain Growers, two successful and highly diversified farmer joint-stock companies involved in the grain trade and in the wholesale commodities business. Yet the aim of the dissidents was not so much to overthrow capitalism as to bring about adjustments to permit farmers to retain a favourable position within the system. Unable to obtain federal government assistance in marketing through the re-establishment of the Wheat Board, they turned to consumer co-operative pooling as a panacea for their problems.

Pools, the farmers believed, would minimize marketing costs, maximize returns, and provide greater consideration for small-scale farmers through co-operative action and a central selling agency. In 1923 the Farmers' Union leaders brought Aaron Sapiro, an American lawyer experienced with producer pools in the United States, to Canada to propagandize the benefits of pooling. Provincial wheat pools were established in Alberta in 1923, Saskatchewan and Manitoba in 1924, and Ontario in 1926. The Wheat Pools created a central selling agency, the Canadian Co-operative Wheat Producers' Company, to market their grain. Financial assistance and personnel were obtained initially from the United Grain Growers (who soon dropped their support of the pools, however) and the provincial governments. Differences over the length of contract and whether to include coarse grains along with wheat were resolved by 1928 and the Pools became in effect grain pools. The Pools and the selling agency provided an alternative to the private grain trade and the farmers' joint-stock companies, attempted to control the flow of wheat to market, and provided patronage dividends and service at cost.

The improved agricultural situation from 1925 to 1929 corresponded with the period of the Pools' success. Production, agricultural prices, weather, and pest conditions improved, and farmers' energies were directed towards organizing and supporting the Pools. Pool leaders such as L.C. Brouillette, A.J. McPhail, Colin Burnell, and Henry Wise Wood de-emphasized political involvement to concentrate on farmers' economic improvement. Pool strength increased significantly from 1924 to 1929, when membership totalled approximately 140,000.[19] Pools handled more than 52 per cent of western Canadian wheat and by 1930 owned and operated 1,640 country elevators.[20]

The growing strength of the Pools was shown in the struggle for primacy between them and the older farmers' joint-stock companies. In 1926, after two quarrelsome years, the SCEC sold its facilities to the Saskatchewan Pool. In Manitoba there was constant friction between the UGG and the Pool between 1926 and 1930. Crerar, who retained the presidency of the UGG while in the Commons from 1917 to 1925, opposed selling the company's elevator facilities to the Manitoba Pools and only his astute move in questioning the legality of such action at the 1925 annual meeting saved the company from consummating the transaction. The UGG supported the private grain companies in opposing the Pools' demand that the farmers have the right to designate the terminal elevator for their grain, a dispute which was resolved in the Pools' favour in 1927. Other differences, such as the recurrent complaint against mixing to upgrade poor quality wheat, also divided the UGG and the Pools. In 1929 the UFC and the Pools ousted the UGG from the Canadian Council of Agriculture because many farmers equated the company with big business. The following year the UGG resigned from the Co-operative Union of Canada because of opposition from these same farmer organizations, which denied that the UGG was a co-operative because of its reluctance to implement patronage dividends. By 1929 the Pools were ascendent.

The depression wreaked havoc on Canadian farmers and their attempts to break free from their quasi-colonial economic status, particularly in the prairies where agricultural effort had to be concentrated on simple survival. A very large but poor quality crop was harvested in 1928; markets were contracting and prices decreasing. The loss of agrarian income by 1929 was sufficient to decrease national income figures. The Pools, which had withheld their wheat from the world market in hopes that prices would rise, watched helplessly as wheat prices dropped in the face of an international wheat glut. Canada number 1 Northern plummetted to 38 cents a bushel in 1932, the lowest in its history, and agricultural prices as a whole dropped 66 per cent. Prairie provincial governments assisted the Pools, but as their financial resources dwindled so too did the Pools'. In 1931, with the Pools facing bankruptcy, R.B. Bennett appointed J.I. MacFarland, an experienced grain businessman, to administer the Pools' central selling agency, but ruinous prices and a virtually stagnant market were almost impossible obstacles to overcome. Natural calamities such as unparalleled drought worsened the farmers' situation. Lack of money, clothing, and food was common. Farmers abandoned their homes in droves. Others remained, perhaps mesmerized by the alluring promise of the region that Jean Burnet has called 'Next-Year Country'. Relief assistance was provided through federal, provincial, and municipal agencies for more than 125,000 destitute prairie farm families.

In 1935 the federal government became more directly involved in trying to offset the impact of the depression on the farmers. The Prairie Farm Rehabilitation Administration was established in that year to help farmers save themselves and the soil and water of the prairies. Still conditions worsened. Drought, hordes of grasshoppers and caterpillars, rust, and uncommonly cold winters combined to turn large areas of the prairies into a dust bowl. Indeed, within two years approximately 18,000,000 acres of land, or one-quarter of the arable land of Canada, were rendered uncultivable.[21] Farmers' net income remained disastrously low. Additional aid was supplied to complement the Farm Loans Act of 1927 by the Prairie Farm Assistance Act of 1939 which provided direct cash payments to farmers in low-yield areas of the prairies and the Peace River district of British Columbia. Assistance was contingent, however, upon municipal funds and the relief program in effect; in most instances farmers interpreted it as being too little too late.

Another expedient of the Conservative government was the replacement of the selling agency of the Pools by a Canada Wheat Board in July 1935 to conduct the marketing of wheat. The Board was retained reluctantly in 1939 by the King government, which also encouraged private marketing. The Board set quotas on the amounts the farmers could deliver and instituted a price supports system, which, nonetheless, fell short of western grain growers' expectations.[22] Wheat prices remained depressed at 54 and 53 cents per bushel from 1939 to 1941. The farmers' situation improved by 1943 as the price support minimum for wheat was increased and price supports were provided for other agricultural products like milk and cheese. A number of international wheat agreements were concluded in the post-war years in an attempt to stabilize the marketing and price of wheat. The Board became the sole wheat marketing agency and in 1949 was given control of western coarse grains. It has since undergone minor changes and displays a grudging sensitivity to farmers' demands for increased price supports.

Farmers' interest in direct political action also revived during the depression. In Saskatchewan in 1926 some members of the UFC formed a Political Association, independent of the UFC, and at the 1931 annual meeting successfully urged the UFC to endorse direct political action. The UFC pursued a different type of expansion from that suggested by earlier Progressives, this time expanding along class lines. They helped form a Saskatchewan Farm-Labour party with a New Economic Policy that was admittedly socialist yet included planks from the Progressive platform of 1921.[23] In 1932 UFC and UFA leaders such as George Williams and Robert Gardiner contributed significantly to the founding of the Co-operative Commonwealth Federation. It was organized somewhat like the Progressive party as a loose federation of provincial affiliates which exercised considerable autonomy from the national body. The new party was unable to reconcile farm and labour organizations, however, and its proposals for agriculture did not attract widespread support from other farm organizations. CCFers were also attacked, as had been their Progressive predecessors, as being communists or bolsheviks. The UFO initially endorsed the CCF but officially

UFA/CCF

withdrew its support in 1934. The UFM was not attracted to the CCF. In Alberta the UFA was unable to convert supporters to the CCF and in 1939 the UFA officially withdrew from politics. In Saskatchewan, where the industrial labour force was very small, the CCF was able to make appreciable gains for farmer politics. In 1937 it became the official opposition and seven years later formed the government, remaining in office for twenty years and being returned again in 1971. In other provinces, British Columbia, Ontario, and Manitoba, CCF strength relied on urban voters. The federal CCF returned seven members in 1935, two each from Manitoba and Saskatchewan and three from British Columbia. The UFA was wiped out in that election even though MPs such as W.T. Lucas campaigned as supporters of Social Credit theory.

Soc.Cr.

CCF

Social Credit and the CCF inherited the farmers' organizational structure and practice and used them for political purposes. The former, an amalgam of small businessmen and farmers, quickly lost its reformism and became ultra-conservative. The latter continued its legacy of agrarian political protest premised on agrarian socialism. The CCF retained Progressive reforms like abolition of the Senate, nationalization of transportation, communications, and energy resources, and belief in participatory democracy. But farmer political activities have never attained the fever pitch reached between 1919 and 1921. Most subsequent farmer organizations have not affiliated with political parties and have eschewed direct political action in favour of economic activity.

The privations of the depression contributed to the regrouping by farmers along economic lines. The Canadian Council of Agriculture had died by 1932 and no national body was created to fill the vacancy. As the United Farmers of Canada was unable to provide it, organizational leadership passed to the commercial farmers' organizations. In 1935 farmers' commodity and co-operative business enterprises in the prairies, Ontario, and Quebec formed the Canadian Chamber of Agriculture, renamed the Canadian Federation of Agriculture four years later. It is a loose association of farmer organizations, centred in Ottawa, whose major functions are to unite farmers, encourage improvement by better farming techniques and education, and lobby as a pressure group submitting farmer companies' demands to the federal government. The CFA represents farmer organizations from all Canadian provinces except Newfoundland.

The CFA has become a prestigious body, its legitimacy confirmed by appointments to various international agricultural conferences. Membership of its constituent organizations in 1972 was approximately 350,000. Not all farmers, however, were satisfied with the CFA.

From 1939 to 1960 a resurgence of farmer dissidence in the Progressive tradition occurred. Provincial farm organizations developed because of opposition to the influence of the farmers' commercial leaders in the CFA, its conservatism, and the desire to provide an effective voice for small farmers. The UFC was reactivated from 1939 to 1947 in Manitoba, Saskatchewan, and Alberta. The militancy of these new bodies was evident with the 1942 prairie farmers' March on Ottawa demanding increased wheat prices. They represented independent farmers and formed an Interprovincial Farm Council in 1947. Differences over the method of affiliation with the CFA, the co-operatives' right to speak for rank and file farmers, the means of organizing farmers provincially and pursuing farmers' demands, seemed insurmountable obstacles to unity within the farmers' movements.[24] The Farmers' Unions in 1946 struck and picketed agricompanies to back up their demands, while the CFA deplored the action. Farmers' Unions were established in Ontario and British Columbia in 1952 and 1955 respectively.

The National Farmers' Union, a loose federation of provincial farmers' unions centred at Saskatoon, was formed in 1960 to present a farmers' popular front. In 1954, amalgamation discussions between the CFA and the provincial farmers' unions broke down as they did in 1962 between the CFA and the NFU. Drought in the early 1960s, decreased income, costly transportation, an inadequate feed grains distribution policy, and the lack of assistance or consideration for small farmers increased the militancy of the NFU. It was reorganized under a federal charter in 1969, purports to represent rank and file farmers regardless of the type of agriculture pursued, and emphasizes provincial autonomy. Farmers from all provinces except Newfoundland and Quebec are represented and concerted effort has been made since 1970 to attract French-Canadian farmers from Quebec. Membership estimates vary from 30,000 to 75,000. The NFU is more critical than the CFA of government agricultural policies and advocates more radical proposals, such as collective bargaining and the check-off system for all marketing agreements. The NFU also submits formal recommendations to the government on agricultural policy.

Unlike the CFA, the NFU endorses direct confrontation by strikes, pickets, tractor parades, marches, boycotts, and the free distribution of produce to advertize their grievances to governments and the public. Neither the CFA nor the NFU endorses independent political action.

The verve and intensity of the farmers' movements have abated since the activity of the first three decades of the twentieth century and farmers have returned, with some success, to their earlier role as a pressure group. Farmers' agitation has prompted federal governments to provide greater assistance to agriculture. Legislation has provided increased credit and crop insurance, marketing boards and commissions, and programs to assist the rural community to adjust to social, economic, and technical change. Government action has been piecemeal, however, and, as V.C. Fowke pointed out in 1957, remains largely premised on the competitive system rather than introducing a system that produces secure higher returns for the farmer.[25] This assumption is only slowly changing as governments consider the extension of price supports and other programs to protect the small-scale or marginal farmer.

Despite the assistance offered farmers, difficulties remain. Factors such as weather are uncontrollable, but farming methods have changed drastically since the early years of the century. Although wheat is still king on the prairies, there has been considerable diversification and specialization with ever larger, more efficient farms. Farm income fluctuates, but generally farmers depend on outside sources to supplement it.[26] The farm labour force and the number of farmers and farms have decreased sharply in the past twenty-five years.[27] For many, farming is a precarious vocation. It is evident that a government agricultural policy encouraging larger farms, modernization, mechanization, increased production, and greater efficiency has not solved farmers' troubles.[28] Agricultural grievances include insufficient and badly structured marketing boards, high transportation costs, continuing rural depopulation, rising costs of production, and, as always, insufficient income. These grievances are not confined to western Canada, although western farmers are frequently the most vocal. Many prairie farmers believe that they are discriminated against by large private agribusinesses, railways, banks and financial institutions, and the manufacturing-industrial complex of central Canada which is favoured by the federal government. An unsympathetic, insensitive, and uninformed urban public has difficulty understanding the farmers. The status of farmers in Canadian society has clearly declined and their influence on the federal government's agricultural policy, despite the various marketing boards and other programs established under government aegis, has been limited.[29] On the other hand, the world-wide demand for food in the early 1970s meant significant short-term increases in the financial returns from farming in Canada, although prospects for the rest of the decade are uncertain.

Whether or not the impact of the agrarian movements to 1924 was beneficial to Canadian society is debatable. The objects of their political platforms were laudatory. Proposals like direct taxation, female suffrage, a degree of public ownership of utilities, energy sources, and transportation, and improved credit facilities were implemented. But when farmers' organizations gave priority to economic rather than political action after 1924 they lost much of their reforming zeal. Consequently the basic class and power structure of which they complained remains intact. The abuses of party politics have not been removed. The Senate has not been abolished, sources and amounts of campaign funds are only gradually coming under public scrutiny, political patronage is freely distributed, the House of Commons is predominantly a lawyers' club, and undue weight is given to the business community's demands. Crucial natural resources and transportation systems are not nationalized. The taxation system burdens those least able to pay, while corporations return attractive profits and receive generous tax concessions from the federal government. In a contest between organized business and organized farmers, the farmers were naïve to think they could confront the expertise and power of big business and win. In this sense L.A. Wood's *A History of Farmers' Movements in Canada* is a history of hopes still unfulfilled.

ACKNOWLEDGMENTS

I would like to acknowledge assistance from several individuals and institutions. Information was generously provided by Dr Wood's daughter, Mrs Lenore Hyslop of Eugene, Oregon, and his son, Fergus J. Wood of Silver Spring, Maryland. The registrars' offices of the University of Western Ontario, London, the University of Toronto, Montreal Presbyterian College, the University of Heidelberg, Germany, and Robertson Presbyterian College (now St Stephen's), Edmonton, Alberta, replied patiently to my many queries. The staff of the special collections libraries at the University of Western Ontario, the University of Toronto, the University of Heidelberg, and the University of Oregon also willingly assisted. Professor Robert Campbell, Chairman of the Department of Economics, University of Oregon, offered useful information. Carleton University provided financial assistance for research. Special thanks are extended to my wife Jean, who was a captive listener to the unravelling of Wood's career, and to Professor Michael Bliss, who has been an efficient and critical editor. Any errors that may remain are my responsibility.

NOTES

1 'Lebenslauf,' L.A. Wood, 'The Form and Origin of Milton's Antitrinitarian Conception' (London 1911) np
2 Eugene *Register-Guard,* 4 February 1955, p 1
3 See Stewart Crysdale, *The Industrial Struggle and the Protestant
Ethic in Canada: A Survey of Changing Power Structures and Chris-
tian Social Ethics* (Toronto 1961) chapter 2
4 *Western University Calendar 1919-1920* 104, 105, and subsequent
calendars up to 1923-4
5 Oregon's reform leadership in direct legislation and women's suffrage
was one of the models for farmer reformism and likely contributed
to Wood's decision to move there.
6 Queen's University Archives (QA), T.A. Crerar Papers, J. Kennedy to
Crerar, 23 May 1918
7 Firmin Letourneau, *Histoire de l'agriculture (Canada français)* Montreal 1959) 301-6, 273-6, 264-5
8 See, for instance, R. Cook, 'Stephen Leacock and the Age of Pluto-
cracy, 1903-1921,' in J.S. Moir, ed., *Character and Circumstance:
Essays in Honour of D.G. Creighton* (Toronto 1970); R. Allen, *The
Social Passion: Religion and Social Reform in Canada 1914-1928*
(Toronto 1971); R.W. Armstrong, *The Salt of the Earth* (Ottawa
1929); and Sir A.J. Macphail, *Essays in Politics* (London & New
York 1909).
9 See, for instance, F.J.K. Griezac [sic], 'The Honourable Thomas Alexander Crerar, Marquette Riding and the Union Government Election
of 1917,' *Transactions, Historical and Scientific Society of
Manitoba*, Series III, #28 (1971-2).
10 Public Archives of Canada (PAC) William Lyon Mackenzie King
Papers, J Series, LI, Alexander Smith to King, 25 August 1919. See
also J.D. Smart, 'The Patrons of Industry in Ontario' (unpublished
MA thesis, Carleton University 1969).
11 Regina *Leader,* 5, 7 August 1925; Winnipeg *Tribune,* 2, 3, 9, 14
September 1925; *Western Producer,* 10 September 1925
12 H.A. Scarrow, *Canada Votes* (New Orleans 1962) 35, 77. See also J.
Murray Beck, *Pendulum of Power* (Toronto 1968) 160-1, 202-3, and
M.C. Urquhart and K.A.H. Buckley, eds., *Historical Statistics of
Canada* (Toronto 1965) 620
13 Paul F. Sharp, *The Agrarian Revolt in Western Canada: A Survey
Showing American Parallels* (Minneapolis & London 1948) 161-2,

W.L. Morton, *The Progressive Party in Canada* (Toronto 1950) 212

14 Urquhart and Buckley, eds., p 358. See also *Canada Year Books 1919 to 1925*, particularly 1922-3, p 1009. Sharp, pp 167-8, 174-5

15 *Census of Canada* 1931, VII (Ottawa 1936) 18. A.E. Safarian, *The Canadian Economy in the Great Depression* (Toronto 1959) 22, 25. Also see M.A. Tremblay and W.J. Anderson, eds., *Rural Canada in Transition* (Ottawa 1966) 267, 325-6, and Urquhart and Buckley, eds., pp 351-2, 59

16 *CYB* 1922-3, 830-3, 870-3, 1008-9; Sharp 167-8, Safarian 25-6

17 S.M. Lipset, *Agrarian Socialism* (Berkeley & Los Angeles 1959) 60

18 Safarian 22-3, 25-6. See also James H. Gray, *Men against the Desert* (Saskatoon 1967) 21, 54. This is perhaps the best, but least known, book on the prairie farmers' struggle during the depression.

19 After 1926, when the UGG Annual Report began to show a marked decline in the number of shareholders, they were no longer recorded. The Pools recorded increased membership. See for instance, *Manitoba Wheat Pool Reports for Financial Year ending July 31, 1930*, p 3, and *Annual Reports* from 1926 to 1929. In 1926 the comparable totals were: UGG, 35,109 for the three prairie provinces, Manitoba, 18,628, Saskatchewan, 80,410, Alberta, 38,460. Ontario Grain Pool membership in 1927 totalled 13,200.

20 V.C. Fowke, *The National Policy and the Wheat Economy* (Toronto 1957) 241, 244

21 Gray 3

22 Fowke, *The National Policy and the Wheat Economy* 263ff.

23 Lipset 79-80. Cf. Morton, *The Progressive Party in Canada* appendix.

24 For an illustration of these differences see J.C. Gibson, et al., *Report of the Manitoba Commission on Farm Organization* (Manitoba 1962) chapter 1.

25 Fowke, *The National Policy and the Wheat Economy* 292

26 *Canada, Agriculture: The First Hundred Years* (Ottawa 1967) 114. J. Saywell, *Canadian Annual Review 1964* (Toronto 1965) 348, 351. See also H.E. Bronson, 'Continentalism and Canadian Agriculture' in G. Teeple, ed., *Capitalism and the National Question in Canada* (Toronto 1972) 124-5.

27 Bronson 124

28   Fowke, *The National Policy and the Wheat Economy* 289ff. For a
sympathetic analysis of farmers' problems in recent years see
Bronson.

29   V.C. Fowke, *Canadian Agriculture Policy: The Historical Pattern*
(Toronto 1946) 270-1, 280, *Canada One Hundred 1867-1967* 121,
and Bronson, p 124, all point out the weakness of farmer influence;
cf. W.L. Morton, *The Progressive Party in Canada,* 267ff.

SUGGESTIONS FOR FURTHER READING

In the main, interest in the farmers' movements in Canada has been confined to Ontario and the prairies. Full studies of the farmers' movements in Nova Scotia, New Brunswick, Prince Edward Island, and Quebec have yet to be produced. The farmers' movements since 1930, although the subject of a few scanty monographs, still require scholarly investigation. Newspapers, journals, and magazines of farmers' organizations or which were directed towards the agricultural community, although important research sources for studying the farmers' movements, have not been recorded and assessed here because of lack of space.

Facets of agricultural practices and agriculture's position in the Canadian economy have been explored. Vernon C. Fowke, *Agricultural Policy: The Historical Pattern* (Toronto 1946) demonstrates how the Canadian farmer has been outside the pale of governmental decision-making. Pertinent chapters of *Canada and its Provinces,* volumes IX, XIV, XVI, XVIII, XX, and XXII (Toronto 1912-14) contain information on early agricultural conditions in the provinces, *Canada, Agriculture: The First Hundred Years* (Ottawa 1967) provides a brief sketch of the Department of Agriculture's activities since confederation. R.L. Jones, *A History of Agriculture in Ontario 1613-1880* (Toronto 1946) includes a succinct summary of early agricultural societies. A fine piece of work is Firmin Letourneau, *Histoire de l'agriculture (Canada français)* (Montreal 1959), which describe the development of agriculture, agricultural societies, and the co-operative movement in Quebec. The *Canadian Annual Review of Public Affairs* 1902-38 includes valuable contemporary information on the conditions and activities of the farmers; the *Review* of the 1960s is skimpy on agriculture and perhaps reflects its decreased importance. Three reports on the dairying and livestock industry are J.A. Ruddick, *An Historical and Descriptive Account of the Dairying Industry of Canada,* Department of Agriculture Bulletin 28 (April 1911), H.A. Innis, ed., *The Dairy Industry* (Toronto 1936); and J.G. Rutherford, *The Cattle Trade of Western Canada* (Ottawa 1909). The prairie agricultural economy is well recorded in the Canadian Frontiers of Settlement series: R. Murchie et al., *Agricultural Progress on the Prairie Frontier* V (Toronto 1936) and W.A. Mackintosh et al., *Economic Problems of the Prairie Provinces* IV (Toronto 1935).

Vernon C. Fowke, *The National Policy and the Wheat Economy* (Toronto 1957) analyzes the western grain growers' problems created by the National Policy. Kevin Burley, ed., *The Development of Canada's Staples, 1867-1939*, Carleton Library series 56 (Toronto 1971) contains useful excerpts on the grain trade. The best volume on this important staple in the early decades of the twentieth century is D.A. MacGibbon, *The Canadian Grain Trade* (Toronto 1932). Indispensable statistical information is included in M.C. Urquhart and K.A. Buckley, eds., *Historical Statistics of Canada* (Cambridge & Toronto 1965).

Biographies and autobiographies of agrarian leaders are few. W.K. Rolph, *Henry Wise Wood of Alberta* (Toronto 1950) recounts the activities of a fascinating agrarian leader. W.L. Morton, 'The Social Theory of Henry Wise Wood,' *Agricultural History* XXI (1947) is an incisive analysis of the development of Wood's ideas. A.R. Turner, 'W.R. Motherwell: The Emergence of a Farm Leader' in Donald Swainson, ed., *Historical Essays on the Prairie Provincies,* Carleton Library Series 53 (Toronto 1971) and Ralph Hedlin, 'Edmund A. Partridge,' *Historical and Scientific Society of Manitoba Transactions,* Series III, 15 (1960) offer sympathetic insights into the careers of two vastly different prairie farmer leaders. An assessment of T.A. Crerar's early activities is F.J.K. Griezic, 'The Honourable Thomas Alexander Crerar: The Political Career of a Western Liberal Progressive in the 1920s,' in S.M. Trofimenkoff, ed., *The Twenties in Western Canada* (Ottawa 1972). W.C. Good, *Farmer Citizen: My Fifty Years in the Canadian Farmers' Movement* (Toronto 1955) and E.C. Drury, *Farmer Premier* (Toronto 1966) are defensive autobiographies by two Ontario farmer leaders who differed on how the farmer could improve his position. They contain useful information on the Grange, the Farmers' Associations of Ontario, the United Farmers of Ontario, and the UF Co-operative ventures; neither acknowledge the assistance received from the prairie grain growers' associations, or the Grain Growers Grain Company.

The farmer movements in the late nineteenth century in Canada have not attracted academics. H. Michell, 'The Grange in Canada,' *Queen's Quarterly,* XXII (1914; and in pamphlet form, Kingston 1914) presents a narrative of the Patrons of Husbandry (the Grange). H. Glendinning, a former grandmaster of the order, 'The Grange in Canada' in J. Castell Hopkins, ed., *Encyclopedia of Canada* V

(Toronto 1898) is disappointing. The Farmers' Protective Union and the Farmers' Alliance of Manitoba and the Territories continue to require scholarly research although Donald F. Warner, 'The Farmers' Alliance and the Farmers' Union: An American-Canadian Parallelism,' *Agricultural History* XXIII (1949) attempts unsuccessfully to fill some gaps in the Canadian scene.

The Patrons of Industry in Ontario is described briefly by former grandmaster Caleb A. Mallory, 'The Patrons of Industry Order' in J. Castell Hopkins, ed., *Encyclopedia of Canada* V (Toronto 1898). Additional information on the complexities of the order's political activities is provided in the article by Janet Kerr, 'Sir Oliver Mowat and the Campaign of 1894,' *Ontario History* XV (March 1963). J.T. Watt, 'Anti-Catholicism in Ontario Politics: The Role of the Protestant Protective Association in the 1894 Election,' *Ontario History* LIX (June 1967) and 'Anti-Catholic Nativism in Canada: The Protestant Protective Association,' *Canadian Historical Review* XLVIII (March 1967), suggest an important dimension of the movement's social composition and attitudes which affected the Patrons politically. Two recent studies of the Patrons in Ontario are weak. J.D. Smart, 'The Patrons of Industry in Ontario,' (unpublished MA thesis, Carleton 1969) does little to clarify the muddled 1894 provincial election and its after-effects, but the political collusion between federal Liberals and some prominent Ontario Patron leaders in the 1896 federal election is reconfirmed. S.E.D. Shortt, 'Social Change and Political Crisis in Rural Ontario: The Patrons of Industry 1889-1896,' in Donald Swainson, ed., *Oliver Mowat's Ontario* (Toronto 1972) leaves the field open for investigating the social implications of the Patrons of Industry Order in Ontario. The movement in Manitoba has been capably discussed in Brian R. McCutcheon, 'The Patrons of Industry in Manitoba, 1890-1898,' *Historical and Scientific Society of Manitoba Transactions,* Series III, 22 (1965-6); also in Donald Swainson, ed., *Historical Essays on the Prairie Provinces,* Carleton Library.

Considerable writing of an uneven quality has been produced on farmers' co-operation and their co-operative activities. *The Bibliography of Canadian Writings on Co-operation 1900 to 1959* (Ottawa 1960) contains an inadequately organized list of works and the bibliography needs to be updated.

Hopkins Moorhouse, *Deep Furrows* (Toronto 1918) is a popular sympathetic account of why the prairie grain growers organized provincial associations and how they attempted to improve their economic situation. M.H. Staples, *The Challenge of Agriculture: A History of the UFO* (Toronto 1921) deals with the development of the Ontario farmers' movement. Two other short monographs are helpful to an understanding of the UFO. H.H. Hannam, *Pulling Together for Twenty-Five Years: A Brief Story of Events and People in the United Farmers' Movements in Ontario during the Quarter Century, 1914-1939* (Toronto 1940) recalls the problems confronted by Ontario agrarian leaders in building the UFO; R.A. Farquharson, 'The Rise and Fall of the UFO,' *Saturday Night* (21 June 1950), based on material gleaned from the unpublished memoirs of J.J. Morrison, reflects his view of UFO difficulties. D.S. Spafford, 'The Origins of the Farmers' Union of Canada,' *Saskatchewan History* XVIII (Autumn 1965), and 'The "Left Wing" 1921-1931' in Norman Ward and Duff Spafford, eds., *Politics in Saskatchewan* (Toronto 1968) provide significant information about the radical agrarian movement spawned on the prairies in the early 1920s. A succinct insight into the importance of radical elements on the farmers' movement in Saskatchewan is Lorne Brown, 'A Hinterland Rebels: The Story of the Saskatchewan Farmers' Movement,' *Canadian Dimension* VIII (August 1972; it should be noted that C.A. Dunning was first appointed Minister of Finance by Mackenzie King in 1929, not in 1935 as stated on p 34). J.C. Gibson et al., *Report of The Manitoba Commission of Farm Organization* (Winnipeg 1962) investigates the farmers' attempts to organize and compares their actions with other groups that organized. H.H. Hannam, *Forging Ahead for Twenty-Five Years, 1935-1960: The Canadian Federation of Agriculture* (Ottawa [1961]) briefly surveys the attempt by the CFA to become the national farmers' organization. Jake Schulz, *The Rise and Fall of Farmer Organizations in Canada* (Winnipeg [1955]) is an attractively titled but slim record by a farmer organizer. J. Hulliger, *L'Enseignement social des évêques canadiens de 1891 à 1950* (Montreal 1958) assesses the position of the bishops towards the Quebec farmers' movements but ignores the organizations that flirted with the Progressives in the early 1920s.

The founding and development of the United Grain Growers a farmers' joint-stock company (sometimes called a co-operative) created to combat the eastern interests and grain trade monopolists, is narrated in R.D. Colquette, *The First Fifty Years* (Winnipeg 1957). Ian MacPherson, 'The Search for the Commonwealth: The Co-operative Union of Canada, 1909-1949' (unpublished doctoral dissertation, University of Western Ontario 1971) centres on the movement in Ontario and illustrates the confused interpretation of a co-operative and its functions. Differences between the prairie farmers' co-operative business ventures are illustrated in Ian MacPherson, 'The Co-operative Union of Canada and the Prairies 1919-1929' in S.M. Trofimenkoff, ed., *The Twenties in Western Canada*. The standard work on co-operatives and pooling is H.S. Patton, *Grain Growers Co-operation in Western Canada* (Cambridge, Mass. 1928). W.A. Mackintosh, *Agricultural Co-operation in Western Canada* (Kingston 1924) contains a less optimistic view of wheat pooling. H. Boyd, *New Breaking* (Toronto 1938) and L. Nesbitt, *Tides in the West* (Saskatoon 1956) are readable accounts of the co-operative activities of prairie farmers and judiciously consider the effect of the UGG on the development of the co-operatives and pools. H.A. Innis, ed., *The Diary of Alexander James Macphail* (Toronto 1940) contains intimate recollections of Pool problems. The earlier co-operative activities in the Maritime provinces are generally discounted. Most works concentrate on the post-1930 period. The Reverend M.M. Coady and the Roman Catholic church's influence in the Maritime co-operative movement is underscored in A.F. Laidlaw, ed., *The Man from Margaree* (Toronto 1971). J.S. Croteau, *Cradled in the Waves* (Toronto 1951) similarly emphasizes this influence for the farmers' co-operatives in Prince Edward Island. For Quebec the attitude of the Roman Catholic bishops towards co-operatives is concisely summarized in J. Hulliger, *L'Enseignement social des évêques canadiens de 1891 à 1950* (Montreal 1958). Gérard Filion, 'La Co-Opération agricole dans Québec,' *L'Actualité économique* XIII (October 1937) and Yves Roby, *Alphonse Desjardins et les caisses populaires 1854-1920* (Montreal 1964) depict the direction of co-operatives in Quebec.

The history of the Canadian Council of Agriculture, the first attempt to establish a national farmer organization, is uncritically examined in the following: J.C. Mills, 'A Study of the Canadian Council of Agriculture, 1910-1930' (unpublished MA thesis, University of Manitoba 1951), J. Ward, *The Canadian Council of Agriculture: A Review of the History and Work of the National Farm Organization in Canada* (Winnipeg 1926), and A.E. Darby, *The Canadian Council of Agriculture: A Review of the History and Work of the Canadian Council of Agriculture 1925-1930* (Winnipeg 1930). Some pertinent information on the activities and the development on the CCA can be culled from these narratives.

O.J. McDiarmid, *The Commercial Policy in the Canadian Economy* (Cambridge, Mass. 1946) provides basic groundwork for understanding the organized farmers' advocacy of free trade. E. Porritt, *Sixty Years of Protection in Canada 1846-1907* (London 1908) and *The Revolt in Canada against the New Feudalism* (London 1911) are two solid arguments in support of free trade which farmers were encouraged to read. The organized farmers' demands in 1910 are presented in G.F. Chipman, ed., *The Seige of Ottawa* (Winnipeg 1911). Clarus Ager (pseudonym), *The Farmer and the Interests* (Toronto 1916) and W.C. Good, *Production and Taxation in Canada* (Toronto 1920) are reasoned arguments for greater consideration for agrarians. Two other contemporary articles briefly sketch the history and objectives of the farmers' movements. W.C. Good, 'The Farmers' Movement in Canada,' *Dalhousie Review* III (January 1923) concentrates on the aims, significance, and difficulties of the farmers' actions from about 1919 to 1922. John A. Stevenson, 'The Agrarian Movement in Canada,' *Edinburgh Review* CCXXXII (July 1920) offers a succinct exposition on the movements' activities and defends the Crerarite party advocacy against Wood's economic class philosophy. Two different works are Anonymous [C.W. Peterson?] 'The Agrarian Movement in Canada,' *Quarterly Review* CCXXXV (January 1921), which contains glaring inaccuracies as it repudiates the farmers' objectives, and C.W. Peterson, *Wake Up Canada! Reflections on Vital National Issues* (Toronto 1919), which is the reaction of an agribusinessman and former employee of the Canadian Pacific who denounces the reformism of the farmers' party and of labour or anything that hints at socialism, attempts to divide labour and the farmer, and opts for the status quo and a business government.

The effect of the farmers' movements on prominent politicians is contained in the following works: O.D. Skelton, *The Life and Times of Sir Wilfrid Laurier* II (Toronto 1921); Henry Borden, ed., *Robert Laird Borden: His Memoirs*, 2 volumes (Toronto 1938); Roger Graham, *Arthur Meighen*, I, *The Door of Opportunity* (Toronto & Vancouver 1960), *And Fortune Fled* II (Toronto & Vancouver 1963); R. MacGregor Dawson, *William Lyon Mackenzie King*, I, *A Political Biography 1874-1923* (Toronto 1958); H. Blair Neatby, *William Lyon Mackenzie King*, II, *The Lonely Heights, 1923-1932* (Toronto 1963); C.B. Fergusson, *The Honourable W.S. Feilding*, II, *Mr Minister of Finance* (Windsor, Nova Scotia 1971).

The farmers' political activities in the twentieth century have attracted attention. W.L. Morton, *The Progressive Party in Canada* (Toronto 1950), although weak in some areas, is the most important work for the political movement of the 1920s. Paul Sharp, *The Agrarian Revolt in Western Canada: A Survey Showing American Parallels* (Minneapolis 1948) discusses the influence of the American movements, particularly the Non-Partisan League, on the Alberta movement. Four unpublished MA theses contain useful material: F.W. Anderson, 'Some Political Aspects of the Grain Growers' Movement 1915-1935 with Particular Reference to Saskatchewan' (Saskatoon, University of Saskatchewan 1949); M.J. MacLeod, 'The United Farmers' Movement in Ontario 1914-1934' (Kingston, Queen's University 1958); G.E. Panting, 'A Study of the United Farmers of Manitoba to 1928,' (Winnipeg, University of Manitoba 1954); and A.A. MacKenzie, 'The Rise and Fall of the Farmer – Labour Party in Nova Scotia, 1920-1924' (Halifax, Dalhousie University 1970). R. Cook, ed., *Dafoe-Sifton Correspondence 1919-1929* (Winnipeg 1970) presents shrewd comments on the farmers' political activities. W.L. Morton, 'Direct Legislation and the Origins of the Progressive Movement', *Canadian Historical Review* XXV (September 1944) outlines the contribution direct legislation made to the farmers' politicization. His 'The Western Progressive Movement, 1919-1921,' *Canadian Historical Association Report* (1946) summarizes the origin of the farmers' party in the crucial post-World War I years. Two articles describe the fate of the Progressive movement in Saskatchewan in the 1920s: W. Calderwood, 'The Decline of the Progressive Party in Saskatchewan, 1925-1930,' *Saskatchewan History* XXI 3 (Autumn 1968) and J.W. Brennan, 'C.A.

Dunning and the Challenge of the Progressives, 1922-1925,' *Saskatchewan History* XXII 1 (Winter 1969). Margaret Ormsby, 'The United Farmers of British Columbia: An Abortive Third Party Movement,' *British Columbia Historical Quarterly* XVII (1953) explores how the farmers' movement in the Pacific province was exploited and undermined. Doris French and Margaret Stewart, *Ask No Quarter: The Story of Agnes Macphail* (Toronto 1959) is a sympathetic political biography of a UFO activist who in 1921 became the first woman elected to the Canadian House of Commons. The Ontario farmers' 1919 provincial electoral success has fascinated academics. The UFO success, according to the analysis of Peter Oliver, 'Sir William Hearst and the Collapse of the Ontario Conservative Party,' *Canadian Historical Review* LIII (March 1972) was due more to the ineptness of Hearst and the Conservatives than to general agrarian discontent. W.R. Young, 'Conscription, Rural Depopulation and the Farmers of Ontario 1917-1919,' *Canadian Historical Review* LIII (September 1972) argues that the impact of demographic change effected by rural depopulation spurred the Ontario agriculturalists to independent political action. Firmin Letourneau, *Histoire de l'agriculture (Canada français)* (Montreal 1959) briefly outlines the development of the Fermiers-Unis de Québec and tersely attributes its demise to Liberal misconstruction in the election of 1921. He also recounts the growth of its non-political successor, l'Union des Cultivateurs Catholiques in L'UCC (Montreal 1949).

The social composition of the farmers' movements has yet to be fully analyzed. A provocative chapter which equates farmer leaders and social gospellers appears in Richard Allen, *The Social Passion: Religion and Social Reform in Canada 1914-1928* (Toronto 1971). The socio-economic background of some farm leaders is considered in J.N. McCrorie, *In Union is Strength* (Saskatoon 1964). M. Lipset, *Agrarian Socialism: The Co-operative Commonwealth Federation* (Garden City, NY, revised edition 1968) is a sociologist's interpretation of the farmers' movements leading to the formation of the CCF and its success in Saskatchewan.

W. Irvine, *The Farmers in Politics* (Toronto 1920) and *Co-operative Government* (Ottawa [1929]) defends the group government idea against the old party traditionalists. C.B. Macpherson, *Democracy in Alberta: Social Credit and the Party System* (Toronto

1963) includes a tidy analysis of Henry Wise Wood's group government theories.

The relationship between organized labour and the organized farmers is discussed in Martin Robin, *Radical Politics and Canadian Labour 1880-1930* (Kingston 1968). K. McNaught, *A Prophet in Politics: A Biography of J.S. Woodsworth* (Toronto 1958) describes the creation of the Ginger Group of Progressives, which contributed to the birth of the CCF. The Reverend A.E. Smith, *All My Life* (Toronto 1949) is a slanted autobiography of a Methodist minister sympathetic to organized labour and farmers who, disillusioned, became a communist. Duff Spafford, 'The 'Left Wing' 1921-1931' in N. Ward and D. Spafford, eds., *Politics in Saskatchewan* (Toronto 1968) compares the influence of labour on the Farmers Union (Saskatchewan Section) and the attempt by opponents to paint the new farmers' organization as a communist movement. W. Rodney, *Soldiers of the International: A History of the Communist Party of Canada 1919-1929* (Toronto 1968) also contains useful information on the unsuccessful attempts by the Communist party to infiltrate and join the farmers' movements. Two master's theses are germane to the topic of farmer-labour relations. J.D. Hoffman, 'Farmer-Labour Government in Ontario, 1919-1923' (Toronto, University of Toronto 1959) explains the relations between the two groups that formed the administration. A.A. MacKenzie, 'The Rise and Fall of the Farmer-Labour Party in Nova Scotia 1919-1924' (Halifax, Dalhousie University 1970) unintentionally demonstrates that there was no farmer-labour 'party' in Nova Scotia. It is critical of the farmers' movements and emphasizes labour's activities. G.A. Rawlyk, 'The Farmer-Labour Movement and the Failure of Socialism in Nova Scotia' in L. Lapierre et al., *Essays on the Left* (Toronto 1971) relies heavily on MacKenzie's thesis.

Studies of the remnants of the farmers' movements that evolved into the CCF are legion. Their political success in Saskatchewan as a farmers' movement is recorded in D.E. McHenry, *The Third Force in Canada: The Cooperative Commonwealth Federation 1932-1948* (Berkley & Los Angeles 1950) and C.H. Higginbotham, *Off the Record: The CCF in Saskatchewan* (Toronto 1968). A recent analysis, Walter Young, *Anatomy of a Party: The National CCF 1931-61* (Toronto 1970) considers whether the farmers' movement should have been a movement or a party and opts for the latter.

A history of farmers' movements

in Canada

LOUIS AUBREY WOOD

TO
MY WIFE—DORA ISABEL

CONTENTS

CONTENTS—*Continued*

PART III

The Rise of Grain Growers' Movements on the Prairies, 1898-1912

PART IV

The Launching of the Tariff Struggle, 1896-1911

PART V

The Farmers' Movements in More Recent Years

A HISTORY OF

FARMERS' MOVEMENTS IN CANADA

CHAPTER I

INTRODUCTION

UNCOUNTED axes were swinging in the sombre-hued pineries of the Trent and Crow river basins. It was the logging season of 1873-4 when the despoiler was busily at work in the southern rim of Canada's woodland heritage. Timbers, nobly upstanding, tottered—crashingly they fell, to measure their length on the floor of the forest.

Millions of feet of virgin white pine and hardwood were being cut in what was soon to be the provisional County of Haliburton. Lumbering operations of magnitude were being conducted by the water-stretches of Cardiff Township. There in his neat log home a settler was pondering the situation. He had been fourteen years out from Lancashire, and had experienced all the hardships of clearing land with a dense forest cover. His Cardiff farm was rocky; its soil was a mere mantle of glacial drift. During the winter time he had been accustomed to go into the service of the lumbermen in order to eke out a bare existence for his family. He had watched the lumbermen prosper as the finest stand of merchantable timber had been borne downstream to feed the mills.

Something was wrong with the social, economic and political status of the Canadian farmer. This the Cardiff settler believed, and he had a message which he was eager to indite. Taking up paper he began the composition of a letter* to the monthly farm journal that entered his household.

*Written in December, 1873, and signed by Philip Harding, this letter appeared in the *Farmers' Advocate* of London, Ontario, early in 1874. Philip Harding was reeve of the townships of Cardiff and Monmouth-Glamorgan in 1874 and 1875. When Harding was over fifty years of age Bishop Bethune, of the Diocese of Toronto, "took knowledge of him as of superior education and a godly spirit," and ordained him deacon of the Church of England in October, 1876. He was located at Apsley as a missionary and priested in 1877. Later he was appointed to the prebendal stall of Haliburton. For twenty-eight years he prosecuted his mission in portions of four large townships where he brought about the erection of various churches and halls. Described as a "courteous gentleman of the old school," Canon Harding died in June, 1905.

"Organize!" The word was fraught with deep significance to the writer. Thrice in succession it dripped from his pen as he bade the farmers join forces for their common welfare. Individually, to his mind, the Canadian farmer was at a serious disadvantage, and his efforts must continue to prove unavailing unless he sought by united action to achieve his ends. Organization was the only avenue toward a positive solution of agrarian difficulties.

Political impotence, moreover, had been the Canadian farmers' bane. Surely it were possible to find "honorable and intelligent" men on the farm lands of the Dominion who would be capable of representing their constituents in parliament. "Is there not one amongst us," he queried, "wise enough to win the support of his fellows?" Why should the farmers' franchise be consistently pledged to those in other walks of life? "We have too many lawyers and lumbermen in parliament," he complained; "we must have more farmers." By voting for men of their own occupation the farmers would soon gain a voice in the halls of legislation. No longer would they be thought of as "rurals," "bucolics" and "bushwhackers," but they would form "the great country party, influencing and ultimately ruling the affairs" of the nation.

The despoiler has been thorough in his work. Few axes now swing in the spacious confines of the Trent and Crow river basins. Young stands of birch and poplar cluster in the denuded and fire-scarred areas where once the white pine reigned in majesty. Farm homes, crumbling into ruin, and untilled, abandoned acres testify to the exodus of such as were not able to wrest a living from the soil.

But the utterances of the settler of Cardiff Township survive the desolation, for, although they lie on forgotten pages, they were winged with prophecy. Moving to action, as will be related, the farmers of Canada have established their organizations in every province. They have set on foot economic projects, large and small, in order to win a greater measure of justice for the agricultural industry. They have formed their "country" parties which already have exercised an influence upon, and to some extent have ruled the affairs of the nation.

PART I

THE GRANGE IN CANADA SINCE 1872

industry. Yet this period had about it distinctive features that must not be overlooked, inasmuch as they exercised a formative influence on the events which were to follow. A naive, though purely localized, class-consciousness had begun to grow up in the farming communities in pioneer days. The evolution of this class-consciousness was due in the main to the similarity of each pioneer's fight for supremacy; to the common, economic problems that were presented to each in turn, and to the status of isolation from town life which was the pioneer's lot. It remained for a later day to witness the vitalizing of such class-consciousness upon a wider plane.

Again, pressure of circumstances drove the early settlers on Canadian farm lands towards primitive forms of co-operation. By united effort work could be done which was beyond the capabilities of the individual farmer or at least very difficult for him to perform. The story of pioneer life is replete with many a picture of neighborliness which became of unquestioned value in an economic sense. Buildings were raised by the combined man-power of the whole community; sheep were sheared and animals slaughtered through the rendering of mutual assistance. Heavier farming operations were often performed by a group of fellow-workers, and the burden of road structure and maintenance was distributed, as a rule, among all the members of the settlement. To the quilting-bee foregathered the women-folk for miles around, zealous in their labor, eager though they were to recount the happenings of the hour. To the paring-bee came the tottering elder and the active youth, memories of the past engaging the attention of the one, romance quickening the pulses of the other. Here, indeed, were forms of co-operation that were largely adventitious, and which for the most part have passed from view in rural Canada, yet which were to have a lasting effect in predisposing the minds of the people towards the acceptance of the systematized and more scientific co-operation of the modern period.

During the pioneer era, also, numerous organizations that had as their object the betterment of the farming industry began to arise in the several provinces of Canada. As a rule these were known as agricultural societies* and were cus-

*There is faint trace of an agricultural society having existed at Windsor, Nova Scotia, as early as 1765. In 1789 the establishment of an agricultural society was fostered at Quebec City by Lord Dorchester, intended for both French and English-speaking farmers, and the same year other societies were formed at Halifax and in Hants and King's Counties,

tomarily supported in part from the provincial coffers. Having jurisdiction in a larger district, or in a county or section of a county, such organizations worked along identical lines to realize the purposes they had in view. Arrangements were made by them for the exhibition of farm products upon specified dates at certain points throughout the country, and in this way arose the custom of having annual fairs. Prizes were offered by the societies for the competitive display of products, and for the composition of essays pertaining to agricultural matters. Besides the interest of the farmer was stimulated in more profitable methods of cultivating his land and in improving his live stock, while at the same time his notice was drawn to new labor-saving implements arriving on the market, the use of which would simplify his toil. It is easy to understand how societies of this type became of inestimable worth to agriculture in pioneer days, just as they have remained quite serviceable to the same industry until the present time. On the other hand, it would be an error to assume that agricultural societies have ever borne any close relationship to the development of the farmers' movements that have played such a rôle in Canadian history. From this standpoint their influence, if exercised at all, has been exercised indirectly or has been of subsidiary importance.

The Organization of Farmers' Clubs.

New economic conditions intruded upon this idyllic, though stern and rigorous, life of the pioneer about the time that Upper and Lower Canada were united in 1840, and constitutional reforms were becoming imminent in the Maritime Provinces. So far the farming populace of the British North American provinces had been almost entirely dependent for their livelihood upon the products which nature supplied, and upon goods of their own making, giving little heed to the industrial world without. Now a transition period was at hand: capital had been accumulating at the main centres; manufactories were steadily growing more diversified; and

Nova Scotia. New Brunswick's first society was created at St. John in 1790. Lieut.-Governor Simcoe organized one at Newark, Upper Canada (Ontario), in 1792. A series of thirty-eight letters appeared in the *Acadian Recorder* in 1818, written by John Young, a Nova Scotian, who signed himself "Agricola." These touched upon almost every phase of farming practice, and excited such wide attention that under the patronage of Lord Dalhousie a provincial agricultural society was formed for Nova Scotia to which a money grant was made by the legislature as well as to the county societies. Financial support was given to the societies in Upper Canada by the provincial government from 1830 onward. In what is now Western Canada an agricultural association was first set up at Victoria, on Vancouver Island, in 1861; societies were established on the prairies on the influx of settlers after 1870.

the farmer was acquiring fresh tastes and demanding added comforts. Water transportation by river, lake and canal, as well as overland travel by ox-cart, were losing their importance as railways rapidly sprang into existence in every direction during the thirty years prior to 1870. Tariff discussions also became rife in the farming communities when Great Britain went over to "free trade" in 1846, eliminating thereby the preference market that the provinces had formerly enjoyed, and burst forth again when a few years later the question was mooted of securing a measure of trade reciprocity with the United States. The farmer suddenly awoke to find himself caught in an industrial network of which he had heretofore known nothing, and was driven to relate the problems of agriculture, already thronging for solution, to all the other variegated phases of production.

It was while the foregoing changes were in progress that a type of organization was launched by groups of farmers in the British North American provinces which was to be the first real token of a movement abroad among them, and gave them a vehicle of expression unthought of before. Here and there, from the great lakes to the sea, farmers' clubs, associations, or leagues as they were called in the Maritime Provinces, started to arise which were quite distinct both in form and purpose from the agricultural societies already in existence. Just where the first of these organizations had its beginning is wrapped in mystery, but once their utility was recognized, they were established in one district after another. References to them occur in the agrarian literature of the fifties of last century, and the probability is that they had begun their activities in the preceding decade.

No definite model was evolved for the organization of these clubs, but the scattered data that is available would indicate that they were mainly alike in constitution and procedure. Ten to twenty farmers coming together quite informally would oftentimes form a club, and then and there proceed to the election of its officers. A simple constitution was forthwith drawn up, a nominal fee assessed upon the members to meet incidental expenses, and the club was prepared for business. Regular meetings were held generally at a farmhouse or in the section schoolhouse. Discussions and debates on agricultural issues were inaugurated and essays read by club members on topics of current interest. When a meeting was held at a farmer's private home, "pot luck" re-

2—F.M.

freshments were customarily served by the mistress of the household to those who had assembled.

Among organizations of this character the Markham Farmers' Club, one of the most progressive in Ontario, may be regarded as an example. It had for its constituency a portion of York County, noted at that time for its well-tilled farms. "If a bad ploughman was to show himself along this road," wrote a traveller of the early seventies on a York County highway, "we believe the farmers would drum him out of the section." The Markham Club met at two o'clock in the afternoon on the first Saturday of each month. Occasionally when its sessions became protracted, an adjournment was made for supper, and its members gathered again to conduct business at an evening hour. During a meeting of this club, held in the early summer of 1874, the theme under consideration was the problem of fencing. As the discussion became animated, many points of value were brought out by the individual club members who took the floor. The consensus of opinion among the farmers seemed to be that the pine or cedar, zigzag rail fence was still the most economical for all purposes. Board fences, some thought, might be used to advantage; portable fences were generally classed as too expensive. A divergence of views emerged respecting hedgerows and living fences. The native thorn was conceded to have the greatest utility as a hedge builder; the sweetbriar, though meeting with approval, was said to have the habit of "pulling the wool off the sheep;" the willow tree came in for censure—in the words of one speaker it was "only fit to amuse old people."

Everything points to the conclusion that the farmers' clubs of this era were entirely unfederated; there is no trace of any special intercourse occurring among them. It may be taken for granted, however, that in the main their objects were the same. In some sections a sort of huddling together of clubs might be discovered within a circumscribed area. For instance, seven or eight clubs are known to have been in operation at one time in the vicinity of Brantford. Four clubs were located in Grey County, Ontario, several in the Eastern Townships of Quebec, and as already indicated, a number in the Province of New Brunswick. Certain clubs appear to have been set up in an isolated manner apart from any organizations of their kind, while it would seem that many localities had no clubs at all.

The institution of such a form of local combination among farmers must have been due to a contemporary demand. These clubs may be described as having arisen spontaneously; plainly they were not a mere vogue of the day, but had come into existence with the object of supplying a felt want. Moreover it would be a mistake to list them along with agricultural societies under the heading of betterment organizations. True, like agricultural societies, they aimed to cultivate among their membership a more extended knowledge of the farming industry. But, on the other hand, the social functions of the clubs carried them into new channels of endeavor; co-operative buying was in some cases practised among the members, though on a limited scale; even political matters came under review at club gatherings and time after time comment was made upon the scarcity of farmer representatives in the legislative bodies of the provinces. Bonds of unity were created by the farmers' club that no agricultural society could have effected, bonds of unity, indeed, hitherto unimagined in connection with rural life. To what extent the farmers' club might have become the starting-point for a wider manifestation of agrarian class-consciousness in the British North American provinces had not the field been occupied beforehand by an exceedingly virile movement, that of the Grange emanating from abroad, will always remain a matter for pure conjecture. It will be necessary first to examine the origins of the Grange movement and the characteristics that it assumed in the United States. Then an effort will be made to show how it was transplanted over the border, and attained a high degree of florescence on Canadian soil.

CHAPTER III

DEVELOPMENT OF THE GRANGE IN THE UNITED STATES

THE MAJORITY of the insurgent movements which have affected the life and thought of North America since the Civil War period in the United States have had their origin, or at least have had their greatest development, in the broad basins of the Mississippi and its confluent streams. During the last few decades the prairie provinces of Canada to the north and west of these rivers, being within the same orbit of influence, have revealed similar characteristics. Just why a proneness to revolt has been so manifest in the mid-section of the continent is not easy to determine. No doubt—though tradition has had its influence—the cause has been largely environmental. Dwellers in this region have been peculiarly jealous of their heritage of democracy. They have moved to its defence even as standing grain sways before the elfin breeze of summer.

So it happened that Greenbackism arose as an aftermath of Civil War conditions in the states comprising the Middle West with its bold bid for "cheap money" and its powerful onslaught on the financial interests of the East. So it happened that in the same area the Patrons of Husbandry reached their ascendency, offering to the agriculturist an elaborate programme of social improvement and economic amelioration. Here, too, in the eighties of last century, grew up the two divisions of the Farmers' Alliance, one in the south drawing unto itself the Farmers' Wheel and the Farmers' Union, another flourishing in the corn and grain states farther north, each of them castigating the evils of speculation and advocating the benefits of co-operation. Here, too, Populism first reared its head to the terror and amazement of the old-line politician; here the beacon fires of reformatory Bryanism have burned their brightest; here Progressivism put forth its sturdiest efforts to release men from the ancient shibboleths of party connection; and here, within more recent years, the Non-Partisan League, militant and unrelenting, has preached its doctrines of a new era for the producing classes. Across

21

the forty-ninth parallel of latitude grain growers' movements have arisen on the western plains of Canada which have had a very decisive influence in shaping the social, economic and political history of the country. A narrative of them will be given occupying many separate pages in this volume.

INCEPTIVE STAGES OF THE GRANGE.

One of the best-known and most attractive of the movements to which reference has just been made was that of the Patrons of Husbandry, or Grange. Although the Grange throve most vigorously in the Middle West, it had its beginnings on the Atlantic seaboard. The procreator of the Order was Oliver Judson Kelley, a New Englander, who had cultivated land as a pioneer in Minnesota, and then in 1864 accepted a clerkship in the Federal Bureau of Agriculture at Washington. In January, 1866, at the conclusion of the war, President Andrew Johnson commissioned Kelley to make a tour of the southern states in order that he might bring back first-hand information to the government with respect to their agricultural and mineral resources. Kelley's observation of the wretched state of the farm lands in the south led him to ruminate upon the general bleakness of the farmer's social lot in America, and his economic helplessness. As he was a firm believer in the efficacy of organization, he began to form the opinion that only through taking collective action could the farmer hope to better his conditions. Whereupon, in keeping with the tendencies of the day, Kelley envisaged a Fraternal Order for the farmer as the best way out of the impasse. Upon his return from the south he went on to Boston and there sought the advice of his niece, Carrie Hill— later a distinguished songstress of the Grange—who urged him to admit women to full membership along with men in whatever form of organization he might choose to advise.

Next Kelley imparted his ideas to a number of Washingtonians, among whom may be mentioned William Saunders, a superintendent in the Bureau of Agriculture, and two government clerks, William M. Ireland and John R. Thompson. Soon he had gathered together an interested group who, after repeated deliberations, succeeded in drawing up a constitution and arranging an appropriate ritual for the proposed Order. Descriptive and informative circulars were at once sent out in various directions with a view to drawing attention to the embryonic movement. Then, on December

4, 1867, seven men, the so-called founders of the Order, meeting at Washington, declared themselves the National Grange of the Patrons of Husbandry, and accepted its constitution and ritual. William Saunders was named as Worshipful Master, or head official of the Order; Kelley became its Secretary, and Ireland its Treasurer. Shortly afterward a local unit, or as it was entitled, a subordinate grange, was created to test out the ritual, and within a few months the Order was ready for transference to the farming communities.

Upon Secretary Kelley was laid the burden of first propagating the movement, and he entered upon his duties with no little apprehension concerning the outcome of his venture. As a matter of fact he underwent the hardships and encountered the rebuffs which are usually incidental to the dissemination of new ideas amongst a doubting public. He believed that the Order should make an instant appeal to the western farmers, and so decided to begin work near his old home in Minnesota, organizing granges wherever possible on the journey out. In pursuance of this plan he was able to authorize the launching of four granges on his way to Minnesota, but of these only one, situated at Fredonia, New York, ever came to maturity. However, the good hearing he had expected to get from the Minnesota farmers did not materialize for a time and he was disappointed at the indifference shown to his pleading. But at length the farmers thawed out and began to acknowledge the merits of an Order committed to the advancement of their own welfare. The first grange in the West was set up by means of correspondence, at Newton, Iowa, in the spring of 1868. Then in August of the same year another was established at St. Paul, Minnesota, and so rapidly did the Order take hold in this state that by the end of 1869 it had thirty-six more. Kelley meanwhile had gone personally into Iowa in October, 1869, to scatter more seed, and thence he had proceeded into Illinois, Indiana and Ohio, leaving permanent organizations in his wake in each of these states. The following year he was busy in Missouri where the advent of the Order was acclaimed with enthusiasm. By January 1, 1871, the Patrons of Husbandry had granges actively in operation in nine states of the Union.

So far the work of planting the Order had been in the main an uphill struggle. Nevertheless, beginning with 1872, the movement began to sweep through the United States with unexampled celerity, and even penetrated into Canada. January 1, 1875, found nearly 22,000 subordinate granges in existence in forty-one states and the Indian Territory. The major portion of these, numbering in excess of 12,000, were located in the North Central states. Of the total, Missouri had 2,009 subordinate granges, Indiana, 2,000, Iowa, 1891, Illinois, 1,533, Kansas, 1,332. In the South Central states there were on the same date over 5,500 subordinate granges, of which Kentucky had 1,493, Tennessee, 1,642, and Texas, 916. East of the Alleghanies, Pennsylvania led in the North with 428 granges, while in the South, Georgia had 683 and North Carolina, 477; in the western division the Order was fairly strong in both California and Oregon. Viewed from the standpoint of the relation of granges to the agricultural population, the movement had reached its high point in Nebraska, where there was a grange for every ninety-six persons.

As the Order expanded, the functions performed by the National Grange steadily increased in importance. State granges were set up as intermediary bodies to attend to business that the National Grange could not be expected to transact. Finally a revision of the constitution and by-laws of the Order became imperative, and this was accomplished at the sixth annual session of the National Grange held in January, 1873, at Georgetown, D.C. Simultaneously a charter of incorporation for the National Grange was secured from the Congress of the United States. O. H. Kelley was retained as Secretary, but from now on the control of the Order was surrendered almost entirely into the hands of bona fide farmers.

Grievances Fostering the Spread of the Order.

While agriculture was in a more or less debilitated state all over, following the Civil War, few complaints as to their lot were offered by those engaged in one type or another of diversified farming. Producers of staple commodities, on the other hand, such as wheat, corn or cotton, were much harder hit by economic conditions, and began in no uncertain terms to decry the situation. More particularly in the Middle West where one-crop methods were still fully in operation, were loud remonstrances heard, as the farmer noted the sluggishness of his own industry and the comparative prosperity of those in other walks of life. Accordingly when the

Grange came into this section it was heralded as an instrument whereby wrongs might be righted, and tillers of the soil protected from further victimization. The farmers accepted the "cardinal maxim that only in union can the agricultural class show its strength," and believed that the Grange would give them "a means of combination, of harmony of action, such as they had never before possessed."

The most vital economic problem which the farmers of the Middle West had to face at this time related to the transportation of their surplus products to the eastern markets and the bringing in of manufactured articles in return. During the post-bellum period numerous railway lines had been built to the banks of the Mississippi and beyond, to supplement those already in existence. The boon which these lines would unquestionably confer on the farming communities was instantly recognized and they were given a cordial welcome. Not only were they dowered with public lands, but governments, central and local, assisted them with funds and special privileges, and thousands of unsuspecting farmers bought up the securities which they had to offer and so helped to supply the outlay for their construction. But in process of time the same investing farmers were subjected to a rude awakening. Stock-watering and stock-jobbing were practised in the most artful manner; company reorganizations gave the designing manipulator his chance to squeeze out the lesser fry. Anticipated dividends either failed of realization, or in some instances the farmers' holdings of stock became absolutely worthless. Little wonder then that the farmers, as they saw themselves well plucked in these transactions, renounced their earlier attitude of friendliness to the railroads and turned against them with bitterness and loathing.

To make matters worse the railroads, aware of the monopolistic powers that had been vested in them, generally adopted an overbearing and often thoroughly discourteous manner towards those for whom they were acting as common carriers. Moreover they were accused of seeking to gain influence and further their own ends by debauching legislators, public officials and even the courts of the land. More important from the economic standpoint, they were charged with fixing exorbitant rates in hauling farm products to the eastern markets and with showing unjust discrimination between shippers, to the farmers' evident disadvantage. Taking it all in all, the farmers had many counts in their indictment of the railway corporations, and when the Grange appeared they made haste to use it as a rallying-point for attack against these corporations' pretensions. Government control over and regulation of the railway services became a slogan among granges in every state of the Middle West during the early seventies. In one way and another they impressed their views upon the state legislatures, and a great array of restrictive measures, known as "granger laws," were passed, which put a check on discrimination, sometimes fixed maximum rates and strove in general to make the railways submit to the dictation of public authority. Grangers also began already before 1880 to agitate for a federal regulation of the transportation services, and had their part in bringing about the passage of the notable Interstate Commerce Act of 1887.

Another incentive toward organization among the farmers of the Middle West, and in fact elsewhere in the United States, lay in the system of commercial distribution in operation whereby a fair recompense was denied them, they said, as sellers, and they were overcharged as buyers. In disposing of their agricultural wares the farmers claimed that they were at the mercy of the local produce buyers and commission men among whom there was little competition; in making their purchases they were forced to take goods at the prices set by the retail dealers upon whose books they were carried, or buy from agents who exacted heavy gains in the process. The introduction of the Grange gave an opportunity for combined action against these middlemen which was seized upon with avidity. Forms of distributive co-operation were established under the sanction of the Order in every quarter of the United States. A multitude of local grange agencies were created with the object of purchasing goods directly from the manufacturers and jobbers, and of sending their staple products to more extensive markets where better prices would prevail. State agencies as well were set up to do business on a larger scale and at the same time to facilitate the work of the local agencies. In 1875 the National Grange formulated rules for the establishment of co-operative stores under the Rochdale plan, and soon hundreds of such stores were dotted across the country in the grange constituencies. The majority of these co-operative undertakings were rather short-lived, but they had cut down the number of middlemen in the field, and brought others to better terms; besides, they had indicated how in future co-operative projects might possibly be made to succeed where theirs had failed.

When the Grange first made its appearance dissatisfaction was also rife among the farmers over the financial and monetary situation, and over the tax burdens that they had to carry. Loans to farmers in the Middle West were bearing interest rates at this time as high as fifteen or even twenty per cent. The currency was badly depreciated at the end of the war and, when its supply was contracted, the value of money rose and the repayment of loans took proportionately more out of the farmers' pockets. In addition the extraordinary war tariff of 1864 with its duties on imports averaging forty-seven per cent. was continued with only slight modification until 1883, and as a result the farmers when making purchases of clothing, implements, provisions and building materials, subject to taxation, were forced to pay enhanced prices while the foreign market for their agricultural produce was curtailed. Nothing of a really comprehensive nature was done by the Grange to lighten the farmers' financial difficulties, although co-operative banks were set up in California and Kansas and in a number of states legislation was sought reducing the legal rate of interest. The Order confined its efforts to passing resolutions on the currency question; on the problem of the tariff sectional interests were so strong that unanimity of opinion was impossible.

Constitution and Ritual of the Grange.

According to its constitution as given in 1873, membership in the Secret Order of the Patrons of Husbandry was confined to farmers and horticulturists and to their womenfolk who might care to join. No religious or political test was required of members nor was discussion of such topics allowed in the meetings of the Order. The subordinate grange when duly formed must have thirteen officers, four of whom were women and nine of whom were men. As soon as fifteen subordinate granges had been set up in any state, a State Grange might be established with jurisdiction in that area, which would meet annually and consist of the masters and past masters of the local organizations and their wives. The National Grange, or Central Bureau of the Order, had general supervisory and legislative powers, and was made up, when it gathered in annual convention, of the Masters and Past Masters of the State Granges and their wives. Each subordinate grange transmitted a pro rata membership payment to the State Grange, and a portion of this found its way into the coffers of the National Grange.

The ritual of the Order was symbolic and was said to be "pleasing, beautiful and appropriate—designed not only to charm the fancy, but to cultivate and enlarge the mind and purify the heart, having at the same time strict adaptation to rural pursuits." Altogether seven degrees were conferred upon Patrons of Husbandry, the first four of which might be obtained in the subordinate grange. For male members, in ascending order, these were entitled the degrees of: Laborer, Cultivator, Harvester and Husbandman. The corresponding degrees for female members were: Maid, Shepherdess, Gleaner, and Matron. The fifth degree, Pomona or Hope, which might be acquired by either sex, was conferred only in the State Grange. The National Grange was empowered to bestow on male and female members the sixth degree, Flora or Charity, and the seventh degree, Ceres or Faith. Those who had entered into the knowledge and mysteries of Ceres were given oversight of all the secret work of the Order.

The Grange did not serve alone to protect the farmer and advance him economically. From the outset it fulfilled a very high purpose through the educative and cultural influences which it brought to bear on the agricultural communities. The procedure of its meetings, assisted by the observance of its symbolic ritual, was both enriching to the moral fibre and stimulating to the mind. An opportunity for social intercourse was given which warmed the solitary cheerlessness of farming life. In this regard the inclusion of the wives and unmarried daughters of the farmer in the organization with full membership rights was a matter of happiest augury, since women on the farm lands of the United States and Canada were at that time, and, in fact, always have been, subject to a daily routine more unvarying and inexorable than have their men.

CHAPTER IV

THE GRANGE ENTERS CANADA

NEWS of the rapid extension of the Order of the Patrons of Husbandry in the United States was disseminated throughout Canada in a variety of ways. Items in the daily press and articles in farm journals dealt with the significance of the new movement for the rural dweller. Many who travelled across the line into the United States brought back stories of the Order's success in that country. Migrating sons of Canada, more especially those who in their wanderings had gone to the American West, told of the Grange in the budget of chit chat which they transmitted to friends and relatives at home. Information with respect to the Order, however gleaned, only led to wider inquiries, and soon a desire to have the advantages of the Grange system conveyed into Canada made its appearance, notably amongst the membership of the existing farmers' clubs who were quick to recognize the superiority of an organization with a centralized and stable form of government.

The setting up of granges in Canada, if permitted, would involve a new orientation in the policies of the National Grange; it would mean a legalization of the Order outside the bounds of the United States. Difficulties on this score might naturally have been expected, but, when an appeal came from Canada for the benefits of the Order, National Grange officials, burdened at the moment by many problems and exercising little forethought, readily complied and placed no bar against the advancement of the Order into foreign territory. This decision, loosely rendered, but far-reaching in its consequences, brought the movement into Canada by the time that it had established itself in one half of the states of the American Union, and at first occasioned no trouble; subsequently, however, it caused a jurisdictional dispute to break out that led to a period of embarrassment in the relationhips of grangers in the two countries. For purposes of organization officials of the National Grange regarded Canada as a single territorial entity, and when they sent in a deputy, as will be related, he was authorized to set up granges anywhere within the Dominion.

THE GRANGE ENTERS QUEBEC.

Reports submitted to the headquarters of the Patrons of Husbandry for 1871 indicated that at the end of that year the Order had been implanted in sixteen different states. During 1872 nine more states were added to the list, and, as a supplementary fact, the annals of Grangeism record the extension of the movement northward into Canada. It is a rather noteworthy incident in the Order's history that, whereas it had grown up chiefly in the Middle West, it did not enter Canada from that direction, but instead was admitted by way of the New England states into the ancient province of Quebec.

Grange emissaries in carrying on their activities in the farming communities of the United States had during the inceptive stages of the movement met with little response in New England. The only state in that section of the country showing any degree of friendliness to the Order had been Vermont. A subordinate grange had been established there in July, 1871. But when O. H. Kelley visited the state later in the same year, he had been given a cold reception and the outlook was distinctly unpromising. Nevertheless such inconstancy on the part of Vermont proved to be only temporary, as the events of the next year amply demonstrated. In January, 1872, Eben Thompson, a native Vermonter, with the powers of an organizing deputy for the state, set to work and by March 1 had established nine new granges, and so continued was his success that by midsummer he had added four more. O. H. Kelley, having learned of the circumstances and having returned to the state, was now accorded a fervid welcome, and on July 4, at a gathering in St. Johnsbury, Caledonia County, organized the State Grange of Vermont.

These events had made Vermont a sort of Grange island surrounded by several of her sister states and one lone Canadian province, all of which had either heard little or nothing of the new agrarian movement, or having heard had repudiated its principles. But the situation in Vermont was to be meaningful for Canada, since the rich agricultural Eastern Townships of the province of Quebec lie directly contiguous to that state on the north, and it was from this quarter that the first Canadian appeal was uttered for the introduction of the

Order.   Owing in part to racial and bilingual differences existing in Quebec, the inhabitants of the Eastern Townships have
always regarded Vermonters as their close kinsfolk.   Indeed
at no place along the international boundary between Canada
and the United States has there been, historically speaking, a
greater interchange of ideas or have the relationships of the
two peoples been more cordial.   Fate had decreed that the
Vermont-Quebec line was to be the point of transit for the
Grange upon its entrance into British Territory.

The torchbearer of the movement as it now swept into
Canada was Eben Thompson, the deputy whose achievements in Vermont have just been chronicled.   Thompson
in 1872 was a youth of but twenty-four who during the previous
year had been graduated from the Chandler Scientific School
at Dartmouth College, N.H.; later in life he was to attain the
degree of doctor of medicine, and become a practising physician.*   As to the actual sequence of events which drew
Thompson into the province of Quebec, data is largely wanting.
But of one fact there is full assurance and that is that he
went into Canada as the result of an invitation that had been
extended to him.   Upon this point he was absolutely clear
when giving an explanation of his presence in Canada to a
farmers' meeting held in 1874 at Pond Mills, in southern
Ontario.   He stated on that occasion that he had been bidden
to the country, and further with respect to the authority that
had been vested in him asserted that "the National Grange
had given him instructions to proceed to Canada to attend
to organization there."   It is almost certain that the request
for Thompson's services, which he speedily answered, came
from farmers in Stanstead County, Quebec, as that was the
portion of the province which he entered on first crossing the
border.

---

*Eben Thompson was born in North Danville, Caledonia County, in the State of
Vermont, on August 7, 1848; his parents were Ebenezer and Abigail Randall Thompson.
A paternal ancestor had settled in the Green Mountain State in 1787, and had made the
first survey of a portion of Caledonia County.   After retiring from Grange activities in
Canada, Thompson entered Poultney Medical College, in New Hampshire, where he was
graduated as a Doctor of Medicine in 1877; he secured a Bachelor of Science degree from
Dartmouth College in 1883.   He began the practice of his profession at Newton Upper
Falls, Mass., near Boston, in 1877, and, as the records would indicate, became "loved and
respected in the community as a friend, a physician, and a public servant."   In 1885 he
married Mary Wallace Tripp, daughter of Professor Alonzo Tripp, of Boston.   He interested himself in municipal politics as a non-partisan, and served two terms on the board
of aldermen of Newton Upper Falls, holding the chairmanship of several important committees.   He was a prominent Mason, and a member of various other secret orders and
societies.   His death on December 9, 1897, appears to have been deeply regretted in the
Massachusetts community; his obituary notice supplies the information that he had "built
up a large practice, but was better known for his generosity to the poorer residents of the
village than for his success in his profession, which was great."

On August 6-7, 1872, a public meeting was held at Newport, Vermont, under the auspices of the Board of Agriculture, Manufactures and Mining of that state at which Eben
Thompson was known to have been present, and to have read
a paper on the Patrons of Husbandry. Newport is located
only a few miles from the international line, and some time
during the succeeding eight or nine days Thompson journeyed
thence into the province of Quebec. New railways had
recently been opened for service to the north of Newport, and
it is likely that he went by these on his trip into Canada.
In that event he took the Connecticut and Passumpsic River
Railroad as far as its border station of North Derby; there
he transferred to the Massawippi Valley Railway* which
conveyed him to Rock Island in close proximity to Stanstead,
the point he had chosen as his objective. At Stanstead a
throng of young people from the adjoining farm lands were
called together,† and Thompson earnestly instructed them
in the merits of the Grange. As he warmed to his subject
he is said, to have exclaimed, with a show of pride "that his
father was a farmer who was the son of a farmer who worked
on the farm six days in the week and preached on the seventh."

Information was forthwith sent through to American
headquarters that International Grange, the first in Canada,
had been established at Stanstead on August 16, A. P. Ball,
master, and J. G. Field, secretary. Yet, notwithstanding this
statement, recorded as official, there exists much uncertainty
as to whether the organization of a subordinate grange at
Stanstead was ever completed. Albert Clark who was at
the meeting asserts that Thompson left before the grange
had been fully instituted, promising to come back and set it
going, but had failed to reappear; to his knowledge no subordinate grange ever functioned in or about Stanstead.
Whichever version is taken, the official or that of a farmer on
the spot, the episode is interesting in that it marks the incipient stage of the propagation of Grange doctrines within
the Dominion of Canada. International Grange, if it ever
became an actuality, was like a graceful but delicate flower

---

*These lines had by 1870 offered transportation facilities into Quebec as far as
Lennoxville. Subsequently they became part of the Boston and Maine Railway system
which obtained running rights over the Grand Trunk Railway from Lennoxville to Sher-
brooke in 1873.
†The names of those present at this meeting, enrolled by Thompson as charter
members, included the following: Albert P. Ball, George Bachelder, D. A. Mansur, M. A.
Noyes, Albert Clark, Mrs. G. L. Russell, Mrs. D. A. Mansur, Mrs. L. R. Robinson, W. S.
Hunter, George L. Russell, L. R. Robinson, J. G. Field, Mrs. Mary L. Ball, Mrs. W. S.
Hunter, Mrs. E. A. Bachelder, Miss Mary A. Field, and Miss L. Clark.

that perfumed the dayspring for a moment and then withered away before the rising sun.

Thompson on departing had gone to the eastern end of Stanstead County, where he set up two more granges during 1872, one at Barnston and another, entitled the Golden Grange, at Dixville. In a report submitted to the National Grange at its sixth annual session in Georgetown, D.C., January, 1873, mention was made of the fact that three granges had already been established in Canada, and that Eben Thompson, special deputy, had been paid $60 for his work of organization and travelling expenses. Thompson was again busy in the province of Quebec during 1873, with a record of five granges to his credit as the result of diligent effort. Due to scantiness of data on the subject one of these granges is as yet unlocated; two of them are known to have been organized at Melbourne* and Danville in Richmond County and two others at Freiligsburg and Dunham, respectively, in Missisquoi County. On January 16, 1874, a ninth grange, if International Grange be included in the count, was formed by Thompson at Abbott's Corners, Missisquoi County, this completing the total number established through his agency in Quebec. On the whole the Quebec granges may be characterized as having been of somewhat ephemeral growth, and, though a few of them persisted for a time, the majority had soon languished. A great deal more importance must be attached to the work that Thompson was about to begin in the province of Ontario.

THOMPSON'S SUCCESS IN ONTARIO.

The portal of admission for the Grange into Ontario lay by way of Prescott County on the right bank of the Ottawa River. Acting in response to an appeal from farmers in that county, Thompson proceeded thither from Quebec early in 1874. Here at L'Orignal, an old town on the river, he established Longueuil Grange, J. F. Cass, master, and C. A. Cass, secretary. Then almost immediately Thompson left Prescott County to attend the seventh annual session of the National Grange held that year in St. Louis, but before going away empowered J. F. Cass to serve as a deputy for the Order in the eastern section of the province. Some weeks later

---

*It is interesting to note that the seventh Baron Aylmer was chosen as master of the grange at Melbourne, which was entitled Aylmer Grange.

Cass paid a visit to Dundas County, and on March 17 set up Winchester Grange at Cass Bridge.

The St. Louis meeting of the National Grange, February 4-12, 1874, has been described as "the most representative gathering of farmers which had ever taken place in the United States." On February 6, Eben Thompson appeared before it, and was asked to make a report on the condition and needs of the Order in Canada. "He said," according to the minutes of the National Grange, "that there were ten granges in Canada, some of them numbering over one hundred members; that they desired to establish a Dominion Grange, in order to have a fixed headquarters for the Order, and that they most earnestly desired to see the organization international." The National Grange awarded Thompson $205.75 for his year's services, but for some unexplained reason allowed his authority as special deputy in Canada to lapse. Possibly it was thought that from the optimistic trend of Thompson's remarks the movement in Canada was robust enough to stand upon its own feet. Again, the purport of his statement that the Canadians were anxious to have in their country a "fixed headquarters" for the Order may have impressed the National Grange somewhat unfavorably, and have caused it to become reluctant to spend any more of its money upon what from its own standpoint might result in a profitless venture.

Nevertheless Eben Thompson believed that Ontario offered him a very promising field for his organizing abilities, and decided to continue the spade work he had begun there for the Grange, although in a different part of the province. Accordingly he halted at London in southern Ontario on his homeward journey from St. Louis. Considerable sentiment had already manifested itself in the London district and in the County of Grey, to the north of London, in favor of testing out the merits of the Grange as a farmers' organization. Some time previous Alfred Gifford,* of St. Vincent Township, Grey County, had been instructed by the farmers' club of which he was a member, to write to O. H. Kelley about the

---

*Alfred Gifford had the distinction of having been actively connected with three different farmers' movements in Canada. He was born in Durham County in 1839, and migrated to Grey County when twenty-three years of age. His forbears were early settlers in the colony of Massachusetts; his father's people were of Puritan stock, his mother's people Quakers. When Canada was still a French possession, Gifford's paternal great-grandfather explored the northern shore of Lake Ontario and the left bank of the St. Lawrence; his grandfather on this side came to Upper Canada soon after the British occupation. His maternal grandfather entered the country as a U. E. Loyalist following the Revolutionary War.

movement, and Gifford had drafted a letter to the Grange leader in which, in his own words, he asked "for information as to the objects and aims of the institution so that he might decide whether it could be adapted to our circumstances and used to advantage." Kelley had replied promptly to this communication from Des Moines, Iowa, inclosing a copy of the constitution and by-laws of the Order, and had suggested that a request should be sent in from Grey County for an organizing deputy. The St. Vincent Club, following this advice, had submitted a plea for a deputy to Grange head-quarters, and an answer had been forthcoming that Eben Thompson had been vested with the necessary authority to set up granges in the Canadian provinces. This club and others in the county were aware how readily their several local units might be converted into granges; moreover, there was general approval of the secrecy attached to the proceed-ings of the new Order. "The accounts we saw of it," as Alfred Gifford has since explained, "convinced us that it would be an improvement on our club system, as, under it, we could ex-clude outsiders whose interests in many cases conflicted with ours."

At London an urgent appeal that the Order might be given a trial in Canada had been made by William Weld, publisher and editor of the *Farmers' Advocate*. He instanced in the columns of his paper what advantages, he believed, would accrue from its introduction, and drew attention to the granges already established in Quebec and in eastern Ontario. "Shall we farmers in Canada," he asked, "unite in action for our mutual interests?" As if in answer to his query Eben Thompson, just arrived from the St. Louis meeting, walked into the *Advocate* office on Dundas Street, in February, 1874, and announced that he was ready to plant the Order in that section of Ontario. After some colloquy on the subject, Westminster Township, immediately south of Lon-don, was selected as a fit spot for him to begin operations, and having made his way there, he delivered an able address at Pond Mills and organized Advance Grange, the first in the district, at Glanworth, on February 27, with the following as its leading officers: William M. Beattie, master; John H. Elliott, secretary; and Henry Anderson, lecturer. After a short interval he was found in Elgin County where he set up Elgin Pioneer Grange in Yarmouth Township, on March 18, Stephen Wade, master. The *Farmers' Advocate* in its March issue made special reference to the presence of Eben Thompson in the neighborhood, and, having emphasized the fact that very few persons were needed to start a grange, intimated that Thompson would go with organizing powers wherever the farmers might choose to summon him.

Ere long Thompson decided to give answer to the petition for a deputy which had come in from Grey County. Late in March, therefore, he hied himself to that county where he remained for upwards of a week. During his stay he instituted three granges in quick succession: the Georgian on March 27, Alfred Gifford, master; the Sydenham, on March 1, master unknown; and the St. Vincent, on April 1, Henry Palmer, master. Thompson's method of organizing granges here and elsewhere was simple as well as effective. On visiting a community he learned the names of a number of representative farmers whom he approached while at their work in the fields, or at the barn, or wherever they might happen to be at the time. Once having elicited the support of a few men of this stamp, he then arranged for a public meeting. In this way he had sufficient backing when he proposed the creation of a grange, and the local organization when formed had the nucleus of a body of officers. Canadian farmers were won by Thompson's lucid explanations of the aims of the Order, and found him a man in many ways admirably suited for the task he had in hand. For one who was chiefly instrumental in getting a new movement under way in Canada he possessed the fundamental qualification of being able to inspire others. In address he was affable and plainspoken, in the conduct of affairs businesslike and distinctly resourceful. Alfred Gifford who came in contact with him when he was in Grey County, mistook Thompson for a person of greater maturity than he was, but the description which he gives of him is worthy of quotation. "Mr. Thompson," he says, "was a man, I judge, of about thirty years of age—tallish, of slight build, and a real Yankee in character."

Signs were not wanting that the Grange movement was beginning to take a firm hold upon the farmers of Ontario. Especially were they influenced by the fact that for the first time in Canadian history an opportunity was being given them to join a widely-extended social organization that would minister to their long-pent-up desires for self expression. Thomas Doherty, an early Canadian granger, writing from Plympton in April, 1874, epitomized the yearnings of his fellow agriculturists. "I cannot see," he protestingly declared, "why the farmer shall not have an association as well as the mechanic, the merchant, and the professional man." Still, it is interesting to note that from the inception of the movement in Ontario, efforts were made to throw cold water on it by individuals of hostile bent. Such individuals, as was pointed out at the time, employed their best skill in an attempt to "write down" the Grange by "holding forth on its imaginary evils, danger of annexation, injury to traders" and other disabilities. So strong was the opposition, indeed, that a story went the rounds to the effect that a counter-organization had been formed to block the progress of the Grange in Canada, but this story was likely without basis. The newspapers on the whole were disposed to be friendly to the movement, though some of the politicians threw capers when they saw it spreading. The main objection raised to the Grange by politicians concerned the question of possible annexation. "One M.P.P.," wrote William Weld, in satirical vein, "spoke of the probability of our being taken up for high treason for favoring such a movement." The same legislator is quoted by Weld as having remarked, in addition, that farmers ought to stay on their farms and not be so anxious to assemble together. Eben Thompson indignantly denied that he himself, or the grangers across the line, were conspiring to help bring about the annexation of Canada to the United States. Relative to this matter he stated upon one occasion that there was no thought or intention of the kind ever dreamed of by him or the American granges; at another time he said that the talk of possible annexation constituted merely a "bugbear objection" to the introduction of the movement into Canada.

THE PROBLEM OF GOVERNMENT.

Consequent upon the increase in number of the Ontario granges the necessity was foreseen of arranging a proper type of central government for the Order in Canada. The officialdom of the National Grange had adhered to the principle of establishing a State Grange just as soon as fifteen subordinate granges were set up within the confines of any state. Eben Thompson intimated that a similar method of procedure might be followed in Canada where the provincial divisions corresponded approximately to those formed by the American states. "When there are fifteen subordinate granges in this province," he affirmed in a letter published, March 11, in the London *Advertiser*, "a Provincial Grange will be organized." But in the same letter he made a weightier proposal when he declared that the Canadian granges might be allowed the opportunity of instituting a form of self-government for the Order in Canada which would link up the movements already under way in Quebec and Ontario. In the course of his Pond Mills address Thompson had discussed this same idea; he had told his audience that the Canadian membership might conceivably favor a separationist policy, and prefer the establishment of a Dominion Grange having sovereign authority within their own country; this, as he explained it, would give them a "head centre" which would be the equivalent of the National Grange in the United States.

Little hesitation was shown by farmers who had entered the Order in Canada in accepting Thompson's lead on the question of government. By April 1, sixteen subordinate granges had been organized, and from now on the problem of what form of rule should be evolved was lifted out of the realm of theory and had become a matter of practical importance. Few of the membership seemed inclined to the view that Provincial Granges would be satisfactory, but on the contrary there was a rapid crystallization of opinion in favor of the creation of a national governing body which would be more or less independent of the parent organization in the United States. Beyond the shadow of a doubt, occasional grangers were led to this opinion through anti-American sentiment which they often took little pains to conceal; it may be stated, however, that the great majority of the membership were swayed entirely, or at least in part, by questions of expediency. William Weld, for instance, was unable to conjure up any reason why the Grange should not have international ramifications after the fashion of the Masonic Order, or the numerous temperance societies of the day. At the same time he thought that the Grange in Canada should develop along its own lines and have its own identity, more particularly in order that all funds collected in the country might be retained by it and administered by it for its own purposes. Delaware Grange, of which Weld was master, took the lead in advocating a proper settlement of the constitutional issue.

The stage was now set for action. Obviously a plan must be devised whereby a consensus of opinion on the question of government could be reached among Canadian grangers. Either it might be feasible to secure the views of the individual granges in writing, or a deliberative conference might be summoned at which the crucial topic would be threshed out. Delaware Grange, it would appear, authorized the sending out of letters to other granges in which the problem of the control of the Order in Canada was taken up, but unfortunately both the text of these letters and the replies received are no longer extant. The probability is that this undertaking on the part of Delaware Grange was not labor misspent, and that information of a valuable nature was transmitted to it on the matter requiring settlement. It may even be surmised that certain of the answering granges advised the holding at an early date of a gathering that would be truly representative of such units of the Order as had already been established in the country.

Delaware Grange gave over its self-allotted task at this juncture to the Forest City Grange, which had recently been formed at London. The latter body was now destined to play a rôle in the history of the Grange in Canada that was in a measure determined by the favorableness of its location, but above all, by the fact that its secretary, Thomas W. Dyas, was a person who had seen the need for action and had responded to it. Dyas was an Ontario Government land surveyor who made his home in London; having interested himself in the Grange movement, he had come out as a strong champion of the independence of the Order in Canada. He believed that the conference method was the only one applicable to the situation as it stood. Accordingly on May 26, with the full knowledge and consent of his own grange and of leading members of the Order, he issued a general appeal to all subordinate granges in Canada to participate in a meeting which would, he announced, be convened at London on June 2, and which would deal primarily with the constitutional issue. Each grange was requested by Dyas to send its master, secretary and lecturer to the meeting as delegates. It was intended that this should be merely a preliminary assembly whose decisions must of necessity be ratified at some later time.

CHAPTER V

ORGANIZATION OF THE DOMINION GRANGE

IN ORDER to signalize a day of fateful consequences in their lives, the people of ancient Rome were in the habit of marking it on a calendar with a white stone. The historian of agrarian movements in Canada would fain, in drawing up his narrative of events, have the opportunity to indicate in as graphic a fashion as the Romans the importance of June 2, 1874. Contemporary press-writers, it is true, gave very scant attention to the proceedings of the meeting convened on that date at London. But time has wrought a change in opinion, and has lifted this event from its pristine obscurity. It has become possible within recent years to view the London meeting in its true perspective, and to estimate its great significance in shaping the dynamic of the farmers' movements.

Judged by the fact that Dyas had issued his call to the granges only a week before the scheduled meeting, the results attained from the standpoint of attendance were eminently satisfactory. As was fully expected, the majority of the grange officials who responded—twenty-five in all—were from close at hand. Some, however, had journeyed a hundred miles or more from Grey County and from the Niagara Peninsula; the Sarnia district, too, had its quota of representatives. The grangers from a distance were lodged at the city's hotels. Responsibility for completing all arrangements in connection with the meeting had been left with the Forest City Grange, and it had decided that its own hall might be fittingly used for the occasion. The Forest City Grange held its regular meetings in what was then known as the Victoria Buildings, on the east side of Richmond Street, directly opposite the site of London's former City Hall. Thither the assembled grangers wended their way on the afternoon of June 2 to determine the policy and formulate a scheme of government for their Order in Canada.*

---

*The official list of those who attended, together with their place of residence in Ontario, where known, is as follows: Squire W. Hill, Ridgeville; Alfred Gifford, Meaford; Captain James Burgess, Masonville; William L. Brown, Hyde Park; Captain Henry Bruce, London; James Armstrong, Camlachie; H. Payne, Delaware; Matthew Gardner, Woodford; Stephen

41

The day was summery and nature blithesome. Within the Victoria Buildings the grangers approached the task they had in hand with careful optimism and the best of good-fellowship. Captain Henry Bruce,† master of the Forest City Grange, acted as temporary chairman, and guided the meeting through its first and most crucial stages. Thomas W. Dyas, at the request of the chair, set forth the reasons why the meeting had been called, and gave it as his opinion that for financial and other reasons the Order in Canada should adopt a policy of independent action. Straightway after this explanation the grangers focused their attention upon the problem of whether or not they should create a separate body for Canada, as apparently the settlement of this question must take precedence before everything else. While no comprehensive account can be given of the debate which ensued, it is known that it lasted all afternoon and that it was precipitated by a resolution laid before the meeting by Thomas W. Dyas to the effect: "That the time has now come when it is necessary to establish a Dominion Grange." Dyas was plainly one of those who favored the severing of all ties as speedily as possible with the Order in the United States.

Without question Dyas' resolution struck a responsive chord in the breasts of most of the attending grangers; yet some of them demurred at accepting it in the form in which it had been presented. Would the Grange in Canada, asked a number fearfully, be strong enough to stand by itself? Again, what attitude would the National Grange assume towards the Canadian membership if they were to terminate their connection with it in so abrupt a fashion? Evidently no objection was interposed in the meeting to the proposal

---

Wade, Union; Adam Nichol, Wilton Grove; Thomas W. Dyas, London; Henry Palmer, Strathnairn; William Cole, Sarnia; Dr. Henry Hanson, Hyde Park; Henry Anderson, Wilton Grove; Thomas Doherty, Uttoxeter; Henry Weld, London; D. Ferguson, Wyoming; William Weekes, Calder; Thomas Weekes, Calder; W. Pemberton Page, Fonthill; E. D. Scott, Union; John Elliott, Wilton Grove; William Hoskin and A. K. Spencer.

---

†Born on the island of Jamaica, the son of Major Henry Bruce, a British army officer, Captain Henry Bruce had been brought to Canada as a child when his father had been gazetted to a new command at Quebec. The father had been formerly in the 82nd Regiment, and had fought at Waterloo. For many years Captain Bruce and his sister, Mary, lived on a small farm just west of London where they were known for their quaint whimsicalities and their ardent love of nature. Captain Bruce read a paper before the Forest City Grange soon after its formation, deploring the wanton destruction of native birds. He long had one of the finest flower gardens in Middlesex County. Mary Bruce had a name for every beast and fowl on the farm, many of them high-sounding and ornamental. Because King Robert, the Bruce, had refused to kill a spider, she never would kill one, and was horrified when others did so. As she lay dying at the hospital in October, 1920, she requested that her father's swords be laid crosswise on her bed.

that a central administrative body should be organized for the Canadian movement, but it was finally decided that in the adoption of such a policy it would be a matter of wisdom to proceed with due circumspection, and a proper regard for the continuing goodwill of the National Grange. An amendment was accordingly introduced by William Cole, of Sarnia, whereby the original resolution was altered to read in the following manner: "That the time has come when it is necessary to establish a Dominion Grange; be it therefore resolved, that we hereby consider ourselves a Dominion Grange; that we apply to the National Grange to organize us as such; that in the meantime we grant dispensations to subordinate Granges until a final separation from the United States is effected." Upon a vote, the meeting carried Cole's amendment.

Force of circumstances then had placed the Grange officials who had gathered at London in a somewhat anomalous position. Although bent on exercising the functions of a constituent assembly, they had been checkmated in their desire by the need of maintaining pacific relations with the National Grange. The die, however, had been cast and there was now no turning back. The meeting had failed to give any serious thought to the question of establishing dependent Provincial Granges in the country, but on the other hand had, unless the parent body could successfully intervene, taken steps which would eventually bring a full measure of autonomy to the Order in Canada. One interesting feature about this decision on the constitutional issue was the fact that, while no delegates were in attendance from Quebec, the Dominion Grange was expected to have sovereignty not only in that province, but in any other province where granges might be subsequently established.

The same day a provisional list of officers were selected for the Dominion Grange who were to act until the first annual meeting of the Order should be held. The following were chosen, some of them in their absence: Master, Squire W. Hill; Lecturer, Alfred Gifford; Overseer, T. Leet, Danville, Quebec; Secretary, T. W. Dyas; Treasurer, Adam Nichol; Steward, William Weld; Assistant Steward, Captain James Burgess; Chaplain, William Cole; Gatekeeper, L. Galer, Dunham, Quebec; Ceres, Miss Steed, Sarnia; Pomona, Miss Whitelaw, Meaford; Flora, Miss Ellen Weld, Delaware; Lady Assistant Steward, Miss Ellen Armstrong, Camlachie.

An Executive Committee was also appointed for the same period, comprising: Stephen Wade, Matthew Gardner, James Armstrong, Captain Burgess, Henry Anderson and J. F. Cass.

The Declaration of Principles.

The speeches delivered at this gathering where the Dominion Grange "issued into glorious birth" are said to have been uniformly of a high degree of excellence. Directness of manner and clarity of reasoning marked the utterances of those who participated in the debates; a few representatives showed true eloquence. According to a comment of the time, there was in evidence at the meeting "no hesitation, no stuttering, no want of words to convey ideas." In short, the proceedings were throughout of such a character as to demonstrate beyond peradventure that the more intelligent farmers of Canada were associating themselves with the Grange movement.

On June 3 a method of securing representation at the first annual meeting of the tentatively-formed Dominion Grange was drawn up and given sanction. It was arranged that the meeting should be held at Toronto beginning on September 22, and that each subordinate grange in existence on that date should have the right to send two delegates; in addition the provisional officers of the Dominion Grange might attend as well as the wives of officers who had attained the fourth degree. The Quebec granges, in case they could not send delegates, were to be permitted to exercise their voting strength by proxy. In order to avoid jurisdictional disputes during the interval, an agreement was reached to the effect that subordinate granges might not be set up closer than five miles apart. The remaining time at the London meeting was almost entirely devoted to the acceptance of a body of principles for the Order in Canada, and to the drafting of its constitution and by-laws.

The things for which the Grange movement has stood in Canada were set forth in what was entitled its declaration of principles. This document was a compound from two main sources. Its introductory clauses or preamble was taken from a general preamble explaining the objects of the Patrons of Husbandry, adopted at the sixth annual convention of the National Grange held at Washington, D.C., in January, 1873. The bulk of the document, however, was formed of selections made from the declaration of purposes of the National Grange, accepted at its St. Louis sessions, February 4-12, 1874, and of which J. W. A. Wright, a California granger, was the leading author.

The preamble to the declaration of principles states that instruction in the art and science of husbandry is to be above all the aim of the Grange in Canada. "The products of the earth," it asserts, "are subject to the influence of natural laws, invariable and indisputable; the amount produced will consequently be in proportion to the intelligence of the producer, and success will depend upon his knowledge of the action of these laws and the proper application of their principles. Hence knowledge is the foundation of happiness." Membership in the Grange gives the farmer an opportunity to combine in order to attain his ends. "Unity of action," continues the preamble, "cannot be acquired without discipline and discipline cannot be enforced without significant organization; hence we have a ceremony of initiation which binds us in mutual fraternity as with a band of iron; but, although its influence is so powerful, its application is as gentle as that of the silken threads that bind a wreath of flowers."

Heading the declaration proper is found the motto of the Order, to wit; "In essentials, unity; in non-essentials, liberty; in all things, charity." Canadian grangers' ideas on the economics of agriculture are therewith outlined in pithy language. They plan to give added attention to the diversification of crops, and in general to make their farm lands more self-sustaining. With the object of reducing the weight of their exports, grangers will adopt the policy of selling "less in the bushel, and more on hoof and fleece." Knowing too the value of foresight in their industry, they intend to "calculate intelligently on probabilities." And to avoid the influences that have militated against the success of agriculture in the past, the Order will "discountenance the credit system, the mortgage system, the fashion system, and every other system tending to prodigality and bankruptcy."

Upon the question of the business relations of Canadian grangers, the declaration is very explicit. The Order holds no enmity to capital; legitimate business must obtain; transportation companies are necessary to agricultural development. On the other hand the Grange in Canada is firmly determined to bring producer and consumer more closely together. "We must dispense with a surplus of middlemen," contends the document, "not that we are unfriendly to them, but we do not need them—their exactions diminish our profits." Any "tyranny of monopolies" would be distasteful to the granger just as he would be "opposed to excessive salaries, high rates of interest, and exorbitant per cent. profits in trade."

No hesitancy is shown in repudiating the idea that the Grange in Canada has in any sense been established for political purposes. "No grange, if true to its obligations," is the emphatic statement, "can discuss partisan or sectarian questions." It might not call political conventions, nominate candidates, or permit of the discussion of questions on which its members stood divided on party lines. At the same time, the granger must perforce take a deep interest in political issues. It must be his business to do everything in his power to put down "bribery, corruption and trickery" in connection with public affairs. The principles of the Order, it was thought, should be of great value in the realm of government, because those principles "underlie all true politics, all true statesmanship."

The declaration states quite candidly that the Grange movement in Canada is meant exclusively for the farming population. A barrier must be imposed to the admission of the non-agriculturist, since he has "not a sufficient direct interest in tilling the soil, or may have some interest in conflict with our purposes." But sex distinctions are wholly eliminated within the Order; more than that its aim is "to inculcate a proper appreciation of the abilities and sphere of women." While an advocacy of better agricultural education is considered a watchword among Canadian grangers, they desire to obtain better facilities for education all round. "We shall advance the cause of education," is emphatically promised, "among ourselves, and for our children, by all just means within our power."

CONSTITUTION AND BY-LAWS.

Owing to the fact that the Dominion Grange has been in existence for more than fifty years, its constitution and by-laws as promulgated at London in 1874, have been variously revised and amended to meet changing conditions. Nevertheless, as the original constitution and by-laws were operative with only minor alterations during the period when the Order reached its greatest expansion in Canada, a brief study of these documents will be instructive.

Under the terms of the constitution a subordinate grange might be established by nine male persons, eighteen years of age or over, and four female persons, sixteen years of age or over, who in all cases must of necessity be "directly interested in agricultural pursuits." The fee for admission to the Order and for the acquisition of the first four degrees was for male candidates three dollars, and for female candidates, seventy-five cents. At least thirty dollars, therefore, was collected when a grange was formed; but the cost of securing a dispensation for the grange to carry on its functions was two-thirds of this, or twenty dollars. Minimum monthly dues of ten cents per capita were assessed upon the membership of each subordinate grange. No political or religious tests were required of those desiring entrance to the Order, but three negative votes cast by members already in good standing might debar a candidate; at a subsequent meeting, however, the same candidate might again seek admission. It was compulsory for subordinate granges to hold a regular meeting at least once in every month.

Five subordinate granges or a larger number might unite to form a division grange. The expectation was that division granges when set up should have jurisdiction over a single county or, under certain circumstances, over a more extended area. Division granges met as often as the need was felt, and consisted of the masters of subordinate granges and their wives who had been invested with the fifth degree. The finances accruing to subordinate granges were taxed for the benefit of the division grange in whose territory they lay, according to the following plan: seventy-five cents for each male member and thirty-seven cents for each female member enrolled, and a per capita tax of six cents a member payable four times a year. In addition, ten dollars, or one-half the sum necessary to secure a dispensation, was received by the division grange whenever a subordinate grange was formed under its jurisdiction. Not only was the division grange allowed to exercise general powers of oversight with respect to grange matters within its territory, but it was duty-bound to make out a report at regular intervals on the business affairs of each subordinate grange and to transmit this to the secretary of the Dominion Grange.

The Dominion Grange when in session, consisted of its own office-bearers who had been elected at the previous annual meeting, together with their wives, and a body of delegates representing the division granges. Each division grange chose and sent one delegate to the Dominion Grange for every five subordinate granges under its control. Members of the Dominion Grange were eligible to have conferred upon them the sixth and seventh degrees of the Order. The Dominion Grange was supported financially by payments made to its secretary by the division granges, namely: twenty-five cents for each male member, and twelve cents for each female member admitted to the Order, and a per capita assessment of two cents for each member, levied quarterly. It also received one-half of the amount paid in by subordinate granges when a dispensation was granted for their establishment. The issuance of charters and dispensations rested entirely with the Dominion Grange, while organizing deputies secured their powers through its master. A two-thirds vote of the Dominion Grange was always necessary to legalize any amendment to the constitution.

The by-laws as at first drawn up referred principally to the methods of electing the various officers of the Order and the duties that were expected of them. The Executive Committee of the Dominion Grange, which under the constitution consisted of five members elected annually, was empowered to take care of all the necessary business transactions of that body during the time when it was not in session. It was given the right to direct as it saw fit expenditures of money from the treasury of the Dominion Grange in the recess period. And if by way of anticipation it be mentioned that the Dominion Grange assembled for only a few days in each year, it will not be hard to understand why a great deal of the work and worry connected with the advancement of the Order in Canada soon fell upon the shoulders of the Executive Committee; so, too, the Master and Secretary of the Dominion Grange, as its leading officers, were kept more or less permanently active throughout the year in attending to its affairs.

THE GRANGE BECOMES INCORPORATED.

With the object of securing a proper legal status for the Order in Canada, Grange leaders sought and obtained legislation to that end from the federal government. A bill to incorporate the "Dominion Grange of the Patrons of Husbandry" was given its third reading in the House of Commons on March 21, 1877. This measure was introduced by Joseph Rymal, member for South Wentworth, in whose district the Grange was in vigorous condition at the time. By its terms the Dominion Grange received authority to acquire and hold property, both real and personal, and to dispose of the same according to its desire. It could issue regulations and by-laws for the government of the Order, but only in so far as in so doing it did not interfere with the laws of Canada or of the several provinces. The power of the Dominion Grange to establish subordinate and division granges under its corporate seal was granted full recognition; nevertheless, in every instance, these bodies when created were to be allowed to control their own property. The dissolution of subordinate and division granges might be effected through the Dominion Grange revoking their charters, but a subordinate grange could not put in a claim for dissolution unless two-thirds of its members were in agreement. It was also stipulated that the management of the business affairs of the Dominion Grange should be vested in a board of directors which would comprise its Master and Secretary and the five members of the Executive Committee.

The bill of 1877 was re-enacted by parliament in an amended form in March, 1880, under the sponsorship of Lachlin McCallum, representative at Ottawa for Monck. Two important alterations were made in the original measure. In the first place the Dominion Grange was now authorized to set up Provincial Granges in Canada wherever it might be deemed advisable. Further, it was made impossible for a subordinate grange to seek dissolution if seven of its members in good standing were to register their objection to such a move.

CHAPTER VI

Expansion of the Movement in Canada

THE WARM months of 1874 intervened between the organization of the Dominion Grange in June and the opening of its first annual meeting on September 22. Consequently farmers who were interested in the movement had, on account of the season of the year, given little thought to anything but their harvest operations. None the less, during this period twenty new subordinate granges had been established, bringing the total number already in Canada up to forty-four. Moreover, two division granges had been created, the first at London on July 21, and another during August, in Grey County. Secretary Dyas of the Dominion Grange had been busy sending out circulars to various manufacturers asking them what special prices they were prepared to quote to members of the Order, and had received a batch of satisfactory communications in reply. Besides he had superintended the printing of two thousand copies of the constitution and by-laws, a like number of copies of the ritual, and one thousand song cards. For this work Dyas was a good deal out of pocket, but later he was reimbursed from the coffers of the Dominion Grange.

Midsummer, too, had been marked by a joust with Grange officials from across the border, which for the moment looked as though it might have a serious outcome. Though due notice had been given to the parent organization of the formation of the Dominion Grange, National Grange headquarters had not deigned to remit an acknowledgment. Instead, the Master of the National Grange, Dudley W. Adams, of Waukon, Iowa, wrote to certain of the Canadian granges bidding them send representatives to a meeting to be held at London, on August 18, where it was proposed to set up what was intended to rank as a Provincial Grange. Having learned of this move, Master Hill and Secretary Dyas countered with a letter to the granges in which they endeavored to explain the situation, and doggedly affirmed that the "Dominion Grange is an established fact and will so continue." To make

51

sure, indeed, that the cause of the Dominion Grange might
not go undefended, the Executive Committee was also asked
to convene at London on the day named in Adams' letter.
A clash seemed to be imminent. But when Master Adams
appeared on the scene in person at the appointed time, accompanied by the Master of the Michigan State Grange, he
found that his last-minute effort to corral the Canadian
movement had gone awry. One lone farmer, the master of a
subordinate grange, name unknown, had come in answer
to his summons. A parley therewith ensued, and the upshot
was that the Executive Committee graciously invited the
Iowan and his Michigan fellow-granger to lunch at the Albion
Restaurant. Here matters were lengthily debated, and oil
evidently poured on the troubled waters. At any rate the
confabulation ended in friendly manner, and it was announced
that a settlement had been reached which would be of singular
advantage to the Order in Canada.

But Master Adams, having betaken himself home, apparently still nursed feelings of resentment because of the
waywardness, as he thought, of the Canadian movement.
He spoke of affairs in Canada before the National Grange in
session at Charleston, S.C., during February, 1875, and
accused the Canadian granges of having perpetrated acts
of defiance. In consequence his charges were referred to a
special committee for adjudication, and its report, no longer
extant, seems to have been equally as censorious. However,
neither Adams' invectives, nor the committee's report were
given much publicity throughout the Grange, as they were
stricken out when the minutes of the convention were issued
in printed form. Master Hill visited Charleston at the time
to discover the attitude of the National Grange toward
developments in Canada, but is said to have met with a
very frosty reception; only William Saunders among American
Grange leaders appears to have proffered him a welcome hand.
As will be seen, several years were to elapse before a full
measure of harmony was achieved between the two sections
of the Order.

THE FIRST ANNUAL MEETING.

Seventy-three delegates answered the roll call at the first
annual meeting in Toronto, which lasted from September
22-25. A trio of delegates who were in attendance from the
province of Quebec were allowed two votes apiece on account

of the large Grange constituency that they represented in proportion to their numbers. The rather substantial notices of the meeting given in the Toronto newspapers were indicative of the fact that the press had begun to recognize the growing strength of the Patrons of Husbandry in Canada. The *Globe*, in addition to printing a detailed report of Master Hill's address, commented editorially upon the governmental form which the Order in Canada had adopted. "It was wise," it opined, "of the Dominion Grange to sever itself from the parent institution in the United States, with the view of carrying on the movement in a thoroughly national spirit." Confidence was expressed by the newspaper that the introduction of the Grange movement would better the condition, generally speaking, of the Canadian agriculturist; for one thing, the farmer's home would be made a brighter place in which to dwell. Drudgery in connection with farm life, sad to relate, had been leading toward rural depopulation. It was an unfortunate, though common, sight to witness farmers' sons "rushing into law, or trade, or some other calling—only to escape from monotonous and unpalatable duties." The new Order, thought the *Globe* editor, might materially assist in remedying such a deplorable state of affairs.

Among those present at the meeting was Eben Thompson who had come to Toronto following an address that he had delivered to a throng of Grange picnickers at Bond Head, Simcoe County, on September 19. Thompson evidently thought that a wrong construction had been placed on certain of his earlier remarks, since he argued that Canadian grangers had gone altogether too far in the manner in which they had dissociated themselves from the National Grange. But this opinion had not prevented him from acting as an official organizer for the movement in Canada after the formation of the Dominion Grange. According to the secretary's report he had been paid fifty-five dollars for deputy's services during the intervening period. William Weld, who was also at the meeting in virtue of his appointment as provisional steward, requested that he might no longer be continued in that office. He pointed out that, although quite friendly to the new movement, he occupied a rather invidious position as an editorial writer and the publisher of an agricultural paper. He preferred, he said, to be a humble member of the Order without official rank, able, as he put it, to "freely cut and slash into the doings" of the Dominion Grange in case it should in his opinion misuse its powers. For a time after his retirement from office, Weld did criticize the activities of the Order in a constructive manner; later his attitude towards the movement changed, becoming tinged with indifference.

Master Hill was re-elected by the meeting and the following chosen to form the Executive Committee for 1874-5: U. S. Campbell, Brantford; J. Manning, Schomberg; Captain J. Burgess, Masonville; B. Payne, Delaware; and C. C. Abbott, Abbott's Corners, Quebec. The receipts of the Dominion Grange up to date had been $290.20, its disbursements, $219.53. Various standing committees were appointed for the purpose of instituting a division of labor in connection with the administrative functions of the central body. These, according to their objects, were severally named as committees: on Constitution and By-laws; on Preamble and Resolutions to the National Grange; on Songs and Ritual; on Good of the Order; and on Manufacturers. The employment of the committee system in this way met with instantaneous success and has been a permanent policy of the Dominion Grange during its long history.

Phenomenal Growth of the Order.

By New Year's Day, 1875, upwards of seventy-five subordinate granges were in existence in Ontario and Quebec. "New granges," announced the *Farmers' Advocate*, "are forming daily, and the old ones are adding scores to their membership." To be sure, that farm journal was beginning to scent a possible danger in the movement's too rapid and immature development. "Some," it sagely cautioned, "wish to drive the Order too fast." Already with the ushering in of March, the total number of subordinate granges had reached the hundred mark, while division granges were being steadily organized as needed. During the second quarter of 1875 the movement spread like wildfire with the result that by the middle of the year two hundred subordinate granges had been granted charters.

Fragmentary notices, meanwhile, with respect to the advance of the Grange in Ontario and Quebec had reached the Maritime Provinces, and letters began to pour in from that section of Canada, soliciting more information about the Order and its value to the farmer. Accordingly William

Clark, of Caledon, Peel County, was selected to proceed thither as organizing deputy for the Dominion Grange and instructor in the aims of the movement. Clark first set to work in New Brunswick in the early summer of 1875, and soon had established Douglas Grange (No. 220), Charles McGibbon, master, near Spring Hill, York County. Next he went to Colchester County, Nova Scotia, where he met and attracted into the movement Col. William M. Blair, who for many years was to be the most active and distinguished granger in the Maritime Provinces. Acadia Grange (No. 221) was formed close to Blair's home at Onslow, and he was appointed as its master. Also during 1874-5 a few new granges were erected in the province of Quebec; one of the ruggedest of these was at Knowlton, Brome County, Levi R. Whitman, master. Apparently, though, the most of the granges originally set up by Eben Thompson in Quebec had either vanished or become emaciated organizations.

THE ANNUAL MEETING OF 1875.

Little wonder, therefore, that when the second annual session of the Dominion Grange was convoked at Toronto, on October 27, 1875, there was manifest jubilation in the innermost circles of the Order, and a display of enthusiasm among the sixty-one accredited delegates who attended the meetings in Shaftesbury Hall. The Secretary announced that a total of 247 subordinate granges and 22 division granges had been formed to date; the membership of the Order at the time was roughly estimated at 6,500. The treasury was reported to be well filled; the receipts for the year had been in excess of $4,500. But it must be remembered that a considerable portion of this revenue had been derived from the Dominion Grange's share of the regular charter fees assessed upon the newly-organized granges.

Mindful of the ever-widening responsibilities which the Grange in Canada was assuming, the delegates conducted their business with painstaking decorum; the meeting of 1875 has been likened to a farmers' parliament. Master Hill's annual address was not only impressive, but aglow with ardor for the future of the Order. However, there seemed to lurk in the speaker's mind a fear lest the Canadian movement might be in danger of manipulation by artful schemers for their private ends. "The Order," he said, "has now arrived at an important point in its history in this country. We will find many, who are opposed to us, putting forth every effort to stay our progress." On the other hand there would be some who, having noted the growing strength of the movement, would begin to make use of it to increase their influence in the community. In view of these circumstances it became the duty of each member to guard against the intrusion of such as were only "prompted by selfish motives," and to remember that granges were "banded together for a higher and holier purpose than to be the instruments in the hands of designing men."

Items in the list of disbursements for the year ending in 1875 included $125 paid to William Clark and $179 expended for other deputies' services. Eben Thompson had been engaged in organization work during the year, but does not seem to have accomplished much; a portion of the $179 likely went to him. No further reference to Thompson occurs in the annals of the Dominion Grange, and at this point he fades out of the story. Still a young man, he returned to his studies, and can be pictured in after life as often, when making his rounds as a medical practitioner, calling to memory his romantic wanderings here and there through Canada as the Grange's emissary. On the evening of October 28, the Committee on Good of the Order advised a policy of retrenchment with respect to financing all subsequent extensions of the movement, recommending that, so far as possible, the task of organizing new granges be performed without fee by the officers qualified to do so in the already-existing granges. This plan worked well in Ontario, but only to a limited degree in the other provinces.

PEACE EFFECTED WITH THE NATIONAL GRANGE.

A visiting granger from the United States was fraternally received at the 1875 meeting in the person of Dudley T. Chase, Master of the State Grange of New Hampshire. Though Chase was a member of the Executive Committee of the National Grange, there is no evidence that he had come to Toronto on an official mission from that body. His appearance was evidently due to a personal desire that better relations might be established between members of the Order in the two countries. He extended the olive branch to Canadian grangers, expressing the hope that the National and Dominion Granges might be able to co-operate on an amicable basis. In the course of his opening address Master

Hill had stated that the Canadian membership unhesitatingly acknowledged the parenthood of the National Grange, but were eager in turn that their American brethren should accept the independent status of the Dominion Grange without qualification. "The desire is still apparent," he had pointed out, "in all our subordinate granges for a recognition by the National Grange of the United States." Sentiment north of the border, he believed, was strongly in favor of a "fraternal union of the two Granges." An interesting sidelight was thrown on the question of international relations when a report was submitted to the meeting by the Committee on Songs and Ritual. From certain quarters the suggestion had come that the song book in use was too American in its character, and for that reason ought to be discarded. The Committee admitted that it did not find the song book entirely suited to Canadian tastes, but approved of it from the standpoint of general merit, and recommended that the book be still employed, as no case had been made out against its retention.

It must be remembered that the goodwill expressed by Chase was as yet scarcely general among American grangers, and that without question a great deal of antipathy toward the independent Canadian movement still slumbered in the minds of at least a portion of the delegates to the National Grange, when it met at Louisville in November, 1875; however, this feeling did not show itself in any overt act. Thenceforward, in fact, the National Grange appears to have accepted the quasi-defection of the Canadians as a matter of course, preparing meanwhile for the possibility of similar occurrences in other lands to which the Order might be carried. At the Louisville meeting a Committee on Foreign Relations was organized, which during the next few years was to concern itself not only with affairs pertaining to Canada, but with the various efforts put forth to introduce the Order into Great Britain, Germany, and elsewhere in Europe. The farmers of the Old World, it may be mentioned, were visibly influenced by the new movement, but in no country with the exception of Canada did the Grange obtain a foothold outside the United States.

Immediately upon its creation at Louisville the Committee on Foreign Relations outlined, in somewhat grandiose style, its attitude toward the spread of the Order into other lands. Dealing specifically with Canada, it told of the beginnings of the movement there and advised that, although dispensations had been issued to granges in Canada since 1874, this policy should now be discontinued by the National Grange. During the session a resolution was adopted to the effect: "that when fifteen subordinate granges shall have been duly organized in any foreign country, and the same shall have been organized as a foreign State Grange—the Secretary shall receive no more applications for dispensations for subordinate granges within the jurisdiction of such foreign Granges." In this diplomatic manner the sovereignty of the National Grange in Canada was virtually negatived, and the status of the Dominion Grange given recognition without the necessity of a formal vote being put on the subject.

A fuller measure of concord was achieved between the American and Canadian sections of the Order during the years 1876 and 1877. At the tenth session of the National Grange, held at Chicago, in 1876, Mortimer Whitehead, of New Jersey, Assistant Steward, presented a resolution which was approved, requiring that steps should be taken to bring about "close fraternal and business relations" with the Patrons of Husbandry in Canada. Furthermore, Dudley T. Chase read a letter to the meeting from the Secretary of the Dominion Grange, notifying him that he had been appointed to act as an official delegate for the Dominion Grange at Chicago, and empowering him to deal with any matter of interest to Canadian grangers that might come up. The following year Chase's appointment was renewed, and this time he read the National Grange another letter indicative of the quick growth and healthful condition of the movement in Canada. The National Grange, now in a much more friendly mood, decided that Chase might fill a dual rôle by going also as its official representative to the next meeting of the Dominion Grange; nothing, however, was voted him in the way of expenses.

The above-mentioned action on the part of the National Grange, though unsupported from its treasury, meant the endorsation of an interchange of fraternal representation between the two bodies, and was tantamount to a complete acceptance of the claims of the Order in Canada. Only for the acquisition of the annual password and the securing of instruction in the higher degrees of the Order was the Dominion Grange any longer subservient. A just meed of praise was bestowed upon Dudley T. Chase for his services as a peace-bringing intermediary when the Dominion Grange met in January, 1878. "It affords me great pleasure," said Master Hill, "to announce the happy results of the negotiations which have been pending in regard to the recognition of the Dominion Grange by the National Grange of the United States, and for the result of which I believe this Grange has contracted a debt of gratitude to our worthy brother, Dudley T. Chase—for his untiring efforts with the parent institution for our recognition." When the National Grange assembled at Richmond, Virginia, in November, 1878, its Committee on Foreign Relations commented favorably upon the growth and prosperity of the Canadian movement.

In 1879, for the first time, a Canadian-born granger, E. H. Hilborn, then Master of the Dominion Grange, went as a properly-accredited delegate from that body to the National Grange when it met at Canandaigua, New York. Master Hilborn presented himself on November 20, accompanied by his wife, Past Master Hill and W. Pemberton Page. Mutual felicitations were the order of the day after the Canadians had been introduced to the meeting. "On behalf of the National Grange of the United States," said Master Samuel E. Adams, of Minnesota, addressing them, "I welcome you to our fraternal assembly. We are truly glad to take by the hand of friendship those who are coadjutors with us in the noble work of human progress and happiness." Both Hilborn and Hill spoke, depicting the rise and enlarging activities of the movement with which they were identified. "This, Sir," exclaimed William W. Lang, a prominent granger from Texas, who followed Hilborn, "is a pleasing occasion to us—to meet under filial obligations those who are knit together by the strong affinities of agriculture from another country." In 1880 Master Hilborn was again sent as a delegate to the fourteenth session of the National Grange, and in later years the names of other Canadian representatives are to be found inscribed in the records of National Grange proceedings. Jabel Robinson, for six years all told an incumbent of the Master's chair in Canada, was especially assiduous in attending the meetings of the American organization and in bringing back a graphic account of his experiences.

THE MOVEMENT REACHES ITS ZENITH.

The history of the Grange in Canada during the next few years was one of uninterrupted growth in a numerical sense. This was the period also, as will be set forth in Chapter VIII, in which the larger economic ventures of the Order began to take their material form. The subjoined tabulation will show the increases occurring in the number of division and subordinate granges, and in the size of the Order's membership between the annual meetings of 1874 and 1879:

Annual Meeting	Date	No. Subordinate Granges	No. Division Granges	Estimated Membership
First	Sept., 1874	44	2	1,300
Second	Oct., 1875	247	22	6,500
Third	Oct., 1876	530	33	17,500
Fourth	Jan., 1878	635	44	25,000
Fifth	Dec., 1878	711	47	28,500
Sixth	Dec., 1879	766	51	31,000

The membership of the Grange in Canada reached its highest level in 1879, and thenceforward began to decline. Of the 766 subordinate granges reported to the sixth annual meeting as in working order about 650 were located in the province of Ontario. On that basis the Ontario membership may be computed as having been, in round numbers, 26,000 at the end of 1879. An analysis of statistical data leads to the belief that the population of Ontario actually dependent upon agricultural pursuits at that time was in the neighborhood of 900,000. In other words, a grange had been set up in the province on the average for every 1,400 persons dwelling on the land. However, it must be borne in mind that granges were by no means evenly distributed throughout the province. In fact they were often thickly clustered together, as was the case in Grey County where sixty-five live granges were said to have been in operation at one time. Conditions in the County of Bruce must have been quite similar, as it has been estimated that something like eighty-five granges were organized there during the Order's period of expansion.

Wherever granges were plentiful in any district community effort was fostered among them. They united especially for purposes of sociability and pleasure, and an outstanding feature of the halcyon days of the movement in Canada were the open-air picnics held by grangers at the lakeside or at some central point to which excursions might be run. These picnics were mostly set for June 2, in commemoration of the institution of the Dominion Grange upon that day. The event was made attractive as a rule by enlivening band music, an outflow of oratory, and a bountiful repast. The speakers for the occasion were customarily officials of the Order, though politicians angling for grange influence sometimes took the platform to state with winning plausibility their abiding interest in the farmers' cause. Large picnics of this description were held as early as 1876 at Port Hope, Bradford, Flesherton, Brantford, Port Stanley, and in the northern part of Middlesex County. Twenty-two granges combined to make the affair at Flesherton a success. So widely common had Grange picnics become by 1878, that at least one hundred of them occurred in Canada during that year. The most pretentious outing of 1878* was at Port Stanley, where, on June 4, 6,000 persons are estimated to have attended from the surrounding country.

*This year June 2 fell on Sunday so that the Port Stanley Picnic was held on the following Tuesday.

CHAPTER VII

THE RECESSION OF THE ORDER

DESPITE the remarkable expansion of the Order of the Patrons of Husbandry in Canada which took place between 1874-9, signs were not wanting that so far at any rate as Ontario and Quebec were concerned it had reached the apex of its strength. Not only were there evidences of too rapid development in these provinces, leading to the acquisition of certain weaknesses detrimental to the Order's welfare, but outside antagonisms must also be noted which had roused themselves against it and were thirsting for its overthrow. Letters had begun to appear in plenty in the press vilifying the business methods of the Grange, its secrecy of procedure, and its alleged attempt at class dominance. It is plain now that leaders of the Grange would have been better advised had they held its progress more strictly in leash, adopting as they might have done a selective policy with respect to its membership, in order that greater loyalty might have been observable in the ranks, and that the movement might have had added powers of resistance in its days of trial. As it was, immediately after 1879 it began to decline numerically speaking almost as fast as it had arisen.

Grange leaders themselves were among the first to discover that something was wrong; as they were in close touch with the situation, indeed, they were unable to blink the facts. It would seem that while the total number of subordinate granges had been steadily growing, this did not reveal the actual state of affairs. The truth is that the movement had already begun to slip backward in 1878, although to the eyes of the average observer such was hardly the case. During the eleven months from January to December, 1878, the list of subordinate granges had increased, according to the Secretary's report, by seventy-six. But—and here is the rub—during the same interval sixteen granges surrendered their charters, and two more were forced to combine with other granges in their neighborhood. In reality then, ninety-four new granges had been created in order to effect an addition of seventy-six to the total number still rated as active. The official year from December, 1878, to December, 1879, saw a repetition of the same thing: the movement as a whole expanded, but various granges had meanwhile become dormant.

The foregoing considerations lead directly to the belief that the recession of the Grange in Canada started first in 1878, rather than in 1879, when from the standpoint of numbers it attained its greatest success. Master Hill, in discussing the Order's condition before the sixth annual meeting of the Dominion Grange in 1879, acknowledged that it was losing a measure of its pristine vigor. "It is true," he said, "that signs of decay are apparent in some parts of the heritage, which our returns clearly show." In extenuation he offered the explanation that the time must come when in an organization like the Grange, "lifeless branches have eventually to be pruned off." The Secretary, speaking with commendable frankness at the same meeting, declared that in various districts an "apparent apathy among subordinate granges" was discernible, and pointed out that, in his opinion, a stabilization of the Order was becoming absolutely essential. Nor could the fact that the new movement among Canadian farmers, though outwardly powerful, was being sapped of a good deal of its original vitality long escape the attention of carping critics. A foe of the Order, writing in 1880, to whom the wish was unmistakably the father of the thought, endeavored to dismiss the Grange altogether from the scene. "Like most novelties," he averred, "the Grange spread rapidly, put forth a sort of mushroom growth, and has passed —or is passing." Moreover, he was thoroughly convinced that the movement "never took a firm hold of our people,"— possibly, as he jingoistically affirmed, because it was a "Yankee institution."

IN THE MARITIME PROVINCES, QUEBEC AND THE WEST.

Delegates appeared for the first time from the Maritime Provinces at the 1876 meeting of the Dominion Grange, when J. A. Dickson, of Colchester County, Nova Scotia, was elected to the office of Gatekeeper. Already there were seven subordinate granges active in New Brunswick and four in Nova Scotia. The movement in Nova Scotia took a remarkable spurt forward in 1878 when E. H. Hilborn at the invitation of George Creed, of Hants County, visited the province and succeeded as the result of an arduous campaign, in setting up twenty new granges. Next year George Creed himself took up the work of organization and twenty-one more granges were added; he received well-merited encomiums from the Dominion Grange at its regular meeting in December. In 1878 Col. William Blair had been appointed Overseer of the Dominion Grange, and was elevated to the Master's chair in 1881. A report of February, 1882, indicated the existence of sixty subordinate granges in Nova Scotia, distributed among the following counties: Colchester, Hants, King's, Annapolis, Pictou, Lunenburg, Queen's and Cumberland; and of sixteen in New Brunswick in the counties of: Westmoreland, Albert, King's, Shediac and Kent. One subordinate grange, No. 910, was formed during this period in Prince Edward Island at Searltown, Prince County. By 1876 the Quebec granges had risen in number to sixteen, but by 1882 had slumped again to eleven; thereafter the movement crumbled in that province although one organization lingered on at Randsboro until 1894.

Grangers migrating westward from the older provinces of Canada carried a knowledge and love of the Order with them to the lands beyond the Great Lakes. As early as 1876 a subordinate grange was set up at High Bluff in the province of Manitoba. This quickly disappeared, but within a few years seven others were established at Carberry, Mekiwin, Wellwood, Florenta, Gladstone, Arden and Eden. It will be seen from a glance at the map that these were confined within the triangular strip of Manitoba territory which has as its base the main line of the Canadian Pacific Railway, from High Bluff to Brandon and as its apex the town of Florenta to the north. Several of the Manitoba organizations flourished until 1907. Two granges were formed at Morningside, Alberta, in 1905, and one at New Westminster, B.C., in 1908, each of which ran a brief course.

THE ERECTION OF PROVINCIAL GRANGES.

As the Grange waxed stronger in the Maritime Provinces, the contention arose that a greater measure of home rule should be permitted in that section of the country. While it was stated emphatically that the granges there had no desire to separate from the Dominion body, on the other hand, it was resolutely urged that they had local interests to serve, which they could best administer by themselves. "So far as Nova Scotia is concerned," said Col. Blair, at the annual

5—F.M.

meeting of 1878, "we must have a Provincial Grange." To his mind the Dominion Grange had "become too large, too unwieldy, partaking too much of a local or subordinate character." In Ontario as well the home rule principle had numerous advocates. The matter was up again for consideration before the Dominion Grange in 1879, and a decision reached to apply for a revision of the act of incorporation in order to allow for the creation of Provincial Granges. The issue had been determined in a large measure, it must be confessed, by its financial bearing: the cost of bringing delegates from the Maritime Provinces to Ontario had been shown to the meeting to be a heavy drain on the income of the Dominion Grange.

A year later on December 8, 1880, representatives from the division granges in Ontario gathered at Toronto, and the Ontario Provincial Grange was established, Jabel Robinson, Master, and Alfred Gifford, Secretary. This organization, which had a rather checkered career, remained in existence almost six years, holding five annual sessions. The requirements of the granges in the Maritime Provinces were attended to by George Creed, and through his efforts the Maritime Provincial Grange was set up in 1880, embracing under its jurisdiction all of Nova Scotia and a portion of New Brunswick. Levi R. Whitman had been deputed to act if need be in Quebec, but grangers in that province evinced no disposition to launch a governing body of their own and none was ever formed.

From the outset the Ontario Provincial Grange was hampered by difficulties that militated against its success. In the first place Ontario, as the active centre of the Order, was preponderatingly represented in the Dominion Grange, with the result that the problems brought before it were largely identical with those commanding the attention of the Provincial Grange. Accordingly the discovery was made that to a marked extent a dual authority had been inaugurated with consequences oftentimes perplexing. Again, whenever the Ontario Provincial Grange was in session, it was by no means easy to reconcile the divergent elements that had come to it representing the various parts of the province, and for that reason the home rule principle was more or less inoperative. However, the Ontario organization's chief stumbling-block lay in the unproductiveness of its sources of revenue. Under the revised constitution fixed dues had to be paid to it by the lower granges; then, as a supplementary form of income, it had been awarded a certain percentage of the gate receipts taken in on Grange Day at the Toronto Exhibition. But after 1880 the Order was on the down grade in Ontario, and the regular dues fell off in amount. To make matters worse, Grange Day was shifted to an undesirable place in the Exhibition calendar, so that the monetary return therefrom became negligible.

By 1886 the Ontario Provincial Grange was seriously in debt to the Dominion Grange, and was obliged to abandon its annual meeting of that year. The Dominion Grange in consideration of the other's plight delayed its own meeting for eight months during 1886 in order that the Provincial Grange might have time to assemble and elect its delegates. At length the two bodies met, one immediately after the other in November, and, as the situation of the Provincial Grange appeared to be hopeless, the Dominion Grange legislated it out of existence. The Maritime Provincial Grange, which was still functioning in 1886 with over eighty subordinate granges under its control, was set adrift by itself. There is little to relate concerning its further history. A commercial enterprise, fostered at Halifax (vide Chapter IX), grew wobbly in 1887, and its ultimate collapse had a disruptive influence upon the membership. No new granges were formed in the Maritime Provinces after 1889, and in the nineties the Order disappeared in that section of Canada.

THE DOMINION GRANGE, 1879-1907.

To a limited degree a correspondence may be traced between the ups and downs experienced by the Grange movement in Canada and in the United States. Having gotten an earlier start, the Order had achieved its greatest numerical success in the United States by 1875, when its total enrolled membership was estimated at 858,000. In Canada, as has been stressed before, the movement reached its high tide of membership in 1879 with approximately 31,000 under the jurisdiction of the Dominion Grange. Subsequent to these dates in the respective countries a decrescendo occurred by graduated stages until the era "of fat things full of marrow" had given way to days that were lean and hungry; both Canadian and American grangers went through a period of struggles and anxiety. Here the parallelism may be said to end. Whereas after 1900 in the United States a revival of the Order took place which won for it a measure of its old-time prestige, in Canada, on the contrary, no permanent reawakening among grangers has ever transpired.   For a brief season, it is true, there was a spurt forward after 1907, when the Farmers' Association of Ontario was united with the Dominion Grange; but by this time other movements were germinating on Canadian soil and the Grange soon fell back into a state of semi-quiescence.

From 1880-1907 little clue is furnished in the successive annual reports of the Secretary of the Dominion Grange as to the actual membership of the Order in Canada; possibly under the circumstances such omissions are forgivable.   Nevertheless the reports as a rule candidly admit, or leave the inference to be drawn by the reader, that the Order was slowly losing ground.   It is noteworthy that in 1884, ten years after the formation of the Dominion Grange, the membership had lapsed to 12,500.   A decade later only eighty-four subordinate granges were in working order, and the number of Canadian grangers could be more graphically represented by hundreds than by thousands.   The opening years of the twentieth century found the Order in Canada but a shadow of its former self.

The financial statements submitted annually to the Dominion Grange also afford a commentary upon the gradual disintegration of the movement.   During the fiscal year which ended in 1879, the sum of $6,160 was paid into the treasury of the Dominion Grange.   No report was issued in 1880, but that for 1881, covering a period of twenty months, showed a reduction in income to $3,887.   Figures taken at five-year intervals after 1881, as follows, are suggestive of the manner in which the receipts continued to taper off; 1886, $1,655; 1891, $560; 1896, $344; 1901, $195.   When the amalgamation with the Farmers' Association of Ontario occurred in 1907, the revenue of the Dominion Grange had sunk to $134 for the preceding year; thereafter given fresh stimulus it rose to $1,022, in 1909, but only to drop back again to low levels.*

*The following have been occupants of the Master's chair of the Dominion Grange since its inception: S. W. Hill, 1874-8; E. H. Hilborn, 1879-80; Col. W. M. Blair, 1881; Alfred Gifford, 1882; Jabel Robinson, 1883-4; Robert Wilkie, 1885; Robert Currie, 1886; Charles Moffatt, 1887-8; George Copeland, 1889; Henry Glendinning, 1890-1; Peter Hepinstall, 1892-3; Dawson Kennedy, 1894-5; George E. Fisher, 1896; W. F. W. Fisher, 1897-8; Jabel Robinson, 1899-1903; Henry Grose, 1904-5; J. G. Lethbridge, 1906-8; E. C. Drury, 1909-10; N. E. Burton, 1911; Henry Glendinning, 1912; W. C. Good, 1913-4; W. E. Wardell, 1915; J. C. Dixon, 1916-20; Howard Bertram, 1921-4.

SUMMARY OF EXPANSION BY PROVINCES.

An index to the territorial distribution of division and subordinate granges in Canada as they were established until February, 1907, is furnished in the table below. No division granges were set up after 1907, but a column has been added to show where subordinate granges have been formed since that date.

	Organized 1872-1907		Organized after 1907
	Division Granges	Subordinate Granges	Subordinate Granges
Ontario..................	47	800*	64
Quebec..................	..	23*	1
Nova Scotia..............	7	84*	..
New Brunswick	2	38*	..
Prince Edward Island......	..	1	1
Manitoba................	1	8	..
Alberta..................	..	2	..
British Columbia	..	1	..
	57	957	66

The aggregate of all bodies, therefore, created by the Patrons of Husbandry in Canada since 1872 may be given as follows: Dominion Grange, 1; Provincial Granges, 2; division granges, 57; and subordinate granges, 1,023.

THE PRESS ORGANS OF THE GRANGE.

On account of the restricted sphere of its operations, the Grange in Canada has never been able to develop during its lifetime a press which has been the equal of that maintained by the Order in the United States. At its inception the Grange in Canada had to depend upon editorials and news items in the columns of such periodicals as the *Farmers' Advocate* or the *Weekly Globe*, and upon the stories of its progress appearing in the daily papers, more especially those which had a section devoted to agricultural matters. Very soon the conviction grew that the Order must needs have a press of its own. A suggestion was made at the annual meeting of 1875, that the Dominion Grange should consider the advisability of securing a printing plant. At the same

*This summary was compiled for the author after a close analysis of all existing records by Hattie Robinson, secretary of the Dominion Grange. She states that in the case of subordinate granges formed before 1907 only approximate figures can be given for Eastern Canada; she believes that the estimate of 800 granges for Ontario is somewhat too large, while the totals for Quebec, Nova Scotia and New Brunswick may possibly be too low.

meeting Dr. Hanson, of Hyde Park, went further and introduced a resolution calling for the establishment of a paper which would be conducted in the interests of the Canadian membership, but no action followed.

The demand for a Grange organ was met shortly afterward by private enterprise. In 1876 the first issue took place of a monthly known as the *Canadian Granger*, edited by William L. Brown, secretary of the London division grange. Brown had been a school teacher at Hyde Park and is accredited with having been a man of many parts. He opened an office at 13 Market Square, London, and had his paper printed by the Free Press Publishing Company of that city. The *Canadian Granger* was a four-page issue, large folio size, and contained a great amount of intelligence relating to the Order. It reached a maximum circulation of about 3,000 among subscribing grangers. Unfortunately its editor did not possess adequate financial backing, and as advertising was difficult to obtain for his ambitious little paper, he was soon harassed for funds. In June, 1878, Brown went before the Executive Committee of the Dominion Grange and proposed to hand over the paper to that body, on certain conditions, in order that it might be run as an official organ of the movement. The Committee did not incline to the task. Consequently the *Canadian Granger*, a promising publication, suffered an untimely demise; Brown was taken on the staff of the London *Free Press* as its agricultural editor.

Meanwhile another monthly had been launched in the hope that it might supply a channel of communication for the Order. The *Canadian Farmer and Grange Record*, published at Welland, had grown in favor with the membership, and in 1879 became the recognized organ of the movement. This paper, also under private ownership, had as its editor N. B. Colcock, while W. Pemberton Page, then Secretary of the Dominion Grange, assisted in its issue. Within a few years, however, the *Canadian Farmer and Grange Record* had piqued the majority of its grange subscribers by the attitude it had assumed as an interpreter of the affairs of the Order. Grange news according to their complaint was relegated into the background, and other matters of lesser importance given prominence. Hence the Executive Committee of the Dominion Grange reported on it in 1882 as follows: "Your committee regrets to inform you that the *Grange Record* has not realized our expectations as the organ of the Order in advocating the principles for which we labour." In 1885 the paper was moved to Toronto where its name was changed to the *Rural Canadian and Grange Record*, and henceforward it played only a minor role in Grange history.

Rather oddly, just as a recession of the Order was occurring in Canada during the eighties, its periodic literature became more plentiful. Almost simultaneously in 1881 two papers budded into existence, the one in September of that year at Toronto, designated the *Grange Bulletin*, the other in October, entitled the *Canadian Co-operator and Patron*, with Owen Sound as its place of publication. At basis these were really both trade sheets, although in each case they carried an assortment of Grange news. In short time strife had broken loose between them, or rather between the business interests which each paper represented, and the silent mass of grangers were obliged to witness a factional fight within the Order that was very damaging in its consequences. The individual editors, having unburdened themselves of all restraint, entered into a campaign of charge and counter-charge which reeked with personalities, and oftentimes grew most spitefully virulent. Upon several occasions the Dominion Grange was forced to take cognizance of abusive statements that had been printed. All this, of course, made sensational reading for those who took the papers but was lamentable in its effect upon the fortunes of the Grange. The *Canadian Co-operator and Patron* became later an organ of the Patrons of Industry; when it ceased publication in 1903 upon the death of its editor, R. J. Doyle, its title had been shortened to that of the *Canadian Co-operator*. The *Grange Bulletin* had expired years before.

The Dominion Grange, having in 1891 found itself without an official organ, entertained an offer made by the *Farmers' Advocate* to open once again its news columns to contributions relative to the Order. The constitution of the Order in Canada was reproduced in the *Advocate* as a beginning, but apparently the matter ended at that point. Then, for something like sixteen years, from 1891 to 1907, the Canadian movement was bereft of any special means of communication. Finally upon the amalgamation of the Order with the Farmers Association of Ontario in 1907, the *Weekly Farmers' Sun*, of which more anon, became the organ of the enlarged Dominion Grange. Still it must not be forgotten that throughout its long history the Order in Canada has drawn considerable inspiration from Grange journals issued in the United States. Ardent grangers began subscribing for American publications at an early date.   Among such papers coming into Canadian homes might be mentioned: the *Husbandman*, of Elmira, N.Y.; the *Farmers' Friend*, of Mechanicsburg, Pa.; the *Dirigo Rural*, of Bangor, Me.; and the *Journal of Agriculture*, of St. Louis, Mo.

CHAPTER VIII

ECONOMIC ACTIVITIES OF THE GRANGE IN CANADA

A PROPOS of the declaration of principles which it had adopted in 1874 as its guiding norm, the Grange in Canada was inevitably drawn into business activities. As a matter of fact, there was no realm of endeavor into which Canadian grangers entered with more verve and enthusiasm than into the realm of business; none proved more disappointing to them. Individual granges soon began to engage in trade to the hoped-for advantage of their membership; various industrial, commercial and financial enterprises were launched under the ægis of the Dominion Grange. Needless to say critics of the Order have dipped their quills deeply to employ harsh terms of censure in referring to its ventures into business. In some cases the Order has been placed in an invidious position through misrepresentations as to the extent and ultimate effect of its mishaps. For instance, the unwarranted statement has been made that the Grange was brought to its low estate almost entirely by means of its ill-starred business undertakings. It is true that the decline of the Order was hastened in this way. But the reverse is equally true, namely, that other causes making for the decline of the Order helped to deprive it of its membership, and as a result the patronage of its various enterprises fell away. A comparison of the Grange's failure and half failures with those occurring in the every-day business world might not be greatly to the Order's disadvantage.

SUBORDINATE GRANGES ENGAGE IN TRADE.

The discontent which had fostered the development of the Grange movement in the Middle-Western States, as previously noted, had been occasioned in large measure by the power exercised by the railroads. In Canada it was otherwise; hostility to the alleged exactions of the railroads did not manifest itself among Canadian farmers for ten or fifteen years after the institution of the Dominion Grange. The *bête noire* of the Canadian agriculturist during the seventies and eighties of last century was the middleman in trade. Whether he be wholesaler, retail dealer or travelling agent, any one who occupied an intermediate position between manufacturer and final consumer was considered an encumbrance.

The travelling agent with whom the farmer and the farmer's wife had personal dealings had become a subject for obloquy. Against some of these agents there was little cause for complaint; others, however, had stirred up resentment. In the popular mind, when disposing of agricultural implements, sewing machines, fruit trees or other goods in the rural sections, the average agent was thought to be in receipt of excessive commissions. It was stated that the rate of commission varied from 25 to 100 per cent. of the cost price of the articles. These "swarms of travelling agents" occasionally figured in letters to the press. "Some plan," indignantly wrote a farmer, in 1874, who had noted how plentiful they were, "should be devised to check the flood of non-producing, hindering, talking persons." In a further letter the same farmer told of the obeisance made to the travelling agent at the village inn. "Go to any hotel in the country," he fumed, "and there are one or two of them on their travels. They have the best rooms, the chief seats at the table; the host and hostess run to do their bidding. Common farmers can wait. I say, who pays for all this?" In return for attacks of this character, the agent was impelled to take up cudgels on his own behalf. He argued that without his initial labors many articles would never have reached the farming communities, and that his was surely a work of service.

Relations between the farmer and the country store-keeper were on a better footing. At the time when the Grange arose the long-time credit sustem was fully in operation whereby the farmer was carried on the merchant's books, if desired, for a year or sometimes longer. Credit was regularly extended from January 1 to December 31, so that purchases became heavy after New Year's Day. Customarily, the merchant looked for good-sized profits to take care, as he said, of the volume of his credits. Even the more prosperous farmers ran accounts at the country stores, and spent their money in the urban centres. Produce was often hauled long distances to the city or larger town, there converted into money, and goods bought therewith that were necessary back home on the farm. In this way the farmer made a comparison of the prices prevailing in the city with those charged by the local merchant. The farmer believed that he was being defrauded in his district store. The merchant contended that he was doing the best he could in view of the credits that he was forced to carry.

When a large percentage of well-to-do farmers were attracted to the Grange upon its introduction, these especially began to realize that a change might be wrought in the methods by which the farmer secured his supplies. The plan evolved must be to circumvent the credit system by the introduction of co-operative purchasing. This could be accomplished by the secretary of a subordinate grange, on behalf of his fellow-grangers who wished to participate, getting in touch with manufacturers or other dealers from whom they might buy directly. Immediately upon the creation of the Dominion Grange, Thomas W. Dyas, its newly-appointed secretary, as related in Chapter VI, had sent a circular letter to a number of manufacturers, asking what special rates they could offer on direct sales to members of the Order. There had been a liberal response in the way of quotations, and as a consequence price lists had been prepared and transmitted to the subordinate granges. A considerable proportion of the granges began to make purchases of not only farm implements and other farm necessaries, but sometimes as well of staple articles for the household. Little uniformity, though, was observable in trading; whereas one grange bought meagrely and casually, its neighbor often went into business on an elaborate scale.

Trade carried on in this manner could never be permanently successful unless all knowledge of the manufacturers' terms were withheld from the general public. Strict injunctions were therefore given to members of the Order to preserve their trade secrets. But in spite of every precaution taken, information steadily leaked out as to the prices at which grangers were making their purchases. The country merchants, having learned what these prices were, made haste to seize the opportunity to regain their trade. Immediately they adopted the policy of selling to those who would pay cash at the same rates as were set forth in the manufacturers' lists. In other cases grangers, on presenting a token of membership, were enabled to buy at prices which were identical with those offered through their local secretary. The merchants could not have kept up this competition indefinitely, but as a result of their stratagem the practical advantages of co-operative buying were more or less lost to view.

The charge frequently made that a number of farmers joined the Grange for pecuniary reasons only is without doubt quite justifiable. Trade secrets were likely to be revealed by individuals of such type rather than by men of loftier principles. As soon as the terms offered through the Grange might be obtained elsewhere, many who had trooped into the Order with alacrity, trooped coolly out again or became dispassionate in their zeal. Considerable harm was done the Order in this way, although the rolls of the subordinate granges were much better purged of such self-seekers.

The trade in agricultural implements was by long odds the most profitably conducted. Local secretaries found difficulty in persuading many farmers to buy groceries or dry goods in anything but small quantities; for instance, the distribution of tea in one or two-pound lots, as was oftentimes demanded, proved a constant source of worry. "This pettifogging grocery trade," wrote William Weld in 1875, "is, or ought to be, below our sphere of action." Just what saving was effected in the purchase of implements co-operatively is not a matter of record. A few figures supplied by Thomas A. Good, of Brant County, on this subject, during the seventies, will, however, be illuminating. He states that reaping machines were bought at $88 which otherwise would have cost $110; ploughs at $12 instead of $20; turnip drills at $12 rather than for $18; and forks for 55c. which ordinarily retailed at 75c. He further declares that through co-operative buying the price of apple trees had been cut in two, namely from 20 to 25 cents a tree to 10 to 12½ cents a tree.

Isolated cases of granges selling in common also occurred during the early period of the Order's history. In the autumn of 1878 grangers in the Belleville district sold together about 10,000 bushels of barley at $1.12½ a bushel, gaining a few cents a bushel on the transaction. Wheat is known to have been shipped in bulk from Grey County directly to the larger markets with the result that the local grain buyers lost their commission and the farmers made the difference. But members of the Order near Belleville, according to the story of a captious journal, made upon one occasion a sorrowful miscalculation in arranging to ship their grain. They set out to load a schooner with barley, but forgot that in so doing they were intruding on some one else's property, and that wharfage charges might be required of them. "They made themselves quite at home," states the journal in tones of amusement, "using the handcar and railway track, and doubtless would soon have loaded the vessel but for an interruption, which presently came in the appearance of the wharfowner and his attorney; and a stop was put to the proceedings at once." Accused of trespass the luckless grangers had to pay two cents wharfage charges on each bushel assembled for shipment.

The Grange Wholesale Supply Company.

A step beyond the simpler methods of trading described above was taken through the inauguration of the Grange Wholesale Supply Company. This business concern had its origin in Addington County where a division grange set an example in co-operative buying by contracting for orders of farm implements. In due season a company was organized among grangers in the same district with the object of bringing out immigrants who might be employed as farm help. Within a year this company broadened out its activities by applying its funds towards the erection of a grain warehouse from which it began to market barley and other cereals. At length it went further, and opened up a grange co-operative store in the town of Napanee. The leading promoter of these several enterprises had been W. N. Harris, the owner of a four-hundred acre farm in Addington County. Harris, now agreed to leave his farm, and become manager of the Napanee store.

The Dominion Grange noted with interest the opportunities which were offered by the venture at Napanee and decided to give Harris the title of Grange Agent so that through his special efforts the facilities of the store might come into more general use. It was arranged that orders for goods might be sent in from the granges to Harris, who would have them filled by the Napanee store or in some cases directly from the maker. An annual trade of considerable proportions soon grew up under this plan in implements and general hardware, dry goods, boots and shoes and groceries. But the view was currently expressed that the expansion of the store's activities was seriously hampered through the remoteness of Napanee and the unavoidable delays that were frequent in completing the shipment of goods. Accordingly it was proposed to remove to Toronto where the company would be put on a reorganized basis, and be prepared to do business on a larger scale. A prospectus of a new organization, entitled the Grange Wholesale Supply Company, capitalized at $50,000, was drawn up in December, 1879, and stock disposed of among members of the Order. The Company opened for business on Front Street, Toronto, in 1880, with Squire W. Hill as president and W. N. Harris as manager.

Favorable reports respecting the G. W. S. Co. were submitted to the Dominion Grange for several years after its formation until about 1884-5 when trouble had begun to brew between factions of the Order at Toronto and Owen Sound. The company's total sales for the year ending in 1883, according to its financial statement, were $237,000, and a dividend of eight per cent. had been declared; at this time the business necessitated the services of twenty to twenty-five employees. It was also announced that stock subscriptions to the value of $20,000 had been secured although only in the neighborhood of $7,000 of that amount had been actually assessed. Judged by the company's annual turnover, it would appear that $7,000 was a rather low figure for a wholesale concern, and had it set out with a higher paid-up capital the likelihood is that it would have stood up to better advantage under the strain of later years. In 1883 a plea was voiced by grangers in the Maritime Provinces for the establishment of a branch of the G. W. S. Co. in the East, as they claimed it was too far to send all the way to Toronto for goods. The directors authorized the raising of share capital in the Maritime Provinces, and a branch store was opened in 1884 at Halifax.

Unfortunately, at this juncture the first symptoms of wrangling within the Order became manifest. R. J. Doyle started the trouble in the May number of his Owen Sound paper, 1885, by levelling an attack upon John Burns, manager of the Halifax branch of the G. W. S. Co., in which he asserted that Burns, when visiting the granges in the Maritime Provinces, had belittled the Order's fire insurance company that had been instituted with headquarters near Owen Sound. The Dominion Grange inquired into the matter and exonerated Burns, but already blood had been spilled and there was war in the camp. Uninterruptedly thereafter for years Doyle and Harris were at daggers drawn, the former defending the companies in which he was interested, and scoring the manager and directorate of the G. W. S. Co., the latter, through the *Grange Bulletin*, lampooning Doyle and criticizing the organizations he had fathered in the north.   The Halifax store never prospered.   By 1887 a dispute had arisen over its business proceedings and the eastern shareholders upon call refused to pay up their stock in full.   Ultimately the branch had to close its doors, and the shareholders were badly pinched in the collapse.   The home company, too, was partly involved and lost $5,000 in the failure with the result that it could declare no dividend in 1888.

The rest of the story may be briefly told.   W. N. Harris shortly afterward was charged with having mismanaged the affairs of the G. W. S. Co.; lawsuits ensued and he was released from his position.   In the early summer of 1889 there was some talk of winding up the company altogether, but the directorate took fresh courage and found a new manager in the person of R. Y. Manning, of Schomberg.   Manning lacked experience, but he was wise enough to retrench.   He moved the business from 1-7 Jarvis St., where it had been at the end of the Harris regime, to cheaper quarters, and curtailed his expenses in various other ways.   But to win back the trade lost during the Doyle-Harris fracas was next to impossible.   The plan of dealing with Grange secretaries had been discarded while Harris was in office, and the policy introduced of selling directly to individuals.   The *Grange Bulletin* had deridingly stated that the secretaries were antiquated in their business methods, calling them "mossbacks."   Selling directly to individuals meant that the G. W. S. Co. was now disposing of its goods in large measure to outsiders, as throughout this period the Grange had been gradually waning in strength.

Manning continued an uphill fight for several years, and then gave way to G. W. Hambly as manager.   Goods valued at $125,000 were marketed by the Company in 1896, but by 1898 its sales had dwindled to $87,000.   It was still considered a fair risk by commercial agencies, and was carrying out its engagements, but its credit was low, and the old Grange trade was almost non-existent.   On June 15, 1899, the company suspended payment, and called in its creditors.   The stock, estimated as worth $15,000 was put up at auction, on July 19, and sold at fifty-six cents on the dollar.

In the Field of Production.

Visions of the Grange engaged in the co-operative manufacture of goods essential to the farming industry oftentimes seized upon the minds of members of the Order in Canada during its palmier days. Not only did they hope to benefit by the introduction of various forms of producers' co-operation, but they expected that by selling directly to the consumer they might assist in getting rid of the middleman in trade. With the single exception of the salt company organized in 1882, which will be described below, none of these visions became realities. In the spring of 1876 Alfred Gifford was deputed by the Executive Committee of the Dominion Grange, meeting at Brantford, to formulate a plan for a manufacturing company, but the matter was allowed to drop as the time did not seem opportune. The same year J. P. Bull, Treasurer of the Dominion Grange, paid an informal visit to Patterson and Brothers' implement factory near Richmond Hill, in York County. He found this manufactory "in the tidy little village of Patterson" equipped to turn out grain drills, ploughs, rakes, fanning-mills, reapers, mowers, and other forms of agricultural machinery, and employing a labor force of about sixty men. He was peculiarly struck by the neatly-constructed workmen's cottages built in the neighborhood of the factory. He advised the Dominion Grange that the plant was possibly worth between $75,000 to $100,000 and that the owners, in case the Order might wish to acquire it, would leave the question of value to a board of arbitration. Bull's report was referred to the Committee on Commercial Relations, but nothing came of it.

The origin of the Grange's decision to engage in the manufacture of salt lay in its knowledge that a monopoly was being exercised in Canada by producers of this commodity so valuable on the farm. A ring or combine, known as the Canadian Salt Association, had been set up, it was alleged, with the object of arranging price levels to suit its members to the bane of the farmer and other consumers of salt. Accordingly in 1882 initial steps were taken to launch a co-operative company under Grange auspices which would fight the combine, and in April, 1884, a suitable property was acquired in Bruce County near the shore of Lake Huron where mining operations were soon begun. Deposits of salt had been found in Bruce County in 1868 at the depth of about 1,000 feet where the Onondaga rock formation emerges at the mouth of the Saugeen river. At first a crude and expensive method of extracting the salt was utilized by boiling the brine in potash kettles set in a row. Then as the possibilities of the industry became apparent, American capitalists arrived, a number of wells were sunk at Kincardine, and more up-to-date processes of manufacture were introduced. For a time during the seventies large consignments of salt were shipped by lake to Chicago, but the American tariff rates against the commodity proved so burdensome that the industry flagged, and most of the outside capital was irretrievably lost. The Grange thought it might resuscitate one of these properties on the Saugeen river for the benefit of its membership.

In November, 1882, a prospectus was issued from Owen Sound stating that the Order was about to establish a company which would "furnish the people of Ontario with salt at a fair price." References were made in this document to the way in which producers of salt, hiding behind the protective rate in the Canadian tariff, were enabled to fix prices through their combine. The Grange company, on the other hand, proposed to market salt at quotations that would never allow it more than a ten per cent. profit over actual costs of production. Subscription lists for stock were forthwith opened at twenty dollars a share upon an assessable plan, and in October, 1883, a circular was sent out to the granges declaiming once more against the "iron grasp of the monopolist," and asserting that each grange which took five shares of stock in the company would be allowed to supply all its members with salt. By December 31, 1884, 1,464 shares of stock had been disposed of, and already what Kincardiners called the Scott and Gray salt block had been purchased for $12,000 and put in good repair for purposes of production.

Doing business under the name of the Ontario People's Salt Manufacturing Co., Ltd., the Grange organization sold 270 cars of salt to farmers in 1885. It has been claimed that immediately it had entered the field the Canadian Salt Association dissolved and the price of coarse salt fell from one dollar to sixty cents a barrel. A period of stiff competition ensued with the result that the Grange company, which had spent more than was originally anticipated on its works, and had lost custom through the decline of the Order, was in a rather precarious condition by 1888. In that year its deliveries of salt to farmers amounted to but seventy-nine cars. Accusations were made by the Grange company that its rivals, forgetful of good business ethics, were in the habit of adulterating their product with lime and of using short-

6—F.M.

weight barrels in shipping salt to the trade.   Finally to avoid liquidation the Grange Company was driven to conclude an agreement with the association, which had come to life again, whereby it would market its surplus output through the association's agency.   Thus began a period of some four or five years during which the co-operative company was in Egyptian bondage to the salt combine, although the latter was no longer in a position to indulge to the same extent in the reprehensible practices of an earlier day.

Another complexion was put on the situation by the rise of the Patrons of Industry after 1890.   This budding organization, keen for the elimination of unnecessary profits, saw the advantage of striking a bargain with the co-operative salt company.   Accordingly, in 1892, an arrangement was made with the company by the terms of which the Patrons contracted to take annually for three years at least 40,000 barrels of salt at sixty-five cents a barrel.   This gave the company a great impetus forward, so that it was able to sever its relations with the combine and augment its sales until they reached the sum of $31,470 for the year ending May 31, 1894, as compared with a total of $12,267 three years previous; a dividend of seven and a half per cent. was declared in 1894. Many Patrons renewed their contracts at a lower quotation of sixty cents a barrel for the five years from 1895-1900, at the expiration of which time their movement had run its course. Beginning with 1895 the company set about installing a plant for the manufacture of bicarbonate of soda and chloride of lime, but the attempt was a failure and considerable money was wasted.

Advancing costs of production after 1900 due to business expansion and a general fall in the value of money led the Grange company to raise its price of salt on several occasions prior to the outbreak of the European war, although it steadfastly continued to undersell the combine.   In 1901 its price for coarse salt had mounted to seventy cents a barrel; the association quoted eighty cents for the same salt.   In 1904 the Grange company's price was eighty cents a barrel whereas the association was selling at ninety-five cents.   On the eve of the war in 1913 the Grange company found it necessary to hoist its price to eighty-five cents a barrel.   Then, under the stress of war conditions, this organization, which for thirty years had been quite prosperous except during a short interval and which might properly claim to have broken the strength of an insidious monopoly, became a prey to the circumstances of the hour.   Its markets were in disarray; the transportation services out of Kincardine were interrupted; an efficient labor force was increasingly difficult to secure; and to make matters worse, a series of mishaps befell the plant at a time when costs of replacement were exceptionally high.   After 1915 no dividends were paid, and in an effort to stabilize itself the company decided to sell preferred stock yielding interest at seven per cent.   This did not permanently mend matters, and the situation became so acute that the company was forced to make an assignment on January 16, 1922.   All preferred stock and other secured claims were paid in full; unsecured creditors received a final dividend of 35.83 cents on the dollar.   Thus passed the most successful of all the business enterprises of the Grange.

Insurance Projects.

Immediately upon the institution of the Dominion Grange, leaders of the movement in Canada began to discuss the feasibility of organizing Grange fire and life insurance companies upon the mutual benefit plan.   The proposal to launch a fire insurance company was well received, and at the Toronto meeting of the Dominion Grange in October, 1875, a committee of five was selected to inquire into the matter. The committee's report was presented to the third annual meeting in November, 1876, and adopted by it in a slightly revised form.   Straightway the same committee was empowered to proceed to the establishment of a company under the terms of Ontario act which governed the creation of mutual insurance companies.   As a result the Dominion Grange Mutual Fire Insurance Company was formed with head office at Sarawak, in Grey County, and began to write policies in March, 1877.

Mutual insurance companies were already numerous in Ontario, and some of them were in a thriving condition. Unlike the joint stock insurance company, where business is done entirely at the risk of the stockholders, the mutual insurance company allows its members to "insure each other." In other words, the participating member belongs to an association where he becomes liable for his pro rata share of all assessments for loss.   The commonest mode of assessing the membership has been to take an annual levy from them in accordance with the losses sustained by fire during the year. The Dominion Grange evolved another scheme: each member was required to pay a small cash deposit when taking out his policy or renewing it in proportion to the amount of insurance carried. A fund was thus created from which to indemnify such as had suffered loss by fire. This money drew interest at a chartered bank, and in case there was a surplus over losses sustained in any given year, it was applied to reduce the deposit required for the next term of insurance.

No difficulty was experienced by the D. G. M. Co. in securing business. It took risks on farm property only, though it did not restrict its policies to members of the Grange. By 1882 its total risks amounted to five and one quarter million dollars. "I consider it," wrote an Ontario government inspector, "one of the best mutual companies, both as to its plan of operation and management, that we have in the country." At the termination of its fiscal year in 1886 the D. G. M. Co. was doing business far in excess of any farmers' mutual in the country; it had 6,987 policy-holders and had contracted for risks totalling more than seven and one half million dollars. The company was reputed to have the best safety vaults north of Toronto. But again the internecine strife raging at this time within the Order exercised a deterrent influence upon its fortunes. When R. J. Doyle, its manager, assailed the G. W. S. Co. from Owen Sound, the *Grange Bulletin* in turn let loose its fulminations against him and the D. G. M. Co. from Toronto. The *Bulletin* charged that "a company nurtured by the Grange" had now passed outside the Order's control, and Doyle, the "all-wise bungler," was lord and master of the situation. He had intrenched himself at Sarawak, it asserted, "away back in the woods," and there "hide-and-seek meetings" were held at which the interested granger had no chance of appearing or of making his voice heard.

These and sundry other aspersions cast upon the D. G. M. Co. helped to lower it from its proud estate. Besides Grange support was falling away as the Order steadily weakened. December, 1891, saw the company with only 4,329 policy-holders. Doyle went over to the Patrons of Industry in 1892, and the feeble connection still maintained with the Grange was broken; the association then took the title of the Dominion Mutual Fire Insurance Company. A temporary period of success ensued, but finally as its risks began to shrink again, the company went into voluntary liquidation on September 13, 1899; at the time of its demise, it had 3,196 policy-holders and was carrying risks of a little over three and one half million dollars.

A life insurance company was also organized under the auspices of the Dominion Grange but only after opposition to such a venture had died out. In 1875 a committee of investigation was selected to look into the matter but reported adversely to the Dominion Grange at its annual session of 1876; the committee affirmed that where secret societies had ventured into the field of life insurance they almost invariably lost both prestige and membership as a result. The question lay dormant for several years but eventually a company was organized to provide life insurance especially for grangers known as the Canadian Mutual Aid Association for which letters of incorporation were taken out in Ontario on August 20, 1880. It established headquarters at 19 King St. East, Toronto, and selected William Rennie, the seed merchant, as its president. The association was understood to have placed $60,000 in bonds with the provincial Treasurer to guarantee its charter, but it was disclosed under criticism that this amount had only been pledged as personal security with the minister and that no bonds had come into his hands. Nevertheless the organization throve rapidly so that by 1886 it had 3,457 members who held policies valued at close upon eight million dollars. The claims assessment for this year on the mutual plan had been $25.68 per member; in addition there had been an expense assessment of three dollars a member. R. J. Doyle, bespeaking his hostility to a Grange company controlled in Toronto, ridiculed this in his Owen Sound broadsheet as high-price insurance, and accused the company's directorate of gross mismanagement and lack of economy. The company's business slumped as the Order became enervated and in 1891 its name was altered to the Canadian Mutual Life Association. Soon afterward, being in difficulties, it was taken over by the Massachusetts Benefit Association, of Boston.

IN THE SPHERE OF FINANCE.

The most daring of the economic proposals of the Grange in Canada have been in connection with the principles of banking. The Order early expressed a strong conviction that farm lands and the improvements thereon, because of the fixedness of their value, should constitute a logical basis for the capitalization of either a loan society or a bank, and even for the issuance of paper money. Hence the effort made by Canadian grangers to embody their ideas in the formation of a trust and loan society, and their open advocacy of the establishment of an agricultural land bank, or as they chose to call it, a real estate bank of issue. The trust and loan society was organized and had a brief history; the bank scheme never got beyond the stage of theory, although its leading features, as will be shown, were presented to the House of Commons by a non-granger for its consideration.

The idea of forming a trust and loan society which would provide farmers with money at a low rate of interest was sanctioned by the Executive Committee of the Dominion Grange in 1878, and as a result letters patent were taken out for the incorporation of the Grange Trust, Limited, in the province of Ontario, on April 10, 1879. Its charter allowed this organization to issue 20,000 shares of stock at fifty dollars apiece, and to borrow funds up to five times the amount of its paid-up capital. The plan of its promoters was to seek capital in Great Britain and Europe and to reloan it to the stockholders of the company who would not only, it was hoped, obtain cheap money on easy terms, but share as well in any profits that might accrue. A cash payment of ten per cent., or five dollars on each share, was required, and as the membership of the Grange was very large at this time 19,739 shares had been subscribed for by December, 1880; T. J. Staples, of Northumberland County, had been the chief stock salesman. But efforts made abroad to secure capital, especially from the British and French co-operative societies, proved abortive. In order to widen the company's opportunities and, if possible, to enhance its borrowing powers, Dominion incorporation was sought for it in 1883 by means of a bill introduced into the House of Commons by Thomas White (Cardwell). This bill which raised the capitalization of the Grange Trust, Limited, to $2,000,000 was carefully dissected by the Committee on Banking and Commerce before it was allowed to go through the House. However, the practical difficulty of attracting funds to the company from outside sources could not be overcome, and at a special meeting of shareholders held in June, 1886, it was decided to wind up the business which in a small way had operated at a profit. Another act of parliament was, therefore, passed in 1887 appointing the directors of the company as its liquidators, and, as it was entirely solvent, its assets were distributed among the shareholders.

Periodically the question of starting an agricultural land bank in Canada arose for discussion during the first decade or so of Grange history, but no plan for such a bank ever reached sufficient maturity for action to follow. In 1878 a real estate bank of issue was recommended to the Dominion Grange as the type of financial organization which would be peculiarly suitable to the conditions and needs of a farming country. According to those who outlined this project the capital of the bank was to have been built up upon the basis of trust deeds or first mortgages, and a form of paper currency to have been emitted with these documents as security. Note issue would have been altogether dependent upon credits held against the land. The scheme impressed the delegates assembled, but was allowed to rest at that point. In 1884, when the Dominion Grange was in session at Ottawa, a deputation came before it on March 5th with the object of explaining the details of a certain proposal for the erection of a farmers' bank which had recently been brought to the attention of the House of Commons by Dr. George C. Orton, member for Centre Wellington. The Dominion Grange after due consideration went on record as favoring Dr. Orton's plan.

The Wellington County member had set forth his views on the subject in a lengthy speech delivered to the House of Commons in February. He was convinced, he said, that farmers' banks should be established in Canada to arrange for short-term loans to farmers at reasonable rates of interest. In periods of depression, to his mind, the farmer was in the position of an under dog, and was forced to pay high interest charges for temporary accommodation. Invariably under these circumstances he was driven into the fold of the loan societies since the chartered banks did not desire his business. At such times the stock of currency was always very scarce in Canada, especially in the agricultural districts. Orton thought that the currency situation might be relieved if farmers' banks were established by the government and given authority to issue legal tender notes up to one-half the assessed value of improved farms belonging to either stockholders or borrowers. In this way a farmer who had deposited a first lien or mortgage against his holding up to one-half its assessed value could, as the case might be, occupy on the one hand the position of an investor in the bank or on the other a borrower from it. Orton contended that five per cent. ought to be the maximum rate charged for loans by these banks. Moreover, he was strongly of the opinion that the Canadian banking system should be brought completely under the government's control, and that the government should regulate the entire note issue of the country. S. R. Hesson (North Perth), upholding Orton's point of view, spoke in a similar strain. Sir John A. Macdonald, who had listened intently to the debate, complimented Orton on his address, but said that he had not been convinced by the arguments presented. "However," remarked the Premier with his accustomed adroitness, "as I am not a financier, I have no objection to our having a full opportunity of examining into the subject." Orton's proposals were then referred to the House's standing Committee on Banking and Commerce, and there, as might be expected, died a natural death. Meanwhile, in high financial circles, the Wellington County member's heretical preachments had stirred up vigorous antipathies. "As an exhibition of ignorance," bitingly commented the *Monetary Times*, "it has never been surpassed in Parliament." The same journal, alluding to Orton and his associates, considered "their talk about financial matters," to be the "veriest nonsense." "Parliament sometimes jokes," it went on remorselessly,—"Dr. Orton's Bill was a contribution to the funny element."

THE COLONIZATION SCHEME.

In consequence of the passage by the Macdonald administration of the Public Lands Act in 1879, numerous colonization companies were formed with the object of purchasing tracts of virgin soil in the Canadian North-west to which settlers might be attracted from the eastern provinces. Discredit was brought on the Grange through the activities of one of these companies, known as the Temperance Colonization Society, by reason of the fact that leading members of the Order were partly responsible for its promotion. The aims of this society were first set forth in a prospectus issued in October, 1881; then in March, 1882, it was duly incorporated, and on the 25th of the same month extensively advertized in the Toronto papers. G. M. Rose, publisher, was named as its president, W. Pemberton Page as vice-president, J.

Alpheus Livingstone as secretary-treasurer, while Squire W. Hill was listed on its board of directors. The company claimed to have perfected an arrangement with the Dominion government whereby it was to receive 2,000,000 acres of land in a "compact block" in the West, and—better still—was to be permitted by the government to keep this territory absolutely free from the sale of intoxicating liquors. Subscriptions for land would be taken from purchasers at the rate of two dollars an acre, ten per cent. of which must be paid in immediately.

Directors of the society hit upon a novel method of presenting its claims to the public by appearing personally at Toronto Exhibition. President Rose mounted a platform near the horse ring, together with other directors, and there expounded upon the merits and possibilities of the organization, using a large scale map to give point to his remarks. By one method or another the company was quite successful in disposing of its scrip contracts to eastern investors who put faith in the lavish claims made. The temperance idea appealed to many, including Dr. John Potts and Dr. W. J. Hunter, Methodist ministers, who were placed on the society's initial board of directors. These reverend gentlemen, later scenting fraud, withdrew from the rather conspicuous position they had occupied in relation to the venture, and can in no sense be implicated in the company's wrong-doing.

By 1886 the Temperance Colonization Society was headed full tilt into difficulties. An exposé of its alleged practices was given publicity through front page articles appearing in the Toronto *World*, January 14-16 of that year, and thereafter a whole medley of lawsuits occurred, in which the company was involved, lasting until 1890. It now became known that the government had never definitely agreed to sell the company 2,000,000 acres in a compact area; as a matter of fact the Public Lands Act precluded such an agreement since it had stipulated that even-numbered sections of land in the West must be reserved for homesteading and pre-emption. Neither had the government promised to give the society authority to forbid the sale of intoxicating liquors in the land allotted to it for the simple reason that to do so was beyond the scope of its federal powers. It would seem that on June 6, 1882, the society did acquire from the government 213,760 acres of land adjoining the present city of Saskatoon, but only about 200 settlers had migrated to this area. The price charged by the government for land had been $1.10 an acre. In making its disclosures the *World* asserted that the company had already taken in $400,000 from the resale of its holdings, but that so far only $84,000 had been handed to the government on account.

The court proceedings made it quite plain that the promoters had been guilty of flagrant misrepresentation in submitting their scheme to eastern investors. However, no one was decisively laid by the heels as a result of either litigation or newspaper dispraise. Questions were at different times propounded in the House of Commons respecting the society, and in 1890 a member read an exceedingly doleful letter to parliament from an embittered scripholder who told in minute detail how he had been fleeced through the company's transactions. At length Hon. E. Dewdney, Minister of the Interior, announced in 1891 that a settlement had been reached with the society, and that its total holdings in the West were to be restricted to 100,000 acres; he further stated that it had paid in $100,000 to the government and upon that basis had been discharged of all indebtedness. Just how many grangers put their money into this enterprise it is impossible to say— probably a goodly number. The Order itself was in no wise culpable in the matter as it had no official connection with the society; the presence, though, of Hill and Page among those who engineered the scheme assuredly exercised a deleterious effect upon the interests of the Grange in Canada. While it is hardly conceivable that $400,000 ever accrued to the society from its resales, as the *World* had intimated, the belief, long current, that certain persons had profited richly by the enterprise and that the scripholders had paid the piper, was doubtless well founded in fact.

CHAPTER IX

THE GRANGE'S INTEREST IN MATTERS OF LEGISLATION

TO THE credit of Patrons of Husbandry in Canada it may be stated that never have they forgotten the fundamental precept of their Order that as an organized body they must keep out of partisan politics. In the United States the Grange has not always been so careful on that point. Not only at an early date did politicians creep insidiously into the Order in the United States, but here and there Grange organizations became immersed in the affairs of independent political parties which brought harm to the Order when those parties fell by the wayside. In Canada, on the other hand, grangers have confined themselves to the criticism of existing political conditions, and the open advocacy of measures deemed of importance to the agricultural population.

In a few cases men identified more or less with the Grange movement have sought election to the Canadian House of Commons or to one or other of the provincial legislatures, but they have done so in a private capacity and not as representatives of the Order. In January, 1875, Squire W. Hill, then Master of the Dominion Grange, contested Monck for the Liberal Party in the Ontario elections but was defeated, receiving 1,100 votes to his opponent's 1,412. Col. W. M. Blair was a successful candidate in Colchester County, Nova Scotia, in the provincial elections of 1878; he sat for Colchester during two terms of the legislature until 1886. Charles A. Drury, although unable to gain a seat in the House of Commons when he contested North Simcoe in 1882, was subsequently elected to the Ontario House of Assembly in 1887. The following year Sir Oliver Mowat, Premier of Ontario, having established the new combined portfolio of Agriculture and Public Works selected Drury as the first executive head of those departments. John Tolmie, first a granger and then a Patron of Industry, sat at Ottawa for West Bruce from 1896-1904, and for North Bruce from 1906-1911; his lusty rendition of Annie Laurie in Gaelic during an all-night session of parliament never failed to attract a throng. In

1900 Jabel Robinson was returned to the House of Commons with a good-sized plurality from the West Riding of Elgin County. He had run as an independent, with the result that he played the rôle of a free-lance during his four years at Ottawa. Though sixty-nine at the time of his election, Jabel Robinson proved himself an active and skilful debater in the House, and his speeches, largely on matters pertaining to agriculture, fill many pages of the Canadian Hansard. Of the parliamentarians of more recent years who were nurtured in the Grange more will be related in due course.

VIEWS ON THE TARIFF, 1872-78.

As an organization addressing itself especially to agrarian problems, the Grange in Canada has always during its history been vigilant to the effect of customs and excise tariffs upon the lot of the farmer. Since 1907 the Order's attitude on tariff issues has been more or less bound up with the policies of concurrent farmers' movements, and will be treated in other chapters. Prior to that date, however, an evolution of opinion on tariff matters had occurred within the Order which forms the basis of an interesting study. Whilst recognizing the fact that the National Policy with its protective features was officially set up in Canada by the government of John A. Macdonald in 1879, it is well to remember that a step toward the introduction of that policy had already been taken by Macdonald in 1870. Especially significant is it, indeed, that Macdonald permitted an uptrend of duties in 1870 in the schedules affecting the mine and the farm. Coal, wheat, and flour of different kinds, hitherto on the free list, were made dutiable in the tariff of 1870. Imported coal was charged fifty cents a ton on entering Canada; likewise wheat, four cents a bushel, wheat and rye flour, twenty-five cents a barrel, and other flours, fifteen cents a barrel. Within a year Macdonald found himself compelled to cancel this revision, but for all that the farmer had been given a taste of what a tariff might mean that afforded protection to agriculture as well as to the manufacturer.

When the Conservatives went into opposition in 1873, their chief appeal to the farmer for a number of years was that he should favor a National Policy of protection because it would build up an extensive home market for his products. This argument, while proving attractive enough to the farmer of the day, was not wholly satisfactory. The farmer claimed that his industry might reasonably expect protection also. If the tariff rates on manufactured articles were to be raised as the Conservatives desired, above the average of seventeen and one half per cent. maintained by the Liberal government, then it would be only just and fair that agriculture, in like fashion, should receive a measure of protection. Such a demand coming from the agricultural communities did not escape the observation of protectionists who foresaw that it might be used to their advantage; to wit, the *Monetary Times* suggested that a scheme of co-operation between manufacturers and agriculturists on the tariff might be brought about in order to facilitate the propaganda for a National Policy.

Just as the Conservative campaign for higher tariff rates was gathering full momentum during the winter of 1875-6, discussions occurred in the granges as to whether a petition should not be drawn up incorporating the Order's views on the tariff question. Eventually blank forms were issued to the subordinate granges to which might be appended the signatures of those favoring protection for the agricultural industry. These forms were upon their return to have been transmitted to the government as an expression of the Grange's opinion. The result was somewhat disconcerting to the Executive Committee which was managing the affair. A proportion of the granges made no return of the forms; others sent letters disapproving of the action that had been taken. Approximately 5,000 names were inscribed on the forms which came back, or about one-third of the membership of the Order at that date. The Executive Committee under the circumstances did not feel justified in presenting the petition, and held the matter over for further consideration. This was the only attempt made by the granges at joint action on the tariff question previous to the election of 1878 in which Macdonald came again into power. Although the petition was withheld, the fact that 5,000 grangers had signed themselves in favor of protecting their own industry in 1876 is a good criterion that the Order as a whole was inclining to the support of Macdonald's National Policy. There is reason to believe then that the majority of grangers went to the polls in 1878 and helped in the downfall of Mackenzie by voting for higher tariffs. They were rewarded by the incoming government. Sir Leonard Tilley, the newly-appointed Minister of Finance did not ignore agriculture when he abandoned the old seventeen and one half per cent. average, and embodied duties which ranged from twenty to forty per cent. in his tariff bill of 1879. Wheat imported was to be taxed at the rate of fifteen cents a bushel; other rates in the tariff were: rye, ten cents a bushel; wheat and rye flour, fifty cents a barrel; oatmeal, one half cent a pound; bacon, hams and smoked meats, two cents a pound.　The wheat tariff at this time was almost the equivalent of that of the United States which was fixed at twenty cents a bushel in 1883. While Macdonald was in office the wheat flour rate was hoisted to seventy-five cents a barrel.

Desertion of the National Policy.

Nevertheless, during the long Conservative regime, 1878-1896, a gradual revulsion of opinion took place within the ranks of the Grange towards the policy formerly endorsed by the bulk of its membership. Several reasons may be adduced to explain this change of front.　In the first place, the National Policy, though broadening the home market, had done little or nothing, according to the grangers' view, to relieve the agricultural depression of the eighties; whereas the fluctuations in wheat prices had been from $1.02 to $1.76 a bushel in 1877 on the Chicago market, they had so declined that by 1887 the range was from 67c. to 95c. a bushel. Again, the rise of combines and monopolies in Canada, a phenomenon of the period 1880-90, implemented as it was by protection and the bounty system applied to the iron and steel industries in 1883, had been an eyesore and offence to the farmer who had to sell his wares in a competitive market. Besides, the drift toward the cities had begun in Canada; the farms were being robbed of their workers, and immigration was at a low ebb.　As early as 1883 Master Jabel Robinson was found delivering an ardent attack upon the evils of protection before the assembled Dominion Grange.　During the next decade hostility to protectionism grew apace within the Order. "It is useless for us to cry out against rings and combines," lamented George Copeland, in his Master's address of 1890, "so long as our tariff invites them, and encourages their continuance in our midst."

In November, 1893, the Executive Committee of the Dominion Grange drew up a petition for presentation to the government in which they expressed themselves in part, as follows: "We are practically and painfully aware of the fact that protection has not increased the value of farm products, which seem after fifteen years of this tariff to be shrinking in value all the time." Two years later, in 1895, the Secretary of the Dominion Grange sent a memorial to Ottawa in the name of the Order, asking "that the tariff of the Dominion be reduced to a revenue basis, as we disapprove of bonusing any industry at the expense of the country." Indisputably, then, Patrons of Husbandry in Canada as a body had taken up a position antagonistic to protection and the bonus system previous to the overthrow of the Conservative administration in 1896. But it will be borne in mind that, when the grangers had helped Macdonald to power in 1878, they were a stalwart host; on the other hand, when they rallied against the government which Tupper led in 1896, they were a decimated band of the faithful. "It now commands no attention," pessimistically acknowledged Robert Wilkie, Secretary of the Dominion Grange, with reference to the Order's waning influence in 1896, the very year that Hon. Wilfrid Laurier took over the reins of office at Ottawa.

SPECIAL TARIFF CONSIDERATIONS

Because of the peculiar burden which certain tariff rates were said to impose upon the farmers of Canada as a class, these rates were specially protested by the Grange from time to time. Possibly the most lengthy agitation conducted by the Order during this earlier period was for a reduction in the taxation on coal oil. As the wax and tallow candle disappeared from use in America, refined petroleum came to be looked upon as a necessity for the illumination of lamp and lantern on the farm. Oil began to flow in quantity in southern Ontario after 1860, so that not only was the Canadian demand met thereby, but there was a surplus for export as well. Between 1870-5 the output of these wells fell off rapidly, with the result that, instead of exporting millions of gallons annually, Canada was compelled in 1875 to secure 700,000 gallons of refined oil from the United States. At that date the customs duty on coal oil was fifteen cents a gallon, the excise duty, 5 cents a gallon, and coal oil was selling in Canada at thirty to forty cents a gallon or at about fifteen cents more than was obtained for it in the United States. In 1875 the Dominion Grange decided to champion the farmers' cause with respect to this article of daily use, and a committee consisting of J. P. Bull and A. J. Hughes was selected to draw up a memorial requesting the government to reduce the customs duty on oil to five cents a gallon, and to remove the excise duty altogether.

The same year a debate was precipitated in the House of Commons by Charles C. Colby, Conservative member for Stanstead, who, though moderately protectionist in principle, argued that the customs duty on coal oil should be cut in two. He said that oil was being smuggled across the border in large quantities, and that a lowering of the duty would likely put a stop to such illicit traffic, and as a sequel the revenue from the article would remain the same. It was argued on behalf of the refiners that they needed the ten cents a gallon they were receiving in the way of protection, because the Canadian oil was inferior in quality and the refining process for that reason more costly. The excise tax, it was said, would surely have to go if the customs duty were reduced, or else the Canadian oil industry would be ruined. A resolution moved by Colby on the subject in 1875 was defeated in the House. However Sir Richard Cartwright, minister of Finance, proceeded to grapple with the situation in 1877 by eliminating the excise duty on refined oil, and reducing the customs duty on it at the same time to seven and one quarter cents the imperial gallon. The protective feature was thus retained in connection with the industry, but the Canadian consumer obtained cheaper oil. The Macdonald government on assuming office in 1878 continued the rate of seven and one quarter cents a gallon until 1893, when the duty was fixed at six cents a gallon. Meanwhile the Dominion Grange had been pressing for a reduction of the duty to three cents a gallon, and when it petitioned the government to that effect in 1893, it pointed out that five and one half million gallons of coal oil were being imported annually into Canada. Finally under the Laurier administration the rate was lowered to five cents, and then after the election of 1904, to two and one half cents the imperial gallon.

Another import tax that was particularly irksome to the Canadian farmer was the duty on binder twine, since he realized the fact that the incidence of the tax fell on him alone. The Dominion Grange, along with the Grand Association of the Patrons of Industry in Ontario and Quebec, strove to have this tax removed from the Canadian tariff. The binder twine industry, it might be mentioned, having obtained a foothold in Canada about 1880, had grown sturdy behind a protective *ad valorem* duty of twenty-five per cent. levied on all kinds of twine entering the country. By 1890 the farmers were using binder twine in immense quantities, and were disturbed at the prices they paid for it in comparison with those charged their fellow-agriculturists in the United States. The Dominion Grange in 1891 boldly importuned the federal government that binder twine should be put on the free list. Almost simultaneously William Mulock, member for North York, introduced a like proposal embodied in the form of a resolution into the House of Commons. A ponderous debate ensued in the House on the question which spread into the sessions of 1892 and 1893. Mulock quoted figures to show that binder twine was selling for three cents more in Canada than across the line, and produced evidence to demonstrate to the House, as he believed, that the manufacture of binder twine in Canada was under the monopolistic control of the National Cordage Co., of New York.

Henry Glendinning in his Master's address to the Dominion Grange in 1892, asserted that the revenue accruing to the government from the binder twine tax was practically nil, and that the manufacturers of twine, if the duty were removed, would "be willing to take a smaller percentage of profit, rather than allow manufacturers of another country to undersell them." Memorializing the government the same year, the Executive Committee of the Dominion Grange asked once again that binder twine be allowed to enter Canada duty free, and in the body of their petition alluded to the fact "that the operations of trusts and combines are conducted with great secrecy—but there seems scarcely room for doubt that the supply of binder twine is controlled by an American combine—with a branch office in Montreal to supply the Canadian trade." Copies of this petition were sent to the Cabinet and to about one hundred private members of the House of Commons; Sir J. J. C. Abbott, the Premier, formally acknowledged its receipt. That the petition bore fruit was indicated by the announcement made by Hon. George E. Foster, minister of Finance, that the duty on binder twine would be lowered to twelve and one-half per cent., the change to take effect at once. The Executive Committee transmitted its thanks to the government, though it still persisted in the opinion "that the duty should be abolished, and the Canadian farmer should be permitted to benefit by the competition of the world." No further concessions were won from the weakening Conservative administration, but when

7—F.M.

Laurier came into office, as will be noted, he trimmed the duty down to ten per cent., and provided that on and after January 1, 1898, binder twine was to be admitted entirely free into the country.

Upon the first introduction of the National Policy, a uniform tax rate of twenty per cent. was laid on all imported agricultural implements. This duty was maintained in the tariff for five years, when suddenly in 1884 under the suasion of its protectionist principles the government increased the rate to thirty-five per cent. The Dominion Grange appeared somewhat apathetic regarding the tax on implements, as it accepted the thirty-five per cent. rate until 1893 without remonstrance. In a petition sent to Ottawa by the Executive Committee in November of that year, the following clause was inserted: "We ask that the duties on agricultural implements be reduced to fifteen per cent., as we consider this would leave the Canadian manufacturers a sufficient advantage over the foreign manufacturer." Just what influence this request had with the government it is impossible to state, but in the extensive tariff revision of March, 1894, Foster abandoned the thirty-five per cent. rate and returned to the pre-1884 duty of twenty per cent. It is more than likely that the Conservatives, by this reduction, were endeavoring to conciliate the farmer in anticipation of a general election. During the budget debate of 1894 James McMullen, member for North Wellington, argued strenuously that, even with the twenty per cent. duty in force, the Canadian manufacturers were receiving fourteen dollars protection on each binder made in the country. The stand-pat attitude assumed by the Laurier government between 1896-1906 respecting the tax on imported agricultural implements will be considered in Chapters XIX and XX.

THE NOXIOUS WEEDS ACT.

The Grange, however, has been deeply interested in other matters of legislative importance than the tariff. During its short tenure of life, for instance, the Ontario Provincial Grange took up the question of the damage done by noxious weeds, and the means that might be employed for their eradication. Just before Confederation an act had been passed by the legislative assembly of Upper Canada in 1865 with the object of safeguarding the farms of the Province from the inroads of the Canada thistle. This legislation was still on the statute book fifteen years later, but in the interval a rapid propagation of other weeds than the thistle had occurred, and there was a crying need for a wider and more scientific measure. The Provincial Grange, in order to meet the situation from the farmers' standpoint, decided upon the appointment of a special committee to deal with the subject. The committee after due investigation recommended that a deputation should wait upon the Ontario government with the suggestion that the township councils be compelled to appoint inspectors who would have power to supervise the destruction of weeds in the township areas. Up until this time the highway overseers had been responsible for the work of cutting down and destroying the Canada thistle. The committee also thought that penalties should be enforced against those who allowed noxious weeds to flourish on their farms, or who vended grass or other seeds in which the germinating element of harmful plants might be lurking. The government gave close heed to the Provincial Grange's advice, and in 1884 drew up a bill based in the main upon its suggestions. By this it was enacted that a township council must choose an inspector of noxious weeds upon the application of fifty or more ratepayers. Each inspector so chosen had to see that all noxious weeds were cut down and destroyed on the farm lands of the township, and also that the diseases of black-knot and yellows were exterminated from the orchards. The noxious weeds mentioned for destruction were: the Canada thistle, ragweed, ox-eye daisy, wild oats, and burdock; but the municipality could list as noxious whatever other weeds it saw fit. Ten days' notice must be given to the owner or occupier in which he could clear off weeds that had been discovered on his land. At the expiration of the ten days the inspector must take action, either superintending the destruction of the weeds himself at the offender's expense, or haling the offender before a Justice of the Peace where a fine could be imposed on him of from five to twenty dollars. A similar fine must be collected from any farmer who sold contaminated seed. In 1891 the original act was amended so that grain diseases were brought under the supervision of the township inspectors, and, at the suggestion of the Dominion Grange, the occupant of the land now became entirely responsible for the destruction of weeds. In addition it was enacted that any one who knowingly sowed smut with his grain seed would be liable to a fine. In 1893 the provisions of the act relating to the diseases of fruit trees were deleted and embodied in a separate measure.

THE QUESTION OF TILE DRAINAGE.

Credit must be given to the Dominion Grange for having originated a plan whereby the farmers of Ontario might secure money for the purpose of underdraining their lands. As practical tillers of the soil members of the Order knew the injury done to their land by stagnant, subterranean waters; they had seen their cattle stand hungry and emaciated upon it; they had watched the hoary exhalations rise from it in spring and autumn, and a myriad insects breed upon it in summer. The best-known expedient for getting rid of under-lying waters of this sort was to arrange a conduit of tile drains set in at a proper distance below the surface. Most farmers found this a burdensome expense, and few of them could pay for all the work necessary in a lump sum. The Dominion Grange sent three representatives to the Ontario legislature in 1878 to ask that body to devise a method of loaning money to farmers who desired to drain their property. The outcome was the Ontario Tile Drainage Act assented to in March of the same year.

According to the terms of this act, a township council might procure a sum of from $2,000 to $10,000 out of the provincial treasury through the authorized issuance of debentures maturing in twenty years. The money thus obtained was to be loaned to any farmer who applied to the council in sums ranging from $100 to $1,000; to requite his indebtedness the farmer might either pay back eight dollars per annum for every one hundred dollars borrowed during a period of twenty years, or he could make other satisfactory arrangements for repayment. Inspectors of tile drainage might be appointed under the act who would investigate the applications coming in to the council, and keep an accurate estimate of the rods of drain and cost per rod of drain laid on each farmer's land. The provincial treasury was protected by the stipulation that all arrears from the township with interest thereon at seven per cent. became a first charge upon the funds of the municipality. This act became very popular among agriculturists and large amounts were taken from the Consolidated Revenue Fund of the province to invest in drainage debentures. In 1887 the necessary annual repayment for each one hundred dollars borrowed was lowered to seven dollars and thirty-six cents.   The measure was quite adequate for the times, and was only superseded when engineers took up their work in the counties, and municipal borrowing was put upon a new basis.   The municipal drainage acts subsequently passed have occasioned expensive litigation that was unknown under the act of 1878.

The Taking of Market Fees.

About forty Ontario municipalities of those which held customary markets in 1879 took regular fees from the farmers and other sellers of goods who made use of their privileges. In that year the Dominion Grange adopted the rather advanced position that fee-taking for the use of markets should be entirely abolished.   In 1881 a similar opinion was expressed by a joint committee representing both the Dominion and the Ontario Provincial Granges in an interview granted to them by members of the government.   In stating their case the grangers pointed out that the farmer by attending a market was conferring a benefit on town and city purchasers, and should not be charged under a system which in their understanding of it was "a relic of barbarism." Urban dwellers came back with the argument that much money had been expended by municipalities in acquiring market sites, and in the erection of buildings to accommodate the farmers; the municipalities, therefore, should be reimbursed for their outlay.   The government found itself between two fires and hardly knew which way to turn.   The draft of a proposed bill dealing with the matter was shown to the officers of the Ontario Provincial Grange, and, although it did not abolish market fees, this bill met with their approval.   Afterward a deputation of mayors, representing market-fee towns and cities, came to Toronto, and put their side of the case to the government.   The government then veered around, and as a result a compromise measure was passed, which, taken as a whole, was quite unsatisfactory to the Grange, but which with some amendments has remained law ever since.

Highly divergent views were uttered in the Ontario legislature when the question was up for discussion.   D. Creighton, Conservative member for North Grey, vigorously advocated the entire disallowance of market fees.   Other men pled the cause of the towns and cities.   It was urged that the rural sections should be forced to surrender their toll gates if market fees were to be eliminated.   Hon. S. C. Wood, Provincial Treasurer, introducing the bill which became law, said that the vested interests of the municipalities had to be respected, but that the fees permitted under the measure were low and that many farm articles were specifically exempted from any charge. According to the terms of the act, fees of from two cents to ten cents might be collected on market days from those purveying butter, eggs, and poultry, and upon the sale of each head of live stock; fees of from two cents to fifteen cents might be charged for the weighing of grain, meat, wood and hay. No levy could be made after nine o'clock in the morning from April to November, nor after ten o'clock during the rest of the year. The weighing of hay, wood, etc., required the mutual agreement of both vendor and purchaser. At a later date municipalities were legally empowered to lease or sell their rights, and the system of taking fees has gradually died out in the province.

The Question of the Size of County Councils.

Even though the county councils of Ontario hold but two statutory meetings in the year, valuable time is usually taken up by the councilmen in attending; it has often been remarked that the June sessions particularly come at a very busy season for the farmer members. Shortly after the organization of the Grange a reduction in the size of the county councils of Ontario was urged by the Order as a matter of public expediency. The composition of the county councils was regulated at the time by an act of pre-Confederation days. By it each township was qualified to send up to the council its reeve, and then possibly one or more deputy reeves, according to the number of voters on its municipal list. In certain of the large and populous counties under this system the councils had more than fifty members and tended to become unwieldy. Also, because of the distances frequently travelled by assembling councilmen, and the days spent by them in transacting business, the councils were looked upon as distinctly uneconomical. Upon various occasions dating from 1879 the Dominion Grange entreated the Ontario government to devise legislation to better the situation. The Grange had a plan of its own to lessen the size of the councils; namely, that only reeves should be sent as representatives from the townships, and that each reeve should have voting power in the council in proportion to the number of seats which his township had formerly held there. But when the government at length took action in 1896, it completely ignored the suggestion of the Grange and introduced a form of representation from the counties quite at variance with that hitherto in operation.

Under the new legislation each county was to be laid out in districts according to the extent of its territory, population and the assessed value of its property, and two councilmen, elected in alternate years, were to come from each district. It was enacted that no council should have less than eight members, while the largest must not have more than eighteen members. A commission made up of County Judges was to divide the counties. Hon. A. S. Hardy, who sponsored the bill, estimated that by means of it the number of councilmen in the province would be cut down to about two-fifths of their former total. But the government did not seem to realize that in formulating this scheme it was trespassing upon what were deemed to be the ancient constitutional rights of the individual townships. It was difficult to persuade the rural people of the province that the townships in which they dwelt should be no longer represented as such in the county councils. Complaints were constantly arising from the weaker townships that the district councilmen neglected their interests to the advantage of other sections, and that they were unable to oust these men from office.

Eventually the question of representation in the county councils was reopened by the Whitney administration in 1906, and the act of 1896 was annulled. The older system of township representation was restored with a stricter limitation of the number of deputy reeves who might come to the council. Owing to the rural depopulation that has taken place in Ontario, few deputy reeves are now in evidence in the county councils; besides, better roads and better means of transportation have made it easier for the farmer members to get to the meetings. It remains to be seen whether the Grange's proposals to appoint only reeves with graded voting power will ever become an issue in Ontario again after the population of the counties has reached or surpassed its quondam dimensions.

RELATIONS WITH THE TRADE UNIONISTS.

In 1886 a questionnaire was received by the Dominion Grange from the Secretary of the Trades and Labor Congress of Canada inviting it to state its attitude upon a number of matters of public interest. A reply was drawn up by a committee of seven from the Dominion Grange which is of historic value in that it supplies a commentary upon the respective views of labor and farmer organizations at the time. Manifestly the Grange's committee in answering the twenty-one questions propounded had only a hazy knowledge of some of the issues involved; on other questions it was evidently better informed. The committee was frankly opposed to the abolition of the contract system in public works; neither did it believe that educational and other state property should be subject to taxation. It doubted the wisdom of debarring Oriental labor from Canada, of introducing a plan to elect officials which were then appointed by the Crown, and of abandoning the policy of furnishing assisted passages to immigrants. So, too, the committee did not favor the grouping of constituencies and the application of the principle of proportional representation in elections; moreover, it was unwilling to grant that municipal offices should be thrown open to those without property qualifications. On the question of the eight-hour day in industry it stated its hostility without ambiguity as representing the farmers' viewpoint. "It would be impracticable on the farm," was the committee's response, "a waste of valuable time, and must necessarily lead to an increase in the price of the products of labor."

Yet on several important points the Grange was unhesitatingly in accord with the views of the trade unionists. In setting forth the Order's position on the subject of co-operation, the committee took a very definite stand: the application of co-operation, it affirmed, was "one of the principles of the Grange Order, and should have our sympathy and support wherever justly and fairly carried out." Similarly, with reference to the public ownership of communications within the Dominion of Canada there was absolute concurrence between the Grange and Labor. "We believe that the time has come" ran the committee's dictum, "when the government should assume control of railway, telephone and telegraph communications." The Grange's support was also pledged to any attempt to establish the Torrens system of land transfer and registration on condition that costs should be held at a reasonable level. Again, the committee was of one mind with the trade unionists respecting the appropriation of Canada's public lands which it contended should be held for actual settlers, and, like Labor. it was ready to demand the amendment of "all laws which delay speedy justice or discriminate against any class or creed of our people." Answering the question whether the Grange was in favor of legislation that would provide for arbitration in labor disputes, the committee declared its opinion "that the time has arrived when the enactment of some equitable and efficient laws for the settlement of labor disputes has become a necessity."

INTEREST IN OTHER MATTERS OF LEGISLATION.

Space does not permit of a full treatment of the miscellany of other matters upon which the Grange sought legislative action from time to time. In only a minority of instances was the Order able to get the ear of the ruling powers, but for all that some of its successes are noteworthy. In 1887 it made a plea to the government of Ontario that live stock should no longer be a subject for taxation in the municipalities; the following year, when the Assessment Amendment Act was passed by the legislature a special clause was inserted effecting this desired exemption. At the instigation of the Grange an Act respecting Steam Threshing Engines was put through the Ontario House of Assembly in 1889, whereby it became necessary for manufacturers of engines to equip them with proper spark arresters before placing them on the market, and which forced those who ran the engines to keep their spark arresters in good order.

Standardization of the size of both salt and apple barrels; an amendment to the Free Library Act allowing libraries to be set up in unincorporated villages with a minimum of fifty book readers; a change in the school law compelling township councils to pay $200 out of their funds for every new school constructed—these were other reforms achieved in Ontario mainly through the Grange's influence. Nor must it be forgotten that as early as 1892 the Order requested the federal government to reduce the postage on letters from three to two cents an ounce, that in 1901 it advised that an experiment should be made with rural-mail delivery in one or two sections of the country, that together with other farmers' organizations it solicited the appointment of a railway commission for Canada, and that it was steadfastly in favor of the compulsory teaching of the art and science of agriculture in the rural schools. For many years, too, the Dominion Grange with zeal unabating took cognizance of the Senate of Canada and yearned for its total abolition—"a haven" as it called that body, "for discredited politicians, and a means of rewarding party service."

PART II

The Patrons of Industry, 1889-1902

The Farmers' Association of Ontario, 1902-1907

CHAPTER X

The Patrons' Movement in Ontario

AGRARIAN discontent, which for twenty years had been gathering potency in the United States, came to a head during the period, 1890-96. A group of restive farmers' organizations, having linked forces and having attracted to their cause an element of Labor, launched the Populist Party which boldly entered the presidential election fight of 1892. The success of this Farmer-Labor *entente* was instantaneous; although a third party and with a more advanced platform than any yet known in American history, it captured twenty-two seats in the electoral college. Both of the old-line parties were staggered at the situation. The Republicans, in view of the circumstances, played a much wiser game than their political opponents, for, having entrenched themselves behind the great financial interests of the East, they prepared carefully for the campaign of 1896. The Democrats, on the other hand, fearing the South and West, adopted at Chicago their now famous eclectic platform with Free Silver as its dominating feature, and sought to draw the Populists unto themselves. The election of 1896 was contested with the acme of bitterness. It ended in the return of the Republicans to power, the almost immediate obscuration of Populism, and a temporary degradation of the farmers' hopes.

Coterminous with these events in the United States occurred a noteworthy ebb and flow in the political annals of Canada. Many Canadian farmers at this time believed that as producers they were being systematically hoodwinked by the professional legislator, and had begun to yearn for a party of their own, through which they might achieve aims of a political character. The Grange, of course, had nothing to offer them, as it had carefully avoided politics, but this desire for independent action was to be realized in quite an unexpected manner. Just as the fateful nineties were being ushered in, an organization known as the Order of Patrons of Industry entered Canada from the State of Michigan and at once took an insistent hold on the farming communities.

109

With unprecedented rapidity—it grew even faster than the Grange had done—this new Order spread through Ontario and into Quebec and the golden West. For a season it left its impress upon the business life of Canada, played an important political rôle, flourished, indeed, like the proverbial green bay tree, and then, like the Populist movement to the south, almost as suddenly withered and passed away. The movement inaugurated by the Patrons of Industry was a social ebullition that could scarcely have been repressed; yet, looking backward, the critic of to-day is driven to the opinion that it came before its time. The farmers of Canada were hardly ready for the extensive programme that it endeavored to make effective, and when the Order collapsed it brought with it a reaction that was very much to the farmers' disadvantage.

Upgrowth of the Patrons of Industry.

The politico-economical association which took the name of the Order of the Patrons of Industry of North America had its origin in 1887 at Port Huron, in the State of Michigan. The founders were: Rev. F. W. Vertican, who had conceived the idea of developing the organization, Dr. David Campbell, a physician, and F. W. Krauss, a printer, all of Port Huron. The Order which had a ritual and was secret, though not pronouncedly so, aimed to give its members an opportunity to discuss together matters of scientific and economic import. A supply of booklets, containing an outline of its purposes and original constitution, were issued from Krauss' press, and Vertican was commissioned to begin field work for the proposed movement in the territory immediately to the north of Port Huron. Vertican* was a convincing speaker, and to

---

*A retired minister of the United Presbyterian Church, Vertican was in the neighborhood of seventy years of age when he began to set the heather afire in Michigan with the doctrines of Patronism. His first work was done in St. Clair, Sanilac and Huron counties, where apparently he was well acquainted. He was selected as president of the Order and Dr. David Campbell as secretary. F. H. Krauss, who was named treasurer, had been drawn into the movement, because, as he has humorously remarked, Vertican, "being Scotch, had an eye to the possibilities of having a job press in the family." In addition to expanding phenomenally in Michigan, the Order had by 1889 been established in Ohio, New York, Pennsylvania, Indiana, Illinois, Wisconsin, Iowa, Minnesota and Nebraska. An estimate made in 1891 placed its total membership at about 200,000, scattered through 3,000 lodges in seventeen different states. The *Western Farm and Home*, issued by Krauss at Port Huron, was adopted as the official organ of the movement. Besides, Krauss published once a month the *Patrons' Guide*, which was used to disseminate news about the Order and at one time had a circulation of 100,000. In the flush of their wide-spread development in Michigan, the Patrons essayed their fortunes in the state elections of 1890. They put up a candidate for Governor who, naturally was defeated, but they elected six members to the state House of Representatives and four to the state Senate. In its westerly ramifications the Order encountered the keen rivalry of the Farmers' Alliance, and this marked the beginnings of its decline. Together, in fact, with the Alliance it succumbed in the United States before 1900.

the surprise of himself and his confrères had little difficulty in enrolling farmers in the lodges or sub-associations which he sought to create under the Order's jurisdiction. "The thing," as Krauss has since tersely put it, "grew like a mushroom."

The Order of the Patrons of Industry developed almost exclusively as a farmers' movement, although its founders had provided for the admission to it as well of mechanics and laborers. Statistics would indicate that within a few years 75,000 Michigan farmers had taken its vows, while in the meantime it had moved out into other states. At the apex of the Order stood its Supreme Association with head-quarters at Port Huron; then, as it spread, Grand Associations were set up with jurisdiction in the individual states. Its membership early showed a reluctance to confine themselves to the prolixities of seemingly resultless debate, and began to turn their energies to more practical ends, consummating business arrangements and even entering into the realm of politics. In Michigan a diluted form of co-operative buying became the vogue among Patrons whereby they undertook to make purchases from storekeepers who agreed to restrict their profits to from ten to twelve per cent. on all goods sold to members of the Order. As a sequel merchants in the state who had not come to terms with the Patrons complained that they were resting under a species of boycott, and asked the wholesaler to intermit sales to their competitors who were deriving benefit from the Patrons' trade. This opposition proved embarrassing but did not prevent a good deal of business being conducted on the aforesaid plan.

Invasion of Ontario.

Only the broad-sweeping St. Clair river, fresh from the limpid waters of the upper lakes, lay between the Port Huron shore line and the town of Sarnia with its fertile hinterland in the province of Ontario. The proximity of this good farming country, even though under another flag, where Patronism might be implanted, could not escape the attention of Port Huron officials of the Order, and as might be expected they debated the advisability of sending in an organizer. An affirmative decision was reached, and in the early summer of 1889 Norman Smith, who had done meritorious work for the Order in Michigan, having crossed the St. Clair river, pro-ceeded to the neighborhood of Mandaumin, in Lambton

County, about eight miles east of Sarnia, where he set up the first primary lodge in Canada. Smith was a native of the islands of Lewis and Harris in the Hebrides, stockily built, and possessed of a ready tongue and compelling manner. He discovered that Ontario farmers were every bit as eager to receive instruction in the tenets of Patronism as had been their fellow-industrialists in Michigan, and soon he was dotting Lambton County with lodges. As the movement grew he enlisted the aid of James McLean and Fergus Kennedy, of Camlachie, in the work of organization, with the result that before long a sub-association had been located in practically every school section of the county, and the Order carried into the adjoining counties of Kent and Middlesex. On May 5, 1890, articles of incorporation were obtained for the Canadian branch of the Order under the terms of the Ontario act governing the formation of benevolent societies.

At a gathering held in Sarnia during the autumn of 1890 and attended by some forty Patrons a county association was instituted for Lambton County. A visitor at this meeting was Caleb A. Mallory who had come all the way from Northumberland County, east of Toronto, to spy out the land. Organizers were now penetrating farther and farther into the province, and the movement had made such headway by the beginning of 1891 that it became imperative that a governing body should be created for the Ontario membership. Steps were accordingly taken to hold a constituent assembly at Sarnia on February 25, which was found, when it had been opened, to have representatives in attendance from eighteen counties. A strong desire was manifested by the delegates present to cut loose from the parent organization in the United States and to set up an autonomous body in Canada. The delegates felt that little community of interest existed between them and their brethren over the border; that it would be better if they had their own financial centre in Canada, and that it was expedient that they should be allowed to draw up a national platform without interference from abroad. Having passed a resolution in favor of separation, the meeting proceeded to form a Grand Association of the Patrons of Industry of Ontario with a complete staff of officers which included the following: Grand President, Fergus Kennedy; Grand Vice-President, C. A. Mallory; Grand Secretary, C. A. Welch, and Grand Lecturer, William Nesbit. Three Grand Trustees were also appointed and a committee named to consider the various points that might be embodied in a national platform.

Word of what the Sarnia meeting proposed doing had brought two leading officials of the Supreme Association post haste across the river to remonstrate and to claim jurisdiction in Canada. As a result proceedings towards independence were stayed until the matter should be considered at the annual convention of the Supreme Association which was set for March 28, at Jackson, Michigan. Following this convention a joint parley was held at Sarnia with Rev. J. W. Vertican, Supreme President, in attendance, when all objection to the Ontario Patrons' action was withdrawn and the promise given that a notice to that effect would be published in the *Western Farm and Home*, the official organ of the movement in the United States. Whereupon the financial and secretarial headquarters of the Ontario Association were located at Strathroy.

At the very moment when the Grand Association of Ontario was being organized a political campaign was in full swing in Canada, as the Macdonald administration had issued writs for a general election to be held on March 5. Patrons in the federal riding of Bothwell, emboldened by the strength of their lodges, had decided to put a candidate in the field in the person of Alexander McLartey, of Dawn Township, Lambton County. A small committee, with Emerson E. Parratt as its mentor, had taken counsel together in the Queen's Hotel, Dresden, and had drawn up a rather sumptuous platform for McLartey's use. A three-cornered fight developed in Bothwell, which ended with McLartey at the foot of the poll, although he had led both his competitors in twelve rural subdivisions of the riding and had done particularly well in Dawn and Sombra Townships. W. E. Taylor, rated as a Liberal candidate, was also endorsed by the Patrons during the election in North Middlesex; he lost out by only six votes.

The special platform committee selected at the Sarnia convention met at Chatham, on March 10, and tentatively adopted a draft of policies submitted to it by one of its members, Grand Lecturer William Nesbit. Sole authorship of this draft may be ascribed to Nesbit, though he has since acknowledged that he was familiar with McLartey's platform and incorporated some of its ideas. The committee then sent on the draft to more than 300 lodges in the province with instructions that they should vote upon it clause by clause

8—F.M.

and report back to the Grand Secretary of the Association. When the results of this referendum had dribbled in and been tabulated, a special meeting of the Grand Association was called for September 22 at London, where it was expected that the platform would be given its final form.

THE LONDON PLATFORM.

None of the clauses in the draft had been seriously opposed in the voting so that the Grand Association in formulating the platform made only slight digressions from Nesbit's original plan. Its special sessions, convened in the London City Hall, were accorded considerable newspaper publicity. Among those present was T. J. Leahy, of Huntingdon County, province of Quebec, where the Order had already been planted. Leahy was admitted to full privileges in the Ontario association, which now decided to take the Quebec movement under its wing. R. J. Doyle's Owen Sound paper was accepted for the time being as the Patrons' official channel of communication, but was soon supplanted in favor by a new journal, the *Canada Farmers' Sun*, issued first at London during 1891 by George Wrigley, a member of the *Advertiser* staff. Wrigley, as the Order throve, took his paper to Toronto in 1893. There it was to have a long period of usefulness and to be the guiding star of successive farmers' organizations.

The Patrons' platform as evolved may be summarized as follows under a few main headings:

(a) Matters of general import: (1) The maintenance of British connection; (2) Reservation of public lands for actual settlers; (3) Rigid economy in every department of the public service; (4) Simplification of the laws and a reduction in the machinery of government; (5) Abolition of the Canadian Senate.

(b) Tariff policies: (1) Tariff for revenue only, adjusted to fall as far as possible on luxuries rather than necessities; (2) Reciprocal trade on fair and equable terms between Canada and the rest of the world.

(c) Transportation: Prohibition of the bonusing of railways by government grants as contrary to the public interest.

(d) Elections: (1) Preparation of the Dominion and Provincial voters' lists by municipal officials; (2) Arrangement of electoral districts to conform to county boundaries as far as the principle of representation would allow.

(e) Special legislative demands: (1) Effective legislation to protect labor and its results from combinations and monopolies that enhance prices; (2) Appointment by the county of all its officials except the county Judges.

Progress and Decline of the Order in Ontario.

At such a pace had the movement swept forward that when the annual meeting of the Grand Association of Ontario and Quebec was convened in Victoria Hall, Toronto, on February 24, 1892, delegates were in attendance from thirty county associations. The paid-up membership was reported as approximately 30,000, distributed among some 1,400 lodges. Fergus Kennedy, in his presidential address, belabored tariffs in general, alleging that nearly everything bought by the Canadian consumer was supplied to him through combines and monopolies. Arrangements were now made to open permanent headquarters for the Ontario and Quebec association in Toronto, and the custom arose of always holding annual conventions in that city. However, Quebec Patrons only sent accredited delegates to the meeting of 1894, and then in December of that year set up a Grand Association of their own.

Whoever will study the record of these Patron gatherings in Toronto must acknowledge that they were energetically conducted; yet he cannot help but note that in a measure they lacked the intellectual stimulus and *bonhomie* so characteristic of all sessions of the Dominion Grange. Albeit a perusal of any list of delegates to the Grand Association of Ontario will reveal the fact that many grangers had evidently sought refuge from their moribund organization in the newer and more active movement. C. A. Mallory was named Grand President of the association in 1893, and retained that office until 1898. Each year he opened the sessions with an elegant and forceful dissertation which carried an immediate appeal and which the newspapers were glad to print verbatim.

The total membership of the Order in Ontario and Quebec was computed at 35,000 in 1893; twelve months later it had mounted to at least 50,000; in fact in some quarters was fabulously rated at thrice that number. Possibly the year 1894 may be taken as the turning point in the fortunes of the Order in Ontario, since by that time, in spite of triumphs in the political field, which will be recounted, disharmonies within and attacks from without were beginning to shatter its prestige. In March, 1895, C. A. Mallory referred to "dark insinuations" and "even occasional positive declarations" that were being bandied about the Province concerning the alleged mismanagement of the association's finances.   Leaders of the movement, he said, in Ontario were being charged with "profiting largely at the expense of the poor, deluded toilers." Because of this criticism a special, investigatory committee was appointed which brought in a report stating that the finances of the association were in a satisfactory condition, and that hints of wrong-doing on the part of the Grand Officers were without foundation.   Still, whatever the reason, the coffers of the association were very low when it made ready for the election contest of 1896.

In December, 1895, Joseph L. Haycock, leader of the Patrons in the Ontario Legislature, submitted a resolution to the Grand Board proposing that the terms of admission to the Order should be made more liberal by extending the rights of membership to all and sundry who would accept the association's platform.   This would entail an abandonment of the Order's ritual together with its tokens and password. Haycock's plea was that an independent party was required to fight the machine methods in vogue in Canadian political life, and that the Patrons would be hindered in their aims unless they opened their doors wider.   But when this resolution was presented at the annual meeting of 1896, a spirited hostility developed against its acceptance, and upon a vote being taken, two-thirds of the delegates lined up in favor of leaving the constitution unaltered.

Then followed the federal election of 1896, disastrous to the Patrons' aspirations.   In February, 1897, the usual throng of delegates found their way to Toronto, but they were in a cheerless mood.   Even the Grand President spoke of the Order's lamentable failure in the election as "a cause for discouragement." With the assemblage in such a frame of mind, a resuscitation of Haycock's proposal of the year before was only to be expected; indeed the matter was now debated with enthusiasm.   As a consequence the meeting decreed that any one, except he be financially interested in a combine, might become a Patron in Ontario by simply pledging his adherence to the political teachings of the association.   The exclusion of combinesters was, needless to say, a mere play on words, as these individuals would scarcely have found themselves at home among their sworn enemies. Nevertheless, Patronism could not be bolstered up in Ontario by broadening out its membership, and after 1898 it slowly withered away until there was but a remnant of it left when the Farmers' Association of Ontario arose in 1902.

Attitude on Various Questions.

Eager to pass judgment upon any idea accredited to be progressive, the Patrons of Industry were in the habit of turning their Toronto gatherings into an open forum for the discussion of many novelties. An instance of this occurred in 1894 when a whole array of propagandists were introduced to the annual meeting and each given time to discourse upon his favorite theme. The president of the Women's Enfranchisement Association—a man by the way—spoke on votes for the opposite sex; others were heard on such subjects as the prohibition of the liquor traffic, the initiative and referendum, and the single tax.

The problem of taking a definite stand on the temperance question was brought up for consideration soon after the Patrons began to organize in Ontario, and in 1891 an effort was made to obtain the voice of the subordinate lodges on the subject. The lodges were dilatory in replying, only 120 of them sending in a report; three-fourths of these indorsed prohibitory legislation. The matter then lay dormant until 1895, when it was again discussed before the Grand Association of Ontario and referred back to the county associations for their verdict. But the official attitude of Ontario Patrons on the issue remained undetermined until the annual meeting of 1897. Seemingly the majority of Patrons were friendly to prohibitory legislation, yet a stubborn minority, contesting every inch of ground, had sought to dictate the policy. At the 1897 meeting it was decided that the advocacy of prohibition would not be placed definitely in the association's platform; nevertheless, a strongly-worded pronouncement was issued which constituted a defence of the temperance cause. The question of women's suffrage was sent for opinion to the county associations in 1895, and lapsed at that point. Henry George visited Canada in 1895, preaching the doctrine of the single tax, but his personal influence was not enough to woo the Order to accept his fiscal plan. While doubtless a fag end of the Patrons believed in the single tax, sentiment did not develop in that direction. Though the initiative and referendum were seriously considered by the association it was unwilling to go the length of incorporating these principles in its platform.

After the fashion of the Grange the Patrons of Industry occasionally sought governmental action on matters in which they were specially interested. In 1893 the Grand Association of Ontario and Quebec transmitted an important tariff petition to the federal government, which will merit treatment in the chapter devoted to the political activities of the Order. The same year an appeal was made to the government of Ontario for: the provincial taxation of corporation stocks and mortgages; a decentralization of the superior courts of the province and an enlargement of the powers of the division courts. The Grand Trustees interviewed the Attorney-General of Ontario in relation to these issues in 1894, but came away dissatisfied. The Attorney-General said that, while not adverse to the taxation of corporation stocks, he was inclined to think that a levy on mortgages would affect the interest rate, causing it to rise; he promised to consult the judiciary on the other matters. Shortly after the federal election of 1896 the Ontario Patrons sent a petition to Ottawa enumerating the disabilities which, they said, were imposed upon Canadian shippers by the Railway Act then in force, and urging the government to afford them the same protection as shippers in the United States had secured through the medium of the Interstate Commerce Act. The government promised suitable legislation, but in 1898 was taken to task for its indolence by two Western members of parliament when nothing had been done.

ECONOMIC UNDERTAKINGS.

Aside from their political activities Ontario Patrons referred somewhat vauntingly to the changes which they proposed to effect in the business life of the country, but in this field they actually accomplished little. As in Michigan, they drew up terms at various points with retail dealers whereby no profit beyond a maximum of ten per cent. was to be taken on their purchases. In the palmier days of the movement a number of these so-called "Patron stores" carried on business to the entire satisfaction of both the merchants and their lodge customers. Again, in keeping with its principles the Order thought that it should endeavor to checkmate the insalubrious monopolies and combines that were known to be growing up on Canadian soil. With this object in view plans were set on foot as early as 1890 to organize manufactories where goods of common use on the farms would be produced.

It was suggested that members of the Order should form a joint stock company to operate its own salt wells and the primary lodges were circularized to that effect. The Grand Trustees reported in 1892 that 175 lodges had indicated their willingness to subscribe for stock in such a venture; others had replied, asking for further information. As the scheme did not elicit the necessary enthusiasm, it was ultimately dropped and, it has been observed, arrangements made with the grangers' company at Kincardine by which large consignments of salt would be purchased annually at a fixed price. A much more robust effort was launched by the Patrons to curb the power of the binder twine monopoly. The House of Commons was reliably informed in 1891 that full control over the output of binder twine in Canada was vested in the National Cordage Company, of New York, which had possession of the mills and did business with subsidiary headquarters at Montreal. Under a protective import duty on twine at the time of twenty-five per cent. the average price in Canada of all grades of that article was three cents a pound higher than in the United States. In the hope of combating this situation the Patrons obtained incorporation on October 25, 1892, for the Farmers' Binder Twine and Agricultural Implement Manufacturing Company which they established at Brantford with Joseph Stratford as general manager. The company made an immediate impression on the binder twine market, and prices began to recede. By 1894 the Patrons' organization was selling a good quality of twine to the farmers at six and one-half cents to seven cents a pound. Moreover, during the first five years of its operation it was in a position to pay an annual dividend of ten per cent. Then came the Spanish-American War in 1898, when luckily Joseph Stratford had bought a large quantity of raw fibre ahead, with the result that the company was in clover for three years, being able to apportion its shareholders successive dividends of 60, 100 and 90 per cent. However, after 1900, conditions in the binder twine industry underwent a change. The Laurier government had wiped out the duty on twine and as a result Canadian and American makers were thrown into direct competition. The Patrons' company had put by none of its extensive gains for lean years; the Order which had given it birth was practically extinct; and finding itself without sufficient working capital it eventually became involved in financial difficulties. It passed into the hands of liquidators in 1912.

THE PATRONS OF INDUSTRY AND LABOR.

The tenets of Patronism as outlined in the London platform, together with the public utterances of leading members of the Order on national issues, provided an allurement to the forces of Labor in Canada of which there is ample evidence. Industrial workers at this time in Canada, except where the Knights of Labor were still extant, were mainly interested in their trade policies and as a class had kept almost entirely aloof from politics. There was a yearning, however, among them for a wider sphere of action. Why could not the Patrons' movement be used as a channel whereby the industrial worker might realize his ambitions in the political field as well as the farmer? Given the proper incentive, primary lodges might easily be set up in the towns and cities. Yet even if urban lodges were not established at all events a working agreement might be formulated which could be subscribed to by Labor on the one side and Patrons on the other.

A definite move towards arriving at a *rapprochement* between the Patrons' association in Ontario and the forces of Labor was made during the winter of 1893, in which the Grange was also asked to participate. A meeting was convened at Toronto on the evening of March 1, which was attended by representatives of the Patrons of Industry, the Grange and important Labor bodies. Among those present were: John Miller and Alfred Gifford, from the Patrons of Industry; Peter Hepinstall, Master of the Dominion Grange, and E. H. Hilborn of the same organization; George T. Beales, President of the Trades and Labor Congress of Canada; T. W. Banton, President of the Toronto Trades and Labor Council, and D. H. Carey, District Master of the Knights of Labor. Characteristic addresses were delivered, in which were emphasized both the need for and possibility of united economic and political action on the part of the toilers on the farm and in the factory. At the close of the meeting it was decided to appoint "a committee for the purpose of effecting combined action for the furthering of their common interests." A committee was chosen, but no tangible results accrued therefrom; for one thing the Grange representatives soon made it plain that they were constitutionally forbidden to embark on any political adventures.

A year later, on March 2, 1894, a group of Labor men,—including among others, D. J. O'Donoghue, T. W. Banton, D. A. Carey and A. F. Jury,—presented themselves at the annual meeting of the Ontario association and discussed the subject of proportional representation for the Patrons' benefit. The Labor men had brought along charts to illustrate their points and they endeavored to show how, if large-scale constituencies were erected in Canada and voting permitted on a cumulative plan, the farmer and industrial worker might assist each other's candidates at the polls on the day of election. When this meeting was over a contingent from the Patrons paid a visit to the Toronto Trades and Labor Council in regular session. According to the lively account of a newspaperman, when the Patrons were admitted to the Council's deliberations they were greeted with "a significant outburst of applause." The farmers must have gone in numbers, or else the news-gatherer was burnishing his imagination, for he states that "towards the close of the session the hall was crowded with Patrons." Some eight farmers took the floor, bringing fraternal greetings from their association and pledging its deep sympathy with every question affecting Labor. "All we want," cried one farmer, "is fair play and to abolish the rings." Grand Auditor William Valens assured the packed assembly that "the ruling powers were beginning to realize that by a combined movement—the farmers and workingmen might in future contest the legislatures." While Valens' utterance had about it certain of the earmarks of prophecy, the "combined movement" of which he spoke and upon which he let his audience ponder was not effected in his day and generation nor in the form that he imagined. No binding alliance was ever arranged between the organized industrial workers and the Patrons of Industry in Canada. Twenty-five years were to elapse before a coalition (1919) was formed in Ontario between a farmers' organization and Labor functioning politically; in this case, as will be noted, the "combined action," if it may be called such, took place only after an election had been held.

CHAPTER XI

PATRONISM IN OTHER CANADIAN PROVINCES

EIGHT years previous to the invasion of Western Canada by the Patrons of Industry in 1891, a movement had begun among prairie farmers which, though it had soon spent itself, is worthy of passing notice. A hectic land boom had energized the West in 1881-2, only to be followed by serious depression as artificial values collapsed, drought and frost visited the crops in 1883, and the country was sobered by actualities. An unappeasable discontent thereupon seized hold of the farming communities, a direct result of which was the launching in southern Manitoba of an organization taking the grandiose title of the Manitoba and North-West Farmers' Protective Union, and having as its object the enunciation of policies that were calculated to relieve the farmers of some of their burdens. Preliminary gatherings held in connection with this projected Union led up to a general organization meeting, convened at Winnipeg on December 19, 1883. Here the Union received its constitution which provided for a central governing committee and a federation of local branches throughout the West. Membership in the Union was not confined to farmers, as any ratepayer might join it who was over eighteen years of age. A declaration of rights was promulgated, demanding: absolute control by the province of Manitoba of its public lands and natural resources; the construction of necessary railways under provincial charters; the granting of power to the municipalities to erect their own grain storage elevators, warehouses and flour mills; the appointment of grain inspectors under provincial authority; the construction of the Hudson Bay Railway; and the removal of duties on agricultural implements and building materials, together with a lowering of such other duties as bore on articles of daily consumption. No computation of the Union's aggregate membership is available, but it is known that 300 delegates attended its annual convention in Winnipeg on March 4, 1885. Having discovered that its purposes were largely akin to those of the Manitoba Rights

League, it had amalgamated with that body during 1884. But the Union began to lose caste when the opinion grew up that it was acting as an arm of the Liberal Party in that party's attacks on the Dominion government.   It also brought disrepute upon itself by advising against further immigration into the West until the farmers' grievances had been remedied. By 1886 the Union was enfeebled, and after having changed its name, became defunct.   Among those who had taken more or less interest in its proceedings had been Clifford Sifton, a Brandon Liberal, and Rev. James M. Douglas, of Morris, bitter foemen in later years, as will be seen, on matters relating to the West in the parliament of Canada.

Note may also be made of the fact that, about the time that the Patrons' organization arrived in the West, the Farmers' Alliance, crossing from the north central American states, gained a brief foothold in the province of Manitoba.   The Alliance entered the district immediately to the north of Winnipeg during the winter of 1890-1, where Balmoral appears to have been its early headquarters.   Its members urged the destruction of unjust combines in Canada, and stressed the value of co-operation in the agricultural industry.   Sub-lodges are known to have been formed at Balmoral, Foxton, Greenwood, Alliance, Stony Mountain, Brant, and Clande-boye; the membership possibly reached a maximum of about five hundred.   At a meeting held in Winnipeg during March, 1892, leaders of the Alliance were found dickering for a fusion with the Patrons of Industry, but before this was accomplished the movement disappeared.

ADVENT OF THE PATRONS.

There is still some doubt as to how the Order of the Patrons of Industry was first planted in the Canadian West, but the indications are that it entered under authority from the Grand Officers of the Supreme Association.   Michigan headquarters, having watched the Order flower rapidly in Ontario, were doubtless confident that seed strewn on the western prairies of Canada would bring equally as bountiful results.   The records show that early in 1891 an organizer, A. L. McLachlan by name, was busily setting up sub-associations in Manitoba, especially in the neighborhood of Portage la Prairie.   By the spring of the year local newspapers had begun to comment upon the expansion of the movement in the rural sections. "The Patrons of Industry," declared the

Weekly Review of Portage la Prairie on May 6, "are becoming very strong on the Portage plains, as there are already six associations." A degree of rivalry was manifested between the Patrons and the incipient Alliance movement, described above, which caused the former to advertise themselves as the "Canadian Farmers' Alliance."

The Order had made sufficient headway in Manitoba by the fall of 1891 to warrant the creation of a provincial association, and with that object in view a meeting was convoked at Portage la Prairie, on November 4. M. E. Hogmire, Grand Treasurer of the Supreme Association, attended to sanction this move and to formally establish the Grand Association of the Patrons of Industry in Manitoba. Connection with the Supreme Association, however, apparently was severed at this point. The meeting proceeded to strike committees and to evolve a tentative platform with the slogan "Manitoba for the Manitobans" as its leading note. The aim of the Order, it was stated, would be to afford protection to both farmer and employee against the machinations of the financial and commercial classes; at the same time its members would endeavor to put their trading upon a strictly cash basis. The *Marquette Reporter*, a paper issued by H. C. Clay at Rapid City, was named as an organ through which information respecting Patronism would be disseminated in the province and an executive of nine appointed including among others: Charles Braithwaite, of Portage la Prairie, as Grand President, and Editor Clay as Grand Secretary. McLachlan was retained in the office of organizer for the movement, with a roving commission.

Several months later, on February 24, 1892, another meeting was held at Brandon, when it was announced that one hundred sub-associations were in existence in the West, of which a few had been formed in the North-West Territories. Invectives were hurled against the tariff by Patron orators, and the delegates urged to acquire and operate grain elevators and flour mills at local points. Provincial banks were advocated where borrowers might obtain loans at an interest rate of five per cent. per annum, and a demand voiced that the farmers should have adequate representation on the western board for the selection of grain standards. Steps were taken to establish a distinctive publicity organ for the movement, with the result that some time later the *Patron's Advocate* was started by Clay at Rapid City, apart from his *Reporter*, and gained a fair circulation among the lodges.

Although a few members of the Order took over and operated an elevator at Boissevain, the only considerable economic venture organized in the West was a supply company known as the Patrons' Commercial Union. This concern was incorporated under the laws of Manitoba and began to do business at Portage la Prairie with W. C. Graham, appointed Secretary of the Grand Association in 1892, as its manager. It sold goods on the mail-order plan, distributing them mostly from Winnipeg, and keeping only a small stock on hand at Portage la Prairie. Agricultural implements, binder twine and other farmers' supplies were disposed of to the membership, while to a limited extent the company acted as a selling agency for the farmers' grain and farm produce. In 1894 the Commercial Union handled over 500,000 pounds of binder twine at the remarkably low quotation of seven and one-quarter cents a pound on credit.

Leadership in the West.

Light contrasts vividly with shade whenever pen pictures are given of those who led the Patrons' movements on the prairies. Grand President Braithwaite was a romantic figure, masterful and shrewd, though dwelling for the most part in the realm of the emotional. He possessed only the barest rudiments of an education, but withal was an orator of compelling force. When in the fall of 1891 he heard that representatives of the lodges were meeting at Portage la Prairie to set up a provincial organization, he left his threshing-machine hurriedly, rushed among them covered with oil and grime, protested the legality of their action, and forthwith was elected president *pro tem*. Upon one occasion it is related that he kept a Patrons' audience enthralled for an hour and a half at a picnic near Rapid City. In January, 1895, he achieved fame overnight by giving an address in which he depicted the sorrowful plight of the western farmers in that year of financial stringency and low wheat prices. Excerpts from his speech were cabled to Great Britain where they created such an impression that Sir Charles H. Tupper, then in England, took the opportunity to utter a disclaimer before the Wolverhampton Chamber of Commerce, affirming that Canada was in a prosperous condition, that her finances were sound and that this might be traced to her fiscal policy of national protection. Whether Braithwaite's gloomy asseverations turned the trick or not, the fact remains that just at this time Canadian Pacific Railway stock fell in the British market from seventy-three to sixty-nine and three-quarters.

Another stalwart among the western Patrons was John Forsyth, of Neepawa, who, for a period, was a vice-president of the Grand Association, but who unfortunately was cast out of the Order in 1895 for violating one of its principles. The story is told that Forsyth, desirous of reaching a convention at Brandon where he was billed to speak, drove across country through a raging blizzard with his lower limbs swathed in gunny sacks. He delivered his speech with accustomed vigor only to find upon examination that he had been standing with both feet frozen. Then there was G. A. J. A. Marshall, also a vice-president of the association, and one of the intellectuals of the western movement, who on account of the string of cognomens with which he had been blessed was known by the jesting title of "Alphabetical Marshall." Numerous clever editorials were written for the *Patrons' Advocate* by H. C. Clay, even though some of them may be criticized as having been excessively vituperative. In the issue of October 10, 1894, he inserted a scathing polemic on the railway and other policies of Hon. Wilfrid Laurier, opposition leader at Ottawa, which brought down on his head the wrath of the Grand President, and led to unhappy consequences for the Order. The *Canada Farmers' Sun* was pleased with this article and had reproduced it on its front page, but Braithwaite who always had difficulty in forgetting that he had been a Liberal, curtly bade Clay "draw it a little milder." An acrimonious dispute at once ensued between the two at the height of which Clay adopted the unethical and decidedly cruel expedient of printing in the *Advocate* a long letter received from Braithwaite with all its mistakes of grammar and its array of misspelled words. Clay further intimated that the Executive Board were incompetent, and had not supplied him with news for publication. However, when the annual convention met in January, 1895, strong hostility was evinced against the manner in which the *Advocate* was being conducted, and Clay was forced to remove the designation, "official organ," from the paper. He resigned his office in February, and the following month under a new editor, the paper was received back into favor.

EXTENSION OF THE MOVEMENT AND ITS POLICIES.

The number of Patrons' lodges in the West more than trebled between 1892 and 1895. Whereas 209 were reported to be in good standing on January 1, 1894, this total had increased to 330 a year later, and at the same time the membership had reached its maximum strength of about 5,000. Owing to the fact that the movement had made steady gains in the North-West Territories, where the farming population by 1895 was approximately half that of Manitoba, permission was granted to the lodges in that area to form an Executive Board of their own. The earlier agitation for representation on the grain standards board had borne fruit when Braithwaite and another Patron were put on it; the claim was made that through their influence wheat had been graded up so that the bulk of it passed inspection as Manitoba No. 1 Hard.

Politics were equally as bewitching to members of the Order in the West as to their brethren in Ontario. Braithwaite said in 1894 that if eastern Patrons had thought it wise to enter the political arena, then by the same token it was necessary that the prairie association should be "intensely political." John Forsyth was nominated as a Patron candidate for the constituency of Beautiful Plains in a provincial bye-election of 1894 and won handily. Emboldened by his success, the Grand Association resolved to groom candidates, wherever possible, for future elections, though they came far short of this ideal. The western Patrons' misadventures in the Manitoba and Dominion elections of 1896 will be chronicled elsewhere.

When a common platform was evolved for all Patrons in Canada in 1895, members of the Order on the prairies were more deeply interested in certain phases of it than others; as a matter of fact they added a few distinctive planks of their own choosing. The attitude of Western Patrons on the tariff issue was much closer to a "free trade" standpoint than it was in the East. They emphasized the need for a government-controlled outlet for grain by way of Hudson Bay, condemned the policy of making land grants to railways as mischievous, and demanded the ballot box for the West. After a prolonged and heated debate at its 1894 convention the Grand Association of Manitoba had come out in favor of the enfranchisement of women, a reform which it continued to advocate for several years. The acceptance of a railway pass by members of any legislative body in Canada was looked upon with special abhorrence by the Western association; it urged that members so doing should be disqualified for five years from holding office. Moreover, as the federal election of 1896 drew near, it indicated an uncompromising hostility to the restoration of the separate school system in

Manitoba. On the question of the prohibition of the liquor traffic, fundamentally a provincial matter, there was at first a diversity of opinion among Western Patrons, but the principle was finally adopted at the 1895 convention.

THE BREAK UP IN THE WEST.

The jarring set-to staged by Braithwaite and Clay had a more pernicious influence on the fortunes of the Order than either had imagined. The *Patrons' Advocate* never fully recovered from the blow administered to it by the unseemly quarrel, and was withdrawn from circulation in January, 1896. Another paper, the *Patrons' Western Sentinel*, edited by the Grand Board, was started at Portage la Prairie, on March 18, 1896, but apparently only ran for about ten months. Meanwhile another incident had occurred almost as derogatory to the prestige of the Order as the Braithwaite-Clay mêlée. In the autumn of 1895 John Forsyth, of whose achievement in Beautiful Plains his fellow Patrons were justly proud, had committed the unpardonable offence of accepting and riding on a railway pass. A hue and cry straightway resounded through the West, and the Grand Board, aware that its adherence to principle was being subjected to the acid test, was compelled to take summary action. Denying the refractory member a second chance, it stripped him of his rank in the Order, and even condemned him for accepting an extra indemnity of $100 from the province. The Board felt that it had discharged its duty in a prompt and praiseworthy manner, but the whole affair had left a bad impression in the minds of farmers everywhere.

As in Ontario the failure of the western section of the Order in the Dominion election of 1896 was the guide post to its approaching disintegration. Braithwaite, himself a defeated candidate in the Macdonald riding, soon afterwards quit office, and ended his career as an inspector of noxious weeds in the employ of the Manitoba government. The convention of 1897, in a vain effort to stave off the inevitable, decided to relax the membership obligations. Already the movement in the North-West Territories had drifted apart, and the remaining Patrons in Manitoba at the time of their regular meeting date in 1898 formed themselves into a "broadened-out" organization, described as the Independent Industrial Association. This body seems to have expired over-night, thus marking the last stages of possibly the most

9—F.M.

colorful of all farmers' movements in Canada. The Commercial Union, transferred to the management of G. A. J. A. Marshall, took the name of the Farmers' Trading Company, and continued in business until 1912.

IN THE MARITIME PROVINCES.

The establishment of the Patrons of Industry in the Maritime Provinces was mainly due to the efforts of one individual. Tidings of the spread and political achievements of the movement in Ontario had stirred up a desire among farmers on the eastern seaboard to have the Order introduced into their midst, and as a result letters passed between Grand Secretary Welch, of the Ontario and Quebec Association, and William B. Fawcett, of Westmoreland County, New Brunswick, relative to its extension into the last-mentioned province. This correspondence was published in part in the *Canada Farmers' Sun*, and led Duncan M. Marshall, perhaps the most versatile of the Patron organizers in Ontario, to offer himself for service among the Maritimers.

Marshall was unquestionably fired with enthusiasm for the Patron cause, but as he has himself since acknowledged, it was likely wanderlust more than anything else that influenced him in volunteering for work so far afield. Most of his life he had lived in the upstretches of the Bruce peninsula and the call from the Maritime Provinces brought him an alluring opportunity to move out and see a bit of the world. So in January, 1895, he set out for New Brunswick where he was met by William B. Fawcett at Sackville, and organization began with that place as a centre. Marshall resided at the home of Fawcett's father in Upper Sackville, making peregrinations through the counties round about. He formed a number of lodges in Westmoreland and Albert counties, and assisted in the organization of Carleton County. The burden of his story, as he has stated, "always was the tariff," and apparently the precepts which he sought to drive home on that subject were received with acclaim by New Brunswick farmers. Next he proceeded to Nova Scotia, only to discover that the farmers of Pictou County where he began work were less susceptible to his tariff appeal. He created some thirty lodges in Pictou County and then left it seemingly in disgust, convinced that the Conservative farmer in the riding which sent Sir Charles H. Tupper to parliament was hopelessly "joined to his idols of protection."

However, it was in the province of Prince Edward Island, whither he now journeyed, that Marshall's organizing campaign in the Atlantic provinces was to be most effective. Having crossed from Pictou harbor to Charlottetown on July 12, 1895, he inaugurated a series of meetings in the island province. "Here," he relates, "I found 'free trade' arguments were popularly received. I held meetings in between eighty and ninety schoolhouses in Prince Edward Island, and organized some eighty-five associations." Among those proffering Marshall a helping hand in this work were: William Campbell, of Graham's Road, an exceptionally progressive farmer; John M. Clark, of Summerside, afterward a member of one of the island governments; L. U. Fowler and Jesse S. Wright, both of Bedeque; and John Agnew, of Alberton. John H. Bell, who a generation later, 1919-23, occupied the position of Premier of Prince Edward Island, gave encouragement to the independent political action advocated by the Patrons at the time.

Marshall did not finally return from the Maritime Provinces until December, 1896. Prince Edward Island continued to be the stronghold of the Order down by the sea, although further advances were made in the other provinces. A newspaper, launched for the benefit of Patron readers, was sold out within a year as its subscription field appeared to be too limited. During the winter of 1895-6 a Grand Association of Prince Edward Island was formed, with Duncan M. Marshall as its first, and, as circumstances decreed, its only Grand President. The election of 1896 did not find any Patrons offering themselves as candidates in the Maritime Provinces, but as an aftermath of the general route of Patron forces in that election, the movement in the far eastern part of Canada soon fell into a state of collapse. Nevertheless, the brief sojourn of Patronism in the Maritimes had left a tradition behind which was by no means effaced when the more recent farmers' movements invaded that territory.

Development in Quebec.

The Order of the Patrons of Industry was carried from eastern Ontario into the province of Quebec during 1891, where it first took root in Huntingdon County, on the banks of the St. Lawrence River, south-west of Montreal. T. J. Leahy, who attended the London convention on September 22 of that year as a representative from Huntingdon County, intimated that the farmers of Quebec were enamored of the form and objects of the movement and would gladly hear more of it.   Accordingly, in November, Grand Vice-President Mallory travelled to Montreal and thence to Huntingdon County on an organizing expedition.   The twenty meetings, which he held in the county during the next few weeks were so fruitful of results that before his departure on December 22 a convention of delegates was gathered from all the county lodges at the town of Huntingdon, and plans made to extend the movement to other parts of the province.   Within two years the Order was well-established in the Montreal district, and had passed the Richelieu River into the Eastern Townships.   Announcement was made at the Toronto convention of 1894 that seventy-three Patrons' lodges were in working order in Quebec; delegates had come to the convention from the counties of: Huntingdon, Argenteuil, Soulanges and Vaudreuil.

Sentiment among Quebec Patrons had by this time crystallized in favor of withdrawing to institute a Grand Association of their own.   Ontario headquarters acceded to their desire, and at a meeting held in the Albion Hotel, Montreal, on December 11, 1894, Grand President Mallory transmitted the authority necessary for the creation of the Grand Association of Quebec.   Officers were elected from the counties as follows: Grand President, J. N. Vauville, Argenteuil; Grand Vice-President, James N. Smith, Argenteuil; Grand Secretary-Treasurer, Albert Dauth, Soulanges; Grand Trustees, T. A. King, Richmond, James McGibbon, Huntingdon, and A. D. Lalonde, Soulanges.   The meeting endorsed the London Platform, and James N. Smith, the ablest of the Quebec Patrons, delivered an address, flaying the burdensome exactions of the Canadian tariff, calling for an enlargement of the free list, and extolling the Order's success in bringing down the price of binder twine.   In the federal election of 1896 F. F. Willard ran with Patron support in Compton County, but was worsted.   The records give what may be taken as a farewell picture of the Grand Association of Quebec in session at Montreal on February 26, 1897.   James N. Smith, then Grand President, and the orator for the occasion, is shown vigorously assailing the proposal that the Ottawa government should subsidize the construction of the Crow's Nest Pass Railway.   The meeting selected a committee to wait on the government and ask for a railway commission.

CHAPTER XII

PATRONS OF INDUSTRY IN THE POLITICAL FIELD

THE PATRONS of Industry had begun jockeying for political position as early as the winter of 1890-1. The movement, however, which they had inaugurated was still too youthful for co-ordinated action in the arena of politics when the dissolution of the sixth parliament of Canada caused the Macdonald government to go to the country for the last time in March, 1891. One lone Patron candidate, Alexander McLartey, as already noted, was put up in the Bothwell constituency and suffered defeat, although his showing was not inauspicious; in a three-cornered contest he received more than half as many votes as Hon. David Mills, the winner, an expert and seasoned campaigner. Yet, notwithstanding their inactivity in this election, it is easily demonstrable that Patrons had been focussing their eyes wistfully on Ottawa during its progress; not only had they been interested in the contestants and their policies, but they had been gauging the possibilities that might be in store for the Order upon some future occasion.

Without doubt the original predilection of the Patrons of Industry in Canada was for federal politics. The London Platform, while applicable in part to provincial affairs, had laid its chief emphasis upon matters of Dominion-wide concern. Nestors of Patronism in Canada from the very first had declaimed most earnestly against abuses whose rectification was exclusively *intra vires* of the federal parliament. The *Monetary Times* in its issue of November 28, 1890, had taken occasion to sketch the line of action which it thought the new Order had marked out for itself. "The chief objects of the Patrons of Industry," it surmised, "appear to be to fight the combines and insist on a reduction of the tariff." Still, in spite of the fact that the Order was bent on grappling with the question of the tariff and other weighty, national problems, and that Ottawa was evidently the lode star of its hopes, it was appointed to work out its destiny in another and quite unexpected fashion. The Dominion government, weakened by the death of Sir John A. Macdonald on June 6, 1891, and timorous of the electorate, could be counted on clinging to power—unless a crisis were somehow precipitated—as long as it was legally possible. The studied anxiety of an administration but recently returned to office to avoid dissolution might, therefore, involve for the Patrons, impetuously eager to test their strength, a period of from four to five years' irksome waiting. Meantime, the political pot had begun to simmer in Ontario, and a tempting invitation was thereby held out to the Patrons to enter the provincial field. They decided to take opportunity by the forelock, and to make ready for the Ontario election which would likely occur in 1894, believing that they were making a move in the right direction. Through a variety of circumstances, for which they themselves must be considered partly responsible, this venture into the Ontario field was to be their only successful political achievement.

THE SITUATION IN ONTARIO.

The two-party system of constitutional rule had operated undisturbed in Ontario during Sir Oliver Mowat's long tenure of office as Premier since 1872. The Conservatives in opposition had tried without avail to loosen the government's grip on power, but after eighteen years of striving numbered only one-third of the legislature in 1890. Now new forces were emerging that were to interfere with the tranquillity of the Liberal administration, and Sir Oliver had to proceed with added wariness lest he imperil his political existence. Not only did the Equal Rights Association appear about 1890, fostered by D'Alton McCarthy and aiming to abolish the separate school system in Ontario, but there arose shortly afterward an even more ultra organization, known as the Protestant Protective Association which was considered by its founders as a defence society against the alleged encroachments of the Roman Catholic religion in the country. But more formidable than these in the eyes of Mowat were the Patrons of Industry whose strength he knew lay in the farming communities, and whose ardor to enter the vexing labyrinth of politics was only too apparent. The Premier understood that he could not hold the Patrons lightly if he were to remain master of the situation. The "P. P. A." and the Equal Righters might be charged with fanaticism and by skilful tactics might be driven into the camp of the Conservatives.

The Patrons, on the other hand, must be treated with greater deference; in Sir Oliver's opinion every possible effort should be employed to assimilate them to the Liberal Party which so far had owed its ascendancy in Ontario to the farmers' support. The government press, taking its cue from the Premier, declared that the Patrons had no valid reason to be dissatisfied with the policies of the Liberal Party.

The Patrons Prepare for Action.

A deal of misgiving was expressed by some members of the Order when they found themselves thrust unceremoniously into politics so soon after organization. Such objectors were conscientious in their belief that the social and educative features of the Order should be stressed above all else. Many other members thought that no Patron should be nominated for any contest as the Order's representative, provided that a candidate of either of the existing parties would pledge his support to the principles for which they stood. The leaders of the movement, however, backed by a majority of the rank and file, held a different opinion and were strongly seized with the idea of evolving a third party in the country. In process of time, indeed, it was found that many lodges were meeting for none other than political purposes.

At the annual meeting of 1893 a decision was reached that the moment was already ripe for concerted action on political issues, and word was sent out to the county associations ordering a search for candidates who would stand on the Patron platform in the impending provincial election. A resolution, sponsored by George Wrigley, touching upon the responsibilities of members of the Order in their individual constituencies, received the assent of the meeting to the effect that: "Should it be declared advisable to nominate a Patron candidate, the duty of every Patron shall be to support that candidate, and to use every influence in his power to secure his election." At once a cry arose from various local associations that the terms of this resolution were too binding, and that Patrons of unfettered mind must not be coerced in so flagrant a manner. Signs of a gathering storm immediately loomed up—only as quickly to melt away. One lodge, it is true, announcing that its members were freemen, wound up its affairs, and from the surplus funds in hand celebrated its disruption with a farewell supper. In the main, though, marked enthusiasm was displayed by the county associations in bringing out candidates. Two bye-elections were contested in December, 1893, and, when nomination day for the general elections had drawn round, forty-three straight Patron candidates were placed in the running.

The Wrigley resolution to all intents and purposes had given the Patrons of Industry the status of a third party in the province. Accordingly, the exact position that the Order intended to take up with respect to the government on the one hand and to the Conservative opposition on the other was fraught with importance to both of the older parties. Prior to the general election it was semi-officially announced that the Order had not set out to defeat the government; and, if a statement made at the time by Grand Trustee Lockie Wilson may be fully credited, it could not be accused of having had in prospect a coalition with the Conservatives. "They," he said, speaking of his fellow-Patrons, "do not propose on a technical quibble to upset the government. It will be a policy of give and take between them and the government. They may yield one point to the government, if the government yields another to them. They will not indulge in any factious opposition to the party in power." Alfred Gifford, another Grand Trustee, declared that his party would adopt a neutral attitude in the legislature, a pledge which contained, of course, in it little to comfort the Liberals. "There is a thorough understanding," he publicly asserted, "that our representatives are not to be elected to support any want of confidence motion made in the interests of either party."

RELATIONS WITH THE "P. P. A."

A favorite pastime of the election campaign of 1894 was to endeavor, editorially, on the hustings and otherwise, to group the Patrons of Industry under the same flag as the "P. P. A." The latter organization, while not recognized by William R. Meredith, opposition leader, as such, was generally conceded to be an adjunct of the Conservative party. The "P. P. A." on their part set out with zeal untempered to woo the Patrons, hoping no doubt to attract them into the Conservative fold. The Patrons were placed in a dilemma, because many farmers who had enrolled in the Order were also members of the "P. P. A." As accusations of collusion between the two organizations appeared in the public print, and these were circulated widely through the province, several of the Patron chiefs took occasion in December, 1893, to emphasize the non-sectarian character of the Order. "Our organization," stated Grand President C. A. Mallory, "has never had, has not now, and never can have any affiliation, directly or indirectly, with any organization affecting the religious standing of the people." Grand Trustee Alfred Gifford was equally as explicit. "There is not the slightest possible connection," he maintained, "between the Patrons of Industry and the Protestant Protective Association. With the creed prejudices of the 'P. P. A.,' which, as I understand it, is the foundation of the Order, we have no sympathy at all. We have a large number of Roman Catholics in our ranks." But lest these assertions should give the impression that the Patrons and the "P. P. A." were at loggerheads, a qualifying resolution was adopted at the Patrons' annual meeting of 1894 in which the delegates went on record as follows: "We resent the interference of outside parties and papers, and declare it to be no part or purpose of the Patron Order to denounce either the Catholic faith or the 'P. P. A.' organiza- tion." Nevertheless that there was a considerable distribution of "P. P. A." strength among the Patrons was evidenced by the fact that seven candidates nominated in 1894 by the "P. P. A." announced that they were also carrying the Pa- trons' colors. The total number of candidates representing Patronism in one form or another was thus brought up to fifty.

THE BYE-ELECTIONS IN ONTARIO

The Mowat government brought on bye-elections in three constituencies, North Bruce, East Lambton and South Lanark, during the seven months preceding its general appeal to the province. The Patrons of Industry decided to enter candidates in North Bruce and South Lanark. In the former riding their chances of success looked excellent as there were fifty-three thriving, primary lodges in the area. Daniel McNaughton, reeve of Bruce Township, and a man of proven integrity, was accorded the Patron nomination; the Liberals chose as their candidate an ex-warden of the county; the Conservatives for their part picked a well-known business man as standard-bearer. A spirited fight soon broke loose that drew campaign orators from far and near. Premier Mowat appeared in North Bruce in November, 1893, and made a strong bid for the farmers' vote. His government had erected, he said, a Department of Agriculture; it had set up an agricultural college and model farm at Guelph; it had appointed a commission of experts to investigate the condition of agriculture in the province; it had already loaned about $1,000,000 to municipalities for purposes of under-drainage. "Now," he exclaimed, "in face of these facts, can it be said that the Reform party has neglected the special interests of farmers?" The outcome of the bye-election held on December 2, however, was a distinct revelation to the people of Ontario that a new political force was abroad in the land. Daniel McNaughton was declared victor with a majority of 508 over the Liberal, his nearest opponent, and to him belongs the honor of having been the first representative of an agrarian party ever elected to a legislative body in Canada.

Conditions were by no means so promising for the Order in South Lanark where it had become only partly established at the time of the bye-election. Nevertheless, the Patron candidate, James Ferguson, ran well up in a field of four, obtaining 158 votes less than the victor. The *Perth Courier* commented as follows on the struggle that had taken place in this constituency: "The strength of the Patrons' movement has been shown in the contest just closed here. A month ago the party was practically unknown in the riding. After three weeks' time their candidate, Mr. Ferguson, unknown except at his own end of the riding, polled eight hundred votes, which placed him a good third in the political race."

VICTORY AT THE POLLS IN 1894.

The Patrons went into the Ontario elections of 1894 without an extensive platform. The chief point emphasized in their campaign speeches was the need, as they saw it, of a change in the method of appointing county officials in the province. Let Ontario experience, they argued, "a system of civil service reform that will give each county power to appoint or elect all county officials paid by them, except County Judges." Before polling day they announced themselves as favoring local election, rather than local appointment of these officials. Sir Oliver Mowat defended the system of Crown appointment then in operation, and absolutely refused to budge on the issue. The government's principal organ, the Toronto *Globe*, while carefully acknowledging the Patrons' right to gather into associations for political purposes, had no sympathy for this plank in their platform. The alteration which the Patrons advised would in no sense, opined that newspaper, "exorcise the demon of partyism."

Again the Patrons urged from the hustings the necessity of cutting down provincial expenditures which, they claimed, were becoming excessive. In support of this contention the *Canada Farmers' Sun* published a series of articles in which the annual disbursements of the province were shown to be high in comparison with those of various states across the border. By way of rebuttal, the Toronto *Globe* declared that the states picked out by the *Sun* for the purposes of illustration were especially suited to that paper's argument, and that Ontario was not a relatively high spender. None the less, the Patrons made many friends through urging a policy of governmental economy at the time because it was a period of widespread industrial debilitation. Among other things advocated by the Order in the campaign were: a decentralization of the superior courts; an extension of the jurisdiction of the division courts; and a prohibiting of the customary issuance of passes to members of the legislature by railway corporations.

Whereas the Patrons entered the fray well-organized locally and with plenty of self-reliance, they were at the disadvantage of having no party leader and only a limited press. R. J. Doyle's Owen Sound paper, which had always favored co-operative business effort rather than political action, proved a bit of a stumbling-block during the election. It spoke deprecatingly of a number of candidates whom the Patrons had nominated, stating that in some cases they were "the most useless men that could be found in the whole riding." "Some one-idead bigots," it exclaimed, with true Doyle venom, "have become Patron candidates and we hope to see them defeated." Clearly Doyle was here guilty of exaggeration under the sway of personal feelings, yet for all that, in his own pungent way, was unmasking a truth. While the Patrons had many good men in the field, they also had many who could claim little support from the electorate. In this respect they were handicapped to a greater degree than most new parties.

On June 24, 1894, seventeen Patrons were returned to the legislature, when the Mowat government was sustained at the polls.   The following members of the Order had been successful: John S. McDonald, Centre Bruce; Daniel McNaughton, North Bruce; George N. Kidd, Carleton; William Dynes, Dufferin; Joseph L. Haycock, Frontenac; David M. McPherson, Glengarry; David McNichol, South Grey; Thomas Gamey, Centre Grey; Alexander McLaren, East Hastings;

Thomas L. Pardo, West Kent; John Senn, Haldimand; George Tucker, West Wellington; William Shore, East Middlesex; John McNeil, South Perth; John Craven, Prince Edward; Archibald Currie, West Simcoe; and John Bennett, Stormont. The Liberals had secured forty-six representatives, the Conservatives, twenty-seven, and the "P. P. A." and independents, four, in the new House of Assembly. To all appearances Sir Oliver Mowat's government was in danger of a grouping of parties against it, but such a combination never eventuated in fact. The Patrons, much as it would have pleased them, were thereby denied the joys and responsibilities of holding a balance of power. In September, 1894, Joseph L. Haycock, was selected as leader of the Patron group in the legislature. John Senn (Haldimand) was unseated, as prior to the election he had neglected to resign as an issuer of marriage licences, and at a bye-election on March 19, 1895, was defeated by a Liberal candidate. George Tucker (West Wellington) was disqualified on an election petition, but the seat which he forfeited was subsequently captured by James Tucker, another Patron. Hence the Order's representation had suffered a net reduction of one member, and from 1895-8 its bloc in the house consisted of sixteen men.

PATRONS IN THE ONTARIO LEGISLATURE.

The outcome of the election was received with marked jubilation by Patrons everywhere in the province. They decided that they had been fully justified in giving the people an opportunity to vote for a new party. "Patronism," said Grand President Mallory, "is now acknowledged to be a living factor in Canadian politics." The older parties were distinctly taken aback by the startling rapidity with which the Order had gained the ear of the electorate, and began to change their tactics with regard to it. Instead of treating the Patron movement good-humoredly as heretofore, they set out to find flaws in its organization, and at times assailed it bitterly. The *Canada Farmers' Sun* complained of the unfriendly attitude now being manifested toward the movement by the Tory politicians. "Yesterday," it observed, "they extolled the power of Patronism, and lauded our ambition. To-day they sing the new song that we are divided." Nor were the enemies of the Order confined to one party only. "Partisan papers and party politicians on both sides," was the *Sun's* charge, "having contributed their share of literature and slangwhanging to relegate Patronism to oblivion."

The Patrons took their seats in the eighth parliament of Ontario determined to follow a middle course, and to avoid complications with either of the historic parties. For a time they attained their object, meanwhile making a bold attempt to push forward measures that they considered to be both expedient and democratic. But unfortunately the burden of presenting to the legislature the ideas for which the Order stood was thrown entirely upon J. L. Haycock, the party leader. At the outset Haycock made a good impression, but at length, as his efforts seemed for the most part bootless, he became weary in well-doing. Apparently the Patron group did not possess among them a diversity of talents, or if they did possess them, they were allowed to remain undeveloped. Had the party but obtained a militant phalanx of five or six men in the assembly who would have been always up and at it, the political history of the Order in Ontario might have been vastly different.

Possibly Haycock's most notable parliamentary effort was his attempt in March, 1895, to persuade the legislature to agree to the abolition of the Government House at Toronto. To Haycock's way of thinking the Lieutenant-Governor should be remunerated for the routine work that he accomplished, but the upkeep of his official residence, and the other perquisites belonging to the Crown's representative were a needless expense to the state. In the course of an eloquent address he related how, having abstained from making use of a formal invitation to attend the Lieutenant-Governor's banquet, he had walked by the Government House together with a friend on the evening of that brilliant affair. Cabs were drawn up before the official residence, lights flashed from its windows, wondrous music was being wafted on the night air. "We stood," he told the House impressively, "entranced with those beautiful sounds and those beautiful sights, and, just as we passed around the corner, an old, grey-headed man, bent with years, stopped us, and said, 'I am hungry.' Much more seemly would it be," cried the Patron leader, "were the province's money spent in providing homes for such old men in indigent circumstances, than in lavishing it upon the splendid residences and meaningless functions of the Crown's representative." A motion for the abolition of the Government

House was rejected, when a division was called for, by only forty-four votes to thirty-seven.

Following the pre-election pledges of his party, Haycock also introduced a bill during the session of 1895 which would have rendered the acceptance of a pass from a railway company by a member of the legislature a breach of the Independence of Parliament Act. Neither the government nor the Conservative party could be inveigled into lending support to this measure, and the Patrons had to fight unaided. Sir Oliver Mowat said that the giving of passes was a matter of courtesy on the part of the railways, and that he could not conceive of any valid reason why members receiving them should be tied to the cause of these corporations. Gibes were hurled at the Patrons for having accepted free transportation to Guelph to visit the Ontario Agricultural College, and Haycock had to disarm criticism by referring to an occasion upon which he had returned a pass sent to him by a railway company. The Patrons' bill was eliminated in the house by seventy-four votes to thirteen. Nevertheless, here was a question out of which, had the Patron members held relentlessly to their purpose both in and outside the legislature, an issue might have been created that would have increased their hold upon the farming communities. The invidious attention, too, that would have been drawn to the railways by their action would have blended well with the attitude taken up by the Order toward transportation problems in general.

Save for the above-mentioned efforts the Patron group in the House of Assembly did little but engage in sniping operations. They allowed the subject of the election of county officials to fade from their minds. A bill fathered by Haycock to reduce the fees levied from students by the Ontario Medical Council encountered the opposition of both Liberals and Conservatives and succumbed. The government's readiness to investigate any matter in which the Patron members were interested seemed always enough to curb their zeal. The Conservatives, indeed, accused them of sitting dumb, when they themselves were endeavoring to impress upon the government the need for economy. Taken all in all, the Patrons made a poor showing in the legislature, and their doom was sealed ere the election of 1898 drew round, when James Tucker (West Wellington) was their only successful candidate.

In Manitoba and Prince Edward Island.

Sporadic attempts were also made by Patrons of Industry to gain parliamentary honors in provincial elections and bye-elections held in Manitoba and Prince Edward Island. John Forsyth's victory in the Manitoba constituency of Beautiful Plains in a bye-election of 1894 has been previously commented upon. When the Greenway administration submitted its record to the electors of Manitoba in January, 1896, Patrons were nominated in the following seven constituencies: Cypress, Manitou, Emerson, Morden, Beautiful Plains, Saskatchewan, and Dennis. Two only were elected: W. F. Sirett, in Beautiful Plains, and Watson M. Crosby, in Dennis. Candidates were later entered by the Order in bye-elections occurring toward the close of 1896, in Lakeside and North Brandon, neither of whom were fortunate enough to gain a seat. It is, however, noteworthy that the Patron contestant in North Brandon was D. W. McCuaig, a future president of the Manitoba Grain Growers' Association, and that he lost his fight by only a small margin. In a bye-election held in September, 1896, for the office of councillor for the fourth district of Prince County, P.E.I., a Patron named Humphrey was selected to run, but encountered defeat.

The Lure of Ottawa

"The Tory politicians are trembling," declared the *Canada Farmers' Sun*, referring to what it believed to be the federal government's dread of the Patrons' onmarch in Ontario. Be this as it may, the rulers at Ottawa could not blind themselves to the fact that a party at enmity to the protectionist system had received many thousand votes in a province which since 1878 had been the chief stronghold of the National Policy in Canada. The government had first been apprised of the Patrons' attitude on the tariff back in 1891, when a petition with 25,000 names attached had been sent in asking that binder twine, salt, and iron be put on the free list. This had been followed by further representations from Ontario and Quebec during the session of 1892-3, signed by 40,000 Patrons to the effect that the removal of the duties on agricultural implements, coal oil, wire fencing and corn was keenly desired by the Canadian farmer. The task of submitting the latter petition to the government had been assigned to D'Alton McCarthy, independent member for North

Simcoe, who had stated his willingness to assist the Patrons in their quest for tariff revision.

In a lengthy speech on the tariff, which he delivered in the House of Commons, on March 14, 1893, McCarthy stated that he had received 113 documents, not properly in the form of petitions, from sub-associations of the Patrons of Industry in Manitoba and the North-West territories, decrying the Canadian tariff of customs and asking for immediate relief. The plea of a lodge at Clover Bar, Alberta, was read by McCarthy to the House as typical of opinion in the far West: "We, the undersigned farmers, members of Clover Bar, representing Patrons of Industry of the province of Manitoba and the North-West Territories, feel that the duty now existing upon farm machinery and binding twine, coupled with the heavy freight rates we have to pay, bear so heavily on us in our farming operations, that we cannot advise our friends to come to this country to become agriculturists under existing burdens, and we deem it unwise on the part of the government to pursue their proposed immigration policy unless the burdens are reduced."

Interest in federal politics, quiescent in the days of the Ontario campaign, was again aflare among Patrons during the winter of 1894-5. Delegates from Quebec and the West came to Toronto, in February, 1895, and together with Grand Officers of the Ontario Association drew up a platform for use in the impending Dominion election. The most significant clauses in this platform brought the Patrons' views on the tariff up to date. Cottons, tweeds, woollens, workmen's tools, farm implements, binder twine, wire fencing, coal oil, iron and corn should, they contended, be placed on the free list. Luxuries, on the other hand, ought to be taxed to the fullest revenue-producing extent. Moreover, in his annual address of February, 1896, Grand President Mallory took up an even more advanced position when he declared for the free importation of all commodities from Great Britain, and a reciprocity of tariffs between Canada and other trading countries.

The remainder of the Patrons' platform may be epitomized. Upon members of parliament it urged that the following restrictions be placed: (1) that they must not be directors or stockholders in any railroad or other corporation in receipt of aid from the government; (2) and that they should not be permitted to accept fees or emoluments from the government in addition to their sessional indemnities. It advocated a reduction in: (1) the number of cabinet ministers; (2) the list of servants in the public employ; (3) and the militia expenditures in times of peace to an amount not exceeding $300,000 per annum. Besides, the platform stood for the abolition of: (1) the Government House at Ottawa; (2) the Canadian Senate; (3) the Military College at Kingston; (4) the North-West Mounted Police, except in unorganized territories; (5) the granting of subsidies or bonuses to railroad or other corporations; and (6) the payment of any form of pension or superannuation except for military services.

THE DISASTER OF 1896.

The loudly-heralded entry of Patronism into federal politics had a sombre ending. Grand President Mallory asserted that Patron candidates would be in the running from Montreal to the Rocky Mountains, a forecast which, while almost literally true, had only a rhetorical meaning. The Order contested one-quarter of the Ontario seats, but east and west of Ontario very little was attempted. The complete list of Patron candidates numbered twenty-nine, distributed as follows: Ontario, twenty-five; Manitoba, two; Quebec, one; and the North-West Territories, one. Rev. James M. Douglas, of Moosomin, was originally brought out by the Patrons and was strongly supported by them when he sought election as an independent Liberal in East Assiniboia. Only three Patrons were successful at the polls, all of them in Ontario: David D. Rogers, elected for Frontenac County; William V. Pettet, for Prince Edward County, and John Tolmie, for the constituency of West Bruce. Douglas obtained a plurality of 1,054 in East Assiniboia. Among the fallen were: Charles Braithwaite, who ran in the Macdonald constituency of Manitoba, and J. K. McInnis, defeated by the casting vote of the returning officer in West Assiniboia. At a bye-election held February 4, 1897, in North Ontario, Duncan Graham, an ex-warden of Ontario County, was returned on the Patron ticket. The Patrons now had four members in the House of Commons, but not enough to give them any standing as a distinct party.

The failure of the Order in the election of 1896 may be attributed to various causes. Back of all else was the fact that Patronism and Liberalism had too much in common in the principles for which each contended; especially was this the case in the enunciation of tariff policies. As a consequence it was easy for a Liberal candidate to promise the same things as his Patron rival foı political honors, and in a three-cornered fight, if either anti-protectionist candidate were to win, it was more likely for other reasons to be the Liberal than the Patron. Then, as an overshadowing issue in the campaign arose the Manitoba School Question which excited religious prejudices and passions from Atlantic to Pacific, and upon which the Patrons although comprising a non-sectarian organization, were forced to state their opinions. Another weakness lay in the negative and subversive character of the platform that the Patrons had supplied to the electorate. In 1894, the country was in the throes of an industrial depression, and discontent was rampant; in 1896 the skies were brightening, and the public was ready for more constructive policies than the Patrons had to offer it.

The faithless activities of one of the high officials of the Order gave an unsavory aspect to the campaign. Months before the election, it would appear, this individual had begun to betray the trust reposed in him as a member of the Grand Board. By taking careful note of conversations, public and private, that were held, and by selecting items of correspondence, he was able to furnish another political party with material for its campaign literature. The influence, however, of this official's defection upon the results of the election has doubtless been exaggerated; it was only natural that members of the Order should magnify it into one of the principal reasons for their discomfiture at the polls. During the four years, 1896-1900, David D. Rogers (Frontenac) acquitted himself particularly well in the House of Commons, standing by his guns as a Patron. He strongly opposed the granting of a subsidy of $11,000 a mile to the Canadian Pacific Railway to build a line through the Crow's Nest Pass, and discoursed at length upon the evils of members of the House receiving free transportation on the railways. Both Duncan Graham and he were vanquished in the election of 1900; John Tolmie meanwhile had joined the ranks of the Liberals.

CHAPTER XIII

THE FARMERS' ASSOCIATION OF ONTARIO

FARMERS' movements in Canada descended to their lowest abyss during the years from 1898 to 1901. In the West, except where a few subordinate granges still lingered on, the chain of continuity had been broken in 1898, resulting in an almost complete hiatus until new links were forged in the winter of 1901-2 by the grain growers of eastern Assiniboia. (Vide Chapter XIV.) In Ontario, during the same period, the Order of the Patrons of Industry was crumbling away to nothingness, while the Grange was barely holding its own. In Quebec and the Maritime Provinces, both Grange and Patrons' movements had vanished for ever. The historian seeking consolation for these otherwise empty years must focus his attention on the parliament at Ottawa, and trace the beginnings of a remarkable struggle over the grain trade which was soon to embroil the Western farmer. So, too, he may mark the gallant effort put forth by the *Weekly Sun*, at Toronto, during these dark days to infuse fresh courage into the dispirited and disorganized farmers of Ontario, and to lighten the gloom.

The fact that the Patrons' official organ in Ontario had not succumbed along with the Order was due entirely to the unrequited generosity of Goldwin Smith, the eminent litterateur and publicist. Goldwin Smith had first come to Canada in 1870, penetrating to the forks of the Red and Assiniboine rivers, where he had been seized with the conviction that the far-flung prairies were a "land of miraculous promise." The following year he had taken up his abode at Toronto, and from that time until his death in 1910 was an ever-ready and ever-faithful friend of the Canadian farmer. He had watched with interest the rise of the Patrons of Industry, approving of their independence of thought. Then, as their power had begun to wane, and he saw the *Canada Farmers' Sun*, now a mere starveling with a circulation of 4,000, going to the wall, he had hurried to its rescue. He assumed at once financial control of the paper; its name was changed

147

to that of the *Weekly Sun*, and a new company formed in 1896 to operate it, with C. A. Mallory as president. To bring about this rehabilitation of the *Sun* Goldwin Smith had paid its former owner his full investment, yet was more than gratified at the results achieved. "There is nothing in a long and checkered life," he said in 1906, "upon which I look back with greater satisfaction than that when the Patrons' movement collapsed—I was enabled at all events to save its journal from the ruins."

Each week, under the pen name of "Bystander," Goldwin Smith wrote diversified comment for the front page of the *Sun*, touching upon whatsoever themes had captivated his fancy; much of this reflects his best literary style. It was thought that under this new regime the *Sun* might appeal to town and city dwellers, but, though its circulation steadily rose towards normal dimensions after 1896, the paper continued to go almost exclusively to the farmers. Next came the Boer War with Goldwin Smith an uncompromising exponent of the independence of the South African Republics, which caused a wave of adverse sentiment to rise that well-nigh engulfed the paper. However, as the war fever subsided, and an attitude bordering on revulsion permeated the farming communities, the *Weekly Sun* quickly regained its prestige and popularity. In the spring of 1902, believing that the time was opportune for a reawakening of interest in agrarian organization, it invited its readers to express their views as to what type of movement would be most suitable to the needs of the hour.

EVOLUTION OF THE FARMERS' ASSOCIATION.

By way of answer letters streamed in to the office of the *Sun* from every quarter of the province, indicative of the farmers' desire to combine again for their mutual advantage. A potpourri of suggestions were received as to the form which the new organization should take, including an entreaty from the Grange that a solution might be attempted through a revival of their Order. After an interchange of ideas had occurred among the more ardent proponents of the scheme, the *Sun* gave out word that a "get together" meeting would be held in Toronto at the time of the annual exhibition. September 9 was set as the date of the meeting, and when it opened in the Temple Building, with C. A. Mallory in the chair, 150 farmers were found to be in attendance. A spirited debate broke forth upon the respective merits of one type of farmers' organization and another, in the midst of which Jabel Robinson arose to portray the excellencies of the Grange. Alfred Gifford called for a reaffirmation of the Patrons' platform and a movement that would involve political action, while George Wrigley, speaking in the same strain, argued that sooner or later the farmers would be again in politics. Ultimately it was decided to form an organization to be known as the Farmers' Association of Ontario which would be developed locally on the basis of the federal constituencies of the province.

In spite of the importunities of a number of the farmers present, the meeting resolved that the association would eschew politics, though it would always "be ready to bring its influence to bear to secure and promote the interests of the farmer in matters of legislation." Goldwin Smith, introduced to the gathering as a champion of "the under dog," assured the farmer audience that his "under dogs had generally become upper dogs in the end." The avocation of the farmer, he went on to say, was both industrially and politically "the sheet anchor of the country." C. A. Mallory was chosen as president of the new body and W. L. Smith as its secretary, while an executive committee was appointed with representation distributed among the counties as follows: J. Lockie Wilson, Glengarry; C. A. Mallory, Northumberland; L. E. Annis, York; J. F. Bean, Welland; and W. K. McLeod, Middlesex.

The work of planting the movement was begun at Stayner, Simcoe County, in October, and before the close of the year local units had been established in sixteen federal ridings. Twelve more units had been formed by the time of the second annual convention in September, 1903. At this meeting a constitution was drawn up, applying the name, district associations, to the local units, and providing that each of them might send two delegates to the central association. The organization gave its attention at once to a series of transportation problems that were considered of vital importance to the farmer. Besides it advocated the taxation of public service corporations, and raised its voice against the system of granting bounties to manufacturers of iron and steel and to other Canadian industries.

RELATIONS WITH THE RAILWAYS.

The Farmers' Association of Ontario endeavored to implement efforts which were being made at this time in the Dominion parliament to protect the farmers from losses that they sustained through having their cattle killed or injured along the railways. Both in 1901 and in 1902 Edward A. Lancaster (Lincoln and Niagara) had introduced bills in the House of Commons which aimed to place the responsibility entirely on the railways for animals killed or injured on their property except at highway intersections. The Farmers' Association defended the principle of these bills, arguing that if the burden of loss were shifted to the railways they soon would provide well-constructed guards to keep the cattle out of danger. The government referred the Lancaster proposals to the Railway Committee of the House, intimating that it was anxious to find a standard cattle guard the use of which might be enforced on all the transportation lines of the country. Partly with this object in view it named a small cattle-guard commission in August, 1902, to investigate the whole subject. Representatives of the Farmers' Association gave evidence before this commission when it sat at Guelph in November, stating that the government should not concern itself about standardizing the cattle guards but leave that matter to the railways. C. A. Mallory told of the case of a farmer living near Cobourg who had lost three or four head of stock purchased at a sale when, as he was driving them home, they had stampeded across the flimsy, slat guards at a railway crossing. The experiences of an Agincourt farmer were also cited, who, within a period of several years, had had eight horses, and a number of cattle, sheep and hogs killed along the railway track adjoining his home.

Again the Farmers' Association of Ontario demanded a more just and more efficient method of apportioning costs in the many instances where farmers found it necessary to drain across the land of a railway. As the law stood farmers had to petition the Railway Committee at Ottawa whenever they desired such a drain to be built, and costs were adjusted through its instrumentality. In 1901 Jabel Robinson (West Elgin), protesting that this method worked unsatisfactorily, moved a bill in the House of Commons with the object, he said, of bringing the railways under the same law as the farmers in the matter of drainage. Robinson's bill only got as far as its second reading, but he reintroduced it in the session of

1902; simultaneously another more elaborate bill, drawn up on similar lines, was presented to the House by M. K. Cowan (South Essex). The leading feature in both these proposed measures was the stipulation that the drainage laws of the Canadian provinces should apply to the railways operating within their boundaries, or, in other words, that farmers should be allowed to drain across the land of a railway upon the same basis as they would drain across the land of a neighboring farmer. The Farmers' Association not only endorsed this provision strongly, but approved of another clause in the Cowan bill which stated that in case there should be a disagreement as to the costs of construction, arbitration would rest with the county Judge. It might also be mentioned that in February, 1903, a group of association members headed a deputation to Ottawa, which urgently requested the government to establish a railway commission for the Dominion. Upon this occasion L. E. Annis brought up the question of freight rates, complaining that they were exorbitant in Canada for short hauls. He told of a farmer who, desiring to ship a calf forty-seven miles by freight, had been asked eight dollars for the service; later he had shipped the calf by express, for three dollars. About the end of March, a special delegation from the association waited upon Premier Laurier and Ministers Fielding and Patterson at the Capital and gave them a detailed account of the various matters affecting the railways upon which they craved legislative action.

During the 1903 session of parliament the Laurier government brought in a comprehensive railway bill which, after some mutilation in the Senate, became law on October 24, and went into force in February of the following year. By it the appointment of the Board of Railway Commissioners of Canada was authorized with jurisdiction over the rates, services, equipment and operation of all roads in the country. Section 254 of the act was highly significant for the farmers in that it incorporated the principle contained in the Lancaster bills that responsibility for animals killed or injured on their property should lie directly with the railways. However, the railways might shift the burden, if they could prove that the animals were at large through the negligence of their owner or some one acting for him. This modification of the original Lancaster proposal was due to an amendment by the Senate which, when it became known, had caused the executive of the Farmers' Association to telegraph its remonstrances to the Premier, and the Toronto *Globe* to call for a reconsideration of the clause by the House of Commons. The question of drainage across railways was determined to the great satisfaction of the association and farmers generally by section 251 of the act which provided that, where works of this nature were contemplated, provincial laws would apply, although the consent of the railway commission must be secured before operations were begun. Farmers were required to pay the ordinary costs of carrying the drain across the land, while the railways were liable for the balance.

VIEWS ON OTHER ISSUES.

In September, 1903, just as the Railway Act was about to become law, the Farmers' Association of Ontario, meeting at Toronto in annual convention, went on record as favoring a two cent per mile passenger rate on all Canadian lines and a sweeping reduction in freight rates by the commission-to-be-appointed. At the solicitation of visiting representatives of the Toronto Trades and Labor Council it accepted the principles of direct legislation through the initiative and referendum. Also at the same meeting it pledged its unequivocal support to every effort that might be made to obtain the government ownership of public utilities. On September 9, 200 members of the association trooped to the legislative buildings in Queen's Park where they were granted an audience by Premier George W. Ross on the subject of the taxation of railways and other corporations. Since the great corporations in Ontario were assessed lightly, they told the Premier, the farmer, as a property holder, was subjected to an unequal burden of taxation. Comparative figures were adduced to indicate how remunerative was the type of corporation tax then in force in the state of Michigan. The delegation stated that it strongly approved of a bill introduced into the legislature upon two occasions by H. J. Pettypiece (East Lambton) to amend the Assessment Act so as to place an *ad valorem* tax on corporation property, and to return the greater part of the revenue derived therefrom to the municipalities. Premier Ross acknowledged the need for an equalization in provincial taxation, but gave no sign that he would adopt the association's viewpoint. Pettypiece continued to outline his ideas publicly until May, 1904, when the government appointed a royal commission with himself as chairman to delve into the whole question. The Farmers' Association, meanwhile, appears to have lost confidence in the member for East Lambton, believing that he had weakened in his stand, and criticizing him at the convention of 1904 for failing to carry out his pre-election pledges. In January, 1905, several months after the Ross administration had gone out of office, the commission brought in a report in which it advised that corporations should be taxed according to their earning power.

Representatives of the Farmers' Association held a conference with Ontario's new Premier, Hon. James P. Whitney, and several of his ministers, in September, 1905, and were given a sympathetic hearing. In addition to renewing their demand for equalization of taxation, they asked for: government control of the rates charged by electric power companies; conservation of the province's forest resources; the taking of royalties on minerals extracted in Ontario; legislation through the initiative and referendum; and a cessation of the granting of bonuses to railways. Whitney expressed himself as favorable to all these proposals, barring one; he frankly asserted that he did not believe in the initiative and referendum.

About one-half the association's demands received some attention during the next few years. The government dealt with the electric power question by first setting up a commission of inquiry into the possibilities of transmitting power to the municipalities from a publicly-owned hydro plant at Niagara Falls, and then in 1906 establishing a permanent hydro-electric power commission to carry forward this project. The custom of awarding bonuses to railways was abandoned. An act was passed in 1906 doubling the mileage tax on railways in the province, and imposing as well a tax on the lengthier electric lines. However, both the *Weekly Sun* and H. J. Pettypiece censured this measure as disappointingly inadequate. On account of developments in the Cobalt region extensive mining legislation was put on the statute books in 1906, but no provision was made therein for the taking of royalties. The Whitney government proved itself rather lax in its administration of the forests; not only did it deprive the Bureau of Forestry of certain of its main functions, but no forward-looking policy was inaugurated until E. J. Zavitz became provincial forester in 1912.

Brief reference may be made to the attitude of the Farmers' Association of Ontario on questions of military defence and the tariff. Between 1904 and 1906 expenditures for military purposes in Canada were growing rapidly while the association was uttering plaints that evidently went unheard. In 1904 it protested against increases for the department of Militia and Defence being placed in the budget, and the following year in convention acclaimed the denunciatory utterances of President Lockie J. Wilson when among other things he declared that the "Canadian war dogs should be at once called off, and a stop put to Sir Frederick Borden's revelry." In its earlier years the association was rather quiescent on the tariff, confining itself mainly to an attack on the bounty system. But by 1905 it had emerged from its lethargy on this subject, and was found advocating that reciprocal reductions in the tariff be granted to any nation offering Canada an equivalent. In November of the same year, as will be recounted, its president assailed the tenets of protectionism before a federal tariff commission. Then at the association's annual convention of 1906, delegates not only requested a downward revision in tariff rates, but described the system of protection as "a prolific source of political corruption and a moral degradation of our national life, as well as unjust to the great masses of the Canadian people."

UNION WITH THE GRANGE.

Notwithstanding its aggressiveness on many public issues and its unquestioned influence in moulding thought in the agricultural communities, the Farmers' Association of Ontario had never waxed strong in a numerical sense. Meanwhile the Grange had not fallen by the wayside as some had expected, but had been dawdling along, asking for almost the same things from the governments, federal and provincial, as the association; indeed, there appeared to be a wasteful parallelism of effort between the two bodies. Aside from the fact that the Grange was a secret Order, and the association quite informal in its membership regulations, other differences between them were of minor import. Several Grange officials attended the association's convention of 1905 with a suggestion that the organizations should combine; it was pointed out that the admission fee to the Grange had been reduced to one dollar and the annual dues lessened at the same time. Again, in 1906, John G. Lethbridge, Master of the Dominion Grange, accompanied by Jabel Robinson and W. F. W. Fisher, brought fraternal greetings to the association. Lethbridge took occasion to speak commendatory words in support of the association's resolution on the tariff.

A union with the Grange now lay in the offing. When the Farmers' Association assembled in September, 1907, it decided to heed the overtures of the Grange and to accept its proposal to form one organization. This it would seem could only be accomplished by the association losing its identity, and plans to merge it into the older body were finally effected at the annual sessions of the Dominion Grange held in Victoria Hall, Toronto, on December 4-5. Master Lethbridge who presided when the union took place said that the farmers had begun to realize that "highly organized interests" surrounded them on every side, and that efficiency in their own work of organization was essential if they were to safeguard their industry. He told of the enduring qualities of the Grange, which, in a long life's history had "met the surveillance of every opposition" and had shown as it were "the wonderful power of a strong current that runs under a smooth surface." A few delegates who had formerly been members of the association objected to the ritual of the Grange as somewhat of an encumbrance; others defended it. As a result a compromise was reached by which an abbreviated form of ritual was devised, the use of which or the older ritual would be optional for the granges. Among those admitted to the ranks of the Grange in consequence of the merger were: Ernest C. Drury, of Crown Hill, who was appointed to the office of Lecturer, and J. J. Morrison, of Arthur, who was chosen as an auditor. Goldwin Smith was present on December 5 to give, as an old man, he said, his blessing upon the union; this, as it happened, was to be his last appearance before a farmers' gathering in Canada.

PART III

The Rise of the Grain Growers' Movements on the Prairies—1898-1912

CHAPTER XIV

FIGHTING FOR PROTECTIVE LEGISLATION

ONCE upon a time, according to ancient fable, a very thoughtful mouse suggested that a bell should be hung on the cat's neck in order that all the mice, warned of their enemy's coming, might scurry away into the darkness. The plan sounded good and might have been adopted, had not one perky young mouse asked the disconcerting question: "Who will put the bell on?" A Douglas, renowned in Scottish history for his intrepidity in dealing with certain courtiers who surrounded his monarch, was given the name of Archibald Bell the Cat.

On February 14, 1898, a crisp, frosty day, when many arpents of glistening snow stretched away from the brink of the Ottawa river to beyond the horizon, another Douglas arose in the Canadian House of Commons to do and to dare for the prairie settlers who had sent him to parliament. Just after three o'clock he caught the Speaker's eye, and moved the first reading of a bill to regulate the storage and transit of grain in the western country. Douglas' bill did not have government support; as he stood unobtrusively to read his motion it excited the barest of attention among members in the House. *James M. Douglas, member for East Assiniboia, it was understood, was introducing a measure that would be of interest to the scattered settlements of the half kingdom which he represented. It was only later that the House was brought to realize that this Douglas was endeavoring by means of legislative action to bell a cat—the growing elevator monopoly of the West. No one in the august chamber knew, not even Douglas himself, that the first scene of a remarkable

---

*Born at Linton, Bankhead, Roxburghshire, Scotland, on May 26, 1839, James Moffat Douglas, having arrived in Canada as a youth, entered upon the study of theology at Knox College, Toronto. He transferred to Princeton Theological Seminary and was graduated from that institution. He held two churches in Ontario, and was then designated in 1876 as a missionary from the Canadian Presbyterian Church in India. While in India he acted as chaplain to Her Majesty's forces at Mhow. Having returned to Canada in 1882, he took a pulpit at Brandon, Manitoba, and later one at Moosomin, in the North-West Territories. In 1896 Douglas retired from the ministry, and went on a farm, shortly afterward beginning his parliamentary career. On March 8, 1906, he was summoned to the Senate, and became one of that body's most progressive members. He died at Tantallon, Saskatchewan, in 1920.

drama was being enacted which would bring into existence the present-day grain growers' movements on the Canadian plains.

Scarcely had Douglas begun to level his attack on the elevator system than a small band of his Western colleagues, of differing political views, rallied to his support. Notable among those lending him a helping hand was R. L. Richardson (Lisgar), who during the next few years delivered numerous eloquent and informative addresses to the House on the subject of the grain trade. Others participating in the debates on the elevator question in favor of Douglas' claims were: J. G. Rutherford (Macdonald); T. O. Davis (Saskatchewan); Nicholas F. Davin (West Assiniboia) and Frank Oliver (Alberta). However, before depicting the parliamentary struggle which now took place, it will be necessary to sketch briefly the manner in which grain was being marketed at this time on the Canadian plains.

The Grain Elevator System.

As the farming population of Manitoba and later on of the North-West Territories had gradually increased after 1870 an evolution had occurred in the process of grain shipment to the markets of the south and east. The original settlers had been compelled to haul their grain by devious trails over the prairie to where a way freight drew up creakingly on its rusty rails, whence it was borne away to some central shipping point. In time certain enterprising persons began to build flat warehouses by the side of the railway in which the farmers' grain could be temporarily stored previous to shipment. The owners of these warehouses were themselves usually purchasers of grain for the larger markets. The farmers were well satisfied with the warehouse system because they received a fair price for the grain brought in, and were not heavily burdened with storage charges. The railways on the other hand complained that, when the farmers glutted the market with grain, it was difficult to supply enough rolling stock for purposes of transhipment.

As a result grain elevators were built at the solicitation of the railways, structures devised to lighten the strain imposed upon them by the growing harvests of the West. The elevator was intended as a granary into which the farmers contributory to it might pour their wheat and other cereals, and which would slowly be emptied twice or thrice a year by the railway skirting its towering form. A standard elevator was built to hold 25,000 bushels or more of grain, which made its erection costly in a country that had to import nearly all its structural materials. Though some elevators were owned singly, the majority of them were erected by corporations, such as the Manitoba Elevator Company, the Northern Elevator Company, or one or other of the large flour-mill companies that bought grain on the prairies.

It was not long before the imputation was made that these concerns were pooling their interests to the detriment of the farmer, and that they were being aided and abetted by the Canadian Pacific Railway, the leading carrier in the West. The Winnipeg *Tribune* and other newspapers gave currency to this report; it became a topic of conversation among farmers everywhere; finally it led producers to join in passing resolutions condemning the existing state of affairs. The combine, said to have been formed thus among the elevator companies, became known as "the syndicate of syndicates" to grain growers from the banks of the Red River to the out-spurs of the Rockies.

THE CASE AGAINST THE ELEVATOR COMPANIES.

Knowledge of the trend of feeling among their constituents with respect to the elevator companies was doubtless what prompted Douglas and other Western members who rallied to his support to seek remedial action from the Dominion parliament. Douglas assured the House that he fully recognized the value of the elevator system. He said that the building of elevators had caused no trouble until the autumn of 1897, when the Canadian Pacific Railway had made it known that, over a great portion of its lines, no grain would henceforth be received for shipment except through elevators. At one stroke the farmers living along those sections indicated by the C.P.R. were deprived of the right to load cars from their own vehicles, and the owner of a flat warehouse was driven out of business.

There were three main charges laid by Douglas, Richardson and others in the House against the machinations of the so-called elevator combine. They stated that the farmers of the North-West had no longer an open market for their wheat, the principal grain produced and sold. Before the C.P.R. had allied with the elevator combine telegrams had arrived daily for individual buyers at points on the prairie, setting

11—F.M.

forth the price they should pay for wheat, and the farmer had profited through competition among these buyers. Now a few men, meeting in a little room at Winnipeg, arranged the price for each important buying point, and one telegram was dispatched giving a quotation for the day which all, or practically all, the buyers at that point would re-quote to the farmers. In this way competition had been nullified, and in case too much wheat was coming into the market to suit the railroad, prices were artificially depressed and the farmers were forced to sell low or keep their wheat at home. In addition, it was charged that the grain dealers were making large profits through price manipulation. A farmer would be given, for example, seventy-seven cents a bushel for his wheat at an elevator centre in Manitoba; the charges thereafter to Buffalo would be: elevator storage, one and one-half cents, rail to Fort William, thirteen and one-half cents, and lake transportation, two cents for each bushel. The wheat laid down in Buffalo would have cost the grain dealer ninety-four cents a bushel, but if the ruling price in Buffalo on the day in question were ninety-eight cents, he would realize in consequence four cents a bushel on the transaction. The House of Commons was given to understand that the legitimate profit for a large purchaser of wheat was a fraction of a cent per bushel. Roughly estimated, $1,000,000 was said to have been lost by the farmers of the West through the juggling of wheat prices during the year 1897.

In the second place, according to the Western members of parliament, the methods employed by the elevator companies of mixing wheat prior to shipment was a source of both annoyance and loss to the prairie farmer. The actual difference between No. 1 and No. 2 grades of hard wheat was not easy to detect, and gave an opportunity for fraud. The farmers were, generally speaking, at the mercy of the buyers, who often told them that their wheat was second grade and they were paid for that quality. By a process of mixing with wheat just a shade better in the elevators, the whole consignment was graded and sold as No. 1 hard: in this way, two to four cents per bushel was reaped as an extra profit by the dealers. As a result the farmers' incentive to produce good grain was being destroyed. Moreover, the elevator system had worked a hardship to eastern farmers who found it difficult to secure anything but mixed wheat in carload lots from west of the Great Lakes. Formerly, when the farmers had loaded the cars themselves, or the grain was cleared through a flat warehouse, pure Red Fife or other high-grade wheat had been easily procurable in the east for seeding purpose.

Other causes for discontent among the farmers arose from the belief that false weights were frequently recorded by elevator operators, and that excessive dockages were charged for uncleaned wheat. When the wheat was delivered to a flat warehouse, the farmer could watch it being weighed in, and was rarely humbugged in the process. On the other hand, when admitted to an elevator, the wheat was emptied into a hopper and lowered to another storey where the weighing was done. The farmer then received a certificate of weight, the accuracy of which depended upon the honesty of the operator. Suspicions were often entertained that wrong tallies were made at the farmers' expense. The custom of assessing dockages against the farmer was due to the fact that, not having sufficient time or proper facilities to clean his grain after it had come from the thresher, he was forced to send it to the elevator, containing dirt, seeds and other impurities. Some elevators removed the contamination and levied a fair deduction in accordance with its weight. Others cleaned a pound, and having estimated the percentage of waste, assessed a dockage upon all the farmer's grain on the same basis. In some cases a dockage was made without cleaning at the discretion of the operator. Except where all the grain was cleaned, it was argued that fraudulent practices were liable to occur.

THE DOUGLAS BILLS IN THE COMMONS.

The main feature in the bill introduced by Douglas in February, 1898, was its provision that the farmers of Manitoba and the North-West Territories should have the right to ship grain through flat warehouses, as had originally been their privilege. The bill also guaranteed the farmers the right to load grain directly from their vehicles, besides arranging for a better method of car distribution. Before being read the second time, however, the measure was sent to the Railway Committee of the House, and there, after having been vigorously criticized, was finally dropped for the session. Nevertheless, the legality of the C.P.R.'s refusal to let farmers load directly had been openly questioned, and during the debate the Minister of Railways, Hon. A. G.

Blair, had stated that such refusal, if existing, was contrary to Section 246 of the General Railway Act. The C.P.R. thereupon gracefully backed down, and during 1898 accorded the farmers the full privilege of loading from their wagons. Nothing daunted by his initial failure, Douglas again submitted a measure to parliament, on March 29 of the following year, authorizing the restoration to the flat warehouse of its former status in the grain trade. A new and important clause in this bill called for the appointment of a chief inspector, with power to supervise the storage and shipment of grain in the West, including the administration of weights and dockages. An animated debate took place in the House upon the issues involved, during the course of which Hon. Clifford Sifton, Minister of the Interior, declared himself in favor of the proposed inspection, but suggested that the whole matter might better be dealt with by a special committee. Douglas agreed and a committee of eleven members was chosen, five of whom were from the West, namely: Hon. Clifford Sifton, chairman; J. M. Douglas; Frank Oliver; J. G. Rutherford; and R. L. Richardson. The eastern members were: Hon. J. G. Haggart; Hon. Sidney Fisher; David Tisdale; George H. Bertram; T. C. Casgrain; and Bennett Rosamond.

THE QUARREL IN THE LIBERAL CAMP.

The meetings of this special committee in the spring of 1899 were tempestuous and distinctly unpleasant; scarcely indeed were they over when a highly defiant and uncompromising attack was made upon Hon. Clifford Sifton, the chairman, by J. M. Douglas. Whereas supervision of the grain trade had met with the general approval of the committee, the clause relating to flat warehouses, considered by its author the most vital in the bill, had been voted down. Douglas, filled with wrath, turned to the public press, where his declamations were given prominence by both the Winnipeg *Tribune* and the Toronto *Telegram*. "It is a terrible blow to our whole West," he asserted, "and, of course, we know where to place the blame. It was the cold steel of Clifford Sifton that did it—the mischievous scheming of Clifford Sifton is the cause of our defeat."

The Winnipeg *Tribune* was inclined to believe that a trip made to Ottawa by influential grain buyers who "went there in person," and who had money invested in the elevator companies had helped to dictate the result. "Familiar sophistry" had not beguiled the policians at the Capital, but representations made to them "in private" had been enough to win them to the side of the combine. The Toronto *Telegram* claimed that the special committee had been hand-picked under Sifton's eye, and that a mutilation of the Douglas bill was inevitable; the six eastern members, it said, had been selected to safeguard the interests of the corporations. Sifton, speaking in the House on June 3, treated all the charges preferred against him lightly, and reiterated his opposition to the flat warehouse system.

THE GOVERNMENT UNBENDS.

While the Douglas-Sifton fracas of itself was little more than a disturbance on the surface of the waters, the government at Ottawa was awakening to the fact that the currents in the Canadian West were running deep. Douglas' stinging attack on a minister of the Crown meant something, but the opinion which the Western grain growers might have of the government a year or two hence, when the next election would be held, might mean a great deal more. After due forethought the government decided that the best way out of the difficulty would be to conduct an inquiry into the grain trade through the institution of a royal commission. Accordingly on October 7, 1889, a commission was appointed with the following members: Judge E. J. Senkler, St. Catharines, Ont., chairman; W. F. Sirett, Glendale, Man.; William Lothian, Pipestone, Man.; and Charles C. Castle, Foxton, Man.; Charles N. Bell, of Winnipeg, acted as secretary. Before the commission had finished its work Judge Senkler died, and the chairmanship was taken over by Judge A. Elswood Richards, of Winnipeg, in February, 1900.

The secretary of the commission sent notices throughout the prairie country, indicating where public hearings would be held and the principal objects of the investigation. In the main the farmers' grievances under the elevator system, as already outlined, formed the basis of the inquiry. The first hearing took place on October 21, and twenty-two points were visited from Fort William to Edmonton inclusive, before the commission had ended its itineracy on February 8, 1900. Altogether between two and three hundred witnesses representing the producer, the transporter, the buyer and the others interested in the grain trade, attended the sittings of the commission and gave evidence. Commissioner Castle and Secretary Bell also were dispatched to the chief grain centres of Minnesota, in order that they might bring back expert information respecting the storage and shipment of grain in that state.

THE REPORT OF THE GRAIN COMMISSION.

In presenting its findings to the government, the royal commission gave a valuable, explanatory account of the handling and marketing of grain in the prairie country. It reported that 447 standard elevators were doing business in the Canadian West, of which number 206 were owned by three elevator syndicates, 95 by two large milling companies, 120 by individual millers and grain dealers, and 26 by farmers' companies. Wherever the commission had gone the farmers had testified that, so far as the difficulties of the trade were concerned, full freedom of the right to load direct on cars and through flat warehouses would remove most of the trouble. In fact, so widely had this opinion been expressed before the commission that it was led to recommend "that proper relief from the possibility of being compelled to sell under value and of being unduly docked for cleaning is only to be had by giving the fullest obtainable freedom in the way of shipping and selling grain." The evidence taken would indicate that a depression of grain prices had often occurred through a car shortage. The commission therefore urged that an effort be made to increase the transportation facilities necessary for grain shipment, particularly in the months of October and November when most of the wheat was brought to the market. It suggested that loading platforms might be advantageously constructed by the side of the railroad for the use of the farmers. Besides it accepted a distinctive feature of the second Douglas bill in recommending that an officer be appointed with complete authority to superintend all transactions in grain on the prairies.

THE MANITOBA GRAIN ACT.

The Dominion government having received various delegations, and having solicited certain technical advice on the subject, drew up a bill which in large measure was based upon the commission's report. This bill, several times amended, was finally constituted an act of parliament on July 7, 1900, and was described as the Manitoba Grain

Act, although its provisions extended to the North-West Territories as well. High hopes were entertained by the formulators of the act that it would serve to quell the unrest permeating the agricultural districts of the West. The publication of its terms, too, fitted in well with the date of the general election which was to be brought on during November of the same year.

The Manitoba Grain Act provided for general supervision of the grain trade west of Fort William by a warehouse commissioner with headquarters at Winnipeg; all complaints with reference to the weighing or grading of grain were to be filed with this official. Government weighmasters were to be located at the chief receiving points, and the producer was to have access, if he desired it, to the scales. A loading platform must be erected along its track by a railway company free of charge upon the requisition of ten farmers of the neighborhood; a farmer might take twenty-four hours to load a car allotted to him. Flat warehouses could be built of a minimum capacity of 3,000 bushels, if permission were granted by the warehouse commissioner; but when more than one warehouse had been allowed at any point, the cost of site and trackage must be borne by the farmers. If necessary, six days might be taken by the farmers in filling their bins in the warehouses and in loading their cars.

Once more it was around the question of flat warehouses that the conflict raged when the grain bill was in its committee stage in the House of Commons. As originally drafted the bill had stipulated that flat warehouses must have a capacity of at least 6,000 bushels. Such disrelish was manifested for this clause by several of the Western members that many pages of Hansard are occupied with their affirmations of protest. R. L. Richardson tried to secure an amendment which would have allowed farmers desirous of shipping in carload lots to raise any size of warehouse they might choose. It was argued that freedom of trade with no restrictions was what the commission had advised and what was wanted throughout the length and breadth of the West. Hon. Clifford Sifton at length agreed to a compromise which permitted of the erection of warehouses of a minimum capacity of 3,000 bushels, although he did so with reluctance. The ire of the western members was also stirred by the proposal that railway companies might refuse land and trackage to any beyond the first applicant to build a warehouse. Frank

Oliver endeavored to show his fellow-members mathematically how many warehouses could be set up on a railway siding. J. M. Douglas said that the House was busy puddling and the pool was constantly becoming dirtier; in the light of what was being incorporated in the bill he judged that the intention was that "the flat warehouse business should be a failure." The government was, however, insensate to both appeal and condemnation, and, when a division was taken on the question, whipped the bulk of its followers into line, so that with strong support from the Conservatives it was able to carry its motion by ninety-three votes to ten. Three eastern members only supported the negative: W. Stubbs (Cardwell), W. V. Pettet (Prince Edward) and G. Guillet (West Northumberland).

CHAPTER XV

The First Western Associations

DURING a period of twelve years, 1900-1912, the Manitoba Grain Act with the amendments made thereto was the chief governing factor in the grain trade of western Canada.* Flat warehouses, contrary to the expectation of those who had fought for them, were only erected to a limited extent after 1900 along the railways. The farmer turned rather to the loading platform, as he discovered that it afforded him the most economic means of shipping his grain in carload quantities. To meet this new contingency buyers "on the track" appeared at country points, who entered into brisk competition with the elevators for the farmers' grain. Previous to 1900 nearly all grain had been bought "on the street," or in other words while in the farmers' wagons, and then stored in the elevators awaiting shipment. Track buying as it grew in importance quickly revolutionized the whole system of trading.

The price of street grain was, of course, higher than that of track grain on any given day at a shipping centre, although all grain was bought in the interior on the basis of its estimated value when reaching Fort William. For example, wheat sold "on the street" about 1900 would normally command two to three cents a bushel more than wheat sold "on the track" at the same point; the difference was made up of a commission rate of one cent a bushel, plus elevator charges of one to two cents a bushel. Six or seven years later the difference in price or spread, as it was called, amounted to three and a fraction cents a bushel on wheat since elevator charges had advanced in the meantime. Because it was, and is, much cheaper to send grain to the eastern markets part way by boat than by an all-rail route, the main shipping season from the prairies has always been during the three

*Power to administer this act rested with the Department of Trade and Commerce at Ottawa. The department in dealing with grain trade matters had also to carry out the terms of Part II of the Inspection and Sale Act which fixed the standard commercial grades for different kinds of grain, arranged inspection divisions for that commodity, and regulated the methods by which it should be weighed.

months or so from the beginning of threshing operations to the close of navigation on the lakes. Track grain loaded right into the cars would tend to be cleared east so far as possible in this season, whereas street grain might be held in store and subjected to all the influences affecting future delivery. The construction, however, of numerous terminal storage elevators at the lake ports during the period under question visibly altered this situation.

For the better comprehension of what will follow it may be noted that, back in 1887, a non-trading association of divers persons interested in the marketing of grain had been formed at Winnipeg, which four years afterwards became incorporated under the statutory laws of Manitoba as the Winnipeg Produce and Grain Exchange. By 1900 this Exchange was performing many services that rendered it practically indispensable to dealers in grain, and included among its members: elevator men, millers, track buyers, commission men, exporters, insurance brokers and financiers, most of whom had their offices grouped in close proximity. The Exchange collected data for its members concerning grain prices in other markets, concerning transportation facilities and rates, and concerning world conditions of supply and demand; it offered them the advantages of its trading room and clearing house fitted up with mechanical and clerical devices of the most modern type. Besides, it issued rules according to which its members must trade, one of which fixed the uniform margin or commission that might be taken for each kind of grain purchased "on the street."

The enforcement of stricter regulations by the grain act, and the increasing complexities of trading, caused handlers of grain to unite together, as they affirmed, for the protection of their interests, and to form a separate body which would operate in conjunction with the Exchange, known as the Manitoba and North-West Grain Dealers' Association. This organization aimed to strengthen the position of buyers in the market in every conceivable way. One of its chief functions was to telegraph prices regularly to its members' representatives at outlying places. It soon had command of the situation from the buyers' standpoint, though a number of independent dealers still remained in the field. A straight challenge was thereby issued to sellers of grain, that is, to the multitude of producers in the Western country, also to combine for their mutual protection. But growers of grain were widely scattered over the prairies and planless, and if they were to consummate any bond of union it would likely come about through the play of fortuitous circumstances. How they did combine—a story now to be related—is one of the most entrancing episodes in Canadian agrarian history.

THE BLOCKADE OF 1901.

The immediate incentive toward the establishment of a counter-organization among grain growers was supplied by the bounty of nature. The crop of 1901, in striking contrast to that of the previous year, was the heaviest yet known in the annals of Western Canada, and took the railways completely by surprise. During the long period of depression which had stretched across the nineties of the century just closed, the railways had adopted the policy of taking the bad harvest as a guide for the development of their equipment rather than the good harvest. Consequently when 60,000,000 bushels of wheat and a proportionately large yield of other grains were ready for the market in 1901, the transportation companies found themselves in a lamentable state of unpreparedness. The Canadian Pacific Railway, upon which the main burden of handling the crop would fall, was reported to have for all purposes in the West only 7,000 box cars and from 200 to 300 engines. Insufficiency of motive power was without doubt the railways' leading difficulty, and on this point they were roundly criticized for the methods of false economy that they had been practising. For example, the Regina *Leader* pointed out that it had been customary to keep engines running in a delapidated condition during the winter months which, if principles of efficiency had been followed, should have been sent to the repair shops. A member of parliament told of having seen bags of flour carried by engineers on the Prince Albert branch with a view to stopping up all leaks that became too pronounced. To make matters worse a rainy September interfered with threshing operations in 1901, and the lake-and-rail shipping season was not far advanced before it was evident that the value of the year's bumper crop might be seriously diminished through impediments to its transfer.

So congested did the arteries of the grain trade shortly become that talk of a "wheat blockade" was on every one's lips in the prairie country. The situation, though distressing enough in the province of Manitoba, possibly reached its acutest stage in the North-West Territories between Moosomin and Moosejaw. Farmers were at their wits' ends when denied space in the bulging elevators, or saw the grain moving with heartrending slowness towards the export markets. Navigation closed the first week in December, and by that time only 20,000,000 bushels of wheat had reached the head of the lakes. Of the balance, 9,500,000 bushels were in storage, and over 30,000,000 bushels still in the farmers' hands. From early morning wagons loaded with grain began to cluster around the elevators seeking admission, and at Regina where one angry farmer, having discarded his coat, set to work to pommel another, it was suggested that a constable should be put on to regulate the traffic. As the hopelessness of ever getting shipping facilities dawned upon many farmers, they began to improvise what means they could of keeping their grain safe through the winter months; temporary granaries of all shapes and sizes were erected, but as these generally stood upon the bare ground and had ill-constructed roofs, it was manifest that their contents would spoil with the wet weather of spring. One hundred and twenty such granaries were built at Indian Head in eastern Assiniboia where the blockade was especially severe. It was in the district surrounding this little prairie town that the first steps were taken to organize the Western grain growers for the defence of their industry.

A New Movement Begins.

One day in November, 1901, John A. Millar and John Sibbold, two sun-bronzed prairie farmers, were trudging disconsolately towards Indian Head behind brimming loads of wheat. As their wagons jolted and rumbled along the trail they were talking of the car shortage, the favoritism of the railways and the exactions of the elevator companies. Of a sudden Sibbold eyed his companion. "You are secretary of the agricultural society," he said, striving to think of some way in which the farmers might give vent to their feelings; "why not call an indignation meeting?" Millar acquiesced willingly, and in consequence of Sibbold's chance remark made arrangements, soon after, for the holding of an extraordinary session of the Indian Head agricultural society in the town hall. The meeting was intended as a means of protest, and no one thought that it might be the nurturing ground of a new farmers' movement. The fifty odd farmers who attended, however, were so zealous in discussing the wrongs under which

they believed they were suffering, and were so united and
determined in their opposition to the corporations which
they stigmatized as their oppressors, that a clear prevision
was afforded of another movement in the making. It may
be noted that Indian Head was at this time one of the principal
shipping centres in the North-West Territories, and that grain
was hauled to it from long distances; no place of its importance
had been harder hit by the blockade: of the two and one-half
to three million bushels of wheat harvested in the district in
1901, so far only one-quarter had been put on the rails for
shipment. A derangement of such a character in its economic
life, coupled with the fact that a robust class-consciousness
was actuating the producing farmers of the district, made the
town a fit centre for the events that were now to follow one
another in rapid succession.

Let the scene be shifted for a moment to the farm home of
Peter Dayman, a redoubtable pioneer of the Indian Head
country. Memories of the gathering described above were
still bright when W. R. Motherwell, of Abernethy, hitched
up and drove across to Dayman's place for a friendly chat.
Motherwell was a prominent farmer of the section who had
been brooding over the situation for some time, and who had
come to the conclusion that all detached efforts on the part
of the grain growers to have their grievances remedied were
utterly futile. What they needed, in his opinion, was some
form of organization that would allow them to act in unison,
and it was upon this subject that he desired to confer with
Peter Dayman. He found Dayman like-minded, and the
two sat up late into the night* planning how a start might be
made in bringing the farmers together. They decided to call
a meeting for December 18 at Indian Head, when they knew
that, for another reason, many farmers would be in town.
Meanwhile special invitations were transmitted to certain
men whom they thought would be particularly interested in
their proposals.

The reason why Motherwell and Dayman were so sure that
a crowd of farmers would be in Indian Head on December 18
was that the town had been chosen as the site for a lively bout
on that day between two Western statesmen. A joint debate
was scheduled to take place in the evening, in which the par-

---

*J. Hopkins Moorhouse has given a dramatic account of the colloquy between Mother-
well and Dayman in his "Deep Furrows." Use of certain original passages in "Deep
Furrows" has been made by the author in writing Part III of this book.

ticipants would be none other than Hon. R. P. Roblin, Premier of Manitoba, and Hon. F. W. G. Haultain, Premier of the Territories.   Roblin's purpose was to indicate why a portion of Assiniboia might be advantageously annexed to the province of Manitoba and his opponent's task was to rebut these claims.   The fate of a considerable stretch of territory hung in the balance, and an assemblage of notables gathered at Indian Head for the occasion, as well as throngs of farmers from the adjoining countryside.   The debate was held in a fanning-mill factory, which at the time was undergoing repairs, and the eager audience were wedged in along rows of uncomfortable plank benches.   It was far past midnight before the wordy harangue ended, with Haultain manifestly triumphant and Manitoba's pretensions dissipated. During the afternoon, while the thrill of impending battle was in the air, Motherwell and Dayman had managed to get a small group of farmers together in the same factory and divulged their plans.   Various well-balanced speeches were delivered on the benefits that would accrue to the farmers through combined action, and although a few discordant notes were heard, the meeting readily swung into line and endorsed the formation of a new organization.   This was to be known as the Territorial Grain Growers' Association and had Motherwell as its provisional president and Millar as its provisional secretary.   A committee was appointed to draft a constitution for the organization, and a ratification meeting called for January 2.

The Department of Agriculture of the Territories took immediate cognizance of the new movement, and resolved to keep in close touch with its development.   C. W. Peterson, Deputy Commissioner of Agriculture, was detailed to be present at the January meeting to lend whatever assistance he might to the work of organization.   When the constitution was under discussion, Peterson suggested that the already-existing agricultural societies should be permitted to function locally for the association wherever they were prepared to accept its aims; local branches of the association, which he claimed would be very hard to keep alive, need only be set up then as required.   This advice was taken, and the constitution so framed as to provide for the grouping of both agricultural societies and local branches under a central association. Peterson volunteered to take over the secretarial duties of the central body, but the grain growers were loath to have a government official on their executive, and the offer was declined.

The roads were now smooth with winter's snow, and leaders of the movement sped this way and that carrying their message of the value of organization to the farming communities of East Assiniboia. Peterson, they discovered, had been badly astray in the reliance which he had placed upon the co-operation of the agricultural societies, as these were very slow in casting in their lot with the association. On the other hand local branches were created with ease, and after six weeks of campaigning the movement was firmly established along the C.P.R. from Moosomin to Regina. "Those wince that have their withers wrung," remarked the Regina *Leader* as the organization continued to spread, "and it is not surprising that prairie denizens should look for means of relief from the burdens that heavily, unnecessarily and unjustly press upon them."

The first annual convention of the Territorial Grain Growers' Association opened at Indian Head on February 12. Announcement was made that twelve local branches had been formed and four agricultural societies had become affiliated with the association; the total membership was computed at 500. Strictures were passed upon the C.P.R. for its lack of motive power and the consequent grain trade stagnation, and upon the elevators for depressing prices as much as seven to nine cents a bushel by informing the farmers that they had only bins for inferior grades of wheat. The convention went on record as favoring the grading of wheat according to its milling value, and urged that the railways be compelled to take grain direct from the farmers' wagons, no matter what loading conveniences there were at any station. The lukewarmness of the agricultural societies for the cause was commented upon, and the constitution amended to debar any more of them from entering the association. Officers were elected for 1902-3 as follows: President, W. R. Motherwell; First Vice-President, Matthew Snow, Wolseley; Second Vice-President, G. W. Brown, Regina; Secretary-Treasurer, John A. Millar. At the convention was Hon. G. H. V. Bulyea, Commissioner of Agriculture for the Territories, who, when its sessions were over, went with Matthew Snow to Winnipeg for the purpose of bringing the true state of affairs to the attention of C.P.R. officials. The two men set forth the views of the organized grain growers on the transportation issue in unequivocal terms.

Parliament Takes Action.

Any serious obstruction to the trade of Western Canada was a matter of national import and could scarcely escape an airing in the House of Commons. The subject was brought up on March 10, when J. M. Douglas moved a resolution in the House asking for "all papers and correspondence relative to the present wheat blockade in Manitoba and the North-West Territories, and the incapacity and inability of the Canadian Pacific Railway to move the crop of last year in such a reasonable period of time as to prevent the grain growers of the country being subject to serious financial loss." All day long on March 17 the question was debated, and Douglas spoke an hour explaining in detail the operation and mischievous results of the blockade. He said that even in January and February, 1902, the C.P.R. had been to blame in not sending wheat over the Soo line to Duluth, and in refusing to transfer it to other railways at Winnipeg. "Were I to interpret the feeling which exists in the West to-day," he cried, "I would certainly rend my garments and put ashes on my head." It was the government's duty to give the Western producer proper access to the sea. "I am satisfied," said he, "that there is more gold in the soil of the prairies than in the rocks of the Yukon, and we ought to be willing to spend some money in providing such transportation facilities as the country demands." Both Hon. Walter Scott and Hon. Frank Oliver charged that the C.P.R. had been violating the law by explicitly instructing its agents not to furnish cars to farmers. Sir Wilfrid Laurier replied that if tangible evidence were supplied to the government of illegalities of this nature the Department of Justice would be led to intervene.

The ferment in the West and its reflection in the records of Hansard caused the government to inquire into the workings of the Manitoba Grain Act and to decide that it needed revision. The act was accordingly reissued with important amendments on May 19, 1902. The former regulation concerning the minimum size of flat warehouses was rescinded; moreover, it was stipulated that where additional warehouses were constructed the cost of sidings must be borne by the railway. Loading platforms, when required by the farmers, must be built by the railway at sidings where there was no station yard. The demands of the Territorial Grain Growers' Association were met through the provision that "at any shipping point where there is no loading platform, cars shall be furnished, without undue delay, for loading grain direct from vehicles." But the outstanding feature in the changes made was the stringent regulations introduced with respect to the distribution of cars to shippers. It was enacted that an order book for cars must be kept at each station where there was a railway agent. It became the duty of the agent to enter the names of applicants for cars in this book in succession according to the time when the application was made. As the cars came in they were to be assigned one by one to companies or individuals as their names appeared in the order book. These car distribution clauses were intended for the grain growers' protection, and the ignoring of them, as will be seen, gave rise to another period of conflict on the prairies.

VIOLATIONS OF THE LAW.

Another heavy crop was ready for the market in 1902, but the "freight car famine" still went unrelieved. This occurred in spite of the emphatic assurances given by C.P.R. officials during the summer that extensive additions were being made to the rolling stock of their road, and that producers need not fear a second wheat blockade. Just how barren these promises were, although clearly uttered in good faith, was observable as the lake-and-rail shipping season advanced and only a few odd farmers in each locality had cars assigned to them, while the rest went without. Murmurs of resentment arose, to be superseded even before navigation had closed by vehement denunciations of the railways and all their works in every section of the grain belt.

The railways were at length driven to acknowledge that they had neither enough cars nor sufficient motive power to handle the crop in a proper manner. William Whyte, Second Vice-President of the C.P.R., who was held in high esteem by the prairie farmers, declared that business had developed so remarkably all over the line that it had been found impossible to provide adequate service in the grain-growing areas. The farmers on the other hand said that it was not only a question of lack of transportation facilities in the grain trade, but that the distribution clauses of the amended grain act were being openly violated by the railways.

12—F.M.

A portion of the press argued that, were the railways to be able to catch up with the demands of expanding business in the West, the difficulties occasioned by improper distribution would automatically vanish away. The farmers were not satisfied with this explanation; they contended that the railways were exploiting the car-shortage situation, and in so doing were breaking the law and should be brought to book. Shippers who used a loading platform were often "bunched," they said, as if together they composed a single applicant, and were allotted one car in turn for each car supplied to an elevator. Under these circumstances, argued the farmers, the elevator companies by acting in concert had depressed prices since they had been in a position to increase the spread between track and street quotations for wheat. It was pointed out that whereas the track price for wheat had been only two and one-half cents a bushel above the street price at the beginning of October, at the end of the month the difference had widened to ten cents a bushel. Grain growers averred that the existence of a loading platform at any shipping centre should tend to stabilize prices at that point, but as the elevators were receiving the most of the cars they were in virtual control of the market. From data obtainable it would appear that the forcing down of prices was at its worst in those localities where no independent buyers came into competition with the elevators. In proof of this an aggrieved farmer submitted figures to the press in which he compared the street prices for wheat at Hamiota, a centre dominated by the elevator combine, on October 22, with those prevailing on the same day at Shoal Lake where independent buyers were in the majority. The Hamiota prices, less rail charges, for varying grades of wheat were: No. 1 Hard, 52c., No. 1 Northern, 50c., No. 2 Northern, 47c.; for the corresponding grades at Shoal Lake the quotations were: 58c., 56c., and 53c., or a level of 6c. higher.

Feeling was running so high on the prairies in the autumn of 1902, that not only did the farmers gather together to fulminate against the railways, but actions were precipitated that were not far short of violence. At Elva, Manitoba, a group of farmers went on record as stating their belief that the grain act was nothing but a well-devised piece of political chicanery. Ostensibly, they said, it had been passed with the object of securing justice to the farmer in the shipment of his grain; instead, it was discovered to have been "conceived in deceit and hypocrisy, shapen by hands traitorous to the interests of the farming communities." At Minto, in the same province, another body of farmers, desperate when cars were refused to their loading platform, suddenly took the law into their own hands. As a Canadian Northern train drew into the town, they issued to the attack and seized three cars that had been apportioned to the local elevators. Railroadmen interfered and a "lively scrapping took place over the possession of the brakes." Evidently the farmers came out of the mêlée victorious but immediately began quarrelling among themselves over the cars, and the incident ended in a free-for-all fight.

THE SINTALUTA TRIAL.

Needless to state the Territorial Grain Growers' Association was a unit in its opposition to the alleged highhandedness of the railway companies. As yet the young and stirring organization had not won its spurs in the farmers' cause and here appeared to be an opportunity to do so that it must not let slip by. Might not an appeal to the law of the land in this instance serve to establish the fact that the farmer on the plains has his rights as well as the favored corporations? The association's executive was of the opinion that a test case upon the question of car distribution might eventuate to the farmers' advantage. Accordingly W. R. Motherwell and Peter Dayman took a trip to Winnipeg politely to inform western headquarters of the C.P.R. that, unless the car distribution clauses of the grain act were differently interpreted by the railway, the organization which they represented would drag the issue into the courts forthwith. The Winnipeg officials promised to give the matter the attention that it merited, but as time elapsed and action was withheld the association grew hourly more impatient. The breaking point at last came and the farmers' Lilliputian organization set forth daringly to measure its strength against the giant transportation company in the courts of the North-West Territories.

Formal complaints were laid before Warehouse Commissioner Castle that the C.P.R. agent at Sintaluta, A. V. Benoit, had been guilty of infractions of the grain act in his allotment of cars at that centre. The charges preferred were so specific that Commissioner Castle accompanied by T. G. Mathers, of the Department of Justice, visited Sintaluta on

November 28, and after investigation decided that proceedings should be instituted against Benoit on behalf of the Crown. The case was tried in the public-school building at Sintaluta before H. O. Partridge as presiding magistrate, assisted by Magistrates Thompson, of Indian Head, and Magee, of Wolseley, and attracted a tensely-interested crowd from near and far. Evidence was furnished to show that two elevators at Sintaluta had been given priority in the distribution of cars to A. W. Annis, a farmer, although his application had been put in ahead of theirs. It was also proven that W. W. Allen, a farmer, who had signed up early in the season, had waited seven weeks for his car, while in the meantime eighty cars had been received and allotted. So conclusive was the evidence adduced that a verdict against the defendant was inevitable; the three magistrates unanimously decided that he must pay fifty dollars and costs, or be imprisoned for one month.

The Territorial Grain Growers' Association was pardonably exultant at the result of the trial, and everywhere farmers began making inquiries about the organization which had turned the tables against the puissant railway corporation in an inferior court of law. Though Western newspapers gave little space to the event, the meaning for producers of grain of the verdict rendered at Sintaluta was heralded not only in the more populous farming centres, but in far-away nooks and corners of the prairie country. The C.P.R. promptly tried to make amends for its breach of statutory enactment. It is computed that, whereas sixty-seven cars had arrived at Sintaluta during the first two months of the shipping season, of which the farmers had received seven, before spring cars were being dispatched to that point in scores for the farmers' use.

ORGANIZATION IN MANITOBA.

The fires lighted by the grain growers' movement in the North-West Territories were now transferred to the older hearthstone of Manitoba. Information relative to the territorial organization and the purposes it was intended to serve was sought by Manitoba farmers early in 1902, but it was not until the end of the year that a definite attempt was made to introduce the movement into that province. In December the agricultural society at Virden, a town in Western Manitoba, selected a committee to arrange for a special meeting at which the question of establishing a branch of the association would be the main theme for discussion. The meeting was held on January 7, 1903, and was attended by W. R. Motherwell and Matthew Snow, who explained the manner in which their organization was functioning in the Territories. Motherwell was emphatic in declaring that the farmer's occupation was the most important in Canada, and that there was no reason why he should not organize for the maintenance of his rights. A local branch was at once formed with the following officers: President, J. W. Scallion; Vice-President, George Carefoot; Secretary, J. A. Blakeman; Directors, Peter McDonald, Col. C. E. Ivens, and Isaac Bennett.

The example set by Virden was quickly followed by similar organizing activities at other country points in the province. J. W. Scallion travelled energetically, encouraging his fellow-Manitobans to form locals, and found his work implemented by the discontent bred through the mishandling of the 1902 crop. Within a few weeks it became increasingly evident that the movement was bound to have wide ramifications in Manitoba, and a cry went up, especially from the Virden branch, that the membership in the province should cut adrift from the territorial body and establish their own association. No objection was registered by the parent organization, and as a result a convention representative of the existing locals in Manitoba was summoned to meet at Brandon on March 3.

The outcome of this convention was the establishment of the Manitoba Grain Growers' Association, with a constitution modelled quite closely on that of its precursor in the Territories. At the start twenty-two locals were grouped under the new association's jurisdiction. W. R. Motherwell, who had come to give the organization his blessing, regaled the convention with an account of the Sintaluta trial, while J. W. Scallion told it lamentingly of the 40,000 farmers of the West who produced 60,000,000 bushels of wheat and should be prosperous, but who unfortunately were being "done" by the manufacturer, the railway promoter, and the dealer in grain. A decision was reached that no one but an actual grain grower might hold a place on the association's executive. Officers elected for 1903-4 were: President, J. W. Scallion, Virden; Vice-President, R. C. Henders, Elm Creek; Secretary-Treasurer, R. C. McKenzie, Brandon; Directors: William Ryan, Boissevain; W. A. Robinson, Elva; Donald McEwen, Brandon; D. W. McCuaig, Portage la Prairie; John Wilson, Lenore, and H. A. Fraser, Hamiota.

CHAPTER XVI

The Grain Growers' Grain Company

DURING 1903, and again in 1904, the Commissioner of Agriculture for the North-West Territories, authorized experimental tests to be made by a well-known Canadian scientist to determine the relative value of different grades of Western wheat for flour and bread-making purposes. Sample bags of grain were consigned to the inspection department at Winnipeg, whence they were forwarded to this expert with a designation as to their respective grades. Each grade was then milled separately and subjected to a careful baking test. The discovery was made that, while the range of market prices for the several grades of wheat was considerable, the difference in bread-making properties of the various yields of flour was relatively insignificant. Even flour milled from "feed" wheat, though less attractive to the eye, made good, edible bread. These experiments corroborated the view already held among grain growers that their low-grade wheat was affording utilities incommensurate with the prices paid for it, and the Sintaluta local of the territorial association was led to adopt the rather novel suggestion that they should send an investigator to Winnipeg in order that he might secure first-hand information for them concerning the ins and outs of the grain trade. A sum to defray expenses was raised by the Sintaluta farmers, and E. A. Partridge, one of their number, who had been twenty years on the prairies, was chosen for the rôle.

E. A. Partridge, singled out in this manner by fate, was to have a very remarkable influence in shaping agrarian history in the West. A big man, of restless demeanor and flashing eye, he became the seer of the Canadian plains-folk. More ideas have originated with him affecting the farmers' social and economic welfare than with any other dweller in the grain country. Partridge alighted at Winnipeg in January, 1905, and was soon forced to the conviction that the task allotted to him was no easy matter. Though given friendly assistance in some quarters during his four weeks' stay, in the main his inquiry was resented, and he himself regarded

183

as a trespasser on forbidden ground. However, as Partridge made his way about, his mind became more and more impregnated with the thought that the western farmers had surrendered to a motley array of distributors work which they collectively might just as well do themselves. Why should they not combine as marketers of grain and thus save the margins over cost that were going into other men's pockets? This idea took firm hold of him, and he departed with the resolve to urge in every possible way the formation of a distributors' co-operative organization in the grain belt.

On his journey back to Sintaluta Partridge stopped off at Brandon to attend the third annual convention of the Manitoba Grain Growers' Association which opened on February 9. In the course of a piquant address in which he related some of his experiences at Winnipeg, he affirmed that it was "as difficult to get an idea of the grain business there as for a man on the outside of a house with the doors locked and the blinds down to get an idea of the inside contents." He had no fault to find, he said, with those who were responsible for the grading of wheat, but rather with the methods they were compelled to follow, which to his mind were "not a system of scaling intrinsic value." By way of illustrating this point he told of an instance where two cars graded as No. 2 Northern, "right" in color but "off" in weight, had been mixed with a single car of No. 1 Northern, "right" in weight but "off" in color. As the result of skilful blending the three cars had been marketed as No. 1 Hard. Then Partridge launched into his first public pronouncement in favor of the establishment of a co-operative company for the handling of Western grain to be owned and operated by the farmers themselves. This company, he stated, should acquire a string of elevators and might even run its own flour mill. After exercising various economies, it would turn back its profits into the farmers' hands. The audience heard him phlegmatically, and, if appearances meant anything, had slender interest in the proposal; Manitoba grain growers might understand the wisdom of concertedly carrying their grievances before a government or a railway company, but to go into a business undertaking for themselves seemed like taking a leap in the dark. Nevertheless, they were willing to explore the possibilities of the scheme, and appointed J. A. Taylor, of Cartwright, and A. S. Barton, of Boissevain, to act with Partridge in preparing a report on the subject for their next meeting.

But on his arrival at Sintaluta Partridge found himself in quite a different atmosphere when he began to expound his views on co-operative trading among the home folk. They commended him for his efforts at Winnipeg, and, as persuasively and logically, he unfolded his plans for the organization of a grain company, some of the leading farmers of the district were fired with enthusiasm for the project. The matter was held in abeyance during the summer of 1905, only again to become a topic of lively conversation among Sintaluta grain growers after the crop had been cut. An impulsion to do something was abroad, even though neither of the central associations might formally sanction the move. Accordingly in October Partridge and four other farmers: David Railton, Sr., A. J. Quigley, William Hall and Thomas S. McLeod, assembled in Wilson's hardware store on Main Street, Sintaluta, and decided that a company should be formed. Thus was laid the first foundation stone of a business which has become one of the largest of its kind in the world.

In December Partridge reported on his Winnipeg trip to the Territorial Grain Growers' Association in session at Moosejaw, and took occasion to dilate on the need for a co-operative marketing organization in the West, but encountered scepticism and received even less encouragement than at Brandon. Meanwhile, the plans of the Sintaluta grain growers had been taking shape; further preliminary conferences had been held, and by the beginning of the new year it was deemed advisable to bring the scheme definitely to the public attention. On January 27, therefore, at a general meeting in the town hall, an outline was given of the form which the company was expected to assume and the business objects it would pursue. The organization to be established would be known as the Grain Growers' Grain Company, and at the outset would buy grain mainly or altogether on the commission basis, after having purchased a seat on the Winnipeg Exchange. Stock shares would cost twenty-five dollars apiece, but not more than four shares might be obtained by any one person, and shareholders were to be allowed only one vote each at the annual meetings of the company. Without hesitation the gathering endorsed the proposals as set forth and pledged its generous support to a stock subscription canvass. A committee was named to continue the work of organization until enough stock should have been sold to warrant the appointment of a provisional board of directors.

Desk-room was forthwith rented in Wilson's store and the company's sign displayed in the window; a neat prospectus was then drawn up and mailed out to likely subscribers. Stock was selling briskly in the Sintaluta district when the time for the 1906 convention of the Manitoba association drew round and Partridge presented himself to report for his committee. Again he came out flat-footedly for a grain growers' company and was gladdened by unmistakable tokens that opinion was veering in favor of his plea. For instance, when the question of changing the wheat grade standards came up for discussion at the meeting, one delegate interposed the question: "if we have our co-operative grain company, what need we care what the grades are?" Still the association gave no official support to the projected Grain Growers' Grain Company, and President McCuaig took pains to announce that no binding connection was contemplated between the two organizations. The most notable convert to the "business idea" at this convention was John Kennedy, a delegate from the Swan River local, who was shortly to prove a tower of strength to the company in its earlier days of trial and adversity, and subsequently to be its devoted servant in times of expansion.

A decision was now reached to broaden the scope of the stock canvass, and at a meeting held in the Leland Hotel, Winnipeg, later in the spring, several Manitoba farmers were added to the list of those empowered to make sales. Among them was John Kennedy, who soon became the banner salesman of the enterprise. Combining in his person a staid perseverance with a bland geniality, he brought hundreds into the company before its charter was finally secured; in fact three-quarters of the sales effected during the vigorous campaign that was waged within the next few months are attributed to him. Just ten per cent. of the value of the stock was assessed at first, so that Kennedy had only to wheedle $2.50 to $10.00 from each of his "victims," to cover the initial payment.

SECURING THE CHARTER.

Legal counsel was next employed and steps taken to secure a charter from the Dominion government. Application was made that the company might issue 10,000 shares, and have an authorized capital of $250,000. It was not long before the grain growers were led to the belief that the powers at Ottawa were unfriendly to their venture and were bent on putting hindrances in its way. John Kennedy has since asserted that immediately their counsel met the demands made on him from Ottawa some other requirement was trumped up with which he must comply. At length the calamitous news reached Winnipeg that the charter could not be granted at all on the technical grounds that a company capitalized at a quarter of a million dollars might not issue shares below $100 par value.

Despair laid its iron clutch on the promoters of the Grain Growers' Grain Company. Word had been despatched to the members of the organization committee apprising them of the untoward circumstances, and five of them gathered in the Seymour House, Winnipeg, in doleful mood. A crisis had been reached, and four of those present, their faith shattered, were for abandoning the project at once. It was at this juncture that John Kennedy sprang into the breach and by his masterly insistence saved the company from oblivion. "No!" he exclaimed, with dark brow furrowed, while the others quailed at that single word. Proceeding, he said, that even if they had failed to get a federal charter, what mattered that?—could they not procure one from the government of Manitoba and operate as a provincial concern? True, their operations would be more restricted, but they could still establish themselves at Winnipeg, and trade through the Grain Exchange. Confidence was gradually restored among the disheartened group, and they decided to follow Kennedy's advice; John Spencer and he were commissioned to apply for a charter in what it was hoped would be a more favorable quarter.

Negotiations with the provincial authorities went forward smoothly, and the cherished document was procured without delay. Under the statutory laws of Manitoba a company seeking incorporation might begin business with only a provisional directorate, and as the time was not yet ripe for completing the organization of the Grain Growers' Grain Company, it seemed wise to make use of this privilege with the end in view that the company might assist in marketing the crop of 1906. The industrial exhibition, a well-known annual Mecca of western grain growers, would soon open, and it was decided to call a meeting of shareholders while the exhibition was on. Permission was sought to raise a tent on the grounds, and into this tent a throng of shareholders were crowded on July 26. While pandemonium reigned in the grounds outside organization was effected, and the following elected as provincial directors: President, E. A. Partridge; Vice-President, John Kennedy; Secretary-Treasurer, John Spencer; W. A. Robinson, and Francis Graham.

The first problem confronting the newly-appointed directorate was to acquire a seat on the Grain Exchange. This would cost $2,500, but as there was only $1,000 in the company's possession after discharging its organization and other expenses, the directors were in a quandary as to where to obtain the balance. Another call might be made on the shareholders to provide working capital, but before the necessary funds would come in, valuable time must be lost. The president in the pinch resolved to fall back upon the loyalty of the Sintaluta grain growers, and transmitted an earnest appeal to certain of the originals who were known to be blessed with worldly goods asking them to stand by the company in its predicament. Five Sintaluta farmers straightway took their notes to the bank, covering the deficiency of $1,500, and in consequence the seat was purchased. Then a manager and sub-manager with experience in the grain trade, were taken on the company's pay-roll, and a line of credit opened with the Bank of British North America. Special bins were rented in the C.P.R. terminal elevator, an office furnished in the Henderson Block, and on September 5 the Grain Growers' Grain Company declared itself ready for business.

AT CROSS-PURPOSES WITH THE EXCHANGE.

A rosy delineation of the company's expectations was given to the Manitoba *Free Press* for publication in its issue of September 10, and although trade was a trifle dull at first, the directors were bubbling over with confidence as grain was deflected to them that had formerly been marketed through other channels. Their hopes were more than realized, indeed, when, in a few weeks, business became so brisk that the management had all it could do to take care of the incoming grain. By October 1 the company was receiving on an average over fifteen cars a day. Dealers on the Exchange were alive to the situation and watched the strides made by their new rival with no small degree of anxiety. Everything was proceeding thus in happy fashion for the Grain Growers' Company when without warning there came a bolt out of the blue, and the enterprise was again in the throes of trouble.

A letter arrived in October from the secretary of the Grain Exchange, instructing President Partridge to appear before its Council in order to explain why the Grain Growers Grain Company had "offended against the honor and dignity" of the Exchange through the issuance of a certain objectionable pamphlet. Some time previous this pamphlet had been sent out among the farmers with the announcement that the Grain Growers' Company, after declaring a share dividend, would apportion any surplus profits among its customers upon a co-operative basis according to the amount of grain handled for them. Such a system of dividing surplus profits, stated the letter, was in direct contravention of a rule of the Exchange. Partridge on presenting himself said that he did not question the Exchange's right to pass by-laws, but that he hesitated to accept the validity of any by-law which told the members of an incorporated farmers' company how they should divide their profits. The Council pointed out that by-law 19, section 4, of the rules of the Exchange forbade any dealer to allow a rebate to farmers out of the regular commission charges, and that the handing back of profits to the producer by the Grain Growers' Grain Company would amount to the same thing.

The Council of the Exchange was plainly well-entrenched from the legal standpoint in the position it had taken up. But the directors of the Grain Growers' Company were firmly convinced that its action had been dictated through antipathy to their thriving venture, and it is exceedingly difficult for the historian to judge to what extent this was the case. Partridge's outspokenness was quite untraditional and assuredly did not mend matters. He continued to parley with the Council but found it obdurate. The climax came when on October 24 a notice was posted on the board of the Exchange, intimating that the trading privileges granted under registration to the Grain Growers' Grain Company had been withdrawn.

Ejected in this manner when trading was at its height on the Exchange, the company began to rue the fact of its initial prosperity. Grain consigned to it was piling up, but how would it be marketed? Export selling was out of the question, since that could only be done through the Exchange, and apparently the company's single hope would be to unload grain to eastern purchasers with whom independent negotiations might be conducted. This policy was tried but with aggravatingly slow results. Meantime, the farmers had to be paid for their grain, and as little money was coming in, a serious overdraft developed at the bank which bore like an incubus on the minds of the directors. When the company's indebtedness was upwards of $400,000, the local bank manager expostulated with the directors, and prevailed upon three of them, Partridge, Kennedy and Spencer, to sign a personal bond covering the amount.

For the young company, troubles appeared to travel ·in packs like wolves. One splendid sale of wheat, amounting to 310,000 bushels, had been made in the East, and as navigation was about to close this wheat was lying at Fort William ready for shipment. Suddenly the directors began to realize that the days were slipping by and the consignment was still not under way. Should this wheat not get out by vessel, it would mean additional transportation costs by rail, and under the circumstances a financial loss that the company might not weather. There was an Ethiopian in the woodpile somewhere, thought the directors; presumably the shipment was being delayed through manipulation from an unknown quarter. John Kennedy's dependability was again put to the test upon this occasion. He hurried to Fort William, and diplomatically set to work to undo the tangle. So skilfully did he ply his arts that in short order the *J. P. Walsh*, last boat out for the season, was headed with the precious grain under its hatches into the dark, frostbitten waters of Lake Superior. Possibly this episode may be taken as the turning point in the company's fortunes. The Manitoba Grain Growers' Association, as will be noted, had already begun to inject itself into the situation, while a helping hand was lent to the company by the Scottish Co-operative Wholesale Society. Braving anger of the Exchange, where its representative held a seat, the Scottish society made a large purchase of wheat from the Grain Growers' Company, paying full commission on the transaction. The profits accruing from this deal made up in part for the low returns from the eastern sales.

The Manitoba Association Takes a Hand.

At this point it will be necessary to turn back nine or ten months in order to pick up a thread that otherwise would be lost to the story. At its 1905 convention the Manitoba association had passed a resolution stating its belief that the Manitoba and North-West Grain Dealers' Association was "a combine or conspiracy for the restraint of trade," and ordering its executive to bring that fact to the attention of the Attorney-General of the province. Then, in company with other interested bodies, it had importuned the federal government to authorize an official inquiry into the relations subsisting between grain dealers and producers in the West, and into all other matters connected with the grain trade. The government had complied by appointing a royal grain commission on July 26, with plenary powers of investigation, under the chairmanship of John A. Millar, of Indian Head.* This commission had first visited a number of places in Manitoba and Alberta in the fall of the year, and had then returned to Winnipeg for a second sitting on November 20, with the specific object of hearing charges against the Grain Dealers' Association. A stubborn battle was waged before the commission by the opposing forces on that date, at the conclusion of which the Grain Growers' representatives felt that they had established beyond peradventure that the Grain Dealers' Association was a menace to free trading in the West. Nevertheless, one vexing fact had been brought out during the taking of evidence which materially affected the policies of the Grain Growers' Grain Company. Thomas Robinson, counsel for the Winnipeg Grain Exchange, had pointed out that since that trading organization had been incorporated under the joint stock companies' act of Manitoba, any equal distribution of profits made by it would on statutory grounds be illegal.

Two results flowed almost immediately from this hearing before the royal grain commission. On December 6, D. W. McCuaig, president of the Manitoba association, acting in a private capacity, swore to an information accusing three prominent grain dealers with unlawfully conspiring to restrain trade and combining to lessen competition in the market. Next, on December 22, the directors of the grain company, having discovered that Robinson's objection was perfectly valid, adopted the prudent course of renouncing their co-operative plan for the division of surplus profits. Preliminary steps in the proceedings against the grain dealers were taken before magistrate T. M. Daly at Winnipeg, on January 10, who decided that sufficient evidence had been adduced to warrant him sending the case on for trial to a higher court. McCuaig's resort to law was branded as impetuous and very

---

*The two other members of this commission were George E. Goldie and William L. McNair. It continued its work of inquiry in 1907, holding, all told, thirty-eight sittings in Canada and seven in the United States. On May 31, 1907, its members sailed for Great Britain, where they studied marketing conditions, and upon their return, having completed an itinerary of 20,000 miles, laid their report before the government on October 11.

unfortunate, in a jointly-signed letter appearing in the press on January 28, from W. R. Motherwell, then Minister of Agriculture in Saskatchewan, and John A. Millar, chairman of the commission; the writers claimed that the commission's effectiveness was being thereby seriously hampered. E. A. Partridge at once dashed off a reply in vindication of McCuaig, which was printed the following day. So, too, when the Manitoba association met in February it fully sanctioned its president's action.

The provisional directorate's surrender of the co-operative principle of dividing profits was confirmed at a general meeting of the shareholders of the grain company held on February 5. It was thought that the company should, therefore, be restored as a member of the Exchange without any more ado. Elections were now imminent in Manitoba, and this issue together with other disputes affecting the grain trade were projected into the campaign. Premier Roblin asserted his willingness to summon a conference of all parties interested in grain trade matters, but preferred to call it after the elections. A deputation from the Manitoba Grain Growers' Association waited upon the government's agricultural committee and laid before it a long list of suggested amendments to the Exchange's charter. It urged that the Exchange should no longer be allowed to limit its membership; that it should have no jurisdiction over salaries paid in the grain trade; and that its expulsion of any member from trading privileges should not be deemed final until agreed to by the Minister of Agriculture of the province. The deputation also asked that the government should allocate to itself the right to inspect the accounts and records of the Exchange, and that gambling in futures be made an indictable offence. Representatives of the Exchange appeared subsequently before the committee and staunchly defended their institution, declaring that they would rather have its charter torn up than altered according to the demands of the farmers. Towards the end of February the government gave pledges that it would deal with the charter at the next session of the legislature.

The government was sensible of the fact that the company had a strong case for readmission, and, notwithstanding its return with a snug majority in the elections on March 7, foresaw certain political advantages to itself in taking up cudgels on the company's behalf. Evidently that organization was now prepared to abide by the rules of the Exchange, although it was still expressing distaste for a clause in by-law 19 which forbade grain dealers from hiring agents at country points for less than fifty dollars a month; this, it claimed, prevented commission men from operating at small places and threw all business there to the elevators. The government dealt with the Exchange in a summary manner. In Premier Roblin's absence from Winnipeg, Hon. Robert Rogers, minister of Public Works, wrote a letter on April 2 to W. J. Bellinger, president of the Exchange, in which he referred to its "arbitrary and unjustifiable exercise of powers" in refusing to take the Grain Growers' Company back into good standing. Unless, warned Rogers, remedial action were forthcoming by April 15, the government would interpose, and deal with the Exchange through amendments to its charter. On April 4, he gave an interview to the press in which he reiterated the government's intentions in similar terms for public consumption.

The Council of the Exchange discreetly agreed to confer with the government on the issue, and a basis of settlement was reached, the main feature of which was the reinstatement of the Grain Growers' Grain Company to the trading privileges it had formerly enjoyed. The company on its part acknowledged that its proposed method of dividing profits might influence grain shipments, and was "equivalent to a violation of the rules" of the Exchange. The Council promised to repeal the contentious fifty-dollar salary clause. The seat held by the company on the Exchange was transferred to R. J. Spencer, as E. A. Partridge had become *persona non grata* with its governing body. Partridge did not hesitate to expound the view freely that it was the government's ultimatum which had brought the Council to time; his company had accepted the rule, he explained, because the institution through which they must trade had the power to make it. "This, of course," he said defiantly, "has nothing to do with our opinion as to the nature of the rule; in fact, we believe the rule to be arbitrary."

CRERAR BECOMES PRESIDENT.

The permanent organization of the Grain Growers' Grain Company had been effected at the shareholders' meeting of Feburary 5, 1907. As a token of approval of the work they had done, the provisional board was continued in office to fill out the year, while its membership was increased to seven

13—F.M.

by the election of Robert Cruise, of Dauphin, and T. W. Knowles, of Emerson. During the breathing spell afforded while trade was slack, the new board had an opportunity to appraise its position and to lay plans for the future. It was apparent to even the least sanguine of its members that the company would soon be doing business on a pretentious scale and that efficient control would be necessary to development. E. A. Partridge was anxious to retire from the presidency, so the board began to cast about for some one who would be fitted for that position. Few stockholders of the company had the least qualification as business executives. However, the eyes of the board were eventually fastened upon a young man of promise who owned a share in the company, in the person of Thomas Alexander Crerar, of Russell. Crerar, though born in Ontario, was virtually a Manitoban since he had been brought West at five years of age by his parents, who had settled sixty-five miles from a railway. He had experienced a rigorous upbringing, had taught school, homesteaded land, run a saw mill, and at the moment was managing a farmers' elevator at Russell, in north-western Manitoba, and buying grain for a Winnipeg firm. Crerar had already gained a record for shrewdness and integrity, qualities which, combined with his business training and educational attainments, recommended him to the board. At the second annual meeting of the company, on July 24, 1907, he was invited to head the organization and signified his acceptance.

During its first ten months of operation the Grain Growers' Grain Company handled nearly 2,500,000 bushels of grain, and had come through with a slim profit of $790. One of Crerar's initial worries related to his company's line of credit. Just as the crop of 1907 was being harvested the Bank of British North America closed out the company's account without warning, leaving it in a sorry predicament. Nevertheless, the Home Bank, which at this time was fighting for position in the West, was persuaded to assume responsibility for the company's obligations, and established cordial relations with it extending over a period of years. In 1907-8 the volume of grain handled amounted to about 5,000,000 bushels, while a profit had been reaped of $30,000. The nucleus of a claims department had meanwhile been instituted to safeguard the farmers against shortages and overcharges. By the end of its third financial year, on June 30, 1909, the organization had allotted 7,558 shares and had a paid-up capital of $120,708.

CHAPTER XVII

The Exchange Brought to Terms

THE CASE of the Crown against the three grain dealers was entered for trial in the court of assize at Winnipeg, on April 22, 1907, before Mr. Justice Phippen and brought into service the best legal talent in the province. The Crown prosecutor was R. A. Bonnar, Attorney-General of Manitoba, and the indictment was laid under section 498 of the criminal code which held those guilty and liable to punishment who conspired: (a) "to unduly limit the facilities for storing, dealing in an article which may be a subject of trade or commerce; (b) to restrain or injure trade or commerce in relation to such article; or (d) to unduly prevent or lessen competition, et cetera." Bonnar's main charges were that the prices of grain were being regulated by various overt acts, that limitations had in certain instances been placed upon the amount of grain bought, and that the elevator companies were working in combination to fix their rates. Quotations for grain, he explained, were sent out daily from the headquarters of the Manitoba and North-West Grain Dealers' Association, and were accepted by buyers at country points, since there was an agreement among members of the association not to pay in excess of these prices. In addition members of the association had a system of dividing receipts which removed the incentive to "break price." No quotations were sent out between 9.30 a.m. and 1.15 p.m. with the result that sales were few at country points during that interval. Competition, affirmed the Attorney-General, was no longer the governing factor in the grain trade but gambling pure and simple; and then, waxing vehement, he characterized the Grain Dealers' Association as "an offspring of the Grain Exchange to assist them in their diabolical acts."

E. A. Partridge, taking the stand, declared that competition had been obliterated at country points in the purchase of track wheat. The day was, he testified, when buyers had hurried to meet incoming loads, and, after delving into a bag for a sample, had made a bid for the farmers' wheat;

but, since about 1905, they had sat around playing cards and waiting for the farmers "to hunt them up." According to the deposition of another witness summoned by Bonnar, purchases of wheat at one centre had been limited to 5,000 bushels, by prearrangement among the dealers. The defence claimed that the Dealers' Association made no attempt to set prices but merely stated them, and that it was not incumbent upon the buyers to adhere to them rigidly. Bonnar, when cross examining the secretary of the Grain Dealers' Association, on April 24, taxed him so severely that Judge Phippen reprimanded the Attorney-General for insulting a witness. A tense scene followed with presiding justice and Crown prosecutor as the principals. Bonnar declared that the last witness had been the most stubborn he had ever examined in his legal career, and finally left the court. Later he returned without his gown, and went away, having announced that he was no longer acting for the Crown.

An adjournment of the case was ordered until May 6. During the intervening fortnight the Attorney-General, having suppressed his feelings, agreed to go on with the prosecution. However, as the trial proceeded, it was not difficult (from the interpolations of the Judge), to conjecture what decision would be rendered. The defence, at the conclusion of the hearing, moved that the indictment be dismissed as the Crown had not proven a case. Judge Phippen gave out his findings on May 21 in lengthy form, asserting that he did not believe that the public interests had been "unduly impaired" through the actions of the defendants. Restrictions of trade had occurred, but they had been reasonable, more or less necessary, and not criminal in their intent. The main point at issue, said the *Manitoba Free Press*, commenting on this decision, had been the question as to whether grain prices were being fixed or determined in actual trading. The Judge had held that they were being determined; the country producer, on the other hand, was of the opinion that they were being fixed. Disappointment was rife among members of the Grain Growers' Association at the ineffectual outcome of the trial, and a reserve case was stated from Judge Phippen's decision to the provincial Court of Appeal; but upon the same having been argued, a verdict was given completely upholding the findings of Judge Phippen's court.

THE GOVERNMENT CURBS THE EXCHANGE.

The general conference which Premier Roblin had agreed to summon with respect to matters appertaining to the grain trade, met on June 5 and 6; it comprised some two hundred delegates, including representatives of the Winnipeg Grain Exchange; the Manitoba and North-West Grain Dealers' Association; the railways; the Manitoba Grain Growers' Association; and also a number of reeves from the counties. The farmer delegates had prepared a grist of resolutions for consideration, but, as they began to advance them, a sharp cleavage of opinion developed in the conference over the powers that were being exercised by the Grain Exchange. It became evident that the farmers were seeking for ways and means of bringing the Exchange more definitely under public control. The meeting resolved itself into a struggle of two factions, and when a motion was put and passed declaring that no by-law, rule or regulation of the Exchange should become operative until approved of by the Lieutenant-Governor in council, the grain dealers and Exchange men arose in a body and took their departure. One significant resolution offered to the conference by the farmer delegates embodied a request that the Manitoba government should acquire and operate a line of storage elevators in the province.

Scouting any further attempt to bring grain dealers and producers together for the possible settlement of their difficulties, the government of Manitoba proceeded to make good its threat to amend the charter of the Winnipeg Grain Exchange; when the legislature was opened on January 2, 1908, the speech from the throne presaged the introduction of a bill that would materially alter the conditions under which it had been allowed to operate. The bill was brought down almost immediately, and upon its second reading, on January 10, Premier Roblin took the floor to explain its purposes. Striking his desk dramatically, he told the House that if this measure did not receive the assent of parliament his government would resign and appeal to the country. By the terms of the bill supervision of all by-laws issued by the Exchange was to be exercised by the prothonotary of the Court of King's Bench. The Exchange could no longer limit its membership, since any reputable person with proper qualifications must be admitted to it upon application. There was to be a right of appeal against expulsion from membership to the Court of King's Bench. The books and accounts of the Exchange were to be subject to annual inspection by the Minister of Agriculture, and any restrictions that might be placed by the Exchange upon traders with respect to prices or commissions were forbidden.

Efforts were made to stay the government's hand before this bill should become law. On January 21 the Winnipeg Board of Trade passed a unanimous resolution championing the cause of the Exchange, which stated that the "proposed amendments will impair, if they do not utterly destroy, the usefulness of the Exchange in providing the facilities which now obtain for the speedy and safe marketing of grain." Representatives of the Exchange appeared before the agricultural committee of the legislature gravely declaring that such modifications of its charter would drive the organization out of business: would mean, indeed, ruin, and confiscation. On February 13 the president and secretary of the Exchange submitted a petition to the government, alluding to the fact that their charter as it stood, was almost identical with the charters of similar bodies at Montreal and Toronto, and citing commendatory references to the work of the Winnipeg Exchange made in the court decision of Judge Phippen and in the report of the royal commission inquiring into the grain trade. The government, however, could not be deflected from its course and the bill, having been given its third reading, was finally passed on February 19.

Five days later the Exchange suspended business; all trading in grain had to be done through other channels and "official prices" were no longer quoted at country points. The Exchange's position at the time was peculiarly embarrassing, since it had contracted for a fine, new building to house its activities, estimated to cost in the neighborhood of $300,000, and already nearing completion. By the middle of March seats on the Exchange that had formerly sold for as high as $2,800 had fallen in value to $1,000, and it was noised abroad that the organization was in serious financial straits. Its Council reported upon the precariousness of the situation to a largely-attended gathering of members, on March 20, with the result that under the circumstances it was decided that a holding company should be formed to assume responsibility for the unfinished building. Reorganization plans were then evolved for the Exchange, but it was not until November that, with another body of officers and operating under its revised charter, it was again performing its wonted functions in the grain trade.

MOVEMENTS IN ALBERTA.

So far, in tracing the rise of grain growers' organizations on the Canadian plains, this narrative has been confined to the events occurring in the region from Winnipeg to Moosejaw. The constant trek of settlers westward had resulted in a trebling of the population of the North-West Territories during the period, 1901-5, so that by 1905 they contained upward of one-half million souls, and the federal government hearkening to insistent demands for autonomy, had carved out of their domain the two new provinces of Alberta and Saskatchewan by an act which came into force on September 1, 1905. It may be pointed out that in 1901 the district of Alberta, as part of the Territories, had only 9,500 farm holdings, and was chiefly noted for the horse-and-cattle ranges of its southern division. But, previous to the inclusion of that district in the province which took its name, an inrush of settlers had begun to the rich, alluvial lands of its northerly section stretching towards Athabasca, and a movement had originated among its grain growers of striking importance.

Early in 1905, and mainly through the efforts of J. W. Keen, of Turnip Lake, the principles of an organization known as the American Society of Equity* were brought to the attention of farmers in the neighborhood of Edmonton. The American Society of Equity had been founded a few years before, in the state of Indiana, by J. A. Everitt, and already had many thousand adherents in the middle-western states. Its aim was to educate the farmers to methods of "controlled marketing" by means of which they might obtain a better return from the sale of their products. A paper, *Up-to-Date Farming and Gardening*, was issued by Everitt at Indianapolis for the dissemination of the society's views. Rapid headway was made by Keen in his work of organization, and in short order he had formed local unions of the society at Poplar Lake, Belmont, Turnip Lake, Namao, Spruce Grove, Stony Plain and other places.

*Plans for the evolution of the American Society of Equity were first laid in 1902. As profitable ways of marketing were its chief *raison d'etre*, it was to consist of local unions of farmers organized at shipping points. These might join to form state associations. while there would be a national association for the whole body. The society aimed to establish granaries of various sorts, cold storage warehouses, hay barns and other repositories for farm produce. In 1903 J. A. Everitt wrote a work entitled "The Third Power. Farmers to the Front," which was a clarion appeal to the toilers on the land to show their economic strength. In 1905 the society was estimated to have 150,000 members. Its first national convention was held at East St. Louis, Illinois, in October, 1906. Next year an attempt was made to affiliate it with the American Federation of Labor, which occasioned much confusion and led to the society's partial disruption. It has mainly disappeared, although there are still evidences of it in the State of Wisconsin with headquarters at Madison.

From the first a measure of opposition was displayed toward the movement because of its American affiliations. This attitude became more pronounced in the fall of 1905, when an agitation was started for the establishment of some kind of organization that would suit not only the needs of Alberta farmers, already living in a separate province, but at the same time be distinctly Canadian in its character. A branch of the territorial association had been set up at Strathcona, but this body was about to take the name of the Saskatchewan Grain Growers' Association, and it was fully expected that it would limit its activities henceforward to the newly-created province in which its interests almost altogether lay. Rice Sheppard, who was a member of the Strathcona local, became the leading exponent of a Canadian organization for Alberta, while Nestor Noel, of Rivière Qui Barre, a prolific letter-writer, hurried to the defence of the Society of Equity. A controversy between these two flared up, and was given prominence in the *Edmonton Bulletin*. Nestor Noel affirmed that there existed no reason why the Society of Equity in Canada might not become practically independent, if its membership so desired, as information to that effect had been received from headquarters in Indianapolis. Eventually, after certain preliminary negotiations, the local union of the Society of Equity at Clover Bar decided to secede, and to throw in its lot with the Strathcona branch, in order to form the nucleus of another organization to be called the Farmers' Association of Alberta. Not to be outdone and with no intention of quitting the field, the older organization, before the end of the year, then assumed the title of the Canadian Society of Equity.

In this manner Alberta, although still relatively backward as a grain-producing area, had acquired two farmers' organizations, each of which, as will be noted, had its spokesmen before a federal tariff commission that sat at Edmonton, on December 11, and each of which made haste to set up its locals wherever possible throughout the province. The Society of Equity, in keeping with its doctrines, had a penchant for business, and was foolhardy enough to launch a company for the development of a timber limit. This venture came to grief in 1907, a failure which acted as a deterrent to the society's progress. The Farmers' Association of Alberta, while starting no business enterprises, made its influence at once felt in matters of economic import. It undertook the management of a seed-grain fair at Edmonton, and largely at its suggestion a pork commission was established for Alberta. Rice Sheppard was dispatched to Ottawa to plead for the institution of special grades for Alberta winter wheat, and the Inspection and Sale Act was amended with that object in view. Mainly, too, through the association's advice, three creameries were formed in the province under government control.

Although a certain amount of friction and misunderstanding occurred between the two organizations in Alberta, for the most part they were able to live side by side in peace and harmony. Still it was evident that the maintenance of both was a hindrance to progressive action among the farmers, and a bit of an extravagance. An attempt made at Lacombe, in October, 1906, to unite the bodies was resultless, because the Society of Equity desired to establish an organization that would spread all over Canada, whereas the association preferred to limit its operations to Alberta. More than two years elapsed before a proposal to unite was again discussed at a meeting held specially for that purpose at Edmonton, when an amalgamation was effected. The hardest task confronting those who were entrusted with the formation of the new organization lay in securing a name for it, as members of the society clung with a death's grip to the expression, equity, which meant so much to them. From eight o'clock one morning, all day, until one o'clock the following morning, this matter was threshed out in committee. After a variety of titles had been discarded, it was finally agreed that the organization should be called the United Farmers of Alberta, Our Motto, Equity. Local unions were to be grouped under a central association, and after a year's operation this had enrolled 122 such unions and the United Farmers of Alberta had a membership of 2,147; by 1912 the membership had increased to 7,190. Among the first officers of the central association were: President, James Bower, Red Deer; Vice-President, Rice Sheppard, Strathcona; Secretary, Edward J. Fream, Calgary.

THE *GUIDE* ENTERS THE FRAY.

By respecting provincial boundaries in their development, as has been outlined, the farmers' movements in the West were enabled to retain a measure of individuality, and at the same time to take care of local needs. Yet leaders in the three provinces were not slow to recognize that problems were cropping up which must be faced in common, that, in future, these would increase rather than diminish in number, and that it would be a policy of wisdom to create bonds of union among their organizations. Accordingly an Interprovincial Council was formed in February, 1907, which, it was expected, would exercise discretionary powers on questions of wider import to the farmers, and would be representative of the several bodies then in existence. Also, plans were mooted for the establishment of a farm paper which would chronicle not only the various happenings within the organizations, but enunciate the principles for which they stood, and advance any cause that might receive their collective support.

The farm paper was set going through the instrumentality of the Grain Growers' Grain Company, although prior to its first issue it had received the endorsation of the Interprovincial Council, meeting at Regina on May 19, 1908, and had also been accepted by the Manitoba association as its official organ. The Interprovincial Council expressed its pleasure that the grain company was "taking steps to finance a non-political paper" which would deal fearlessly "with economic and social questions affecting the farmers' prosperity and well-being." Named euphoniously the *Grain Growers' Guide*, the paper appeared as a monthly in June, 1908, with E. A. Partridge as editor, and declared its advocacy of the government ownership of elevators, the erection of a sample market at Winnipeg, and the grading of wheat according to hardness and weight rather than color. The publication of the July number was abandoned because Partridge was away on business, so, to avoid a similar mishap, Roderick McKenzie, secretary of the Manitoba association, was appointed joint editor and remained with the paper for three years. George F. Chipman was taken on the staff as associate editor in 1909, and later given full control of the journal. During its first year the *Guide* was authorized to call itself the organ of both the Saskatchewan Grain Growers' Association and the United Farmers of Alberta; by August, 1909, it was strong enough to put out a weekly edition.

The paper had not been running long before it had mixed in a struggle on the farmers' behalf with the elevator combine on the rejuvenated Grain Exchange. By-law 19 had been causing friction on the Exchange because a persistent rumor was current that certain dealers had been quietly evading its terms. Moreover, commission men and track buyers had been pressing for a change in the by-law which would allow them to split the rate on wheat, giving their agents one-quarter of a cent a bushel at country points when they bought it in carload lots. The more powerful dealers on the Exchange, headed by the elevator companies, quashed this plea, and instead forced through an amendment by which the commission rule was to be entirely abrogated for a period of one year. This was described as experimental, but dealers who bought on commission, including the Grain Growers' Grain Company, were inclined to see in it a blow directed at themselves, since the elevator companies, by employing "cut-throat" methods might succeed in driving them out of business. The *Guide*, stressing the fact that sixty per cent. of all Western wheat was now sold in carload lots, warned its readers that the elevator combine, which stored and handled grain in large quantities, controlled its own terminals and received extensive dockages, unfortunately held the whip hand in the market. Its members were in a position to buy wheat on a basis of one-half a cent a bushel or even without commission and still make a profit.

The Grain Growers' Company was well aware that it could not do business long unless it received its regular commissions, and, faced by the imminent danger of underbidding for the 1909 crop, resolved to appeal to the loyalty of its shareholders. A letter was therefore drafted and mailed to all shareholders in August, dilating upon the alleged purposes of the combine and containing a three-question referendum on which the recipients were asked to ballot. "They want to kill us," declared the missive, "and they think that they have at last found a way. Their dodge is simple. By handling cars for half a cent or nothing, they are going to bribe the farmers and our own shareholders to send cars away from us." The referendum sought to discover: whether the shareholders would be willing to pay the usual rates of commission; whether they desired a reduction of rates; or whether they would abide by the judgment of the company's directors in the matter. The *Guide* entered into a strenuous publicity campaign on the issue, tracing the course of the struggle with the elevators, pointing out what the farmers would lose by breaking their ranks, and calling for such answers on the referendum as would decisively outwit the combine. The Grain Growers' Grain Company was overjoyed at the results of the voting: seventy per cent. of the shareholders balloting agreed to pay the regular commission rates and nearly all the remainder were prepared to leave the matter in the directors' hands. Grain, in fact, poured in to the company as it had never done before, with the result that it handled 16,000,000 bushels of wheat during 1909-10, or fifteen per cent. of the whole crop. Its profits for the year were $95,000 on a paid-up capital of $293,000, and it began to consider the advisability of applying for a Dominion charter.* The Grain Exchange restored the commission rule permanently at the end of the twelve-month.

The *Guide* in its callow years also figured in the unearthing of a plot which, had it ever properly matured, might have had a very disruptive effect among the organized farmers. Several farm journals and two Winnipeg dailies began to publish letters over the pen name, "Observer," which attacked the business methods of the Grain Growers' Grain Company and maligned its executive. These were supposedly written by a farmer, and were calculated to breed suspicion of the Grain Growers' enterprise in undiscerning minds. Before they had done much harm, G. F. Chipman had ferreted out the identity of their author, discovering him to be a self-styled financial broker who was contracting for space in the papers at advertising rates. The *Guide* stigmatized the anonymity of the letters, and by rousing adverse sentiment among the farmers compelled their discontinuance. Chipman broke far enough into the plot to learn that it was being subsidized by a small group of elevator men, and that, had everything gone smoothly, in due course "Observer" would have assailed the Grain Growers' views on government ownership. The *Guide* waited several months and then told its readers the whole story, printing photographs of the "men behind" and specifying the annual salary guaranteed to "Observer."

---

*This was secured by a bill which was put through the House of Commons in the spring of 1911 and finally assented to on May 19. The company's capitalization was temporarily fixed at $2,000,000, divided into shares of the par value of $25 of which any farmer might hold as many as 40. Wide powers to produce, manufacture, and trade at home and abroad were given to the company: facts which had given rise to adverse criticism when the bill was in the House. In the midst of a lively debate on the subject the question was asked: was there anything the company could not do? Honoré H. A. Gervais (Montreal, St. James) thought it should be entitled: The General Promoters and Schemers' Company, Limited. J. G. Turriff (Assiniboia E.), however, had come to the organization's defence, asserting that it was seeking no powers that other companies might not obtain by letters patent.

THE CANADIAN COUNCIL OF AGRICULTURE.

The Interprovincial Council had proven such a decided boon to the grain growers' organizations that a proposal was made in 1909 for the inclusion of the Dominion Grange and a reformation of the council on a nation-wide basis. Negotiations were opened with the Grange, and in November three Western leaders, D. W. McCuaig, E. A. Partridge and Roderick McKenzie, proceeded to Toronto to attend the thirty-fifth annual meeting of the Dominion Grange, and to arrange such details as were necessary for the enlargement of the council. On their appearance in Zion Church, where the meeting was in progress, the Westerners were given "a truly royal welcome." "I believe this session," said E. C. Drury, addressing them from the master's chair, "is going to have more important results than any previous one in the history of the Dominion Grange." Roderick McKenzie answered for the grain growers' organizations. "I realize the importance," he declared, "of East and West coming together. Our views on economic questions are the same, and if we bring our united forces to bear, we shall obtain for ourselves the influence in the matter of legislation which we should have." In establishing a national council, he said, "there need be no interference with the provincial work of any provincial organization." But, on the other hand, whenever "great questions such as the tariff" had to be considered it would be possible through federated action to bring their "combined influence to bear for a common end." A joint committee was selected to write a constitution for the new body.

The following morning a draft constitution of the Canadian National Council of Agriculture was presented to the Dominion Grange and received its endorsation. According to its preamble the objects of the council would be: to stimulate organization among the farmers of Canada; to collect data from a variety of sources for the organized farmers' use; to facilitate their demands for legislation; to encourage their interest in political matters so that their views might be given proper representation; and to urge the advisability of co-operative methods of purchase and sale. Any association of farmers that was prepared to give effect to these objects and that was "entirely independent of government control" would be eligible for membership. The council was to be made up of the executives of the affiliated organizations, and was to meet at least once a year. On account of the breadth of Canada it was stipulated that travelling expenses to and from the meetings should be pooled and a flat rate struck for each delegate.

This draft constitution was approved by the Manitoba Grain Growers' Association in December, 1909, and by the United Farmers of Alberta in convention the following month. On February 10, E. C. Drury addressed the ninth annual convention of the Saskatchewan association at Prince Albert, and secured its ratification of the constitution. Next day the council held its first meeting at Prince Albert and elected officers for 1910-1911 as follows: President, D. W. McCuaig, Manitoba; Vice-President, James Bower, Alberta; Secretary-Treasurer, E. C. Drury, Ontario. It was decided that the council should immediately bend its energies towards obtaining evidence for the prosecution of the trusts and combines which, it believed, had been springing up in Canada behind the protective tariff.

CHAPTER XVIII

SOLUTION OF THE ELEVATOR QUESTION

THE PROPOSITION that there should be government ownership of Canadian grain elevators appears to have first been mooted, by the executive of the Manitoba Grain Growers' Association, early in 1907. The association itself, meeting later, gave its imprimatur to the idea, and the June conference at Winnipeg summoned by Premier Roblin, as has been stated, passed a resolution on the subject. E. A. Partridge became the leading exponent of government ownership, and was able to crystallize his views into a succinct plan. His suggestion was that the Dominion government should take over and operate all terminal and transfer elevators in Canada, while the initial or line elevators should be acquired by the provinces within whose boundaries they were situated. Partridge argued that the former ought, logically, to come under federal control because they were intended as repositories of grain that had already passed inspection, but which he claimed, was often subjected to processes of mixing and blending before it reached its ultimate market. The initial elevators, on the other hand, would be more advantageously managed and kept in repair under provincial authority, and should, he thought, be made to provide storage facilities for two-thirds of the crop. In quick succession the "Partridge plan" was endorsed during the winter of 1907-8 by the associations in Manitoba and Saskatchewan and by the Farmers' Association of Alberta. The Interprovincial Council then recommended that the executives of each of these bodies should elaborate their opinions to their respective governments on the question, soliciting co-operation. This advice was followed, and the three provincial governments given a comprehensive outline of the "Partridge plan."

Premier Roblin, whose previous experiences with the organized grain growers led him to the opinion that the issue could not be burked, made arrangements to hold an informal colloquy with Premiers Rutherford, of Alberta, and Walter Scott, of Saskatchewan, at Regina, on May 4, when the elevator situation would be discussed. The three Premiers, putting their heads together on the day appointed, circumvented the necessity of giving a straight answer to the Grain Growers by offering them certain alternative proposals which, as it happened, bore little relationship to the original demands. George Langley, member for Redberry, in the Saskatchewan legislature, was selected as an intermediary to convey these proposals to the Interprovincial Council. In the first place it was suggested that, while private ownership of the initial elevators should remain unaltered, the profits derived from their operation might be limited and their management exercised under the Grain Growers' supervision. Or, in lieu of this, it was pointed out that the provincial governments might influence the railways to build loading elevators, with storage bins sufficient to remove the worst evils of the existing system. Langley had full knowledge of the incongruity of the terms which he bore, and the Interprovincial Council was perhaps more amused than wrathy when it heard them. The *Grain Growers' Guide* remarked that the farmers had asked the premiers for an apple but had "got a turnip instead."

Nothing daunted, however, the Grain Growers' Associations persisted in their demands and by November, 1908, were able to drag the Premiers to a conference with certain of their representatives. But once again the Premiers cleverly side-stepped the necessity of making an immediate pronouncement, stating that they would each take the matter up in Cabinet council and issue a joint reply. This reply was forthcoming in January, 1909, and was sorely discomfiting to the farmers' organizations. In it the Premiers declared that it would be quite unconstitutional for their administrations to embark on the business of operating elevators, since that would involve the enforcement of a monopoly in the handling of grain. Only by seeking additions to the legislative powers of the provinces from federal and imperial sources could they do what the Grain Growers desired. The *Manitoba Free Press* at once challenged the soundness of this position: why, it asked, should competition in the elevator business be entirely eliminated through the introduction of government ownership? The provincial chieftains, it said, had been indulging in "a diplomatic *non possumus*;" plainly they were disinclined to call the Grain Growers' scheme unfeasible, but at the same time were reluctant to endanger their political fortunes in its advocacy. R. A. Bonnar gave out a legal opinion in which he unhesitatingly affirmed that the constitutional difficulties raised by the Premiers would fall down upon close scrutiny.

ATTITUDE OF THE FEDERAL GOVERNMENT.

Meanwhile the government at Ottawa had been apprised of the rôle that it was expected to play in the working out of the "Partridge plan." Already in 1907 certain of the Western members of parliament had learned of the Grain Growers' desire that the federal government should assume control of the terminal elevators, and, when in May, 1908, Rice Sheppard, George Langley, E. A. Partridge, Roderick McKenzie, and R. C. Henders had gone to attend a conference at Ottawa on the question of modifications in the grain act, they brought the matter formally to the government's attention. Sir Richard Cartwright was chairman of this conference, at which were also present representatives of the banks, the railways and the Grain Dealers' Association. At one point in the proceedings E. A. Partridge was given an opportunity to set forth the views of the Western farmers on the elevator question, and he made a strong plea for public ownership and control of the terminals on the ground that in no other way could malpractices in the handling of grain be prevented at the lake ports. The government refused to commit itself on the subject of ownership, but expressed its willingness to intensify its system of inspection at terminal points. Strife broke loose at the conference when the grain dealers and their supporters strove to obtain an alteration in the car distribution clauses of the grain act, claiming that a scarcity of cars was generally brought about through the delinquency of the farmers. This elicited an emphatic denial from the Grain Growers and the counter-charge that, when cars had been loaded and billed out, they often stood motionless for days on the railway tracks. Afterward in relating their experiences at this conference the Grain Growers spoke feelingly of the "warm bond of attachment" that had been discernible among the interests opposing them.

The federal government lived up to its promise to introduce more rigid methods of inspection by amending the Inspection and Sale Act so as to compel its officials to weigh up all grain in store at the terminals during August of each year.* In this way it became possible to check any dis-

---

*This was accomplished by inserting a new section, 126 A, in the act when it was amended on July 20, 1908. Another section introduced classifications of Alberta winter wheat. An amendment of the Manitoba Grain Act assented to on the same date made

crepancies through the records of the warehouse commissioner at Winnipeg. After weighing had been done at Fort William in August, 1909, according to regulation, the head inspector decided that he would catch the elevators unawares at the close of navigation and make a special investigation of their contents. On December 10, together with seventy assistants, he swooped down upon them and measured the grain in storage with a plumb bob. (One elevator was found to have been so skilful in raising inferior grades that it had shipped out 437,884 more bushels of No. 1 Northern wheat than it had received. Discrepancies were detected in the case of three companies and they were haled into the courts, accused of falsifying their reports to the warehouse commissioner, and fined heavily; they were credited with having made extra profits amounting to $50,000 in a period of four months by tampering with the grades. The organized farmers were delighted at these proceedings because verification was thus given to their often-expressed belief that large gains were being taken by the elevator companies through the manipulation of grain at terminal points.)

CHANGE IN FRONT IN THE PROVINCES.

Though temporarily disappointed at the reply of the provincial Premiers, the Grain Growers had put little stock in their apparent hedging and thought that by keeping persistently at it they might eventually induce the prairie governments to take action. In February, 1909, a monster petition, signed by nearly 10,000 farmers, was submitted to the government of Manitoba, asking for a system of storage elevators operated by an independent commission. Again, just before harvest, the directors of the Manitoba association waited upon Premier Roblin, and importuned him to carry out their wishes respecting publicly-owned elevators as soon as possible. In Saskatchewan somewhat similar tactics had been followed: a petition had been drawn up by the Grain Growers' association and sent on to the government urgently requesting it to take over the initial elevators, because the operation of "storage facilities by powerful companies for private gain has proved detrimental to the prosperity of

numerous changes affecting the grain trade, including regulations with respect to: dockages; the deterioration of grain; cleaning methods; preserving the identity of grain; and car distribution. The report of the royal grain commission, presented in 1907, and the influence of the Grain Growers' representatives had impelled the government to authorize these modifications of the two acts.

growers of grain throughout the province." As late as September the Premiers were still ostensibly clinging to their united policy, but soon afterward a break occurred in their ranks. Premier Scott, having diplomatically revised his opinions, politely informed both Winnipeg and Edmonton that his province was no longer bound by the arrangements hitherto made, and that he deemed it advisable for each government to settle the elevator problem in its own way. Then, oblivious of the constitutional hindrances formerly conjured up, the government of Saskatchewan announced on December 14 that it had accepted the advice of its agricultural committee and that it would appoint a commission to make a "searching inquiry into proposals looking to the creation and operation of a system of elevators to effect the objects outlined by the Grain Growers' Association." On February 28, 1910, this commission was instituted with the following three members: Chairman, Professor Robert McGill, of Dalhousie University; George Langley; and Frederick W. Green.

Simultaneously the Manitoba government executed a right-about-face on the issue of seemingly so pronounced a character that it caused no end of wonderment throughout the province. On December 16, Hon. G. R. Coldwell, Minister of Education, appeared at the seventh annual convention of the Manitoba association officially to announce his government's policy. He had a happy disclosure to make, but as he led up to it a chill of apprehension fell on the gathering. A voice from the audience besought him to "break the news gently." Loud and long cheering, therefore, rang through the building when he stated that the government had ceded its opposition and had "accepted the principle laid down by the Grain Growers' Association of establishing a line of internal elevators as a public utility." He asked the organization to make haste in drawing up and submitting a plan to the government in order that this might be considered in formulating an elevator bill for the impending session of the legislature.

The Manitoba association presented its views to the government on January 5. It advised that a system of initial elevators should be purchased or constructed in the province by means of the issuance of forty-year bonds, and that cost of replacement be the sole basis employed in arriving at a fair valuation of the property acquired through sale. Control of the system, it believed, should be vested in an independent commission, named by the executive of the Grain Growers'

Association and appointed for life. At once objection was raised by a number of the elevator men to the proposal that sales must be made according to cost of replacement; some consideration should be given, they said, to the fact that their businesses were going concerns. It was also pointed out that, as only a fraction of the farmers belonged to the Grain Growers' Association, it would be a mistake to allow them to have a "corner" on the appointing power to the commission. The government, indeed, received the Grain Growers' suggestions apathetically, and the conviction grew that the "artless Mr. Coldwell" had depicted its surrender to the principle of public ownership in much too radiant a hue.

R. A. Bonnar drafted a bill embodying the Grain Growers' views, but this was practically ignored by the government in framing the legislation which it put on the statute book. The Manitoba Elevator Act, as this legislation was called, authorized the establishment of a public line of elevators under a commission, but the members of the commission were to receive their appointment from the government and be removable at its behest. A petition signed by sixty per cent. of the farmers contributory to a proposed elevator was necessary before it could be purchased, leased or constructed. If it was impossible to fix the price of an elevator by agreement, then this might be determined in the manner provided for by the expropriation act of the province. Money would be raised to finance the system by the sale of forty-year four per cent. debentures or stock. The organized grain growers made no pretence of hiding their displeasure at the terms of this act: a commission so appointed, they said, would be under the dictation of the party in power and amenable to all whims of political expediency; the sixty per cent. petition requirement would involve compaigns wherever the farmers sought a government elevator; moreover, an appeal to the expropriation act was certain to lead to bad feelings in the grain trade. However, when D. W. McCuaig, president of the Manitoba association, was offered and accepted the chairmanship of the commission, his fellow grain growers asserted that they would give him every assistance in putting the government's plan to a proper test. Gazetted along with McCuaig on the commission were: W. C. Graham, a former Patron of Industry, and F. B. McLennan, a grain commission merchant of Winnipeg.

The Saskatchewan elevator commission went perseveringly at the task assigned to it in May, 1910, and having visited sixteen places in the province and heard upwards of two hundred witnesses, prepared a voluminous report which it submitted to the government in November. Several different schemes of public control had been recommended to the commission, including one from the executive of the Saskatchewan Grain Growers' Association; these were dealt with specifically in the report together with reasons why they were considered unworkable. The Manitoba Elevator Act was rejected as a pattern for Saskatchewan to follow, and comment made upon the fact that it would offer "a government that wanted to discredit the whole principle of public ownership" an excellent opportunity to carry out its purposes. The commission was of the opinion that so far as initial elevators were concerned the solution of the problem "must be sought along the line of co-operation by the farmers themselves assisted in the matter of finance by a provincial loan." It advised, therefore, the formation of a co-operative joint stock company in Saskatchewan to operate storage elevators and with authority to distribute its profits on a co-operative plan. Care must be taken that a "maximum amount of local control" should be allowed in organizing the company, but its general management should be in the hands of a board of directors" entirely independent of government interference."

Early in February, 1911, Premier Scott assumed the personal responsibility of introducing an elevator bill which in all essential points adhered to the recommendations of the commission. One of the most animated debates in the history of the Saskatchewan legislature arose over this measure and it did not become law until March. By its terms authority was given for the creation of the Saskatchewan Co-operative Elevator Company, Limited, to construct, or acquire initial elevators in the province and to buy and sell grain. Stock in the company was to be parcelled into shares of fifty dollars each and sold only to farmers, but no one could hold more than ten shares. A provisional board of six directors was named, who were empowered to take subscriptions for shares and to organize elevator locals. Whenever in any farming district enough shares had been sold to cover the cost of building or acquiring an elevator, a local might be formed, and as soon as twenty-five locals were in existence the company could start business. However, only fifteen per cent. of the local's capital had to be paid in immediately since the government would lend it up to eighty-five per cent. of the cost of its elevator with repayment in instalments stretching over twenty years. Financial control was to be exercised by a central board, which might declare dividends up to six per cent. per annum. As much as one-half of any surplus profits could be distributed to the shareholders according to the amount of business they had brought to their elevators; the balance might either be apportioned to the locals or used to build up an elevator reserve fund. After an all-day debate at its convention in February, the Saskatchewan Grain Growers' Association approved of the government's bill, then before the legislature, asserting that they would rather have "a co-operative system within reach of their hand" than one publicly-owned over which they were denied any influence.

FAILURE AT OTTAWA.

The grain growers' organizations, though pleased at the Fort William disclosures, had looked askance at the federal government's attempt to settle the terminal elevator question by a policy of special supervision and inspection. To their way of thinking this was merely "superficial alchemy" and corruption would only be ended at the lake ports by completely removing "the temptation to transgress." Accordingly, on January 26, 1910, another delegation presented itself at Ottawa again to emphasize the Western farmer's unbending attitude on the elevator issue. Upon this occasion the grain growers were assisted in making their plea by representatives of the Dominion Millers' Association who favored government operation of the terminals in order that grain might be delivered to the consumer in the same condition that it had come from the grower; experience in the grain trade, they said, had taught the milling companies that a toll of one and one-half cents was taken on the average from every bushel of wheat while in transit.

Then as Sir Wilfrid Laurier journeyed through Western Canada in the summer of 1910 the most important theme, next to the tariff, upon which he was memorialized was the subject of the terminal elevators. Speaking at Brandon on July 18, Laurier said that he had talked this matter over repeatedly with Sir Richard Cartwright and was convinced that the farmers had a real grievance arising from the elevator situation; it was not good, he opined, that owners of the terminals should be interested in the purchase of wheat at country points. His government, however, had not yet hit upon a remedy. Other things requested of the Prime Minister while on his tour were: the immediate construction of the Hudson Bay Railway; legislation to permit of the more economic establishment of co-operative societies; and government aid for the chilled-meat industry. The United Farmers of Alberta were eagerly solicitous on the last-mentioned topic, arguing that the marketing of meat was under the dominance of combines and that the government should provide funds to install an up-to-date chilling plant which would either be publicly operated or run by the producers on a co-operative plan. Laurier avowed his sympathy for this scheme when leaving Alberta in September, acknowledging that the United States' market was shut off by its tariff and that the British market "on hoof" was alone being utilized. In December, 1910, a host of farmers—of which more later—besieged Ottawa, under the auspices of the Canadian Council of Agriculture, particularly to lay their views before the government on the tariff, but the opportunity was also taken to submit resolutions and memorials on: the terminal elevator question,* co-operative legislation, the chilled meat industry, the Hudson Bay Railway, and proposed alterations in the statutory laws relating to banking and the railways. A resolution on terminal elevators, supported by a speaker from each of the three prairie provinces, declared that their private ownership had been "detrimental to all parties concerned from the producer to the consumer," and that the only effective solution would be for the government to operate them as a public utility under an independent commission.

But despite the pressure brought to bear upon the Laurier administration by the Grain Growers it could not be induced to take a clear stand for government ownership of the terminals. The direction in which its policies were shaping was demonstrated early in 1911 when a bill was introduced in the Senate, which, although it did not definitely bar the door to

---

*Upon this occasion W. J. Tregillus, vice-president of the United Farmers of Alberta, spoke on the need of terminal facilities at the Pacific coast. Considering the long haul from Alberta to the lake front, he said, was it any wonder that farmers there had "been casting longing eyes upon the year-open ports" along the Pacific. Agitation for a westward route for grain shipments had been launched by Alberta farmers in 1906 just before the United States began to speed up its work on the Panama Canal. In April, 1909, the U.F.A. had sent a special delegation to Ottawa to lay its views on this matter before the government. Again, in 1912, E. J. Fream, secretary of the U.F.A., gave the question further publicity. However, nothing but a flat warehouse at Vancouver was in use on this route until the government took further action in 1916.

public ownership, still placed its main reliance for a solution of grain trade difficulties upon more rigid methods of supervision and inspection. The House of Commons saw, too, the way the wind was blowing, when, on January 25, W. M. Martin (Regina), a government supporter, moved a resolution calling for the adoption of measures to prevent the improper admixture of grades at the terminal ports. In the discussion that followed John G. Turriff (Assiniboia) was the only Liberal who came out unreservedly on behalf of the Grain-Growers' claims. The Conservative opposition deprecated the weakness of Martin's resolution, and having noted the tenor of the Senate's bill, decided to make political capital for itself in the West by exhibiting an attitude of friendliness to the public-ownership idea. Hence, one of their number, Dr. F. L. Schaffner (Souris), brought in a motion, on February 13, that the government should proceed to acquire and operate the terminal elevators. A vigorous debate raged about this subject, in the midst of which the House witnessed the spectacle of Dr. Michael Clark (Red Deer) rising to defend the government and to issue an earnest warning that the Conservative Party was bent on hurrying the country into the maw of socialism. An amendment to Schaffner's motion carried by ninety-six votes to fifty-four, so that it was lost; R. L. Borden, Conservative leader, voted for public ownership.

Bill (Q), as the Senate's measure was termed, aimed to consolidate the Manitoba Grain Act with those portions of the Grain and Inspection Act which specifically dealt with grain-trade matters. In addition it provided for the appointment of a commission to administer its terms instead of leaving control, as heretofore, to the Department of Trade and Commerce. Section 17 of the bill stipulated that the government might build or acquire terminal elevators if, after investigating the situation, the commission so advised. While the bill was being dissected by a committee of the Senate, grain dealers and railway men appeared before it to protest vigorously against certain clauses, especially one which would have forbidden owners and operators of terminal elevators to buy and sell grain. Senators J. M. Douglas, T. O. Davis and P. Talbot fought to retain this clause, but it was finally deleted. The bill reached the House of Commons on May 19, where the government explained that at some future date public ownership might follow its passage. The Conservatives entered a complaint that there was not enough time left in the session to consider the bill on its merits, and it was therefore withdrawn. It is interesting to note that during R. L. Borden's pre-election tour of the West a few months later he declared himself as favoring the government ownership of terminals; assistance for the chilled-meat industry; the enactment of suitable co-operative legislation; and the immediate construction of the Hudson Bay Railway.

THE CANADA GRAIN ACT.

The vanquishment of the Laurier government in September, 1911, put the onus of settling the terminal elevator question upon the incoming Conservative administration. On account of the pledges given by Borden, the grain growers were eager to see how the new government would face up to its task. Their hopes were to be speedily frustrated when, on December 6, Hon. Geo. E. Foster, Minister of Trade and Commerce, sponsored a bill in the House of Commons relating to the grain trade, which on January, 1912, was read for the second time and went into committee. Foster acknowledged that his proposed measure was almost a replica of bill Q that had died on the Liberals' hands in the regular session of 1910-11. After four weeks' rough handling in committee, involving a discussion which covers nearly four hundred pages of Hansard, Foster's bill reached the Senate in March, where a career of vicissitude also awaited it before it became law, as the Canada Grain Act, on April 1.

A delegation from the grain growers' organizations came east toward the end of January and took up quarters at Ottawa to watch the progress of the bill through parliament. On January 30 they interviewed the Minister of Trade and Commerce and informed him that the Western farmer desired: a government-owned terminal elevator system; control by an independent commission; and a retention of the existing methods of grading. Foster readily agreed to the last two points, as his bill called for the appointment of an independent Board of Grain Commissioners, and made few changes in the grading system. On the first point, however, he baulked, evidently seeking to arrange a compromise. The following day the grain growers again consulted with the minister, accompanied by representatives of the Dominion Millers' Association, and the government's purposes were now bared to view. The railway terminals and those owned by commercial companies would be allowed to do business as usual.

The government for its part intended to acquire and operate one or two elevators as an experiment from which public ownership might eventually result.* The grain growers and millers bitterly resented this denouement, and, irate and indignant, filed out of the minister's presence at midnight.

As the bill progressed through the House of Commons in committee, it was decided that section 123 would only be slightly altered, and that, as in bill Q, owners of terminals would be permitted to have money invested in elevators operating in the interior. The grain growers' delegation also noted with dissatisfaction that, whereas one clause of the bill explicitly prohibited the mixing of grades while grain was in store, another section authorized the establishment of sample markets at Winnipeg, Fort William and Calgary where mixing might take place under special regulations. But there was greater cause for aggrievement when, after the delegation, thinking their services no longer requisite, had betaken themselves home, a vital change was made in the car distribution clauses of the bill. On February 20, the House in committee tacked on subsection (E) to section 207 of the bill, giving the Board of Grain Commissioners power to use their own judgment in regulating the distribution of cars whenever it was considered "necessary and advisable in order to relieve congestion and facilitate the dispatch of grain." Grain growers generally had come to regard the car distribution clauses as essential to the freedom of their industry, and when this amendment was made known, there was a loud outcry on the prairies. Upon the third reading of the bill, Robert Cruise (Dauphin) endeavored to secure an elision of the obnoxious subsection, by having the matter referred back to committee, but his motion was defeated in the House.

As a last resort the Western organizations decided to beard the Senate on the issues involved, although to do so was re-

*One public terminal elevator with a capacity of 2,500,000 bushels was erected by the government at Port Arthur in 1913. Along the lake front on October 1, 1923, there were six public terminals at Fort William and five at Port Arthur. Besides, on the same date, Fort William had fifteen private terminals and Port Arthur nine. In other words the commercial companies and railways control almost the entire grain storage facilities at these two ports. However, in 1914-5 the government opened three large interior terminal elevators at Moosejaw, Saskatoon and Calgary. These have brought the work of inspection nearer to the grain-growing areas, and offer a splendid store for grain between the close and opening of navigation. They also provide hospital apparatus for the treatment of damaged grain near to the point of production. It was expected that such terminals would be very serviceable in connection with the proposed Hudson Bay route and the government began to build a terminal at Port Nelson to link up the system, but work on this has been discontinued. In 1916, at the time when the Panama Canal was first coming into use, the government erected a smaller transfer elevator at Vancouver to demonstrate the feasibility of the Pacific route. This elevator has since been given over to the Board of Harbor Commissioners at Vancouver.

garded as a forlorn hope. Another delegation, therefore, made a pilgrimage to Ottawa in March, and began to lobby among the senators; furthermore, it set forth its objections to the bill in no uncertain terms before the Minister of Trade and Commerce. An effort was made to rush the bill through the Senate, but a delay was effected when Senator Arthur Boyer complained that it had not been printed in French and Senator T. O. Davis added his protest. The grain growers denounced the insertion of subsection (E) as a rank injustice, and, on March 21, Roderick McKenzie, a member of the delegation, said that sample markets* were under the circumstances undesirable, since the terminal companies possessing country elevators could buy grain wherever they pleased without using the sample markets and then mix it to their heart's content. The pertinacity of the grain growers brought its reward. Quite unexpectedly on March 28, and to the surprise of seasoned political observers, the government beat a hasty retreat on the contentious clauses of the bill. Senator J. A. Lougheed, government leader in the upper chamber, stated that subsection (E) would be dropped, and that the provision for the creation of sample markets would be rendered temporarily inoperative. "The coon has come down from the tree," vociferated Senator Davis, who had been fighting to preserve the integrity of the car-distribution clauses. The Board of Grain Commissioners was constituted at once, and assumed the duties of its office on April 16.

OUTCOME IN THE PROVINCES.

By this time the system of publicly-owned elevators established in the province of Manitoba had come to grief. In accordance with the powers vested in it the Manitoba commission had set to work early in June, 1910, to build and acquire elevators, with the result that by August 21 it had

---

*Whether sample markets should be established was a moot question in Western Canada for a number of years. Proponents of the plan, who were many, referred to the satisfactory methods of selling grain by sample at Minneapolis, Chicago, Kansas City and other American centres, and argued that better prices would be obtained for particular lots of grain were sample markets set up in Canada. The railway companies were frankly hostile to the scheme because they asserted that transportation of grain would be retarded through the holding up of cars for sampling purposes. The difficulty about introducing the sample market from the organized grain growers' standpoint was that it meant a legalizing of mixing on a scale that they were unwilling to endorse, unless there was government ownership of the public terminal elevators. Accordingly after the passage of the Canada Grain Act sentiment in favor of selling grain on sample became negligible. In August, 1917, the Board of Grain Commissioners devised rules and regulations by which sample markets might be efficiently utilized, but a very few cars have been received for sale in this manner. As mixing is not permitted in the public terminals, this, as well as the treatment of offgrade grain, takes place in private terminals of which the grain growers' companies have their share.

purchased seventy-five and had ten more under construction. Later, when the project went awry, the charge was made that the commission had been allowed a free hand in conducting its affairs until the provincial election of July, 1910, was over and the government returned with a comfortable majority; then immediately the reins had been tightened. The commission, it was said, had at first bought elevators at fair prices in the open market; but after the election the government had begun to interfere, and when elevator companies demurred about selling their property it had been expropriated and purchased by arbitration at what, it was argued, were excessive prices. The report for the first year of operation indicated that $1,001,342 had been spent on the government system, of which amount $852,370 had gone towards the purchase of existing elevators; the balance sheet showed a deficit of $84,145.

The crop of 1910 had been below average and the commission hoped for more encouraging results in the second year of operation, but their expectations were unrealized. A spirit of distrust of the government's enterprise was apparently abroad among the grain growers, who hesitated to give it their business. It was plain that the system was still running behind financially and its condition became a matter for discussion in the Manitoba legislature during the spring of 1912. Premier Roblin declared that the lack of patronage accorded the system was indicative of the fact that the people did not want government ownership, and laid the blame on the Grain Growers' Association for setting him on a blind trail. "I took," he said, "the voice of the demagogue as the voice of the public." The *Grain Growers' Guide* responded that the "elevator fiasco" was due to the government's lack of sympathy for the scheme from the beginning; seemingly it had been intended that the enterprise should fail. The elevators purchased, averred the *Guide*, were only worth one-half the sum that had been paid for them. Chairman McCuaig, who throughout had borne the government's dictation manfully, stated that the commission was engaged in a "losing game," and in May, 1912, announced that the system would close its doors. The Grain Growers' Grain Company, fearing that the 174 elevators already under government control would revert to the line companies, opened negotiations to lease them, and on July 20 arrangements were consummated by which the company took them over for the ensuing year, paying a rental of six per cent. per annum on their total cost; the government was responsible for their upkeep.

Quite different was the fate which befell the co-operative company in Saskatchewan. Since 1910 had been a poor crop year, money was scarce among the grain growers of the province, yet in spite of that fact there was a brisk demand for the establishment of elevator locals during the spring of 1911. As a result the necessary twenty-five locals had been capitalized by June 12. A general meeting was called for organization purposes on July 6, at which it was reported that forty-six locals were ready to function and that 8,101 shares of stock had been sold. The company chose as its executive officers: J. A. Maharg, President; Hon. George Langley, Vice-President; and C. A. Dunning, Secretary-Treasurer. Contracts were let for forty new elevators and work on these begun in August; six other elevators were acquired by purchase. During its initial year of operation the company handled 3,250,000 bushels of grain at a profit. Statistics for its second financial year ending on July 31, 1913, indicated that its shareholders already numbered 9,000, that it had 137 country elevators doing business, and that it had handled 13,000,000 bushels of grain during the preceding twelve months.

Meanwhile the province of Alberta had been forging ahead as a grain-producing area, but, to the detriment of its farming population, the construction of elevators within its borders had not kept pace with the growing demand for storage. The United Farmers of Alberta had repeatedly asked for a government-owned system of internal elevators, only to encounter delay in having their wishes carried into effect. Eventually, when the Saskatchewan plan was put into operation, it won the commendation of Alberta farmers, who then sought legislation from their government allowing for the formation of a co-operative company upon identical lines. A bill was accordingly passed by the legislature incorporating the Alberta Co-operative Elevator Company, Limited, with headquarters at Calgary. Financial aid was to be accorded to the elevator locals upon the same terms as were granted in Saskatchewan. Organization of the company took place on August 19, when forty-six locals had been formed with a list of shareholders numbering 3,500. The executive officers elected were: W. J. Tregillus, President; J. Quinsey, Vice-President; and E. J. Fream, Secretary-Treasurer. The first elevator erected was at Coutts, Alberta, and by June 30, 1914, fifty more had been built or purchased. From the outset the company marketed all its grain through the agency of the Grain Growers' Grain Company in Winnipeg, with which organization, as will be narrated, it was to become amalgamated in 1917. Besides its grain-handling business the company arranged to sell live stock on consignment and opened a co-operative supply department; in connection with this latter it built a large number of flour warehouses and coal sheds at elevator points. During its four years of independent operation, 1913-17, the Alberta Farmers' Co-operative Elevator Company, Limited, handled nearly 45,000,000 bushels of grain, and made profits amounting to $565,000.

PART IV

THE LAUNCHING OF THE TARIFF STRUGGLE, 1896-1911

CHAPTER XIX

Tariff Policies of the Laurier Government

UPON the retirement of Sir Mackenzie Bowell as Prime Minister of Canada, in April, 1896, it became the allotted task of Sir Charles Tupper to take over the dying administration, to gather together as far as possible the serried ranks of the Conservative Party and to bear the memory of Macdonald into the general election of that year. Robust and straight of limb, even if a trifle leaden-tongued, Tupper, a veteran of the political lists, played his part well. Touring the country with the old-time éclat, he presented the claims and extolled the merits of the National Policy as though fully expectant that the people would be won by it again as they had been on four previous occasions. Hon. Walter H. Montague went along with him to excite the imagination and stir the risibilities of those who made up his audiences. But Sir Charles—and perhaps he knew it full well—was taking the pitcher for the last time to the fountain. He professed in his campaign speeches that his party, if returned to power, were ready to modify the old tariff by introducing preferential rates of duty on commodities from the British Isles. Yet neither his temporizing nor the fact that Hon. George E. Foster had made a slightly-downward revision of the tariff in 1894 could disguise the real situation. It was the National Policy of protection and nothing else that the Conservative Party felt itself called upon to save in the momentous struggle of 1896.

The Liberals, in preparation for an election, had formulated their tariff policy at a great national convention held at Ottawa, in June, 1893. Hon. William S. Fielding, then Premier of Nova Scotia, acting as chairman of a special committee, had submitted to the convention a list of resolutions on the tariff, which were vociferously received and endorsed by that assemblage. These resolutions affirmed that the tariff in operation in Canada was "founded upon an unsound principle," and had worked such evil that it had "grievously disappointed thousands of persons who had

225

honestly supported it." The Liberal Party, therefore, believed that the issue between it and the government in power might be clearly defined. Unlike the government it was in favor, not of a fiscal policy that "developed monopolies, trusts and combinations," but of a tariff for revenue "based on the requirements of the public service." Furthermore, the schedules of the tariff proposed by the Liberal Party would be made to bear as lightly as possible upon the necessaries of life.

However, as the election hovered near, the line of demarcation between the two parties on the question of the tariff had become blurred and indistinct. The Liberals for strategic purposes began to offer a mélange to the electors. Sir Richard Cartwright found the resolutions of 1893 if anything too mild for his ardent soul, and ran true to form. Accordingly he was sedulously kept out of the urban constituencies of Eastern Canada during the election, and only allowed to talk of the merits of "free trade" and the "colossal villany of the protective system" to the farmers. In the West Hon. Clifford Sifton preached the same doctrines as Cartwright. No Liberal speaker made more lavish promises relative to the tariff than did Sifton, his pet aversion being the duty on agricultural implements. "Free coal oil, free clothing and free implements," he told an audience at Deloraine, Manitoba, "you shall have if the Liberal Party are returned to power."

Sir Wilfrid Laurier, as party leader, tried valiantly to hold a balance among his following on the tariff issue. He it was, indeed, who had moved the acceptance of the tariff resolutions at the Ottawa convention of 1893, and undoubtedly in his heart he was no friend of protection. At Winnipeg in September, 1894, he had denounced protection as a servile policy. "Yea, bondage," he ejaculated, "and I refer to bondage in the same manner in which American slavery was bondage." Appearing in Toronto at the height of the struggle, on June 12, 1896, he said that he was eager for a tariff that would "produce the maximum of revenue with the minimum of taxation." He held up to scorn what he deemed to be the incongruity of Tupper's attempt to cling to the National Policy and at the same time advocate any form of preferential agreement with Great Britain. "The only way," he informed his auditors, "that we can obtain a preference for our products in the English market over the products of foreign countries is that we must sacrifice, in so far as England is concerned, the policy of protection."

Still, it must be noted that Laurier confined himself for the most part to abstract statements in alluding to the tariff during the campaign.   Moreover, upon two occasions at least he swerved to right or left of the mean course which he had evidently set out to follow.   Upon revisiting Winnipeg on the very eve of the election, he fervidly avowed his devotion to "free trade" in words that would have thrilled the heart of any disciple of the Manchester School.   On the other hand in answer to the solicitations of George H. Bertram, Liberal candidate in Centre Toronto, he had words of assurance for the Canadian manufacturer.   "A revenue tariff," he wrote to Bertram, "being based upon the fixed charges of the country, and, not, therefore subject, to fluctuations and alterations made to suit and please now one interest and now another, would establish those conditions of stability and permanency which experience has shown are essential to the security and prosperity of manufacturing interests."   Conservative organs were sceptical of the Liberal chieftain's advocacy of a preferential tariff, stating that it could not harmonize with the plan for unrestricted reciprocity with the United States which they hinted was still at the back of Laurier's mind.

The work of allaying the fears of eastern business men that their interests would be imperilled by a change of government was left in large measure to two other Liberal stalwarts, Hon. George W. Ross, Ontario's Minister of Education, and William Paterson, manufacturer of Brantford.   These men, while they spoke of the need for tariff reform, gave it as their opinion that incidental protection was still the desideratum of Canadian industries.   So, too, the comforting plea, "we-won't-do-any-harm," was employed by the party in those quarters where it was found to be most effective.   The result of the election, as is well known, ushered in a new epoch in Canadian affairs.   Led by a rising French Canadian who was already the idol of his people, the Liberal Party, having taken a definite stand on the Manitoba school question and having adopted an indecisive, please-all policy on the tariff, gathered its strength from every direction and swept into power with ease on June 23, 1896.

THE TARIFF OF 1897.

The incoming administration had no ready-made tariff measure for the country when it accepted office in July, 1896.   On the contrary it was apparently anxious that the tumult and shouting should have died down and the electorate have had an opportunity to forget a great deal, before it divulged its plans. That no radical revision of the tariff might be expected by the Canadian people became evident when the personnel of the cabinet was announced. Rumor had constantly had it that Sir Richard Cartwright would be Minister of Finance because of his critical activities when in opposition. Instead, Laurier, turning to the East, induced Hon. W. S. Fielding to leave the premiership of Nova Scotia, and tendered him the Finance portfolio. Sir Richard Cartwright, though he remained an important figure in the Cabinet by being appointed Minister of Trade and Commerce, became thereafter, as was said, "a remnant of a bright historic period."

The government, previous to making up its mind on the character of the tariff it would introduce, sent Ministers Fielding, Cartwright and Paterson to some of the leading industrial centres to discover, if possible, what opinions were afloat on the subject. The inquiry was publicly conducted, a method of procedure to which, so far as tariff matters were concerned, the people of Canada had never been educated. As a consequence farmers as a producing class and consumers generally were conspicuous by their absence from the meetings held; the manufacturers and foreign importers, who put in an appearance, had the ground all to themselves. The evidence submitted was to the effect that an extensive revision of the tariff downward would be calamitous for Canadian industries, so that it appeared as if it would be necessary for the Liberals to cast into oblivion the tariff resolutions of 1893.

The inquiry ended, March, 1897, had arrived, and still Fielding had not brought down his tariff bill. Pressure was evidently being brought to bear upon the Minister of Finance to proceed with caution in making his alterations and the word went forth from Ottawa that the government had capitulated to the larger manufacturing interests. The *Weekly Sun* hinted at a betrayal of its pre-election promises on the part of the administration, asserting that the Liberals who helped form the agricultural population were "not in a humor to put up with a deliberate breach of faith." The *Montreal Witness*, which stood in the vanguard of "free trade" journals in the country, was visibly perturbed at the prospect. "We earnestly hope, and have faith," it plaintively told its readers, "that the Liberals will not betray the cause of free trade and tariff reform, and play into the hands of the protectionists." In fact, while in inner circles it was well known that the government was about to legislate with marked circumspection on the tariff, more or less uncertainty reigned throughout the country, even among Liberals, as to what it intended to do, until the Finance Minister made his pronouncement to the House on April 22.

A few sentences from Fielding's lips on that memorable occasion were enough to disillusion low tariff advocates, no matter what hope they might have entertained that the administration would adhere to the resolutions of 1893. Although the minister affirmed that "free trade" would continue to be the ultimate aim of Liberal policies, he said it with little warmth. Nothing, he declared, could be done in a hurried manner; the government must move toward the end it had in view by slow stages; English "free traders"—the Finance Minister quoted the London *Times* in corroboration—expected that the new government of necessity would proceed with moderation. Care must be taken that the industrial machinery of Canada should not be thrown out of gear by deranging measures. "The evil of protection," said Fielding, "like every other evil, is wide-reaching in its influence, and it has become so blended and interwoven with the business of Canada that if we should attempt to strike it down to-day, we should do harm to other interests which are not directly connected with the protected interests." The political situation in the United States, too, had helped to dictate the government's policy on the tariff. When the Liberals had arranged their platform the Democrats were in the ascendency, and better trade relations between Canada and the United States had been awaited; now the Republican Party held power, and its Dingley Tariff would offer instead a rebuff to any attempt at freer intercourse between the two countries. Then, in the course of his address, the Minister of Finance did a peculiar thing. In spite of the open confession which he had just made that his government did not intend to carry out the tariff resolutions of 1893, he began solemnly to read to the House those very resolutions that had been consigned to the limbo. He had gotten part way through with this recital, modulating his voice for the effort, when Hon. George E. Foster, taking humor out of the situation, intonated mockingly across the chamber: "Thus endeth the second lesson."

But Fielding had a titbit reserved for the delectation of those who might feel that their hopes had been frustrated by the government's stand. Announcement was made that for the first time a cleavage would be made in the Canadian tariff, with the result that in place of the single schedule heretofore employed there would now be two schedules, a special and a general. The special schedule would be of a reciprocal character, in that it would be applied to goods coming from those nations which gave Canada equally favorable terms. This arrangement was meant especially for the furtherance of British-Canadian trade relations, but its advantages could not be confined to Great Britain since she had treaties with Germany and Belgium to the effect that none of her colonies might grant her trade concessions that were not immediately accorded to both these countries in turn. The rates of the general schedule applicable to such a country as the United States, according to Fielding, would average up to about the same level as those of the last tariff of the Conservative regime. Until June 30, 1898, the preferential rates to be levied on all commodities except alcoholic liquors, manufactures of tobacco and a few other articles, would be in each case seven-eights of the general rate; after that date the preferential rates would be in each case three-quarters the amount of the general rate. The Minister of Finance and Liberal speakers who followed him contended that by establishing this new schedule a distinct step had been taken toward tariff reduction, and that the government had delivered thereby a blow against the protectionist system since imports from Great Britain would increase, and the Canadian manufacturer be subjected to keener competition.

Several noteworthy alterations were effected by the tariff of 1897 that were of particular significance to the Canadian farmer. Binder twine, upon which the duty had been twelve and one-half per cent., was now to be taxed at the rate of ten per cent., and after January 1, 1898, was to be placed on the free list. A long controversy over the taxation of one of the necessities of the farming industry was thus summarily concluded. Likewise barbed wire, formerly dutiable to the extent of three-quarters of a cent per pound was to be taxed fifteen per cent. *ad valorem* until January 1, and then go on the free list. The duty on Indian corn, used extensively for feeding purposes, had been seven and one-half cents a bushel. Except when imported for the distillation of alcohol, all species of corn under the new regulations were to be duty-free.   A reduction in the tax on corn-meal was made from forty cents a bushel to twenty-five cents a bushel.   Agricultural tools such as axes, scythes, sickles, reaping hooks, hoes, hay and straw knives were to be charged twenty-five per cent. of their value instead of thirty-five per cent. as heretofore. The tax on portable machines, steam engines and threshers was lowered from thirty per cent. to twenty-five per cent. Other reductions were: coal oil, from six cents to five cents a gallon; wheat, from fifteen cents to twelve cents a bushel; and wheat flour, from seventy-five cents to sixty cents per barrel.

The government anticipated that the special tariff schedule would mainly affect the import trade from Great Britain in woollens, cottons and the finer grades of hardware.   The general rate on woollen fabrics was fixed at thirty-five per cent., which meant that the preferential rate would be twenty-six and one-quarter per cent. after July 1, 1898.   Printed cotton fabrics had been taxed thirty per cent. under the old tariff; the general rate on these goods was now raised to thirty-five per cent., which made the special rate also twenty-six and one-quarter per cent.   The former duty of twenty-five per cent. on grey cottons and cotton thread was retained in the new schedule, with the result that these goods when accorded the terms of the special schedule were to be taxed at the rate of eighteen and three-quarters per cent.   Under the last Conservative tariff manufactured articles of steel had borne duties of from twenty-seven and one-half to thirty-two and one-half per cent.; these were now subjected to a uniform tax of thirty per cent. in the general schedule and so of twenty-two and one-half per cent. in the special schedule of the new tariff.   It will be seen that in order to adopt a preferential policy the government had kept the rates of its general schedule up to the old level or even raised them, as in the case of the finer grades of spun cotton goods.   In reality to accomplish its purpose, therefore, the government had been forced to discriminate more or less against the markets of the United States.

Again, Fielding's tariff of 1897 renewed and extended the bounty system which had been introduced by the Conservatives as a phase of the National Policy in 1883, and subsequently developed as a means of giving increased protection to the iron and steel industries of Canada.   It may also be noted that during the Conservative regime crude steel and iron goods, when imported, had been subject to stiff rates of duty in the customs tariff. The policy of the new administration was to lower the rates on goods coming in, but at the same time to increase the bounties as a compensation to Canadian mine owners and manufacturers. The reductions in the rates of duty were as follows: pig iron, from $4.00 to $2.50 a ton; iron and steel ingots, billets, puddled bars and blooms, from $5.00 to $4.00 a ton; bar iron, strips, hoops, etc., from $10.00 to $7.00 a ton. In lieu of these decreases, the bounty on pig iron and puddled bars was raised from $2.00 to $3.00 a ton; while steel ingots, shortly to be made in Canada for the first time, were also given a bounty of $3.00 a ton. As originally provided in the tariff of 1897, these bounties were to expire in 1902, but in August, 1899, an amendment was passed, extending them at gradually lessening rates for five years longer, until 1907. Then, as will be seen, another bounty arrangement was made to cover the years 1907-10.

Reception Accorded the New Tariff.

Hon. George E. Foster, always at his best on the negative side of a debate, spent several busy hours in scarifying the government's proposals. He alluded to the multitude of promises that had been made by Liberal worthies in stalking through the land as to what their party intended to do with the National Policy when elected to power. Whither had these glibly-made promises vanished? "They have adopted," Foster announced jubilantly, "nine-tenths of our tariff." Proceeding, he quoted extracts from the pre-election statements of members on the government side of the House, showing the utter abhorrence they had once evinced toward the principle of protection. Yet, instead of suffering extermination, it would seem that protection was already held in high esteem by the Liberal Party. "It has embalmed that principle," said Foster, "in its tariff." The ex-Minister of Finance took a particular fling at several members of the Cabinet who had gracefully accepted the new tariff. Hon. Louis H. Davies, Minister of Marine and Fisheries, was depicted as a one-time "free trader" who as the farmers' friend had stumped the country on a coal-oil can. Cartwright was upbraided for his apostasy from the faith. However, by far the heftiest shafts of Foster's criticism were directed against Hon. William Mulock, member for York and newly-appointed Postmaster-General. The manner in which, according to Foster, the York County representative had boldly coquetted with the Patrons of Industry, even to applauding their platform, was treated at length. In order that the House of Commons might have a clear idea of the Patrons' views on the tariff and other matters, Foster read their platform word for word, pausing at intervals to chide the recalcitrant Postmaster-General. Fortune had dealt kindly with Mulock; whereas he had risen to high estate, the Patrons had been 'brought low—"the Postmaster-General," as Foster put it, "was where he was, and the Patrons were where they were."

The tariff measures were accepted without quibbling by practically all the government journals, and were only opposed on individual points by a few Liberal members in the House. J. M. Douglas (East Assiniboia) said that he hoped for better things in the future; in his opinion the government had "only administered a homeopathic dose to the manufacturers of the country." Together with R. L. Richardson (Lisgar) and other Westerners from both parties, he thought that a material reduction should have been made in the rate of levy on agricultural implements. A similar view was expressed by the *Manitoba Free Press* which did not believe that the new tariff would be wholly pleasing to the West. "A longer and weightier step," stated that paper, "would have been made if the duties on agricultural implements had been scaled down to ten or twelve and one-half per cent. . . The implement makers are to-day better off than they were under the old tariff." The *Free Press* further argued that while the import duty on the larger implements had been left unchanged, the manufacturers were to enjoy the benefits of a reduction in the duties on the iron and steel goods employed by them in production. N. F. Davin, Conservative member for West Assiniboia, during the debate on the budget, introduced a motion that agricultural implements be placed on the free list. The Liberal members from the West declined to support this proposal as they said that it was intended to embarrass the government, and help Davin with his constituents. On a division of the House only ten votes were recorded for Davin's motion.

DEVELOPMENT OF THE PREFERENTIAL TRADE POLICY.

Besides making changes in the bounty system as already outlined, the federal government put its preferential trade policy upon an entirely different basis during the years succeeding 1897.   Great Britain was aware that the terms of the preferential schedule were intended chiefly for her, and in order that Canada might be able to develop the scheme unhampered, she took the bold step of rescinding the treaties she had with Belgium and the German Zollverein.   As a result the Canadian government in August, 1898, did away with the reciprocal schedule it had originally devised, and in its stead legislated into existence a schedule similar in form but giving preference alone to Great Britain and to any British colony that would treat Canada equally well.   Then in July, 1900, the degree of preference was augmented so that goods entering under the special schedule were to be dutiable to the extent of only two-thirds rather than three-quarters of those coming in under the general schedule.   An outcome of this exclusively British preferential policy was that the German Zollverein refused Canadian imports the terms of its conventional tariff, and in return Canada placed a surtax on German goods which amounted to an addition of twenty-five per cent. above the general schedule; a tariff war was conducted with the Zollverein which lasted until 1910.

THE PARTIAL REVISION OF 1904

(Since the Canadian farmer viewed the tariff almost entirely from the standpoint of the consumer, it cannot be said that, generally speaking, either East or West was he satisfied with what the Liberal administration had done for him.) Still, he had received a measure of relief, partly through the listing as duty-free of articles that he constantly used, but more especially through the instrumentality of the preferential rates, and so he became to a large extent inarticulate when tariff matters were under discussion.   How long under the circumstances the farmer would have remained passive and uncomplaining, it is hard to say.   As it happened, the state of quiescence which the Liberals had been able to establish was fated to last only five or six years.   When the truce—if it may be called such—was broken, and the tariff again became a subject for acrimonious disputation, the responsibility for starting a fresh period of strife rested, not with the farmer, but principally with the large-scale manufacturer.   As the British preference came fully into play after 1900, and the rivalry between Canadian and British manufacturers reached an acuter stage, the fear was expressed by its devotees that the policy of protection was losing ground in

Canada. Presumably the cotton and steel industries were standing up fairly well under the strain of British competition, but difficulty was being experienced, it was stated, by the makers of woollen goods. As a result, the woollen goods manufacturers turned to the Canadian Manufacturers Association for assistance, and also placed their case in the hands of certain high-tariff politicians in the House of Commons. By 1903 the fat was once more in the fire, and another muddled period was about to open in Canadian tariff history.

The protectionist forces used the situation in the woollen industry as the starting point of a general campaign for higher import duties. Without doubt a number of woollen mills, notably those engaged in the manufacture of cloth, were in a wobbly state at this time. But as Hon. W. S. Fielding pointed out in the House, their plight was due in some cases to mismanagement and not to the preferential feature in the tariff. W. R. Brock (Centre Toronto), who was president of the Canada Woollen Mills, Ltd., told parliament that the four mills operated by his company in Ontario would soon have to be closed; a similar pessimistic strain was taken up by R. A. Pringle (Cornwall and Stormont), and Richard Blain (Peel). On the other hand, W. F. McCready (Selkirk), asserted that only the makers of cheaper weaves of cloth were suffering, that the mills turning out knitted goods, blankets and finer worsteds were running full time, and that woollen goods such as sweaters, stockings and mitts were being exported from Canada.

The government finally decided to help the woollen manufacturers and to make a few other changes in the tariff before going to the country in 1904. The Minister of Finance announced, on June 7, that the preferential rate on cloths, tweeds and overcoatings which had been twenty-three and one-third per cent. would be raised to thirty per cent. A further break was made in the principle of having the preferential schedule uniformly two-thirds of the general schedule when the duty on twine and cordage was increased to twenty per cent., and that on chinaware lowered to fifteen per cent. With the object of appeasing the farmer, the tax on coal oil was reduced from five cents to two and one-half cents a gallon, while crude petroleum was included in the free list. At the same time, owing to the claim of numerous manufacturers that Canada was becoming a slaughter market for foreign producers, Fielding incorporated an anti-dumping clause in the tariff, by which the government acquired the power to suddenly levy a duty on goods said to have been thrown into the country for that purpose; the rate of duty was to be equal to the difference between the price obtained in sacrificing the goods and what the customs officials considered should be a fair market price for them. The government was successful at the polls in 1904, but in its manipulations of the tariff it had thrown down a gauntlet to the farmers which, as will be seen, the farmers were quite ready to pick up.

CHAPTER XX

THE FARMERS JOIN ISSUE ON THE TARIFFS

A SECTION of the Canadian press soon after the election of 1904 set out with an aptitude born of experience to impress upon its readers that the day for the introduction of higher tariff schedules was already at hand. Bare thanks was accorded the government for changes already made; while it was acknowledged that something had been done, yet the truly needful industries, it was agreed, had not been given their due; a further revision of the tariff, therefore, was required immediately. The farmer came in for his share of disquieting news. When he picked up his daily paper in the autumn of 1904 or the winter of 1904-5, a variety of annoying references to the tariff had been inserted for his attention. To his surprise he found the suggestion boldly made that binder twine and barbed wire should be removed from the free list. The Western farmer was affrighted by the story that the lumber which he brought in so plentifully from the United States was to be taxed by the government at the rate of two dollars a thousand feet. Largely, no doubt, for the farmer's consumption also, publicity was given to the opinion of the president of the Lake of the Woods Milling Company that an export duty should be laid upon all wheat shipped from Canada abroad. Such propaganda appearing in the newspapers was implemented by representations made directly to Ottawa. Lumber-mill owners in British Columbia and Ontario having agreed upon a joint policy, strongly importuned the government to protect their industry. Then, on April 27, 1905, a deputation from the Canadian Manufacturers' Association waited upon the Minister of Finance and told him that the woollen industry would be in a perilous position unless the preferential duty was increased from thirty per cent. to thirty-seven and one-half per cent.

A wave of alarm swept rapidly through the ranks of those organizations already created for the defence of the farmers' interests. The question of soaring taxes was brought to the notice of the Grange by its Committee on Legislation and

Transportation on February 17, 1905, and strong objection taken to the imposition of fresh burdens on the farmer. Almost at the same time a batch of petitions arrived from the West for presentation to Hon. W. S. Fielding, in which the proposed duty on rough lumber was vigorously assailed since it would add to the load that the prairie farmer had been wont to carry. The Farmers' Association of Ontario, in annual session, while expressing itself in favor of the British Preferential Policy inaugurated by the government, was firm in its hostility to any increase in the scale of duties already in force. Agriculturists everywhere were thinking hard on the situation, and, if the worst came to the worst, would rise to the point of strenuous expostulation.

THE TARIFF COMMISSION OF 1905-6.

The Ottawa government was sparring for trouble. Apparently it was underrating the Canadian farmers' disposition to rebel after long forbearance against what they believed to be an economic injustice. Either that, or the protectionist wing of the Liberal Party so dominated the councils of the government that it was dictating its entire policy. At any rate there is ample evidence in the public records of 1904 and 1905 to show that the suasion of the protected interests was becoming effective with the administration, whereas the farmers, unless they bestirred themselves, were to be left out in the cold. Hon. Charles H. Hyman, Minister of Railways and Canals, and a leather manufacturer, let the cat out of the bag when in a speech at Montreal he promised his audience that the Grand Trunk Pacific, then under construction, by giving cheap transportation in the West, "would go a long way towards making a protective tariff popular." In fact, a statement made by the Minister of Finance in the House of Commons in June, 1904, had gladdened the hearts of high-tariff advocates. While delivering his budget address, Fielding made the forecast that the Canadian tariff in all likelihood would be placed upon a minimum-maximum basis after the fashion of the tariff in vogue in the United States, in order that the maximum rates might be used as a means of retaliation against those nations that refused Canada favorable treatment. It is quite inconceivable how such a maximum schedule could have been introduced in the tariff system of Canada, unless the general level of rates had been hoisted in the process.

In spite, however, of these tendencies and the expressed desire that the Canadian people should become submissively reconciled to the protective system, or according to Hyman's words, that it should become popular among them, the government decided to adopt the prudent course of soliciting various shades of opinion upon the subject of the tariff throughout the country. The Premier, Sir Wilfrid Laurier, was behind this plan; with that native French-Canadian canniness which always stood him in good stead during his political career, he was unwilling to take too much for granted without investigation. On the other hand protectionists, remembering the tariff inquiry of 1897, had little fear but that with proper organization they would get the better of the argument. It only remained to be seen what would be the form and what the scope of the new inquiry that the Government would set on foot.

On July 6, 1905, the Minister of Finance definitely announced that either a commission or special committee of the House would be appointed by the government with authority to take evidence on matters pertaining to the operation of the Canadian tariff. Seven weeks later, on August 23, information was forthcoming that the work of inquiry would be done in a comprehensive fashion, and would be assigned to a group of Cabinet ministers who were to constitute a commission with plenary powers of investigation in all the provinces of Canada. The following ministers were named as comprising the commission: Hon. W. S. Fielding, Hon. Sir Richard Cartwright, Hon. William Paterson, and Hon. L. P. Brodeur, who held the portfolio of Inland Revenue; Marc Sauville and John Bain were chosen to act respectively as its French and English secretaries. When the commission began its sittings Sir Richard Cartwright was indisposed, and could only attend the meetings held at Montreal and Toronto. Hon. Sidney Fisher, Minister of Agriculture, although not a ranking member of the commission, appeared with it at certain points for purposes of special observation.

Thirty-nine places were visited by the commission en route, distributed numerically among the provinces of Canada as follows: Nova Scotia, seven; Prince Edward Island, one; New Brunswick, four; Quebec, five; Ontario, ten; Manitoba, two; Saskatchewan, two; Alberta, two; and British Columbia, six. The first sitting occurred at Winnipeg on September 7, but, as harvest operations were on in the West, was adjourned until a more suitable occasion. The commission thereupon proceeded to British Columbia where it opened on September 15, at Nelson, a series of meetings that were to keep it in that province for three weeks. The next sitting was at Montreal, on November 7, whence the commission moved into Ontario, remaining there until the end of the month. On December 4, it was again at Winnipeg to begin a tour of the prairie country that was to end at Regina, on December 16. On its way eastward once more, it halted at Sault Ste. Marie on December 21, and then went to the Province of Quebec, where its time was occupied until the New Year. On January 3, 1906, it was in session at Newcastle, New Brunswick, and during the whole of that month continued travelling in the Maritime Provinces. The final meeting was held at Ottawa, February 6-8.

THE GREAT SURPRISE.

The voice of the agriculturist was practically unheard while the tariff commission sojourned in British Columbia. Interest in that province was largely divided between the lumbermen's urgent request for a duty on the imported article and the demand of the lead mine owners that they should receive a measure of protection. At Montreal, as had been anticipated, manufacturers were out in force asking for tariff readjustments that would be beneficial to their industries. On the other hand, a few importers in that city were in favor of lower duties, and the commissioners were beguiled for a time by the rather ingenious arguments of Archibald McGoun, K.C., a "free trader," who by close methods of calculation figured that the textile industries of Canada might still do business with a preferential duty of 8.78 per cent. and the iron and steel industries with a duty of 10.44 per cent.

In the province of Ontario, the manufacturers were fully prepared to state their case to the commission at the various points upon its itinerary. Arrangements had been effected that at Toronto, the hub of the province, insistent appeals should be made for a heightening of the maximum rates of duty in the tariff in order that the disabilities suffered under the preferential schedule might be removed; also that a demand should be voiced for a relinquishment of, or a lowering of the duties levied on the raw materials of manufacture. It was thought that if a similar campaign were kept up throughout the province the commission would, willy-nilly, be led to render advice to the government that Ontario, the most populous section of the Dominion, was protectionist in sentiment, and that it must therefore act accordingly.

But, alack-a-day! votaries of protection in Ontario were on the highroad to disillusionment. Not that they thought by any manner of means that representatives of the agricultural industry would fail to put in an appearance before the commission and so allow their case to go by default. Their error lay in ignoring the farmers' organizations of the province, which they either regarded as in a moribund condition or at least incapable of taking any united and effective stand upon the tariff issue. Protectionists did not know that word had gone out to the intelligentsia of these organizations to get ready to brave the commission, and to make an elaborate defence of the farmers' cause. They did not know that data was being gathered and carefully tabulated in farm homes of the province, that dissertations were being fashioned by the wood fires of autumn, and that when the time came the representatives from the farmers' organizations would speak with no uncertain sound. Hence, when the commission arrived in Toronto, a surprise was in store for it, a surprise, indeed, that, as the commission proceeded through Ontario, laid hold upon the press, the politicians of whatever stripe and the public generally, and which even yet has remained a verdant memory in the annals of Canadian tariff history.

Farmers were always given precedence at sittings of the commission, because they came from outside places. On the morning of November 13, when the doors had been thrown open for the Toronto meeting a truly portentous group of Ontario farmers filed in and took up their position in the presence of the Minister of Finance and his fellow-commissioners. Among them were President James McEwing, of the Farmers' Association of Ontario, and W. F. W. Fisher, Master of the Dominion Grange. Nearly the whole of what the Toronto *Globe* chose to call "the first day in this stronghold of protection" was occupied in hearing the farmers present their claims. James McEwing declared that the agriculturist was subjected to constant loss through the protective feature of the Canadian tariff. In his opinion, the home market argument, used so long to buttress up the National Policy, was out of date and distinctly fallacious. In order to show the growing importance of the foreign market to the Canadian farmer, he pointed out that whereas the surplus of farm products for export from the country had been worth only $10,000,000 in 1879, they had been valued at $104,000,000 in 1904. He sincerely regretted the fact that the government had raised the woollen duties to a thirty per cent. level. "No industry," said McEwing, in commenting on these duties, "has the right under the mantle of the protective tariff to take toll of the earnings of another individual or industry manufacturing goods in the country." W. L. Smith, editor of the *Weekly Sun*, in giving evidence to the commission estimated that the increased duties on woollen goods had taken $500,000 from the pockets of the people during the preceding year. "If a municipal tax gatherer," he ejaculated, "went round and levied that amount the farmer would go after him with a pitchfork."

The next speaker was a robust young farmer, of clear eye and resolute demeanour. He gave his name as Ernest C. Drury, of Crown Hill, and had such a ready knowledge of agricultural economics that he soon gained the ear of the commission. Adducing data, he endeavored to prove that a tax burden of $100-$130 fell annually upon goods purchased by the average Canadian farmer through the workings of the tariff. His colleagues and himself were not come before the commission in a supplicatory attitude—tillers of the soil were not in the habit of parading their troubles in the presence of the public authorities. "We farmers," he added, employing a simple picture to illustrate his point, "are not used to asking you for something—if there comes a storm, we duck our heads and take it like men. We don't run to the country for aid." W. F. W. Fisher, speaking for the Grange, made a plea against the imposition of any form of duty on products of the farm; the commission in fact was given to understand at Toronto that both the Dominion Grange and the Farmers' Association of Ontario were prepared to forego any request for protection to the agricultural industry provided that representatives of other industries would manifest a similar spirit of abnegation.

ELSEWHERE IN ONTARIO.

Wherever at other points in Ontario members of the farmers' organizations approached the commission their requests were on the whole quite like those made at Toronto. They asked for lower duties on manufactured articles, approved of the British preference, and a few speakers, in addition, went on record as being in favor of a measure of reciprocity with the United States.   On the other hand, delegations appeared from certain localities seeking the imposition of new duties or the elevation of already-existing rates on vegetables, fruit and tobacco; protection was also sought for the sugar-beet industry.   The commissioners, in view of these latter demands, took pains to tell the organized farmers that there seemed to be a grave difference of opinion among those who worked the soil upon the question of protecting their own industry; the case of the tobacco growers of southern Ontario was singled out by them as offering an exceptionally good example of protectionism operating with successful results in the agricultural industry.

"The farmers' blood is up," ran the bold-faced headline of a press account of the commission's meeting on November 20, at London.   At this southern Ontario centre an able address was delivered by Thomas McMillan, of Seaforth, who had been keeping close estimate of the business done on his 200-acre farm in Huron County.   He showed the receipts from his farm to have been $5,031.64, and the expenditures $4,336.50, leaving a balance in wages for himself and his family of $695.14.   "Dozens of farmers in Huron County," said McMillan, as he pleaded that Canada should have a revenue tariff, "although they have exercised all their ingenuity and economy during the past five years, have only been able to mark time."   James A. Glen, a granger from Middlesex County, protested emphatically against any increase in tariff rates.   "Old Rob Roy," he burst forth, "robbed with his broadsword.   Men nowadays rob under the law, and don't have their necks in danger."   He accused the Canadian manufacturers of dumping goods worth millions of dollars into other countries, and affirmed that a combine was setting the price of hogs at Toronto; he wanted reciprocity with the United States.

Agricultural representatives took up most of the commission's time at Chatham, on November 23.   Thomas Barnes, of Ridgetown, was interrogated by Commissioner Paterson, as to the views of the 500 members of the Farmers' Association of Ontario in Kent County for whom he spoke, upon the question of levying import duties on farm products. "They would wipe them out," was Barnes' rejoinder, "they ask no protection.   They say all protection is a detriment to the farmer. . . . They believe that the tariff is charged back to the farmer in the end, so that it is simply dog eat dog."   At

Brantford, where Paterson's business interests lay, there was a sharp clash of opinion before the commission on November 27. A large group of manufacturers here complained of inadequate protection and solicited the government's assistance for their industries by means of a satisfactory tariff revision. W. C. Good headed a deputation representing the district associations of North and South Brant. The system of protection, he argued, did not benefit the farmer at all, but discriminated against him; he believed that the farmer received the poorest remuneration for his labor of any class in the community. During the preceding year Good said that he had made a clear profit of only $120 on more than one hundred acres of land. Thomas Banks, of the South Brant association, tried to kindle memories of the past in the minds of the commissioners. "I believe that the protective tariff," he told them, "was styled by yourselves as class legislation, as legalized robbery. I believe you were perfectly right at that time. The only difference between us to-day is that you seem to have changed your opinion while I have not." Then he went on to paint two contrasting pictures for the commissioners: in the one he described the manufacturers' wives and children leading a gay life at pleasure resorts of the country; in the other he changed the scene to the farm, where in all humility "the farmer's wife, himself and his family are trudging along."

Thirty members of the Farmers' Association of Ontario living in Wellington County, having met at Guelph, passed a resolution which was submitted to the commission when it opened in that city. In this resolution the existing tariff was blamed for the upgrowth of the combines which, at the time, were under investigation by the government; the only way to eliminate such combines would be to put the tariff on a revenue basis. It was further claimed that the yearly surplus accruing to the farmer represented mere wages. Among those that addressed the commission was J. J. Morrison, of Arthur, who produced a Guelph paper of recent date in which forty-five Ontario farms were offered for sale. "We only want a fair opportunity to live," asserted Morrison, "but we are very tired of supplying the nursing bottle—and replenishing it—for those not willing to stand on their feet. We have to stand on ours." On November 30 the commission was at Peterborough, where Dawson Kennedy, a prominent granger, appeared, asking for a revenue tariff, and also J. A.

Wilmot, a member of the Farmers' Association in Frontenac County, who declared that an Ontario farmer did well when he realized two per cent. annually on his investment.

Opinion on the Prairies

Early in December the commission was again west of the Great Lakes to resume its work of investigation in the grain-growing provinces. The commissioners were not insensible to the fact that on the prairies they might expect to hear numerous diatribes against the tariff then in force. They found, however, that the more radical utterances on this subject fell from the lips of individual farmers who came into the meetings, whereas the agrarian bodies, as the result of having taken council collectively beforehand, had couched their demands in saner and more moderate language. In fact, the views of the Western farmers' associations on the tariff seemed to be only slightly more advanced than those of their organized brethren in Ontario. When the commission sat for the second time in Winnipeg, on December 4, representatives of the Manitoba Grain Growers' Association, and of the Manitoba Live Stock Association presented a joint plea. They urged that the tariff on dutiable goods be placed on a purely revenue-producing basis, with the rates averaging seventeen per cent. They sought an extension of the free list to include such classes of lumber as were subject to taxation and all agricultural products. Furthermore they asked for a reduction in the duty on farm implements, and a restoration of the preference on woollen goods to its original level.

The Manitoba Grain Growers' Association made its main appeal to the commission at Brandon, on December 6. A large delegation was in attendance, including among others: D. W. McCuaig, president of the Association; J. W. Scallion, of Virden; and W. B. Rogers, of Carberry. A memorial was presented to the commission by McCuaig, setting forth the views of eighty local associations in the province upon the question of a tariff revision. Briefly stated, these associations requested that a substantial reduction be made in the duties on agricultural implements, threshing machines and vehicles; that lumber be retained on the free list; that fruit, cement, gasoline, and all gauges of fence wire become non-dutiable; and that the tariff rates be lowered on woollens and cottons. The memorial also informed the commission that if the preferential schedule were again made uniformly two-thirds of the general schedule, the Manitoba Grain Growers' Association would agree to the removal of all import duties on agricultural products.)

The Canadian Society of Equity and the Farmers' Association of Alberta each had its representatives before the commission, when, on December 11, it sat at Edmonton. Both of these organizations were reported to favor a scaling down of duties until Canada should have a tariff for revenue only; both were declared to be bitterly hostile to the imposition of any tax on rough lumber. Then at Prince Albert, on December 14, a sprinkling of members of the Saskatchewan Grain Growers' Association appeared to express an urgent desire for the reduction of duties on agricultural implements. But it was at Regina that the commission was first brought to a realization of the strength already attained by the grain growers' movements in the newly-formed prairie provinces.

A questionnaire on the tariff had been sent out to all branches of the Saskatchewan association prior to the coming of the commission, and upon the basis of the replies received a memorial had been drawn up for presentation at Regina. On December 16 the association's officers, accompanied by a large deputation from far and near, laid this document in the commissioners' hands. In it was evinced a strong opposition to any increase in the Canadian tariff as it stood. It suggested that an approach might be made towards a revenue tariff by a lowering of the duties on agricultural implements, woollen and cotton goods, dressed lumber and other wares. Again it argued that certain articles might advantageously be taken off the free list and made dutiable for revenue purposes. A further extension of the preferential tariff was advised, and the proposed duty on rough lumber was denounced as a serious hardship to the poor homesteader of the West. The memorial contended that there was no more reason for a bounty on iron than on the production of wheat, and closed with a request for the total removal of the duties then imposed on agricultural produce. Seven hours were occupied, all told, in taking the views of farmers at the Regina sitting.

Subsequently, in traversing the territory eastward from Ontario to the sea, the commission heard little or nothing of the agriculturist's case. However, it might be mentioned that, on January 10, a Farmers' Institute deputation appeared before it at Charlottetown, P.E.I., seeking lower tariff rates generally, while at Halifax, on January 29, representatives of the Farmers' Association of Nova Scotia asked that the consumer might obtain relief from the burden of taxation on clothing, implements, and other articles of daily use.)

LAST SHOTS IN THE CAMPAIGN.

(The remarkable aggressiveness displayed by the organized farmers of Canada upon the question of the tariff had spread consternation throughout the protectionist camp. An effort, it was decided, must be made to retrieve so far as possible the ground that had been lost while the commission was on its journey. Accordingly extensive plans were laid to take the commission by storm when it should reach Ottawa for its final meeting on October 6. The Canadian Manufacturers' Association, having drawn liberally from its funds, prepared a voluminous statement in which were incorporated its views on the tariff, and this its president, C. C. Ballantyne, submitted to the commission in printed form, at the Ottawa sitting. Dominating the statement was the idea that protection must be allowed by the government to an extent that would insure the home market to the Canadian manufacturer. The prosperity of the Canadian farmer was dilated upon at length, and an array of figures quoted to show that, while there had been a considerable rise in the price of farm products between 1878-1905, a diminution had occurred in the cost of agricultural implements during the same period. Stress was laid upon the fact that the C.M.A. had nearly 2,000 members in Canada, and represented an investment in manufacturing plants of $400,000,000. When asked by the Minister of Finance whether he was in favor of an increase of duties on British goods, Ballantyne was at first evasive. At length he admitted that he desired that these duties should be raised where the Canadian manufacturer was suffering from British competition, and thought that the tariff should be readjusted with that end in view. "All we want," he explained, "is a competitive tariff, an equalized tariff.")

The mass of data gathered by the commission upon its itinerary was now sifted, analyzed, and placed at the government's disposal. Nevertheless, eight months were to elapse before the government was ready with a coherent scheme of tariff revision, and opportunity was given during this interval to the farmers' organizations to continue their agitation. At a joint meeting of the Dominion Grange and the Farmers' Association of Ontario, held in Toronto on September 4, an undisguised attack was levelled against the protective features in the Canadian tariff. (Later, on November 16, representatives from each of these bodies, and from the Manitoba Grain Growers' Association constituted a delegation which waited upon Hon. W. S. Fielding at the capital. A memorial was laid before the Finance Minister upon this occasion, of which the closing sentence ran as follows: "We therefore ask, in the coming revision of the tariff, that the protective principle be wholly eliminated; that the principle of tariff for revenue only, and that revenue based on an honest and economic expenditure of the public funds, be adopted, and as proof of our sincerity, we will, if this position is adopted by the Government, gladly assent to the entire abolition of the whole list of duties on agricultural imports.")

THE SECOND FIELDING TARIFF.

(The long-awaited announcement of the government's fiscal policy was made to the House of Commons by the Minister of Finance on November 29, 1906. Legislation was proposed whereby the Canadian tariff structure would be materially altered; as a matter of fact so important and fundamental were the changes outlined by the minister that it is better to regard the tariff of 1906 as a new creation instead of as a revision of the tariff of 1897) The general schedule, said Fielding, would be continued in its existing state with a few minor rate changes. On the other hand, the uniform, horizontal reduction allowed by the preferential schedule would be definitely abandoned as a working principle, and the rate of reduction fixed for each individual article. Between the general and the lowest, that is the preferential schedule, an intermediate schedule would be arranged, the rates of which would average about nine-tenths of the general schedule. It was intended that the intermediate rates should be employed to negotiate terms with countries that were eager to trade with Canada, and that would agree not to impose lofty barriers against the entrance of Canadian wares. It will be seen, therefore, that by the second Fielding tariff the system of levying customs duties on goods admitted into Canada became more composite than ever.

No appreciable difference was effected by the tariff of 1906 in the level of rates on cotton and woollen goods, for the lowering of which the farmers' organizations had pled so hard. Moreover, their opposition to measures of protection to the agricultural industry had apparently been ignored by the formulators of the tariff. (The existing duties on beans, peas and other vegetables were subjected to considerable increases as well as were those on horses and cattle. The sugar beet industry was protected by raising the duty on raw sugar to the refineries from forty cents to fifty-two cents per one hundred pounds. Besides, the bounty system on iron and steel wares was continued for four more years, although starting at a little more than one-half of the original rate.)

(But the farmers' campaign against the duties on agricultural implements had borne certain results. The general schedule rate on mowing-machines, harvesters, and reapers, etc., which had formerly been twenty per cent., became seventeen and one-half per cent. in the measures of 1906. A reduction from twenty-five per cent. to twenty per cent. took place in the duty on threshers and separators. Again, a list of small tools, including axes, scythes, rakes, hoes, etc., were to be assessed twenty-two and one-half per cent., instead of twenty-five per cent., of their value upon importation. Hay-loaders, fanning-mills, road-rollers, etc., however, were to be still dutiable to the extent of twenty-five per cent. The request of the Western farmers that gasoline should go on the free list was granted.

The most important set-back received by the farmers' organizations in the second Fielding tariff lay in its abandonment of the scheme of horizontal reduction in connection with the preferential schedule; it is reasonably plain that C. C. Ballantyne's advocacy of a "competitive tariff" as applied to British imports into Canada had carried the day in the government's councils. At the same time the campaign waged by the farmers had resulted in one very significant gain. The forecast made by the Minister of Finance in June, 1904, that Canada would have a minimum-maximum tariff had doubtless been nullified by the stand which the farmers took before the commission. The government—as Sir Richard Cartwright acknowledged—very politely buried this idea when they began to understand the farmers' mood throughout the country and decided to leave the general schedule almost untouched. The establishment of an intermediate schedule was a concession to revenue-tariff advocates because it meant slightly lower duties on goods from nations with which treaties might be arranged. The reductions on agricultural implements, while of some benefit to the farmer, were soon discovered to work little or no hardship to the manufacturer of implements, because the drawback clauses in the tariff were amended in order to allow him a rebate of ninety-nine per cent. of the duties on his raw material when the implements were sold at home, as well as when they were exported.)

CHAPTER XXI

The Renewal of the Conflict

A LULL now occurred in the war over the tariff. More than three years were to elapse before another fiscal crisis was reached in Canada during the summer of 1910. From the very outset, however, after the tariff of 1906 had been brought down, the C.M.A. gave evidence that it did not intend to let matters lie dormant. In January, 1907, the president and secretary of that organization expressed indignation that a maximum-minimum tariff had not been arranged for the country with the maximum rates higher than those of the old general schedule. "The proposed tariff," they wrote, "will not, in our opinion, encourage either the establishment of new industries or the development of those already established." Thereafter, once the government's policy had come into operation, its measures were criticized freely and heatedly at the annual meeting of the association, held in September of the same year. Indeed, it was in the midst of the discussion which took place at this meeting that Edward Gurney gave vent to his feelings in the oft-quoted assertion: "I would make the tariff as high as Haman's gallows, if it would keep the Yankee out."

The new tariff furnished the Conservatives with plenty of opportunity to take the government to task. Foster stigmatized it in the House of Commons as a "scrappy, choppy concern," although he stated his satisfaction that the former flat rate of the preferential tariff had been abolished. Mockingly he told of the joy welling up in his heart that the Conservative Party had won the Liberals to its way of thinking. He ridiculed the average reduction of two and one-half per cent. in the duties on agricultural implements, wondering how much advantage would accrue to the farmer after the implement had gone from maker to wholesaler and then to agent, and finally into the farmers' hands. "If they wanted to help the farmer," he said, "why did they not take off ten per cent." Ostensibly with the object of creating an impression against the government throughout the country, Dr. F. L.

251

Schaffner, Conservative member for Souris, moved on April 3, 1907, that the duty on mowers, binders, etc., be lowered from seventeen and one-half per cent. to ten per cent. It is interesting to note that neither R. L. Borden, Conservative leader, nor Hon. Geo. E. Foster supported the motion, which was lost by fifty-six votes to twenty-two. Borden said that he lacked information on the subject. Most of the western Liberal members absented themselves when the vote was taken, although a few recorded themselves in the negative.

The hostility of the C.M.A. to the new tariff as evidenced in September, 1907, was explained to the Dominion Grange when it met ten weeks later to amalgamate with the Farmers' Association of Ontario. Resentment was expressed against the manufacturers' organization that it had broken what the farmers regarded "as a truce in the battle for reasonable fiscal legislation." The manufacturers had gained, according to the Legislative Committee of the Grange, more than the farmers in the tariff changes that had been made. "The puling infant," stated the committee's report, "that asked for temporary and moderate protection thirty years ago is now a giant demanding that practical prohibition of foreign competition in manufactured goods shall be the permanent policy of this country. This demand must be met by the counter demand that the protective principle shall be wholly eliminated, and the tariff reduced to a purely revenue basis." The manner in which the government had renewed the bounty system was also assailed in vigorous terms. "That extension," opined the committee, "was wholly unjustifiable; it involved a gross misappropriation of public funds, and should be unhesitatingly condemned by the farmers of this country on whom the chief burden of the cost will fall."

CONSOLIDATIONS OF CAPITAL

In 1909 the C.M.A. came out strongly in favor of the establishment in Canada of a permanent, non-partisan tariff commission that would gather statistical data for the government, and assist it in various ways in adjusting the tariff schedules. The farmers on their part had during the same year been gravely concerned over another matter. The knowledge that combines existed among Canadian manufacturers and wholesalers had for a long time been stirring the wrath of agrarian organizations. Nevertheless, up until 1907 such combines were understood to be based in the main upon secret agreements to regulate prices to the consumer. Then there was introduced into Canada that type of business organization known as the merger, whereby individual companies making the same class of goods consolidated their capital to form a new enterprise. Mergers were effected first among manufacturers of knitted goods, rubber, soap, cottons, sugar, enamelled ware, wall-paper and certain kinds of woodenware, with capitalization as a usual thing running up into the millions. The Dominion Grange, having watched this phenomenon for some time, decided early in 1909 to utter a protest. On February 26 a deputation from the Grange appeared before Ministers Fielding and Cartwright, praying for the passage by the government of such anti-combine legislation as would check the abuses of the merger system. They advocated either that the law should be enforced which gave the government the right to cancel the import duties on goods when combines making those goods were charging excessive prices to the consumer, or that a government commission should be appointed to fix the prices at which the combines might market their wares in Canada. E. C. Drury, then Master of the Grange, in supporting this plea traced the growth of capitalistic organizations and the ills of the farmer in Canada to the introduction of the policy of protection. "The rural population of this province," he said, speaking of Ontario, "is decreasing at the rate of six thousand a year. This is because farming is not as profitable as it should be. The decrease began in '78 when the protective principle was first incorporated into the tariff, and I think the coincidence clearly indicates the cause of the decline." But the attitude assumed on the question of anti-combine legislation by the Minister of Finance did not please the delegation. "The reply we received," reported Drury to the Dominion Grange, "was evasive and unsatisfactory."

The pertinacity of the Grange, however, on this issue, was not overlooked by the government; furthermore, a Liberal journal, the Toronto *Star*, began openly to rebuke Ottawa for making no move to place restraint upon the monopolistic tendencies of the new organizations of capital. Finally, in 1910, the Combines Investigation Act was framed by the government with the avowed intention of remedying the situation. Hon. W. L. M. King, Minister of Labor, in piloting this legislation through the House of Commons, said that it was expected to curb "the exercise on the part of combines, or mergers, or monopolies, in an unfair manner, of the powers which they may get from that form of organization." At no time did King state any objection to the introduction of these highly financed corporations; he rather stressed the advantages which might accrue to the Canadian public through their establishment. Under the act it became possible for six or more persons to apply to a Judge of the High Court for an order of inquiry into the activities of an alleged combine. If a case were made out an order of inquiry would be granted, and a board set up consisting of a representative from each side and a chairman whom they might select. All evidence taken by the board would be submitted and recorded to the public in the daily press. Whenever it was discovered that a combine had brought about an "undue enhancement of prices," a penalty of $1,000 a day might be enforced against it until it should agree to a reduction. Some Liberals were dissatisfied with this measure, including Dr. Michael Clark, of Red Deer, who said that it was a "pill to cure an earthquake." With the exception of certain proceedings taken to have a board investigate the United Shoe Machinery Co. of Quebec City, in 1911, the law, until annulled, remained a dead letter on the statute book.

Meanwhile mergers continued to grow apace in the country during 1909 and 1910. Nine manufacturers of cement united in 1909 to form the Canada Cement Co., Ltd., with a capital of $30,000,000. "The cement merger," affirmed the Legislative Committee of the Grange in November, 1909, "has already raised the price of cement from one dollar to one dollar and a half per barrel. It is stated that cement can be made and sold for some seventy-five cents per barrel." Consolidations of capital also occurred in 1909 in the asbestos, carriage-making, felt, and car-building industries. In April, 1910, the canning industry, already subject in part to a combine, was brought under the dominance of a reorganized merger controlling forty-seven factories; in July of the same year the Canada Steel Co. was organized as a merger with an authorized capital of $35,000,000. Other combinations were formed during 1910 in the fishing and lumber industries, and among manufacturers of cereals, boxes, and wood-working tools and machinery. These events, as the farmers' organizations viewed them, had put an entirely different face on the industrial situation. In making their plans for the future they felt that they must match weapon with weapon. It might be all well and good for them to beg the government to make effective its legislation against the combines, but they must do more. (The farmers became thoroughly convinced that their meekness had been their undoing, and that they must resume with intensity the old fight on the tariff.)

LAURIER GOES WEST

Circumstances dictated the time when and the place where the gage of battle should be flung down. During his long term in the premiership, in fact since his historic visit of 1894, Sir Wilfrid Laurier had made no lengthy tour of Western Canada. In the interval great changes had occurred in the West; a heterogenous population had been pouring in from many lands; agriculture was on quite another footing; and problems had arisen that were unknown a decade and a half before. It was officially announced early in the summer of 1910 that Laurier would shortly set out from Ottawa with the purpose of making an extensive journey through the Western provinces to the edge of the Pacific. The main object of this tour, as he himself pointed out, was to get an insight at first hand into conditions of life prevailing on the prairies and farther west. Back of all, no doubt, he was actuated by a serious political motive. The Liberal administration, though to all appearances still rugged, was aging; the next election would be critical; and the Premier and his advisers believed that the time had come to feel carefully the throbbing pulse of the West.

Sir Wilfrid's trip afforded a revelation of the personal esteem in which he was held by the citizenry of Canada. From the time that he arrived at Port Arthur in July, until his return early in September, his journey through the West resembled a triumphal progress. The Premier was accompanied all the way by Hon. G. P. Graham, Minister of Railways; E. M. Macdonald, member for Pictou; and F. F. Pardee, member for West Lambton. Several provincial Premiers and a number of other legislators appeared on the platform with him at different points. Addresses were delivered by Laurier at nearly every important centre in the West, while short stops were made at a great number of railway stations en route.

The Premier was well aware that upon entering the prairie provinces he would be urgently importuned by the representatives of farmers' organizations on the tariff and other

issues which they considered vital. The policy he adopted
was first to hear what the farmers had to say, and then to
frame a careful reply. At a monster mass meeting held in
Winnipeg, on July 12, he gave a masterly address, but completely side-stepped any discussion on the tariff; indeed, it
was only when he reached the town of Morden that he made
his first brief reference to the subject. Meanwhile, the
Manitoba Grain Growers' Association were arranging to
make a powerful appeal to Laurier at Brandon. On the fore-
noon of July 18 a delegation from all the local associations in
the province, 250 strong, crowded the City Hall at that
point, and laid the Grain Growers' case before him. Two
memorials had been prepared, one of which was read by
Roderick McKenzie, secretary of the organization, the other
by J. W. Scallion, its honorary president.

"Of the many economic questions which engage the attention of Western farmers," stated the first memorial, "none
is regarded with so much disapproval as the protective tariff."
Not that the farmers were loath in any sense to paying their
share of money into the public treasury. "What they do rebel
against," continued the document, "is the element in the
customs tariff which compels them to contribute a large percentage of the products of their labor to the privileged and
protected classes. The Western farmers do not want any
protection for their products. In other words, they are willing
that all farm products should be placed on the free list."
The latter part of the memorial then particularized the
burdens which it contended were imposed on the farmer by
the duties on agricultural implements, cement, and woollen
goods.

The benefits to be derived from the consummation of a
reciprocity pact with the United States was the leading theme
of the memorial presented by J. W. Scallion. "There are,"
he read, "no trade arrangements the Canadian government
could make with any country that would meet with greater
favor or stronger support from the farmers of Western Canada than a wide measure of reciprocal trade with the United
States, including manufactured articles and the natural
products of both countries." Yet the Manitoba association
forewarned Sir Wilfrid that any attempt to secure reciprocity
would be diligently fought in certain quarters. "The farmers
know," he was told in the memorial, "that a lowering of our
tariff or freer trade with the United States will be strongly

opposed by the united strength of the protected interests which have developed such strength and grown to such power and wealth under our protective tariff and because of it."

Laurier in reply expressed his sorrow that the grain growers held the mistaken opinion that the tariff had been framed to their disadvantage; this would be news to the Minister of Finance who had aimed to give them justice. Then, at a meeting before which he spoke in the evening, the Premier touched on the question of reciprocity. "Our American friends," he explained, "have been refusing the suggestion of reciprocity for fifty years. So I have said, 'Good-bye, Washington; we will make no more pilgrimages. We will be independent, and try to build up trade for ourselves'—and the next pilgrimage came from Washington to Ottawa." Sir Wilfrid said that he was quite willing to treat with the United States on the matter, but that the British preference would always retain priority in his mind.

At Yorkton, on July 20, where great arches of wheat and oats had been piled up in Welcome, the Premier received the advance guard of several delegations that were to approach him from the Saskatchewan Grain Growers' Association. The Yorkton delegation asked for free trade with Great Britain and reciprocal trade between Canada and the United States. Next day, at Melville, two farmer groups appeared. One, consisting of members of the Saskatchewan Grain Growers' Association, made requests akin to those made by their brethren at Yorkton. The other delegation, coming from a settlement of Welsh radicals at Bangor, advocated free trade as it was in operation in England. "In my youth," said Laurier in answer to the radicals' plea, "I doubt not I would have subscribed instanter to every article enunciated, but my blood is a little cooler now." Thereupon, continuing his journey through northern Saskatchewan, Laurier heard further representations from the Grain Growers' Association at Lanigan, at Humboldt, the centre of an American settlement, and at Prince Albert.

On July 29, when the Premier and his colleagues arrived in Saskatoon, their ears were assailed with bold words against the Ottawa administration. John Evans, of Nutana, a member of the central board of the Saskatchewan association, headed a deputation that presented the farmers' case. Evans was anxious to know why the farmers were not receiving a bonus from the government after the fashion of the Dominion Iron

17—F.M.

and Steel Company. "In 1896," he exclaimed, firing up in the course of his speech, "the Liberal government came into power on the distinct pledge of 'free trade.' The ideal system is British 'free trade.' To-day, you are farther from it than in 1896. In 1896 you promised to skin the Tory bear of protection. Have you done it? If so, I would ask you what have you done with the hide?" E. M. Macdonald immediately went on the defensive and rebuked the speaker. Sir Wilfrid, however, poured oil on the troubled waters, replying decorously. "To abolish the tariff at one stroke," he declared, "would create a financial crisis. It is impossible for us now to raise the revenue as in England. I am a 'free trader.' I am not a protectionist."

The Saskatchewan Grain Growers' most distinctive appearance before the travelling parliamentarians took place at Regina, on August 1. Here F. M. Gates, president of the association, accompanied by a great throng, set forth the opinions of producers at the heart of the great wheat belt. "Whereas Canadian machinery," he said, reading from a carefully-prepared document, "can be purchased from ten per cent. to thirty per cent. less in Great Britain than in the Canadian West; and whereas we believe such conditions are caused by the high protective tariff existing at the present time; Therefore, be it resolved that immediate steps be taken regarding the said tariff so that the home purchaser may at least be able to purchase as cheaply as the outside world; and, further, that the Ottawa government be requested to accept the unconditional offer of the United States government for reciprocal free trade in farm implements." Laurier in answer said that reciprocity was a possibility if the United States would agree to Canada's terms.

"We do not underestimate what you have done," said Frank Sheppard to Sir Wilfrid at Weyburn, where he spoke for the organized grain growers of South Saskatchewan, "nor are we ungrateful; but when we expected you to lay the axe to the root of the tree, and cut it down, you only cut off some of the branches. In conclusion, I must say, if we are free men treat us as such. If we are slaves we ask our freedom. If refused we must demand it. Our resources are not exhausted." On August 8, at Lloydminster, near the borders of Alberta, a mixed deputation from farmers' organizations of the neighborhood asked "that a general reduction of the tariff be made, more particularly on woollen and cotton goods; also, that the duty be immediately removed from farm implements and tools."

Thence on his way to Edmonton Laurier halted at Vegreville, where a group of the United Farmers of Alberta who belonged to that district memorialized him in favor of a lowering of the tariff "as a move toward our ultimate goal of 'free trade.'" Upon arrival at the capital city of Alberta he was greeted by representatives of the same organization from the Edmonton, Clover Bar and Strathcona districts, who solicited a general reduction in the tariff and the placing of agricultural implements on the free list. But the main conference between Laurier and the U.F.A. leaders took place at Red Deer, on August 10. James Bower, president of the U.F.A., addressing the Premier and his confrères at that point, said that the people of the West were to become "the foundation of a great nation." "It is the duty of our government," he went on, "to protect these people, not by unjust tariff laws, but by the removal of these, and by the removal of monopolistic conditions which have grown up here in this Western country." A resolution was submitted deploring the existence of the protective system which was said to levy its tribute from the mass of the Canadian people, and requesting that the duties on cottons and woollens should be lowered and implements and tools be placed on the free list. In amplification of this resolution, James Speakman, an official of the U.F.A., spoke at length, endeavoring by the use of comparative statistics to analyze the working of the Canadian tariff. He pointed out that the dutiable imports of agricultural products were a mere bagatelle in contrast with the articles of manufacture that were taxed under the Canadian tariff; yet it was in the latter case that the tariff was "very much alive." Sir Wilfrid spent a good part of the evening of August 10 in studying the documents that the U.F.A. had placed in his hands, and next day delivered a public address to a Red Deer audience in which he made an elaborate defence of his government's tariff policy; he contended that it had "given a fair measure of freer trade" to the country.

Next Laurier proceeded to British Columbia, where he remained about two weeks and then started homeward by the Crow's Nest Pass route, making a stop at Lethbridge in Alberta, on September 1. Here a contingent from the U.F.A. led by J. Quinsey, of Wheatland, presented a memorial setting forth the views of the southern section of the province.

The Premier once more promised the delegation a downward revision of the tariff, and, touching upon the matter of reciprocity with the United States, asked the question: "Is it not possible that between two peoples of kindred races we can find a common ground on which we can trade for the mutual advantage of both parties?"

CHAPTER XXII

Canada's Rejection of the Reciprocity Pact

THE WEST having spoken, it remained to be seen how far its demands would affect the government's policy. Without question the organized farmers of the grain-growing provinces had shown themselves in favor of lower import duties and an ample measure of reciprocity in the tariff relations of Canada with the United States. But the administration had to bear in mind that the prairie provinces sent only twenty-seven members to Ottawa, or in other words elected but one-eighth of the House of Commons. The problem which had arisen was this: if a tangible effort were made to appease the desires of the Western farmer on the tariff, could the government expect such action to meet with the approval of the more populous East? A great deal would hinge upon whatever decisions the government might reach on this point since it had been a long time in office and any misstep would likely lead to its downfall. Accordingly, when Sir Wilfrid Laurier brought back his message from the West in September, 1910, there were numerous and animated conferences held in the Liberal camp. Very soon the discussion had narrowed down to one principal theme, namely, would it be possible to negotiate a successful reciprocity pact with the United States, and if such a pact were concluded, would it be generously supported by the Canadian electorate? As Laurier had pointed out to the farmers at Brandon, overtures had been coming from Washington with respect to a reciprocity measure, so that Canada's only concern need be the obtaining of proper terms. The Premier, at this juncture, loomed up in the councils of his party as a firm advocate of the tariff readjustment which reciprocity would entail, despite the lukewarmness upon the subject of some of his closest advisers and the plain-spoken hostility of others. In the end affirmative opinion prevailed, the opposition had dwindled down, at least temporarily, and the historian may unreservedly declare that Laurier had been the arbiter of the situation. It was arranged that negotiations would be pushed with

Washington to discover upon what basis a reciprocal tariff agreement might be made with the government of the United States.

The way had been cleared for a parley with the United States through a certain settlement made with that country earlier in 1910. According to the Payne-Aldrich revision of the American tariff in 1909, while freer trade policies had been inaugurated, the structure of the tariff had been changed by arranging its schedules according to a minimum-maximum plan. The maximum schedule was intended for countries that employed any form of fiscal discrimination against products originating in the United States. Seemingly Canada might be debarred from receiving the minimum rates of the Payne-Aldrich measure, both on account of her British preferential policy and the fact that she had recently signed a commercial treaty with France whereby, in return for concessions granted, France was accorded many intermediate or even lower rates in the Canadian tariff. The government of the United States did not complain of the British preference, considering it to affect only inter-empire trade, but it looked askance at the France-Canadian treaty, arguing that this was an act of discrimination against American goods in favor of another foreign nation. Under such circumstances the logical procedure would be for the United States to deny Canada her minimum rates, and levy against Canadian exports the rates of her maximum schedule which were twenty-five per cent. higher. This the American government threatened to do, beginning April 1, 1910, unless in the interval Canada should indicate that she had better terms to offer. President William H. Taft, heading a true-blue Republican administration, endangered by insurgency within its own ranks, was placed thereby in an embarrassing position. The Democrats who stood for lower duties were making advances; Taft did not wish to pose as a high protectionist, and he foresaw trouble for his administration in a tariff war with Canada; hence the United States was ready to open *pourparlers* with Canada in order if possible to avoid a conflict.

As a result, early in March, 1910, an official mission came to Ottawa representing the American Department of State with the object of apprising the Canadian government of the exact situation. Then, on March 19, at the invitation of President Taft, Hon. W. S. Fielding went to Albany, N.Y., where Taft and he gave careful consideration to the points at issue in the controversy. Immediately following this conference President Taft gave a reassuring message to the news services, intended especially for Canadian consumption, in which he asserted his desire to promote better trade relations between the two countries by whatever means lay within his power.) Already it looked as if the conciliatory attitude of both governments would lead to a pacific termination of their difficulties. On March 27, Fielding, in company with Hon. Geo. Graham, appeared at Washington bearing the terms which Canada had to offer, and after having been seriously debated these were found acceptable by the American government. The United States made a last-minute surrender of its objections to the Franco-Canadian treaty on the understanding that it would be granted the intermediate rates of the Canadian tariff upon a number of selected articles. Such concessions were reckoned by the United States as a fair equivalent to allowing Canadian goods to pass her customs barriers under the terms of the minimum schedule.

The restoration in this manner of trading amity between the two countries gave promise of smooth-running negotiations on reciprocity, when seven months later Canada asserted her willingness to deal with the United States on that issue. It was suggested that the first steps towards drafting the proposed agreement might be taken on Canadian soil, and accordingly on November 4, a conference was opened at Ottawa, attended by Ministers Fielding and Paterson for Canada, and C. M. Pepper, J. G. Foster and Henry M. Hoyt for the United States. Undisguised eagerness was shown by the American representatives to help devise a pact which would be mutually acceptable. The Canadians, sensing the strength of their position, are said to have bargained closely during the proceedings. After four sittings the conference adjourned on November 10, with the announcement that it had formulated the ground plan of an international tariff agreement. Meanwhile, political events in the United States were continually shaping to the disadvantage of the Republican administration; the Democrats were making a bold effort to obtain control of both Houses of Congress, and President Taft, facing division in the ranks of his own party, was more anxious than ever for a tariff understanding with Canada that would serve to buttress up his waning fortunes. Secrecy still enshrouds the transactions of the conference which was reopened at Washington on January 7, 1911, and lasted two weeks before the final completion of the pact. Negotiating now for the United States were: C. P. Knox, secretary of State; Chandler P. Anderson, of the Department of the Treasury; and C. M. Pepper. (When the terms of the agreement were published a statement was issued to the effect that there would be no treaty between Great Britain and the United States in order to bring it into operation, but that it would come into force upon the passage of concurrent legislation by the American Congress and the Parliament of Canada. Either country therefore might rescind the scheme at will, although it was hoped by the negotiators that it would be more or less permanent.)

"THE SIEGE OF OTTAWA."

(During the interval between the reciprocity sittings at Ottawa and at Washington a monster farmers' delegation had visited the Canadian capital with the object of clearly setting before the government its views on the tariff and other important matters. The *Weekly Sun* had first suggested the strategic value of this manœuvre; the Canadian Council of Agriculture, having voiced its approval, had assumed the responsibility of filling in the details of the plan. From the West came five hundred representatives of the grain growers' organizations; from Ontario came three hundred more, representing the Dominion Grange, the Fruit Growers' Association, and various other farm bodies; a sprinkling of delegates were also on hand from Quebec and the Maritime Provinces. On December 15 a pre-conference was held in Ottawa Grand Opera House, when a list of resolutions were drawn up for presentation to the government on the following day.)

On the morning of December 16, the delegation was marshalled at a central point and proceeded four abreast to the Parliament Buildings, where it was admitted to the floor and galleries of the House of Commons. Sir Wilfrid Laurier, accompanied by a number of his leading ministers, appeared at ten o'clock, and heard the farmers outline their proposals until two in the afternoon. D. W. McCuaig, president of the Canadian Council of Agriculture, read the memorials that had been prepared, introducing twenty speakers in turn on various themes. The tariff memorial, which was reserved until the last, petitioned for: a reciprocal trade agreement with the United States covering all agricultural, horticultural and animal products; agricultural implements and machinery; vehicles and their parts; fertilizers and spraying materials; illuminating, fuel and lubricating oils; cement; fish; and lumber. It also requested a reduction in the British preferential rates to one-half those of the general schedule and free trade with Great Britain within ten years. Addresses on the subject of the tariff were given by J. W. Scallion and Roderick McKenzie from the Western contingent; E. C. Drury and Thomas McMillan, of the Dominion Grange; Col. J. Z. Fraser; Joseph E. Johnston, of the Ontario Fruit Growers' Association; S. C. Parker, of the Nova Scotia Fruit Growers' Association; M. B. Fawcett, of the New Brunswick Farmers' Association; and Robert Sellar, representing the stock breeders and dairymen of Quebec. Roderick McKenzie's discourse, over four thousand words in length, was a masterpiece of close reasoning. "The purchasing power of a bushel of wheat," he said, "is reduced twenty-five per cent. by our fiscal system." Nothing but what was just and expedient was being asked for by the farmer who had "gone to the frontiers of civilization when the road was dark and the discouragements were great." Sir Wilfrid in his response said that the parley under way with the United States overshadowed all other tariff issues for the moment.

On January 26 the Minister of Finance gave the House of Commons a full report on the scope of the reciprocity agreement that had been arrived at in Washington. The first impression created thereby both in and out of the House was that Canada had made a very successful deal with her southern neighbor. While manufactured goods were involved to some extent the pact mainly referred to the interchange of the raw materials of field, forest, mine and sea. Four schedules had been drawn up: one containing a long list of goods to be admitted free between the two countries; another enumerating those upon which lower or identical duties would be granted; a third setting forth a list of articles to be admitted at special rates into the United States, and a fourth detailing those to be given special rates upon entry into Canada. The Conservatives on listening to Fielding's report were nonplussed at the breadth of the reciprocity proposals; the government and its press were jubilant at the thought that the Liberal party would now be in a very much better position in which to meet the electorate. The opposition press adopted the policy of sparring for time.

RECIPROCITY'S OVERTHROW

(Throughout Canada the various farmers' organizations were quick to show the government that its plan for reciprocal trade with the United States had met with their entire approbation. When, during the annual sessions of the Manitoba Grain Growers' Association, held in Brandon, the news was flashed on January 26, from Winnipeg, that wheat under the agreement was to be on the free list, a cheer, which lasted for several minutes, went up from the throats of four hundred attending farmers. The Canadian Council of Agriculture, meeting at Regina on February 10, since it understood that concurrent legislation would be necessary to bring the pact into operation, passed a resolution to the effect that it "would strongly urge the Parliament of Canada to ratify the agreement." Simultaneously the Council went on record as favoring an increase of the British preference to a point where it would be only one-half that of the general schedule. The Saskatchewan Grain Growers' Association about the same time pledged its unqualified support of the government's reciprocity programme. Various resolutions commendatory of the agreement were drawn up by local branches of the U.F.A., and transmitted to the Minister of Finance.)

(The history of the bitter and highly-spectacular conflict which broke loose in Canada during the spring and summer of 1911 over the reciprocity issue will be recounted briefly. Foes of freer trade relations with the United States soon picked up heart and determined on a fight to the finish. Colonel Sam Hughes (Victoria and Haliburton) is accredited with having been the first to arouse the Conservative party to an attitude of open belligerency. For one thing the antis were emboldened by the array of arguments that they found they could adduce against the pact; their contentions found support in unexpected quarters. The Liberals, on the other hand, believing that they had delivered a master stroke, put too much faith in their laurels. The opposition discovered that it would be possible to set one part of the country against the other, and, moreover, that it would be expedient to play the farmer against the city dweller and the city dweller against the farmer. Such economic arguments as they had were developed and widened. The United States, said the opposition, was faced by diminishing supplies of raw materials and was seeking to draw these from Canada. For many years Canadian railways had been built east and west toward the seaboard; now the tendency would be for trade to move north and south, and Canadian lines, having lost their independence, would become feeders to the American systems. The government on its side emphasized the fact that in the reciprocity measure it was lowering import duties in keeping with its promises, and at the same time securing a wider market for Canadian goods. The United States, according to the Liberals' argument, was surrender ng very much more, if the agreement passed Congress, than was Canada, and a surplus of advantage would accrue to the Canadian people. Stress was laid upon the financial saving to the farmers by the reductions on implements, wagons and other goods, while the town consumer, it was said, would benefit by a downward trend in the cost of living.

In the House of Commons the Conservatives first counselled delay in order that the public might become informed on the question of reciprocity; later they adopted the policy of blocking and impeding the government's actions. In Montreal, the *Star*, and in Toronto, the *News*, came out as the most blatant opponents of the agreement. The *Weekly Sun*, the *Grain Growers' Guide*, the Toronto *Globe* and the *Manitoba Free Press* were perhaps the most influential of its defenders. A revolt soon began to manifest itself within the Liberal fold. On February 20, eighteen prominent Liberals in Toronto signed and published an urgent protest against the reciprocity measure as injurious to Canadian interests. The government's retort was that these men represented purely the Big Interests. The most striking defection from the Liberal ranks occurred, however, when in March, Hon. Clifford Sifton, then Chairman of the Commission on Conservation, announced in the House of Commons that he could no longer follow Laurier's lead, and thereupon proceeded to declaim on the public platform against the terms of the pact. From this time onward an organized opposition to reciprocity arose among an enlarging group of Liberal malcontents which was to be peculiarly disconcerting to the government's cause.

The forces that were now lined up against the agreement gave evidence that they were prepared to go to furthest lengths to accomplish its defeat. Apprehensive lest their economic arguments might not suffice to give them victory, those hostile to reciprocity began to set more store in an appeal to the patriotic sentiments of the Canadian people.

Without compunction they raised the loyalty cry and continued it throughout the length and breadth of the land with untiring zeal. The main issue, they declared, was whether Canada should become a commercial appendage of the United States with political union as the ultimate goal, or, having spurned her tempter, should help Great Britain to cement the bonds of empire. Flaming headlines and the uncanny skill of the cartoonist were used by the opposition newspapers to burn this idea into the minds of their readers. "Wellington did not discuss boot-straps at Waterloo," exclaimed the Montreal *Star*. "Until we are assured that the flag will keep flying, we have no time to revise customs schedules." Moreover, the jingoistic utterances of numerous American politicians supplied abundant material for the loyalty propaganda. For instance, the hope expressed by Hon. James Beauchamp Clark, Speaker of the House of Representatives, that the United States would one day stretch to the north pole, and the word picture of the New York congressman of "a single magnificent country extending from the Rio Grande to Hudson Bay" were seized upon with avidity as betokening what would happen to Canada in due season after the ratification of the pact. Even President Taft's addresses were watched narrowly, and when, on April 27, in an unguarded moment, he told an audience of press writers of the "Chinese wall" that would likely be erected between Canada and United States, if reciprocity were not accepted, on account of Canada's growing imperial affiliations, his remarks were given wide circulation by the opposition in Canada as indicating Taft's distaste for the Dominion's British connection, and his real belief in a policy of continentalism.

When the testing time came in the American Congress on the reciprocity question, only a minority of the Republican members in each House were found supporting the Taft administration. The Democrats, however, were for the most part in favor of such a commercial arrangement with Canada as would give a downward trend to the rates of their own tariff, and since they were now in control of the House of Representatives, the government's bill embodying the draft agreement was readily sanctioned by that chamber on April 21 by 267 votes to 89. The president and his advisers were also able to secure ample assistance in the Senate, with the result that the bill when submitted to it was finally ratified there on July 22. In Canada the fate of reciprocity hung in a more uncertain balance. Sir Wilfrid Laurier was head of a government that had a majority of forty-seven in the House of Commons, and had he so chosen he might have inscribed reciprocity on the statute books of the country despite the renegadism of a part of his followers. But from Atlantic to Pacific public opinion had been thoroughly aroused over the issue, the Conservatives were boldly flaunting the government, and its only course seemed to be to leave the matter to the electorate. Laurier always maintained that the government should make important changes in legislation only on a mandate from the people. Accordingly parliament was dissolved on July 29 and election day set for September 21. During the campaign the work of defending the reciprocity proposals fell mainly to the lot of the Premier, as his colleagues in the cabinet stayed closely by their constituencies in fear of their political lives. The opposition apparently had plenty of money to spend and used speakers galore to enunciate its claims; it took care to end its campaign with a frenzied outburst of patriotic fervor. The election proved singularly disastrous to the government, and at the same time threw proponents of reciprocity into the slough of despond. The Conservatives, having obtained a working majority of forty-five in the House, took over the reins of office on October 10, with Hon. Robert L. Borden as Premier.

SUMMARY OF THE RESULTS.

(It would be wide of the mark to assert that the people of Canada in failing to return a government pledged to reciprocity had rendered their decision under the sway of economic considerations. Albeit numerous economic arguments had been employed by each side in the election, these had served to bewilder the voter rather than clarify the situation for him. There is every reason to believe that the loud-voiced warning against possible annexation by the United States had affected enough susceptible minds to turn the trick in favor of the opposition. So, too, through having been fifteen years in power, the Laurier administration had become subject to the process of erosion, and this had had its influence on the results.

The popular vote cast for Liberal and Conservative candidates, where contests were held, in the general election of 1911 was distributed in this manner:)

	Conservative	Liberal
Ontario......................	269,930	207,078
Quebec.......................	159,262	164,274
Nova Scotia	55,209	57,462
New Brunswick	38,880	40,192
Manitoba.....................	40,356	34,781
British Columbia	25,622	16,350
Prince Edward Island..........	14,638	13,998
Saskatchewan	34,700	52,924
Alberta......................	29,675	37,208
Yukon	1,285	829
	696,557	625,096

An analysis of these figures will show that British Columbia had led the van of the anti-reciprocity forces since sixty per cent. of its electorate had declared themselves for the new government. Ontario, which went Conservative by a plurality of about twelve thousand in 1908, had also taken a determined stand against the pact. Manitoba, somewhat to the surprise of political observers, had been one of the opposing provinces, as had been Prince Edward Island by a slender margin. The prairie provinces of Alberta and Saskatchewan on the other hand had given a clear verdict for reciprocity; Quebec, where Laurier was still supreme in the face of diverse machinations against him, had remained in the Liberal column; lastly, New Brunswick and Nova Scotia might be claimed as having supported reciprocity, although by insignificant majorities. It is interesting to note that the 221 members of the twelfth parliament of Canada, elected in 1911, may be classified according to their occupations as follows: business men (manufacturers, merchants, lumbermen, agents, contractors, brokers, etc.), 76; professional men (lawyers, doctors, journalists, etc.), 112; farmers, 32; and industrial worker, 1.

PART V

The Farmers' Movements in More Recent Years

CHAPTER XXIII

The United Farmers of Ontario

UNDER the spell of a new impetus afforded it by its union with the Farmers' Association of Ontario, the Grange had renewed a measure of its youth in the period, 1907-11. Although the pulsating grain growers' movements had snuffed the Order out completely in Western Canada, it had mounted rapidly in strength in Ontario as groups of farmers who had formerly belonged to the association had applied to it for charters. By the beginning oʄ 1910 some ninety subordinate granges were in working condition in the province. The Order had kept up its agitation for heavier taxation of the railways, and under the suasion of W. C. Good had pronounced itself in favor of direct legislation through the initiative and referendum. It had severely arraigned the country's militaristic preparations. For instance, in 1909, its Legislative Committee had viewed "with grave misgivings the proposal to create a Canadian navy," and the same year its Executive Committee had gone on record as believing that the Canadian people should devote "their whole energies to industrial and moral advancements, rather than to the pounding of drums and the clash of arms." But above all else during this period the Grange had been solicitous on tariff matters, urging that a stay should be put to the evils of the bounty system, and seeking to give the farmers a clearer apprehension of the benefits which would accrue to them were the government to sanction a reciprocity pact with the United States.

While the submergence of reciprocity in the 1911 elections may be regarded as having been a repulse to farmers' organizations everywhere in Canada, its effect in the West was merely that of a parriable thrust. For the Grange, however, whose activities were confined to the province that had turned the scales against the agreement, it proved a sorrier blow. When the Dominion Grange met for its annual sessions in January, 1912, only a handful of delegates made their appearance, and these were in utterly lachrymose mood.

273

No meeting was convened during 1913 until December, by which time the opinion had become prevalent that as a rallying ground for those who desired to fight the farmers' battles the Grange had outlived its day of usefulness. The situation was critical, inasmuch as within a space of little more than ten years the farmers had watched three organizations shrivel in Ontario, and both capable leadership and broad policies would be needed if they were to be gathered into the fold of another movement. One Saturday afternoon toward the close of 1913 a tiny band of "invincibles" gathered in a room at the Kirby House on Queen St. West, Toronto, and asked themselves what course they might best pursue in an endeavor to unite the farmers of the province again for the defence of their industry. These men—Col. J. Z. Fraser, E. C. Drury, J. J. Morrison and W. C. Good—were well aware that the methods of organization so far tried were obsolete, and any repetition of them was foredoomed to failure. After gravely deliberating the question, they separated with the conviction that their only chance of success would be to set off on a new tack just as the grain growers had done in the West.

The effectiveness of the grain growers' movements on the prairies had not only roused the admiration of Ontario farmers but had made them emulous. Yet how, following the same lines, could organization take place in their province where conditions were so unlike those of the West? Farming in Ontario was highly diversified; sectional interests were numerous and must be respected; besides, conservatism was deeply-rooted in the province and might impose a bar to progress. A full meed of praise must be accorded to J. J. Morrison for having formulated the plan whereby organization under these circumstances might become possible. Mention may be made of the fact that in 1885 Farmers' Institutes had been introduced into the farming communities of Ontario by the Mowat government to act as educational stimuli. These met once a year, and were addressed by lecturers specially conversant with the problems of the farming industry. Soon after 1900 clubs arose in conjunction with the Institutes, which assembled much oftener, and at which the farmers threshed out their problems for themselves. In 1905, when Hon. Nelson Monteith became provincial Minister of Agriculture, rules were drawn up and suggested for use in the establishment of these clubs, and their organization vigorously fostered. Some 250 of them had been created by 1913.   But as politics were taboo at their meetings and as they were not encouraged to go into business, the inference was drawn that they were being coddled along by the government in order to neutralize the effect of independent thought among the farmers of the province.

Morrison's plan was simply to form a new confraternity in Ontario out of the hotchpotch of farmers' organizations already existing.   He believed that if the Institute clubs were asked to renounce their leading strings, many of them would gladly abandon their circumscribed position and emerge into a larger life.   The clubs that were ready to break away, he pointed out, together with various co-operative associations and a percentage of the granges might be made the basis of a wide-reaching organization.   This scheme was received with approval by the protagonists of a new movement, and arrangements made to hold a meeting at Toronto, on March 19, 1914, to which the various bodies indicated were invited to send representatives.   Meanwhile, on February 7, five Brant County farmers had secured a charter to establish a co-operative company in Ontario with extensive powers in connection with the business of agriculture, and it was decided to propose to the meeting that this also should be gathered up into the general plan.

The Labor Temple, on Church Street, Toronto, was the scene of the meeting, to which one hundred and fifty to two hundred organizations of one kind and another had sent their delegates.   In an assemblage so motley there was an "outpouring of sentiments," as might be expected, on all manner of themes.   Speeches were delivered by representatives of the fruit-growers, Holstein cattle breeders, seed corn growers, poultry circles and others, while Roderick McKenzie, attending from the West, told of the accomplishments of the grain growers' associations on the prairies.   The outcome of the meeting was the formation of the United Farmers of Ontario, an organization which was to have distinct branches of its own but with which any Institute club, grange or other accredited body in the province might become affiliated. This, it was expected, would constitute an organized farmers' unit in Ontario equivalent to the units already operating in Western Canada.   The admission fee to the U.F.O.—to give it the abbreviated name which soon became popular—was fifty cents, but the local organizations were allowed to raise funds for their individual needs as they saw fit.   At the same time the commercial venture already launched in Brant County was accepted as an avenue through which the branches and affiliated bodies might trade, and was given the title of the United Farmers' Co-operative Company, Limited. In point of government, however, it was to be entirely separate from the U.F.O. at large. The meeting passed various resolutions, one of which condemned the federal government's proposal to continue the bounty system for another term of years as "utterly indefensible" and "an added burden on an already overtaxed public." It also protested against the suggestion that sizes of fence wire on the free list should be subjected to import duties, and reiterated the plea, made frequently by the Farmers' Association of Ontario, that railways should be taxed according to their value in the same way as farm property.

THE MILITARY SERVICE ACT.

Four and one-half months after the establishment of the United Farmers of Ontario the war of 1914-18 began to carry its flame over land and sea, and was to influence that organization's development in a peculiar fashion. When its first annual convention was held on February 25, 1915, it was reported to have in the neighborhood of two thousand members, enrolled in thirty-four local bodies as follows: new branches, fourteen; former Institute clubs, fifteen; granges three, and associations, two. The convention lauded the Ottawa government's introduction of methods of direct taxation for war purposes, but assailed its tariff amendment act which had provided for an *ad valorem* increase in the tariffs of both excise and customs. If production were to be kept up to the high level demanded, was the view expressed, then it would be necessary to remove "all artificial restrictions" and disburden the farmers. R. H. Halbert was elected president and J. J. Morrison, secretary-treasurer.

A year later, when the stress of war conditions was being felt in the farming districts of Ontario as a portion of their young manhood had been drained to the military camps and to the munition and other factories, the convention of 1916 met with gloomy forebodings for the future of agriculture. Though Secretary Morrison hopefully announced that the membership stood at five thousand, and that the number of locals had increased nearly two hundred and fifty per cent., he feared that, when the war was over and sanity was again enthroned among the nations, the terrible costs would in the long run be thrown back upon the farmer. "Are we going to submit," he queried, "to the great burden of taxation that inevitably must follow, and be unloaded upon our industry?" A resolution was adopted at this convention calling for both provincial and federal action to insure a complete prohibition of the liquor traffic in the province. On April 20, 1916, the U.F.O. by a vote of its board of directors formally aligned itself with the Canadian Council of Agriculture; simultaneously steps were taken to distribute informative literature to the locals respecting the aims of the association, and an effort made to discover what principles the locals thought should be incorporated in its platform.

As the year 1916 advanced, discussion was rife in Canada over the possibility of the government introducing compulsory military service, and Ontario farmers were in a state of perplexity as to how they could spare more young men from the farms and at the same time meet the demands for greater production, which were becoming constantly more insistent. At this very moment, too, the war profiteer was taking rich tolls at the expense of Canada's trade and industry, and his unchecked rapacity was sowing seeds of distrust in the farmer's heart. The *Weekly Sun*, cleaving to the Goldwin Smith tradition, agreed that the people must endure the war, but became an out and out foe of conscriptionist policies. Grain and milk, it stated on October 31, were absolutely needed for the feeding of hogs so essential to the rationing of soldiers, and the production of grain and milk would be seriously retarded by compulsory military service. "Hogs," it caustically remarked, "cannot live on the east wind or even on grass alone." And when the third annual convention of the U.F.O. met in February, 1917, it set forth its attitude on the conscription issue in unmistakable terms. "Since human life," ran its pronouncement, "is more valuable than gold, this convention most solemnly protests against any proposal looking to the conscription of men for battle, while leaving wealth exempt from the same measure of enforced service. It is a manifest and glaring injustice that Canadian mothers should be compelled to surrender boys around whom their dearest hopes in life are centred, while plutocrats, fattening on special privileges and war business, are left in undisturbed possession of their riches."

On August 29, the Union government's Military Service Act was finally passed, conscripting, according to stated classifications, all males in Canada between the ages of twenty to forty-five. No answer was given to the farmers' plea for a conscription of wealth beyond an increase of the business profits tax and the introduction of an income tax. Nevertheless exemptions were to be granted to those pursuing special war occupations, to those who had special qualifications for necessary work, and to those whose taking would occasion exceptional hardship. It was doubtless the intention of the act that farmers should be retained on the land with the result that rural tribunals freely exempted them in all parts of Canada. "Farmers' sons," said General Mewburn, Minister of Militia at Dundas, on November 25, "who are honestly engaged in the production of food will be exempt from military service;" moreover, an order-in-council of December 3, allowed Mewburn to override the decision of any local tribunal and grant an exemption if he deemed it wise. Union government candidates, during the campaign which ended in the previous government's retention of power on election day, December 17, expressly promised that the labor requirements of the farm would be fully respected.

The U.F.O., having moved its regular convention date back to December, met two days after the election, but had no comment to make on the results. President Halbert took a fling at economic and political matters in general. "Government by the people," he asserted, "is a myth. The real rulers of Canada are the knighted heads of combines. Financial, manufacturing and food distributing interests are organized, and the individual farmer, standing alone, has no chance against them. Farmers possess but do not control the biggest business asset in Canada." J. J. Morrison, who had been working like a nailer throughout the province, reported that four hundred clubs, as the local organizations were now uniformly designated, were actively listed with the U.F.O., while its aggregate membership had risen to fifteen thousand. The convention resolved to accept the Farmers' Platform drafted in December, 1916, by the Canadian Council of Agriculture, though advising that the question of reciprocity with the United States should be subjected to a referendum.

The Farmers are Set at Nought.

While still believing that wealth should be conscripted in Canada, the United Farmers of Ontario, under the guarantee of exemptions, had acquiesced in the government's policy with respect to compulsory military service. Apparently everything would have proceeded smoothly had not the government been notified by the military authorities that the local tribunals were not securing the requisite man-power. Then warnings were issued for public consumption that, on account of the acuteness of the war situation in Europe, Canada must furnish her full quota of conscripts. Meanwhile, official statements had been made to the effect that food might be the determining factor in the war, with the result that Ontario farmers had been extending their acreage and buying new implements to help in seeding the 1918 crop. On April 19, just as the farmers had gotten nicely on the land, the Premier, Sir Robert Borden, informed the House of Commons that the government desired to abjure its policy with respect to exemptions, and with the House's sanction an order-in-council was published the following day cancelling all exemptions to the twenty, twenty-one, and twenty-two-year classes. Simultaneously the nineteen-year class was called upon to register. The total exemptions granted so far to young farmers in the twenty to twenty-two-year classes had been 41,852.

Immediately a babel of dissent was heard among the farmers of Canada from Halifax to Vancouver. Meetings of protest were held under U.F.O. auspices at leading centres in Ontario, while remonstrances and petitions fairly deluged its head office at Toronto. The issue was so compelling that the association's executive felt itself justified in taking some definite form of action on behalf of the farmers of the province as a whole. Accordingly, it not only lined up its own forces, but sought representation from the rural municipalities of Ontario for a monster delegation which, under U.F.O. leadership, would lay the farmers' case before the government at Ottawa, on May 14. Quebec farmers had also arranged to assemble a great throng in the capital city on the same day, and when the two contingents met they were five thousand in number, a host of rural petitioners such as had never been gathered together before in Canadian history.

The Ontario delegates packed the Russell Theatre on the morning of May 14 for a prearranged conference with Sir Robert Borden, while most of the Quebec farmers met elsewhere. Borden arrived at eleven-thirty and remained until two in the afternoon. He was addressed by W. A. Amos and Manning W. Doherty, representing Ontario farmers, and

Hon. Joseph E. Caron, from Quebec. Amos and Doherty
asked for a relaxation of the new service regulations to allow
for the exemption of young farmers whose work was essential
to the production of foodstuffs, or at least that the conscripts
be given leave of absence until the end of harvest operations.
"We cannot make bricks without straw," was their plaint.
"We cannot produce if our help is taken from us." It was
estimated that 4,400 acres of land would on the average go
uncultivated in each Ontario township through the cancella-
tion of exemptions to farmers between twenty and twenty-two
years, and that production would be thereby diminished one-
quarter. It was strongly urged that industries, manufacturing luxuries and other non-essentials, should be closed down
in the cities. Borden replied at some length, declaring that the
need to reinforce the Canadian troops bulked above everything else, and that the government had broken its pre-election
pledges on account of the military crisis. He said that there
was no possibility of any change in decision on the matter.
Except for a few ejaculations and interpositions the audience
heard the Premier through in orderly silence. A truly de-
risive roar had bellowed forth, however, when he suggested
that inexperienced labor should be brought from the cities
to supplement that on the farms.

A request had been forwarded to the House of Commons
asking that representatives from the Ontario delegation
might appear before it during the course of the day. In the
afternoon a great mass-meeting of Quebec and Ontario
farmers was held in the Ottawa Arena, when felicitations were
exchanged between the two groups and an *entente cordiale*
established that was to be of historical value. Premier
Borden on his return to the House of Commons told it that
no farmers' representatives would be admitted to its presence,
and that the affair over the exemptions was concluded.
Tongues wagged lustily when news of this spread, and in the
evening an enraged crowd of two thousand Ontario farmers
bore down upon the Houses of Parliament seeking admission.
The police informed them that only members might enter,
but eventually let Amos and Doherty in to parley for a
hearing. Nevertheless, despite the fact that a very desultory
debate was on in the House of Commons, the emissaries'
petition was refused point blank and they were turned out
into the night. The crowd then surged off to the Arena to
vent its wrath in inflammatory utterances, although it

reached a decision to do its best to further production. The government's treatment in this manner of the pick of Ontario's yeomen was not only eminently discourteous but a tactical blunder of major proportions. A suspension of the debate might easily have been moved, and, after the Speaker had left the chair, a few farmer delegates have been asked to address the House. Sir Wilfrid Laurier had adopted this method when the farmers came to Ottawa in 1910.

Cachinnations at once rang from the pages of certain Canadian journals at the United Farmers' expense. One professional humorist, writing in the Toronto *Saturday Night* on June 1, strove to furnish a description of the Ottawa expedition, clothed in the habiliments of a parable. His portrayal was steeped in calumny, and a few excerpts from it may suffice to show its descent to coarseness. "They had not baggage," he related, "save their mackintoshes, nay, not so much as a toothbrush." Some gawping here, and others basking there until moved on, had wandered about, and because "pie was ten cents a cut and hollow-chested at that many chewed their nails inasmuch as it was cheaper." While they were in conference with "King Borden" one newspaperman had said to his fellow: "An odor prevaileth. And the other answered: 'Why not? They are five thousand strong.'" And as they were not allowed to enter "the Hall of Council where King Borden foregathered with his wise men," accordingly "the Sons of the Soil remained outside and ate grass." When night came on, "they had no place to lay their heads," and "so the Sons of the Soil slept in the parks and open spaces, but they had no ease, inasmuch as the wind played zizz with their walrus mustaches." Another article which appeared in the Halifax *Herald*, signed by "Cornelius Churchill, V.C.," was so ribald in its composition and malicious in its defamation of the Ontario farmer that the historian may pass it by without further comment.

When the farmer-adventurers returned from Ottawa to the side-lines and concessions to report the inefficacy of their plea with respect to exemptions and to tell of the reception meted out to them on Parliament Hill, a powerful tide of resentment swept the whole U.F.O. organization. Word went forth that a special convention would be held at Toronto on June 7 to consider the situation, which, when it opened in Massey Hall with 3,000-4,000 persons in attendance, developed into the most tumultuous gathering in the long annals of

Canadian agrarian history. A small detachment of police were in the building, alert lest some one should effervesce into treasonable statements. Scorching attacks were made on the federal government for its attitude of sangfroid and incivility, and diatribes hurled at the newspapers for their slandermongering and misrepresentation. Remembering the way in which many Ontario representatives in the Union government from rural constituencies had connived at the treatment accorded the Ottawa delegation, the convention gladly hearkened to a demand from the floor for independent political action. So, too, when a proposal was laid before it calling for the establishment of a U.F.O. official journal, it immediately answered by appointing a board of trustees to finance the matter in its inceptive stages; in fact, many present wanted a daily paper.

Several months later, under the goad of circumstances, U.F.O. clubs on Manitoulin Island brought out a candidate for a provincial bye-election in their riding with, as will be narrated, epoch-making results. On October 28, at a mass meeting of club directors from all parts of the province, it was recommended that independent farmer candidates be put up in any further bye-elections that might occur in rural constituencies. The events of the year had given a tremendous momentum to the work of organization, so that when the annual convention met in December J. J. Morrison delivered an optimistic message to the effect that there were over one thousand clubs in the association, while the total membership stood at twenty-five thousand. Resolutions were passed favoring local option in taxation, and requesting the Ontario government to move slowly in connection with Sir Adam Beck's hydro-radial policy. On September 6 incorporation had been obtained for a publishing company whose directorate set out to inquire from every possible angle into the expediency of starting a daily paper. Finally it was thought wiser to begin more modestly, and, as a consequence, the *Weekly Sun* was acquired by purchase in the spring of 1919. The intention had been to name the association's organ the *United Farmer*, but as it was discovered that this title had already been copyrighted by a foresighted journalist who was willing to surrender it for a consideration, the paper was called the *Farmers' Sun* instead.

The year 1919 witnessed the U.F.O. clubs' famous "drive" into politics, ending with their startling success at the polls, in the provincial election on October 20, and the formation of a Farmer-Labor government with E. C. Drury as Premier. (Vide Chapter XXVI.) The sixth annual convention, therefore, on December 17-19, was a gala event at which members of the new administration were enthusiastically welcomed and pæans of victory sung. Throughout the Drury regime, 1919-23, it was the custom of successive conventions to bring matters to the attention of the government upon which they desired legislation. However, from May, 1920, onward, the tie binding the government and the U.F.O. as represented by its executive, became somewhat insecure when in the first place the latter showed its antagonism to the government's superannuation bill, and then a publicly-stated divergence of opinion grew up between Premier Drury and Secretary Morrison over the question of evolving a People's Party with the farmers' organization as a basis. Statistics for 1919 gave the association a membership of 48,000, enrolled in 1,130 clubs; a year later there were 1,465 clubs and the membership had reached a high-water mark of 60,000. The movement had weakened considerably before the defeat of the Drury government in June, 1923, but is now apparently making quick recovery. An educational secretaryship was created for the U.F.O. in 1920 by means of which information has been sent out to the clubs on questions of public interest, encouragement given to the holding of high-quality debates and entertainments, and short courses arranged for the younger members at Toronto University.

ORGANIZATION OF FARM WOMEN AND YOUNG PEOPLE.

The Grange's rule that women should be initiated into its ranks on equal terms with the men has lent stability to that Order even in its darkest hours. The Patrons of Industry and the Farmers' Association of Ontario, on the other hand, had left the women folk out, as did the U.F.O. until 1918. Soon after the establishment of the U.F.O. farm women of the province had begun to knock at its door for admission, and J. J. Morrison, realizing the value from every standpoint of having them in the movement, bided his opportunity to help form a women's auxiliary. When, in the summer of 1918, it was learned that Mrs. Violet M. McNaughton, a leader among the organized farm women of Saskatchewan, would be in the East, arrangements were hastily made to have her address a gathering at Toronto on June 17. Then and there sixteen farm women who attended decided to get an auxiliary under way, for which they appointed a body of provisional officers, pending ratification by the general association. On July 11, the first branch of what they chose to call the United Farm Women of Ontario was tentatively set up near Georgetown, and two more branches organized before the U.F.O. met in annual convention. This year the convention held its sessions in the Convocation Hall of Toronto University, and hard by, in a room belonging to the University, thirty women, having assembled, endorsed the aims for which the U.F.O. stood, and drew up a short platform of their own. They then proceeded to the great convention with, as may be believed, some tokens of awe, where they were vociferously received, and granted the right to form separate women's clubs under the association's jurisdiction. Their auxiliary would be allowed a complete staff of officers with the exception of a treasurer. It was also stipulated that women who found it impossible to or did not care to set up a club in any locality, might become members of a men's club on equal terms.

The U.F.W.O. flourished at once, announcing the existence of seventy clubs within a year. By December, 1922, it had two hundred clubs and sixty-five hundred members. It has devoted a great deal of its time in annual meeting and locally to problems of rural education and better home-making. Besides it has advocated among other things: the removal of the disabilities of rural women in qualifying as school trustees; the municipal franchise for farmers' wives and daughters; the appointment of county police matrons; the equipment of children's shelters by county councils; the employment of provincial nurses in Northern Ontario; personal naturalization; and the placing of all labor-saving devices on the free list. Through the instrumentality of the women's auxiliary organization work was begun in 1920 among juniors, with the result that a constitution was adopted at the U.F.O. convention of that year for the United Farm Young People of Ontario. With the assistance of any club member, male or female. a junior section may be established by five young people over thirteen years of age. An adult leader must be selected to supervise the activities of the section, and each prospective member is required to take a pledge which includes the promise "to become a good citizen and uphold all that is good and noble in the life of the nation)"

CHAPTER XXIV

Expansion and Work of the Prairie Association

EXCEPT in the province of Manitoba where urban dweller and unorganized farmer turned their faces against reciprocity with the United States, the election of 1911 had only a momentary effect upon the advance of the grain growers' organizations in the West. The membership of the Manitoba association, under the shock of the election defeat, suffered a decline of about one-third, but within two years had forged ahead again, and by 1914 was practically back to its former level. The association in Saskatchewan, where the grain crop was already double that of Manitoba, made steady progress, seemingly undeterred by events in the political world, now being in point of numbers the strongest body on the prairies. The growth of the United Farmers of Alberta during the period, 1911-14, was distinctly unique; even in the year following the election that organization's membership went up twenty-two per cent., and in 1914 was estimated at more than eleven thousand.

For several years previous to the outbreak of the war in 1914 the Western associations took a deep interest in the problems of direct legislation through the initiative, referendum and recall. Examples of the operation of these principles were furnished by various American states, and as early as 1910 a Direct Legislation League of Manitoba had been formed with headquarters at Winnipeg, to explain their advantages in constitutional procedure. John Kennedy, of the Grain Growers' Grain Company, was made vice-president of this league, while among its most ardent officials were: F. J. Dixon, R. L. Richardson and S. J. Farmer. The Manitoba Grain Growers' Association and the *Grain Growers' Guide* decided to lend support to the efforts of the league; moreover, resolutions in favor of direct legislation were passed by the Grain Growers' Associations of both Alberta and Saskatchewan. In May, 1912, a similar league was established for propaganda purposes in Saskatchewan.

285

Exponents of direct legislation in the three provinces brought pressure to bear on their local governments to adopt their ideas, and eventually Premiers Scott, of Saskatchewan, and Sifton, of Alberta, expressed a sympathetic attitude. In fact, laws were put through the legislatures of Alberta and Saskatchewan in 1913, embodying the principles of the initiative and referendum in somewhat limping form, but leaving out the principle of the recall. The Saskatchewan act was subject to approval by a plebiscite. According to its terms any bill passed by the legislature, except it dealt with the granting of supply or was brought into force at once by a two-third vote of the members, might be submitted to a referendum upon a petition filed within ninety days by ten per cent. of the voters in the last election. To exercise the initiative eight per cent. of the electors must petition for a proposed act, which, having gone through the legislative formalities, would then be sent on to a referendum. Grain growers and League leaders regarded the Saskatchewan measure as inadequate, and such apathy was shown in the province when the plebiscite on it was taken on November 27, that only about one-half the number of votes necessary to carry it were obtained. The Alberta act which was along similar lines, though requiring a ten per cent. petition for both initiative and referendum, became law at once. While the *Grain Growers' Guide* considered it to be full of "jokers," it has proven of some worth in the legislative history of the province. A motion calling for a plebiscite on direct legislation was defeated in the Manitoba Assembly in 1913, as was a resolution commending its principles introduced by C. D. McPherson (Lakeside), in January, 1914. Premier Roblin was unequivocally hostile, stating that he would never put direct legislation on the statute books, and terming it "degenerate republicanism." The Liberal Party in Manitoba, on the other hand, was friendly to the idea, and after it had taken over the reins of office, in 1915, enacted a bill to provide for the initiative and referendum at the next ensuing session of the legislature. But this was invalidated, when, after having been tested in the Canadian courts, it was declared unconstitutional by the Judicial Committee of the Privy Council. For the time being the advocates of the initiative, referendum, and recall were thwarted in their desires, but the principles they advanced remained deep-rooted in the farmer organizations and in the minds of individuals.

HAIL INSURANCE AND AGRICULTURAL CREDITS.

Again, at this time the attention of the grain growers' organizations was focussed on the question of hail insurance, which was being extensively contracted for in the West by private companies. The U.F.A. in 1909 had advocated the establishment of a provincial system of writing hail insurance, and two years later the Saskatchewan association, complaining of the business methods of the hail insurance companies, had asked for a government-controlled plan to insure farmers against loss by hail, which would be financed by putting a tax on land of two cents an acre. The Scott government's reply to the last mentioned proposal was to authorize a local option scheme in 1912 whereby municipalities were allowed, if they chose, to go into the hail insurance business and to assess ratepayers a premium up to four cents an acre for indemnification purposes. A special commission was charged with the superintendence of the Saskatchewan plan which, within a year, had been embraced by 115 municipalities. But, after a few years' trial the system was found to be badly in arrears in the discharge of its obligations, and in 1917 a new act was passed, abandoning the form of rule by commission and erecting a self-governing association among the municipalities. A flat rate of four cents an acre was now laid on all assessable lands in the municipalities, while an additional rate, as needed, might be collected from the lands under crop.* The U.F.A. came out for a compulsory land tax to provide for hail insurance in 1912, but obtained no action from its provincial government until 1915. Then a bill was enacted permitting twenty or more municipalities to group themselves into a district where lands would be uniformly taxed for hail insurance purposes. A board was formed to oversee the system and an indemnity guaranteed of six dollars an acre. However, losses in Alberta also ran beyond the intake; objections, too, had been raised to certain features in the insurance plan. Legislation of 1918 made the system non-compulsory by allowing individual farmers in the hail insurance district to withdraw, if they saw fit, and at the same time gave farmers

---

*By a change introduced in 1920 residents of a Saskatchewan municipality belonging to the association who might not want hail insurance could withdraw from paying the tax. The indemnity in Saskatchewan has remained at $5 an acre although recommendations have been made to the government that it be increased to $7.50 or $10 an acre. For the year ending on January 31, 1923, over 12,000,000 acres were assessed in that province at the flat rate and nearly 5,000,000 acres under crop at an additional rate of 12c. an acre. During the ten years, 1913-23, an average of about $1,000,000 a year was paid out in indemnities.

living outside the district an opportunity to apply for protection. Rates in Alberta were to be fixed annually by the board,* varying as the owner or occupant of land desired an indemnity payable in case of loss of six, eight or ten dollars an acre. In 1913 the Manitoba association declared itself in favor of "the principle of inter-municipal hail insurance with uniform appraisements." Nevertheless the government of Manitoba made no move in the matter until 1920, when it put through a bill giving municipalities the right to provide ratepayers with hail insurance by taxing their lands at the rate of four cents an acre. As it was first essential that twenty-five municipalities should agree to the terms of the act, and as this requirement has not yet been met, the proposed system in Manitoba remains inoperative.

Another important departure in which Saskatchewan led the way on the prairies was in connection with the question of agricultural credits. At its eleventh annual convention the Saskatchewan Grain Growers' Association took the stand that the provincial government should devise a method by which farm loans might be obtained at the lowest possible rates of interest. Premier Scott acknowledged that the farmers were handicapped in negotiating both short and long-term loans. In 1913 his government proceeded to appoint a royal commission to inquire into the matter of agricultural credits and to suggest remedial measures. This commission, of which C. A. Dunning, at the time general manager of the Saskatchewan Co-operative Elevator Company, Limited, was a member, brought in a lengthy report in October of the same year. The government, adhering closely to the commission's recommendations, authorized the formation of a Farm Mortgage Association under which were to be grouped local credit societies according to a modification of the German Landschaften plan. Any ten grain growers might set up a society and borrow money on their joint and several liability by means of mortgage bonds guaranteed by the government with repayment extending over a period of from fifteen to thirty-five years. However, the act, which would have brought this system into operation, has remained a dead letter on the Saskatchewan statute books. Subsequently

---

*Since 1918 the Alberta board in its most active years has insured approximately 2,000,000 acres or in other words has handled sixty to seventy per cent. of the hail insurance business of the province. Absence of a flat rate, higher indemnities, and apparently a greater hail risk, have caused the acreage assessments to be much heavier in Alberta than in Saskatchewan. The Alberta municipalities have recently advised the establishment for their system of a sliding scale of rates.

an agitation developed in the West in favor of the prairie governments going into the mortgage loan business in a centralized manner and upon a more elaborate scale. In 1916 the Manitoba Grain Growers' Association went on record as approving of the establishment of an agricultural credit bank under the wing of the government after the fashion of those existing in Western Australia and New Zealand, and ordered its directors to bring this proposition to the attention of the provincial authorities. The Manitoba government by an act assented to on March 9, 1917, created a Farm Loans Association which was to be under the direction of a board of five members, and was empowered to lend money on first mortgages to an amount equal to fifty per cent. of the valuation on farm property. The association's capital stock was fixed at one million dollars, with shares at five dollars, of which the government might hold one-half; borrowers had to own one share of stock for each one hundred dollars of the amount of the loan that was negotiated. Repayment was to be on an amortization plan covering principal and interest so as to extinguish the debt in thirty years.

Farm loan measures were also passed in 1917 by the legislatures of Saskatchewan and Alberta.* In both these provinces working capital might be provided for the scheme through appropriations made by the government or securities issued under the authority of the Treasurer's department. In the case of loans in Saskatchewan amortization could be spread over as many as forty years. A Live Stock Encouragement Act became law in Alberta the same year, allowing associations of five farmers or more to borrow money from the government for the purchase of certain kinds of stock. Furthermore, enactments of 1917 permitted the erection of rural credit societies in Manitoba and Alberta by means of which farmers would be accommodated with minor, short-term loans. A local society might be organized in Manitoba by not less than thirty-five farmers each of whom had subscribed for at least one share in it at one hundred dollars and of which ten

---

*In general loans are advanced under this sytem in the three provinces for: the acquisition of land for agricultural purposes; the making of permanent improvements on the land; activities calculated to increase the productiveness of land; and liabilities already incurred for the aforesaid purposes. In Manitoba and Alberta money can be borrowed for the purchase of live stock and equipment. By way of example it may be mentioned that the Saskatchewan board held first mortgages against land amounting to nearly $8,000,000 on December 31, 1922. It has been lending at six and one-half per cent. but has found difficulty in procuring funds through the government to enable it to quote that rate. Applications for loans have greatly exceeded the funds available.

per cent.* must be paid up at once. Loaning funds were to be obtained from the chartered banks. The maximum rate of interest that might be charged was seven per cent., of which the society would receive one per cent. and the banks the remainder. In 1920 the banks refused to abide any longer by these terms, and funds were then supplied to the societies by the government; a savings office was opened to take money on deposit, which upon being loaned to the government is mainly used to finance the societies. The original Alberta measure was superseded in 1922 by a co-operative credit act authorizing thirty farmers who had subscribed for shares of stock to form a society. Provision was made whereby the financial undertakings of these societies might receive the guarantee of the province of Alberta and, to an extent, of the rural municipalities.

POLICIES DURING THE WAR.

The outbreak of war in August, 1914, greatly enhanced the value of the Canadian grain belt in international economy, a fact which the western grain growers' organizations were not slow to recognize, and which led them to put forward their best efforts to meet all contingencies. In spite of heavy enlistments from the prairies they encouraged the maintenance of grain and live-stock production at their highest possible levels during the four years of struggle. Moreover, the three associations showed great liberality in making contributions, both material and monetary, to war objects. The "patriotic acre" idea took hold on the West soon after the declaration of hostilities; it was endorsed by the Manitoba Grain Growers' Association on January 13, 1915, in the following terms: "Be it resolved that we pledge ourselves, and that we seek to induce our fellow-members to pledge themselves, to give the outturns from one acre of grain, preferably wheat, of the crop of 1915 to the needs of the Empire." The Saskatchewan association on the other hand, soliciting a gift from each of

---

*This was increased to twenty-five per cent. in consequence of a recommendation to that effect made by a commission appointed to inquire into the operation of the act in 1922. The commission, which was composed of Professor W. T. Jackman, of Toronto University, and Francis J. Collyer, stated in its report that the Manitoba system was not properly supervised, that no check was put on the maximum liabilities of the individual societies, that the security offered by the borrowers was problematical and that it would be better to operate on advances from the banks than from the government. A stiff reply was forthcoming from the directors of the federated council of the societies, printed at Dauphin, which took up the criticisms of the report point by point and declared that the system had "more than justified itself." The government made a few changes in 1923, acting, to a limited extent, upon the suggestions of the Jackman-Collyer commission.

its members of the grain harvested from one or more acres, employed a comprehensive plan of having it milled and delivered across the ocean. Arrangements were made by which the Saskatchewan Co-operative Elevator Company, Limited, agreed to accept "patriotic acre" grain at prices quoted "on the track" for carload quantities. It was then ground into flour at cost by the milling companies, and the finished product shipped abroad, under directions from the military authorities, in sacks bearing the emblem of the Saskatchewan Grain Growers' Association. Five thousand acres in the province were devoted to this cause in 1915. The United Farmers of Alberta took steps at their 1915 convention to make a general appeal to their local unions for contributions of farm products and money to assist in the prosecution of the war. However, the Alberta association from the outset was wistfully looking ahead to the day when it was hoped that a suitable covenant of peace would be signed to end the conflict. "The aim," it affirmed in a resolution on this subject, "must be to make future wars between civilized nations impossible." The Grain Growers' Grain Company also adopted the policy of giving freely to war benefactions, contributing twelve thousand dollars to various funds in 1916.

When the federal government proposed in 1917 to conscript the young manhood of Canada there was no unanimity of opinion among organized grain growers on the issue. Nevertheless, once the Military Service Act had been assented to on August 29, its terms were for the most part uncomplainingly accepted. Still the Western associations, after the fashion of the United Farmers of Ontario, thought that wealth should be conscripted as well as men. The Manitoba association, meeting in convention on January 10, 1917, recorded its approval of the government's plan to take a census of the man-power of the country, but indicated its "abhorrence of private profiteering on the part of those engaged in the manufacturing or furnishing of war supplies of any kind," and urged that a census of wealth should also be taken. A national government, it believed, was the need of the hour. The *Grain Growers' Guide* agreed that there should be "a national government in a national crisis," but stated its belief, on May 30, that the question of conscription should be submitted to a referendum as had been done in Australia. Space will not permit of a discussion of the kaleidoscopic series of events which brought several Western political leaders into a Union government Cabinet under Sir Robert Borden in the autumn of 1917, including Hon. T. A. Crerar as Minister of Agriculture. The outcome of the federal election on December 16 gave a clear demonstration of the fact that the prairie provinces were strongly behind the new administration, although the organized grain growers on the whole had accepted Sir Robert Borden as Premier with manifest reluctance.

When the Manitoba Grain Growers' Association met in 1918, it called for a "complete mobilization of the man-power of the Dominion with a special view to the increase of food production," and to that end suggested that bona fide farmers and agricultural laborers should be kept at their occupations, that non-essential industries be closed, and that workers in such industries be drafted for farm operations. Likewise, a few weeks later the Saskatchewan Association, pointing to the non-essential industries that were running in Canada, demanded that they be halted for the duration of the war. But the Union government's abrogation of exemptions to the twenty to twenty-two-year classes of military conscripts, on April 20, while causing much resentment in the West, hardly raised the furore that it did in Ontario. Only in Alberta was any official notice taken of the matter among the grain growers' organizations. The day after the Quebec and Ontario farmers had massed their forces of protest at Ottawa on May 14, a press dispatch was printed throughout Canada stating that the Alberta association had declared that the government's policy of cancelling exemptions was necessary, and that farmers should abide by it everywhere. It would seem that a resolution to this effect had gone through at a meeting of the U.F.A. executive during the absence of H. W. Wood, the president. A controversy immediately broke forth in the ranks of the organization and as a sequel the executive had to change its attitude on the question. Wood appeared at Toronto before the special convention of the United Farmers of Ontario on June 7, and repudiated the telegraphic news that had been sent out. Then on June 13 he presented a memorial from his executive to the federal government, in which it was intimated that the labor situation on the farms of Alberta would be seriously affected by the revocation of exemptions, and that the U.F.A. would not be held answerable for the crippling of production if the young farmers were called up for service.

War conditions hastened the arrival in the prairie provinces of two important reforms which the grain growers' associations had consistently advocated. For a number of years each of them had favored the enfranchisement of women, and this was granted in all three provinces in 1916. Again, they had earnestly stood for a prohibition of the manufacture and sale of intoxicating liquors. Alberta moved first in this direction in 1916, when as the result of a special referendum the sale of liquor was intermitted in the province. The same year Manitoba also went over to prohibition by way of a referendum, and Saskatchewan, having tried the Gothenburg system for a short time, voted out its licensed shops.

Increasing demands for revenue during the war had caused the grain growers in their annual conventions to urge upon the federal government the need for a fiscal measure in the form of a graduated income tax, to which they received an answer in 1917 when the government passed the Income War Tax Act. The United Farmers of Alberta in 1917 advised that the Dominion government should "take over, co-ordinate and operate all railways in Canada with the set purpose of finally owning them at the conclusion of the war." Through force of circumstances this request has been largely met, as the capital stock of the defunct Canadian Northern Railway was acquired by the government the same year, the Grand Trunk Pacific threw itself on the country's mercy in March, 1919, and, after arbitration proceedings, the Grand Trunk Railway was included with other government lines in 1921 to form a unified system of transportation, known as the Canadian National Railways, having over twenty-two thousand miles of track. The attitude of the Western associations on the subject of the tariff since 1911 will be dealt with in chapter XXVIII.

DEVELOPMENT OF THE PRAIRIE ORGANIZATIONS.

That the grain growers' movements had expanded phenomenally during the period of the war is amply borne out by statistical evidence. The aggregate membership of the three organizations had continued to grow until at the close of 1919, some six or eight months before the post-bellum liquidation of grain prices began, it had reached a high total of seventy-five thousand, of whom approximately six thousand were women and juniors. The Saskatchewan association had thirty-six thousand, the U.F.A., twenty-nine thousand,

and the Manitoba association,* ten thousand members. On January 1, 1920, the rural population of the prairie provinces was upwards of a million and a quarter, and of this number it may be computed that there were three hundred thousand to three hundred and fifty thousand males who were in a position to claim admission to one or other of the grain growers' bodies. On this basis it would appear that at least one male person in five employed at farming occupations in the three provinces had definitely cast in his lot with the grain growers' movements. Added significance is lent to the estimate by the fact that a number of foreign-born blocs exist on the prairies which in some cases impose quite a hindrance to the work of organization.

The supremacy of the grain growers' associations in the West has only been challenged by one other body making its appeal to the farming population. In 1916, S. E. Haight, a prominent member of the Non-Partisan League, having arrived in Saskatchewan from North Dakota, took up his abode at Swift Current, whence he began zealously to propagate the doctrines of that organization. Already by 1917 it was estimated that the League had gained three thousand adherents in Saskatchewan and two thousand in Alberta. A paper, the *Non-Partisan Leader*, was started at Swift Current, and a second organ published for a time at Calgary. Advocating as it did the nationalization of not only all public utilities but as well of various major industries and systems of banking and insurance, the League taught forms of agrarian radicalism in which the Canadian farmer had hitherto been untutored. It was intensely political in its aims, placing candidates in the field with some degree of success in the provincial elections of 1917 in both Alberta and Saskatchewan. Yet it became increasingly apparent that the potentialities of the League in Canada were likely to remain circumscribed, and, when an opportunity was afforded the Alberta section in 1919 to join hands with the U.F.A. for political purposes, it gladly acquiesced and then faded out of view. No harmonious relations, however, were ever established between the League and the Saskatchewan Grain Growers' Association.

Before the close of 1921 a wide disparity had arisen in America between the prices of agricultural products and of

---

*On January 7, 1920, this organization became known as the United Farmers of Manitoba.

manufactured articles, which brought economic hardship. This price maladjustment was of special significance for the Canadian grain belt because it was passing through a cycle of drought which lasted until the abundant crop season of 1923. The membership rolls of the Grain Growers' Associations as a result showed a great falling off, although a tendency toward revival is now distinguishable. To deal with even a fraction of the resolutions that have come before their annual conventions since 1920 would be impossible; resolutions numbering all told, for example, 368, were presented in 1923. Questions relating to the marketing of farm products, banking and agricultural credits, alternate shipping routes, and immigration have loomed up most largely for consideration. An outline of the diversity of views entertained on the first topic will be given in Chapter XXVI. In 1923 the Manitoba association asked for a Canadian National Bank to be run by the Dominion government in competition with the other chartered institutions. For some years the U.F.A. demanded a provincial government bank operating under a federal charter, but its 1924 convention was told by the Greenfield administration that this was strictly inadvisable. Modifications of the farm loans systems in the West are being sought, which may bear fruit in the near future. The three associations have continuously urged the completion of the Hudson Bay Railway; in fact, on January 24, 1924, the Saskatchewan Grain Growers' Association spent half a day in discussing this time-worn theme. The Alberta and Saskatchewan bodies have recently shown a very marked interest in the grain-marketing route by way of the Pacific,*

---

*Vancouver has been declared a terminal point by the Dominion government, so that farmers may now ship grain directly to that harbour to be officially weighed and inspected. The Vancouver Harbour Commissioners assumed control of the government's elevator at the port in August, 1923, and already have an addition to that elevator, a large new terminal and a grain jetty under construction. According to the jetty system several boats can be loaded with grain at one time. The commissioners propose to develop a special area where private terminals may be erected. Contracts have been let by a British grain company for a public terminal, and other commercial companies are likely to build elevators in the next few years. Grain can come with advantage to Vancouver from as far east as Medicine Hat, even though freight rates by rail have not been equalized between the Port Arthur and Vancouver routes. The average saving in making a shipment of grain from Medicine Hat to Great Britain by way of Vancouver is two and a half cents a hundred pounds, and from Calgary over the same route six and a half cents a hundred pounds. The movement of a bushel of grain from Calgary to Vancouver costs fifteen cents and thence by ocean to Liverpool costs approximately twenty cents more. Freighters take about thirty-two days for the 8,547 mile journey via the Panama Canal to Liverpool; meanwhile the grain has been in store on board ship. Vancouver will always have superior status because it is an all-year port, although it is slightly handicapped by being at the end of trans-mountain railway lines. 25,000,000 bushels of grain were shipped through it in 1922-3, and it is expected that close to 60,000,000 bushels will follow this route in 1923-4. As the Peace River grain belt is settled, the value for Western Canada of the ocean lane through the Panama Canal, will become even more strikingly manifest.

and the fixation of rates necessary to make it more profitable. Encouragement to immigration in times of stress has been condemned, although the Saskatchewan association has favored a selective policy. Two new journals, the *U.F.A.*, published at Calgary, and the *Progressive*, at Saskatoon, are now being issued with the sanction of the Alberta and Saskatchewan associations respectively.

WOMEN'S SECTIONS IN THE WEST.

The auxiliary organization of farm women on the prairies, now an indispensable phase of the grain growers' movements, came about by an evolutionary process. For the first ten years, 1902-12, grain trade and tariff considerations had weighed so heavily on the minds of those who were directing the movements that they failed to recognize an obliqueness in their development. So vague, indeed, had been their apprehension of the problems that were of special concern to the mothers and daughters of the grain belt that as a rule they had left these entirely untouched. Hence, it was only natural that the women should seek entrance to the associations, believing as they did that they might be of service to their own sex in many practical ways, and ingeniously hoping that they might introduce a humanizing influence where it was badly needed. In 1912 Frances M. Beynon, an editorial writer on the *Grain Growers' Guide*, began to tell the farm women through the columns of that journal that they must gain their appointed place in the sun, and organize for the betterment of themselves and their industry as a whole. As the result of an interchange of ideas, early in 1913, between Miss Beynon and F. W. Green, secretary of the Saskatchewan Grain Growers' Association, arrangements were effected whereby a gathering of farm women was held in February in the Convocation Hall of the provincial university at Saskatoon while the association was meeting in another part of the city. The women were addressed upon a variety of themes by representative speakers, and after some deliberation resolved to launch, if possible, an organization that would be auxiliary to the association at large. Notice of their desire was conveyed to the grain growers' convention, and the following year, when the association assembled in Moosejaw, its constitution was revised to allow for the establishment of a women's section. Full membership standing was accorded to the women in the association; they were permitted to have their own executive officers and might convene apart. It was intended, though, that there should be no "separation of interest" between them and the main body of the association. In this manner the first farm women's organization of its kind in Canada, that is, one entirely free from government tutelage, had come into existence. All dues collected from the women were to be paid into the central treasury, but it became customary to turn back to the section a certain sum every year for organization and other expenses. Convention programmes were drawn up so that the women, having despatched their business, might be present with the men when matters of general import were under discussion. Particular attention has been given by the women's section in Saskatchewan to work among the young farm people, which has led to the formation of thirty to forty junior locals.

An amendment to the constitution of the United Farmers of Alberta, made in 1913, opened the ranks of that association to women, and quite a sprinkling of them attended its annual convention of 1914. Next year a larger group put in an appearance when the association met in Edmonton, and under authority from it created an auxiliary body to be known as the United Farm Women of Alberta. This, as in the case of the women's section in Saskatchewan, was to form an integral part of the general organization, with power to conduct its own affairs and set up its own local unions. The section in Alberta throve rapidly, and in point of membership soon outranked its sister organization in Saskatchewan. The name of Mrs. Walter Parlby, of Alix, appointed president of the U.F.W.A. in 1916, is eminently connected with the pioneer efforts of the Alberta women to make their auxiliary a success. By January, 1920, the U.F.W.A. had nearly two hundred locals and three thousand members. Meanwhile a junior organization which it was hoped would be a nurturing ground for future leaders in the movement had been duly constituted in 1919. A special feature of the junior work was the institution of an annual conference for farm boys and girls at the University of Alberta, where a week's course of study has been given and an opportunity afforded for outdoor sports and other recreations.

According to a revision of the constitution of the Manitoba Grain Growers' Association, which occurred in 1913, farmers' wives, and daughters over sixteen years of age, might become associate members of the organization without fee. But it was not until 1916, at the time of the regular convention in Brandon, that the Manitoba farm women first sat apart. Upon this occasion they appointed a provisional board of directors, and then, within two years having set up a number of locals, they applied for the constitutional privilege of establishing a women's section of the association to further, as they said, "their educational, social, political and æsthetic interests in the way deemed necessary." Their request was granted on January 9, 1918, by a standing vote of the Manitoba association in convention: by the close of 1919 their section had over one thousand members. Steps towards the creation of a national alliance among organized farm women were taken in 1918, resulting in the formation a year later at Brandon of the Interprovincial Council of Farm Women with Mrs. Violet McNaughton, of Harris, Saskatchewan, as president. This body was subsequently taken into the Canadian Council of Agriculture, where it was allowed five representatives who might participate in the council's deliberations on a parity with the men, namely: one from each of the three women's sections in the West; one from the U.F.W.O.; and one from the women's staff of the *Grain Growers' Guide.*

From the outset the women's auxiliaries on the prairies have had a plethora of matters to engage their attention, and their achievements have been noteworthy. In the wider field of endeavor their best work has probably been done in connection with questions of public health and rural education. When the women's organizations arose, facilities for procuring medical aid in many parts of the grain country were of the scantiest, a situation which has been vastly remedied through their efforts. They stressed the imperative need for hospital accommodation and equipment in areas removed from the main centres, which has led both Saskatchewan and Alberta to enact legislation providing for the construction of hospitals under municipal control, and a large number of these have already been built in the two provinces. They have also given effective support to the campaign for public health nurses in rural communities, and for obstetrical nurses to supplement the work of the medical profession in outlying districts. Again, with tangible results they have advocated the institution of child clinics, medical inspection in the elementary schools, and segregation of the mentally defective. On account of the alleged tendency of doctors to throng to the cities, the public health committee of the Alberta section have even suggested a nationalization of the medical profession. A great diversity of recommendations have been made by the farm women's organizations with respect to the betterment of rural education, some of which have borne fruit. They have striven to secure more highly qualified teachers; changes in the curriculum to suit the needs of the farming communities; consolidated schools where expedient; and more efficient and harmonious methods of trustee control. The Manitoba section asked in 1917 that there should be one woman on every rural school board. Besides, in various places hot lunches have been obtained for the children, and the school grounds and buildings beautified and improved.

(Moreover the women's sections in the West have been in the vanguard of the forces fighting for the temperance cause. They have provided rest rooms for the farm women in the towns, taken a strong stand in defence of the property rights of women, delved into the vexing question of the parental custody of children, and elaborated their views on problems of marriage and divorce. They have given close study to the topic of immigration, particularly as it has been related to the introduction of domestic help on the farm lands of Western Canada. Many of their locals have embraced the advantages of having travelling or permanent libraries; some have engaged in co-operative trading; others have been busy fostering community effort; while all have supplied their farm women members with programmes of a social and inspirational value.)

CHAPTER XXV

In the Maritime Provinces, Quebec, and British Columbia

A STUDY of the official census figures issued decennially by the Dominion government will indicate the leading cause for organization among farmers of the Maritime Provinces within recent years. The returns for 1921 as compared with those for 1911 disclose the vitiating influence exercised upon agricultural conditions in that part of Canada during the ten-year period by rural depletion, accompanied by a wholesale abandonment of farms. It will be seen that the rural population of the provinces by the Atlantic declined by 11,544 from 1911 to 1921. On the other hand, 73,917 more persons in the same interval took up their residence in the towns and cities. Meanwhile, occupied farms had been deserted to the number of 6,571, having a total area of 791,215 acres. The Maritime governments have tended to keep this skeleton of theirs securely locked up, and to gloss over an unhappy situation, not yet remedied, by the publication of optimistic agricultural reports. The farmers, living close to the soil and fully aware of their economic disabilities, have been seeking by forms of combined action to make their industry both more profitable and attractive, and to stop, if possible, the trek from the rural districts.

The present-day farmers' movements in the Maritime Provinces burgeoned out in the western counties of New Brunswick. On April 23, 1918, a throng of two hundred farmers gathered at Woodstock from the adjacent counties of Carleton, York and Victoria to discuss the feasibility of establishing an association for protective purposes. J. J. Morrison was present from Ontario in an advisory capacity. After deliberation the United Farmers of New Brunswick were formed, with C. L. Smith, of Woodstock, as the association's first president. The new organization at once pledged its support to the greater production campaign then under way as a war measure throughout Canada. It stated its intention to nominate experienced farmers in rural constituencies to contest all future elections. Besides, it urged: that two farmers be appointed to the Board of Railway Commissioners for Canada; that an abattoir be built at St. John; that public means be devised to break open and snow-plough the country roads in winter; and that there be governmental regulation of the sale of mill feeds in the province. Organization of the United Farmers of New Brunswick proceeded by leaps and bounds during 1918 and 1919, so that by the close of the latter year they had sixty-five local branches and a paid-up membership of five thousand. In the meantime Thomas W. Caldwell had been appointed president of the association and C. Gordon Sharpe, its secretary-treasurer.

On March 25, 1920, the New Brunswick body was admitted to membership in the Canadian Council of Agriculture, and the following week saw the first issue at Moncton of its official journal, the *United Farmers' Guide*. This paper was financed by the *Grain Growers' Guide*, of Winnipeg, and had as its editor G. Grassie Archibald. By 1921 the association was computed to have about ten thousand members distributed among 141 branches. Between 1918-21, at one time or another, it went on record as favoring the establishment of union stock yards and a cold storage plant in the Maritime Provinces; taxation of wilderness and unimproved lands; liberal homesteading privileges and rights of land purchase for all males over eighteen years of age; total prohibition of the liquor traffic; a reliable system of publishing crop statistics and reports; systematic protection of New Brunswick forests from fire and too close cutting; regulation of the stumpage rates to prevent exploitation; better county roads to assist in the marketing of farm products; economic development by the government of hydro-electric power systems; co-operative agricultural credits; government aid for an extension library; and better mail delivery and telephone facilities in the rural sections.

When on January 29, 1920, the Nova Scotia Agricultural Association had concluded its regular annual sessions at Kentville, a few score members, remaining over, held a conference on the subject of farmers' movements in Canada and the possibility of extending their benefits to Nova Scotia. Sentiment at the meeting was rigorously hostile to the machine methods known to be in vogue in connection with provincial politics, and a resolution was passed calling for the creation of an independent farmers' party. A committee was named to discover what success might attend an effort to establish an association in Nova Scotia upon the model of those existing in New Brunswick, Ontario and the West. This committee, having fully explored the situation, decided that the time was ripe for action, and therewith an organization meeting was convened at Truro on April 14. Three hundred farmers attended, and heard an inspiriting address by J. J. Morrison upon the need for an effective development of agrarian class-consciousness. The meeting authorized the formation of the United Farmers of Nova Scotia, accepting for the time being the constitution of the New Brunswick association as a working basis. Henry L. Taggart, of Belmont, was appointed as president of the new body and Frederick A. Chipman, of Nictaux West, as secretary. The *United Farmers' Guide* became the association's organ, and it immediately signified its endorsation of the terms of the New National Policy.

The story of how the United Farmers of Nova Scotia participated with some degree of success in the provincial elections of 1920 will be told elsewhere. On July 13 of that year at a regularly constituted meeting of the Canadian Council of Agriculture the association was given full membership standing. Such headway did the movement make in the counties of Nova Scotia that within a year from its inception it had twenty-five hundred farmers in its ranks. At a convention held in Truro on March 22-23, 1921, support was pledged to a properly-enforced prohibition act, while a very trenchant debate arose over the subject of rural education. One resolution adopted made a rather startling attack upon the administration of schools in the province. "In Nova Scotia," it stated, "the children of the rural parts are not receiving an adequate common-school education. . . . In the opinion of this convention, our school system and management should be revised and reformed, having in view, among other things, a radical simplification of the curriculum, limiting the number of subjects taught, and aiming at thoroughness and accuracy as a mind habit."

Meanwhile, organization of all the Maritime Provinces had become an accomplished fact when the United Farmers of Prince Edward Island were formed as an association on September 29, 1920. By the date of its first annual convention at Charlottetown, January 25, 1921, this body had sixteen locals in working order. Among its original officers were: Horace Wright, of Bedeque, president; and Preston

Ellis, of Tyne Valley, secretary. Special transportation issues at once engaged the attention of the island association; demands were made for a better ferry system to the province of New Brunswick across Northumberland Strait, and for the introduction of a uniform wide gauge on all P.E.I. railways.

The United Farmers of New Brunswick set up a company for the practice of consumers' co-operation and to handle farm produce in 1918, the activities of which were later extended to Nova Scotia. By 1920 this concern had a paid-up capitalization of $268,000 and was operating twenty-three chain stores on a federated basis. Capital in the stores was owned locally, but the system was under the control, financially and otherwise, of a central office. Deflation following the war brought adversity to the company, which was heightened by insufficiency of capitalization and suspicions entertained against the central office. Some stores failed, and at a meeting held in Fredericton in February, 1922, it was decided that reorganization would be necessary. As a result the remaining stores assumed the obligations of the central office pro rata upon the understanding that when these were met each store would be on an independent footing. In 1922 the three Maritime associations were united for economy's sake, and joint secretarial headquarters established. About the same time the official journal was removed to Gardenvale, Quebec, and there published under the shortened title of the *Farmers' Guide*. The movements in the Maritime Provinces are now in a dormant state except in certain localities, but undoubtedly will flourish again, since the grievances which gave them birth are as potent as ever.

LES FERMIERS-UNIS DE QUEBEC.

(In the course of its development in the province of Quebec the Grange had made its appeal almost exclusively to farmers whose mother tongue was English. The Order of the Patrons of Industry, on the other hand, had taken many farmers of French ancestry into its fold, although its spread had been more particularly in the English-speaking communities.) The latest movement, however, to arise in that province, Les Fermiers-Unis de Quebec (The United Farmers of Quebec) has had a preponderating influence among cultivators, or habitants, as they often ingenuously call themselves, of French origin. The rebuff administered by the Borden government to the Quebec delegation which swarmed Ottawa in May, 1918, was not easily forgotten, and may be considered as one of the prime causes of the new organization's formation. The association, Les Fermiers-Unis de Quebec, was established at a gathering held in Montreal on July 2, 1919, presided over by Joseph Forget, of St. Janvier. The movement appears to have expanded first in the counties stretching down the right bank of the Ottawa River, and then to have found lodgement along the St. Lawrence. On January 9, 1920, another meeting was convened at Hull to complete the work of organization. A. H. Clement, of Buckingham, who was of Swiss-French origin, was elected as president of the association, an office which he was to hold for the next four years; J. P. Brady, of Masson, became its secretary. The policy was introduced of dividing Quebec up into districts, each of which sent representatives to a central board of directors. From the outset Les Fermiers-Unis de Quebec had political aims, and in October, 1920, ran Nérée Morin, a typical habitant, in a provincial bye-election in Kamouraska; Morin was elected over his Liberal opponent. J. P. Brady, attending the U.F.O. convention in December of this year, stated that the Quebec association had already set up twenty clubs.

President Clement told the Drayton tariff commission, when it sat at Montreal on November 7, 1920, that a downward revision of the duties was essential to the prosperity of Canadian agriculture. However, from the tenor of his remarks it became clear that the demands of Les Fermiers-Unis de Quebec with respect to the tariff were more moderate than those of their organized brethren in Ontario. Clement asked for "a general lowering of the tariff on all articles required for the cultivation of the soil and for the support of the family." He stated that the average rate of duty on goods required for industrial purposes and maintenance by the agriculturist was twenty-one per cent.; but, he urged, Canadian factories should still be able to operate at a profit if the average rate was cut down to twelve per cent. On May 28, 1921, Joseph Lambert unsuccessfully contested a federal bye-election in the Yamaska riding as a representative of the Quebec organization. Then, as the time for a general Dominion election drew near, Les Fermiers-Unis de Quebec held a special convention at Montreal to discuss the extent to which they should participate in it. It was agreed to put independent farmer candidates in the field, but upon a platform distinct from that of the New National Policy.   This Quebec platform when evolved, demanded: a relationship with Great Britain that would give full play to the interests of Canada; government support for measures looking towards international peace; proper respect in Canada for rights of a social, racial and religious character; development of the Dominion's natural resources; a permanent commission to investigate industrial matters, foreign exchange conditions and questions of fiscal policy; a technical commission to control the national railways; reduction of naval and military expenditures to a minimum; economy in all administrative branches of the government; admission only of immigrants suited to the development of the country; a published statement by parliamentary candidates of their election funds before and after elections, and by newspapers of their ownership; a tax on unearned increments; the appointment of trade commissioners abroad to find an outlet for Canadian products; and a repeal of the conscription act at the next session of parliament.   Some twenty-five candidates were nominated for the election, but on account of the engulfing tide of Liberalism which swept the province none of them were returned. The Quebec association was admitted into the Canadian Council of Agriculture in 1923.

That Les Fermiers-Unis de Quebec has remained a virile organization was in evidence at its annual convention held in February, 1924, at Montreal.   Delegates were in attendance from twenty-two counties of the province.   The movement has now gained firm foothold in the counties south of the St. Lawrence from Montmagny to Châteauguay.   A resolution submitted by habitants from the Lac-Saint-Jean region up the Saguenay river was approved, urging that the provincial government should grant the same aid to settlers in Quebec as was accorded by the Ontario government to settlers in its newer parts.   The convention recorded its opposition to the proposal to place an embargo on pulpwood, and decided to ask the Quebec legislature to assume as a public burden the indebtedness incurred by the rural municipalities in building local roads.   The association's executive committee was authorized to lay before Premier Taschereau the need of immediately creating a system of agricultural credits in the province.   A. R. McMaster, member of parliament for Brome County, addressed the gathering on the tariff and other national problems. Wilfred Bastien, who farms land in Laval

County on the outskirts of Montreal, was elected president. Some years ago, when real estate values were soaring high, Bastien was offered a very attractive sum for his holding, but refused, desiring, as he said, that his ten children should have the advantages of being reared on the soil. The organized farmers of Quebec have two organs: the *Farmers' Guide;* and a well-edited weekly published at Montreal in French, *Le Bulletin des Agriculteurs.*

THE UNITED FARMERS OF BRITISH COLUMBIA.

Down until 1917 the province of British Columbia remained entirely outside the sphere of influence of agrarian movements in Canada, except that in 1897 the Farmers' Alliance had endeavored to set up a few locals within its borders and in 1908 (vide Chapter VII) one short-lived grange had been formed at New Westminster. Strictly speaking, the physical characteristics of British Columbia and the diversity of its farm occupations have been, and still are, the main hindrances to an evolution of class-consciousness among its rural dwellers. Along the coast line no serious obstacle is presented to unity of action, but back in the interior where the fertile lands of the older settlements lie in isolated "pockets" among the mountains, and farther north the river valleys are just being opened to the colonist, there is less response to a broader class appeal. Farmers' Institutes were authorized by the government in 1897 and have spread widely in the province; besides an array of industrial associations have arisen in connection with the production of fruit, milk, cheese and butter, honey and other commodities. Of these latter the British Columbia Fruit Growers' Association began to develop into a closely-knit and influential organization after 1904, when the apple harvests of the Okanagan Valley and West Kootenay grew justly famous.

Interest in the formation of a class organization among farmers of the Pacific province resembling those in existence in other parts of Canada was first stimulated through the efforts of J. L. Pridham, of Victoria, and led to the institution of the United Farmers of British Columbia in 1917. A difficult task awaited the new body. As the majority of its incoming members were also enrolled in the Institutes and industrial associations referred to above, it was faced with the necessity of shaping its policies to suit these divergent elements. More especially did the fruit growers throng into the movement, and as a price of their allegaince impelled the association to favor protection for their industry. Their claim was that the import duty of ninety cents a barrel on apples was essential if they were to withstand the competition of Washington and Oregon growers, and thereby retain the extensive market they had built up in their own province and on the prairies. It is noteworthy that when the U.F.B.C. met in convention on February 20, 1918, its only tariff request was for an abolition of all rates of duty on farm implements. It also advocated at this time the exemption from taxation of improvements on farm lands; development of agricultural education in British Columbia; supervision of the municipal system and schools of the province with the object of securing greater economy in administration; and a prohibition of Oriental aliens from gaining control of agricultural lands.

A marked expansion of the association occurred within the following three years, with the result that by the time of its fifth annual convention in February, 1921, it had 149 locals and about five thousand members. Meanwhile negotiations had been conducted with a view to amalgamating the leading farm organizations of the province into one more effective body, but it had been found impossible to reach a satisfactory basis of agreement among them. Considerable hesitancy was shown by the U.F.B.C. in committing itself to a policy of independent political action; in fact, the 1921 convention expressly declared that the movement must be kept within purely economic channels. Resolutions were adopted at this meeting favoring: a scheme of road improvement in the rural districts; government investigation of the provincial water-powers with the expectation of placing them under a hydro-electric commission; a strict enforcement of the weed laws on the Indian reserves; a system of agricultural credits; representation from the organized farmers on the Board of Railway Commissioners for Canada; and the compulsory stamping on all goods produced by Orientals for sale in Canada. It was reported that a canvass of the locals had shown them to be almost unanimously opposed to an acceptance of the New National Policy, although they had indicated a desire for friendly relations with the other farmers' associations through the medium of the Canadian Council of Agriculture. R. A. Copeland, of Lumley, was reappointed president of the organization for 1921-22. In spite of the convention's dictum with respect to entering politics, seven of the thirteen British Columbia ridings had unofficial Progressive candidates in the federal election of December 6, 1921, and of these three were elected: Thomas G. McBride (Cariboo); Levi W. Humphrey (Kootenay West); and Alan W. Neill (Comox-Alberni).

(The matter of taking political action was again up for discussion at the annual convention of 1922 and elicited warm discussion. It was finally resolved that the central executive should be debarred from participating in politics, but that the locals might bring out parliamentary candidates, if they chose, under the guidance of a special organization committee. So far, however, attempts to form a distinctly agrarian party in British Columbia have proven abortive. The only business activity of the U.F.B.C. has been the co-operative sale of stumping powder to its membership for land-clearing purposes. The association has favored: a national system of marketing grain; development of the Pacific-Panama grain route; establishment of packing houses under the control of the Dominion government; and a plan for the shipment of chilled meats to European markets. But its inflexible stand on the tariff still renders inexpedient its admission to the Canadian Council of Agriculture.)

CHAPTER XXVI

THE GREAT CO-OPERATIVE ENTERPRISES

THE UNITED Farmers' Co-operative Company, Limited, which became in March, 1914, the accepted trading medium of the newly-organized agrarian movement in Ontario (vide Chapter XXIII) well-nigh perished in its first few months of operation. It had started inauspiciously: the farmers were soon after busy seeding and harrowing, and, moreover, during the summer were unsteadied like other classes in society by the lowering war clouds of Europe, which in August burst into deluge. Little heed was given to the company's appeal for investment capital or business, and only by rigid self-denial were W. C. Good, its president, and J. J. Morrison, its secretary-treasurer, able to tide it over safely until winter. The original capitalization was for ten thousand dollars divided into shares at twenty-five dollars apiece, of which as many as ten might be held by any individual or corporate body. By February, 1915, the company had fifty-eight corporate shareholders including U.F.O. branches, Institute clubs and granges, and thirty-three individual shareholders. Its business turnover for 1914, which had been exclusively in farmers' supplies on a commission basis, totalled thirty-three thousand dollars.

During 1915 care was taken to enter into more intimate and lucrative arrangements with manufacturers, and soon the company was making better headway. Sales this year amounted to $226,000; in 1916 they were over $400,000, and by 1917 had crept up to $1,800,000, when a dividend of seven per cent. was declared. A trade bulletin was first put out in 1915, and the company began to consider the practicability of entering the field of co-operative marketing. By February, 1916, 183 shares had been sold, but of these sixty-five per cent. were held by corporate bodies without legal status, which constituted a difficulty in that, whenever a corporate body became dormant, a distribution of profits to its former membership was impossible. As a result, when it was decided in 1917 to increase the company's capitalization to $250,000, and

311

a stock-selling campaign was inaugurated, the policy was adopted of disposing of shares mainly to individuals. It may be pointed out that lack of continuity in its management was an initial difficulty with which the organization had to contend; between 1914-18 four different men were in charge of its affairs.

So far the company had restricted itself to a commission business in binder twine, implements, coal, harness, groceries and other such articles, in the sale of which, more or less directly to the farmers, an economy was effected. However, when a special committee, appointed to inquire into the advisability of the company going into the co-operative marketing of live stock, reported favorably in 1918, steps were taken in Feburary, 1919, to place an expert staff at the Union Stock Yards in West Toronto, and to solicit, in the company's name, shipments of cattle, hogs, etc., from all parts of the province. This department at once leapt into prominence and began to turn in profits; by December 1, 3,682 cars of stock had been handled at the Toronto yards, while the company opened a service at Montreal the following year. Again, in 1919, the co-operative trading department was expanded by setting up eight branch' stores at outside points so that the farmers might be afforded local purchasing facilities. Share capital in these stores was sold to farmers in the neighborhood, but was held through the central company which exercised full jurisdiction over them. W. C. Good had resolutely opposed this plan, urging that individual co-operative societies should finance the stores and operate them as federated units under the company.

After almost seven years of activity the United Farmers' Co-operative Company, Limited, found itself at the time of its annual meeting on December 14, 1920, a large-scale commercial enterprise. Its turnover for the year, reckoned on the basis of after-war, peak prices, had been about twenty millions dollars; fifty-three hundred cars had been consigned to its livestock department; its retail stores had been increased in number to thirty-eight. During the year four new departments had been added under its control, and a subsidiary wholesale company established. The Toronto Creamery had been purchased in the spring, and turned into a department to receive cream on delivery; this has been from the first one of the company's most profitable ventures. Besides, there had been created: an egg and poultry department, later to be known as the produce department; a seed-cleaning department; and a fruit section, which in time became the farm products department, to handle not only fruit but hay, straw, alfalfa, potatoes and mixed vegetables. Then, with the purpose in view of providing supplies for the retail stores and individual farmers and clubs that bought staple wares, separate articles of incorporation had been obtained for the General Wholesalers, Limited, which was housed with the main company. Alterations, meanwhile, had been made in the co-operative company's charter, raising its capitalization to one million dollars, and stipulating that any person or corporate body might hold up to forty shares of stock; before the end of the year this amount had been over-subscribed and the company had more than twenty thousand shareholders. Steps were then inaugurated to arrange the shareholders in groups in order that they might delegate their voting powers at the annual meetings, but this has never been made effective.

However, as trade and industry in Ontario approached a condition of stagnation in 1921, there were manifest indications that the company had been too precipitate and incautious in the development of its retail store system, and was not sufficiently fortified against a deflation in the prices of farm produce. At the beginning of the year it had stocks of merchandise and farm produce on hand which were inventoried as worth over one million dollars. Before the next annual meeting, which was held in January, 1922, the prices of the staple articles in which it dealt had depreciated in some instances as much as sixty per cent., while the egg and poultry market had been disastrously uncertain. Serious losses had been borne, resulting in an impairment of capital and a reduction in the book value of shares in the company to around seventeen dollars apiece. Eight stores had been closed during the year, and, as the remainder continued to drop money for the company, the policy was now pursued of gradually eliminating them. This was accomplished by October 31, 1923, when the company's balance sheet showed that the winding-up process had cut its paid-up capital down to one-third of its original value. The live stock, creamery, and other departments of the business had met with no small measure of success, and the management, in the annual report, was able to show that they had been operating at a profit, and they continued to do so in 1924.

EVOLUTION OF UNITED GRAIN GROWERS, LIMITED.

The leasing agreement for the use of the Manitoba elevator system, to which representatives of the provincial government and the Grain Growers' Grain Company had appended their signatures in 1912, was continued from year to year. Though the company encountered a heavy loss in operating the system in 1912-13, and took small gains therefrom until the harvesting of a plentiful crop in 1915, it decided to keep paying rental for the elevators, since by controlling them it was able to enhance its power in the grain trade. In so doing, however, it had to reconcile itself to the fact that when crops were poor, and competition keen, especially on the part of the milling companies, its profits would be correspondingly low and possibly non-existent. Then, to supplement this leased system, the company adopted the policy of constructing or buying elevators of its own; by 1916 it had fourteen of these in Manitoba and thirty in Saskatchewan. The year 1912, too, was important in the company's history, in that it marked its entrance into the terminal elevator business just as soon as it was discovered that the prospect of the federal government taking over the terminals was becoming very remote. Negotiations were opened with the Canadian Pacific Railway for the acquisition under lease of its great public elevators "B" and "E" at Fort William, with a combined capacity of two million five hundred thousand bushels; upon the completion of terms, these were operated as one elevator. Again, in order that it might be in the market for low-grade or rejected grain, the company purchased the small mixing and cleaning elevator "H" at Fort William; this latter was burned down in March, 1916, but was replaced by another elevator, "H," having a capacity of six hundred thousand bushels and equipped with a modern drying apparatus, on a fine site at Port Arthur, with six hundred feet frontage on the lake.

The company set up a co-operative supply department in 1912 to dispose of staple commodities to the farmers in carload lots or less. Such goods as coal, lumber, flour, binder twine, apples, fence posts, barbed and woven wire, etc., were shipped either to individual farmers or local associations at the lowest possible cash prices. In 1914 the sale of farm machinery and implements was added to the department, but the efficient agency methods of regular companies handling implements and machinery in the West retarded growth in that direction. The same year timber limits, estimated to cut two hundred million feet of timber, were acquired near Hutton, B.C., on the line of the Grand Trunk Pacific Railway, east of Fort George, from which the company hoped to supply lumber and other building materials to the prairie farmers at reduced prices. But, as the war soon intervened, this tract was practically left untouched until 1917, when a saw mill was built at a cost of two hundred and fifty thousand dollars.

Although the Grain Growers' Grain Company had originally set out only to buy grain on commission, its intention had been sooner or later to enter the export market. This it had proceeded to do in 1910, but after a three-years trial found that it was dropping a good deal of money through inexperienced management. Either it must relinquish this end of the business or put it upon a new basis. The solution adopted was to transfer the work of the department to a subsidiary organization, formed in 1914, under the laws of Manitoba, as the Grain Growers' Export Company, Limited. A highly-qualified manager was chosen for the company and substantial profits reaped at once. But owing to the fact that the most of the grain export business was carried on through the United States, it was found expedient to establish another subsidiary in 1916, the Grain Growers' Export Company, Inc., with a charter in New York State. Practically all the stock in these two organizations is held by the parent grain company. The manager of the New York company has supervision over the Canadian concern. When, as a result of war conditions, private exporting of grain was interrupted in 1917, the Canadian company was allowed to send its proportion of wheat to the seaports under authority from the Canada Wheat Board. The American subsidiary, on the other hand, gave its services for twenty-two months to the Wheat Export Company, of New York, taking main charge during that period of the shipment of oats to Europe. Meanwhile, in 1913, a small business had been acquired at New Westminster, B.C., and under the name of the Grain Growers' British Columbia Agency employed to distribute supplies to the farmers of that province; from 1914-16, years of depression on the Pacific coast, it was operated at a loss but then began to pick up; twelve local depots were organized on the British Columbia mainland and on Vancouver Island.

The two most outstanding events in the history of the Grain Growers' Grain Company during the war period were: the formation of its live-stock department, and its amalgamation with the Alberta Farmers' Co-operative Elevator Company, Limited. The live-stock department had its origin in 1916, when an office was opened at the Union Stock Yards in St. Boniface, Manitoba, to receive co-operative shipments of car lots of live stock for sale from farmers or their organizations. A live-stock office, which the Alberta company already had at Calgary, was continued when amalgamation took place, and another office opened at Edmonton. Cars of stock handled in certain years selected for example have been as follows: 1916-17, 1,217; 1918-19, 5,257; 1920-21, 6,065; 1922-23, 6,850. On February 15, 1923, a cattle pool was launched by means of which cattle, instead of being sold in mixed lots at the stock yards to the highest bidder, will be sorted out and sold to suit the purchaser, either locally, in the United States or Eastern Canada, or in the markets of Great Britain and Europe.* An extra profit of 3.11 per cent. was made for farmers in the West during the first four months of this pool's operation. *The Livestock Marketing News*, of July 28, 1924, reported that: "The Co-operative Cattle Pool for the year which closed June 30, 1924, realized a net profit over the initial valuation of cattle, after paying expenses of handling, of $30,974.33."

Proposals looking towards a union of the great co-operative enterprises in the prairie provinces was seriously considered in 1915, but failed of realization when the Saskatchewan Co-operative Elevator Company, baulking at the terms, withdrew from the negotiations. However, the Alberta company, which had been operating its elevators and running its trading and live-stock departments at a profit, agreed to join with the Grain Growers' Grain Company in order to form a new organization to be entitled United Grain Growers, Limited. The charter of the Grain Growers' Company was amended in September, 1917, to legalize the change of name, fix the capitalization of United Grain Growers, Limited, at five million dollars and provide that shareholders might hold as many as one hundred shares of stock. It also became essential that the shareholders should group themselves into local

---

*Pool managers prefer to ship export cattle from Winnipeg to the markets of Great Britain and Europe by way of Quebec rather than Montreal. The distance to Quebec is twenty-two miles less than to Montreal over the Canadian National Railways, and sixty-five miles shorter than the Winnipeg-Montreal route of the Canadian Pacific Railway. Besides the run to Quebec is easier on the cattle, the railway yards are less congested, and loading facilities are better. But cargo steamers do not care to stop at Quebec unless they can load something else than live stock. Undoubtedly as the market for Canadian cattle develops with the lifting of the British embargo, this expeditious route will come more prominently into use.

societies for the purpose of delegating their voting powers. There were at the time approximately thirty-five thousand shareholders and these were divided among 336 locals. T. A. Crerar was elected president of United Grain Growers, Limited, and C. Rice-Jones, formerly of the Alberta company, first vice-president and general manager. It will be remarked that this amalgamated organization is actually a joint stock company with the co-operative feature of limiting the share-holding capacity of its members. Its delegate system of representation, of course, keeps an effective check on its managers who are merely salaried officials. The company has the legal right to distribute its profits on a patronage basis, but so far has made no use of this privilege. Instead, it has placed the major portion of its undivided profits in a reserve fund, at the same time making liberal grants to the provincial associations for educational purposes. Shortly after the amalgamation the company's reserve fund stood at one million five hundred thousand dollars. Its latest sub-sidiary, a securities company, was formed in 1917, which developed: a land commission agency to buy and sell farms at a uniform margin of profit; an insurance department to write hail and other kinds of insurance; and minor departments to deal with farmers' estates and investments.

Deflation following hard upon the war and, to an extent, adverse crop conditions were hurtful to United Grain Growers, Limited, between 1919-22, although in only one year did it have an actual loss over the whole field of its operations. The lumbering venture in British Columbia proved to be the company's "white elephant," when, after spending large sums of money on equipment, it suddenly found the prairie farmers unable to buy lumber and had to stop cutting logs in November, 1920. Plans to open retail lumber yards at prairie points were of necessity halted. The co-operative supply department suffered through shrinkage of inventory values and lessened business, especially in its farm machinery section, so that this and several other unprofitable lines were closed out in 1921-22. Losses were sustained for similar reasons in operating the British Columbia Agency, and in consequence it was sold when a buyer for it appeared in October, 1920. It was also necessary to drop the land com-mission department of the securities company, when its use-fulness waned in times of depression. The balance sheet of United Grain Growers, Limited, for its fiscal year ending on

August 31, 1922, indicated a net loss of over one hundred and eighteen thousand dollars; heavy appropriations meanwhile had brought its general reserve down to one million, two hundred thousand dollars. Nevertheless, a marked return of prosperity was shown in its report for the following year.*

CO-OPERATION IN SASKATCHEWAN.

After having been in business for a year the Saskatchewan Co-operative Elevator Company established a commission and sales department at Winnipeg, during August, 1912, and soon became a prominent dealer on the Grain Exchange. But, unlike its sister organizations in the West, it has consistently refrained from entering into any activities other than the operation of elevators and the marketing of grain. Its annual report for the year ending on July 31, 1914, presented just as the nations were on the verge of war, showed that it was operating 192 country elevators through which, during the preceding twelve months, it had handled nearly twenty million bushels of grain. In 1915 the company began to discuss the advisability of procuring for itself terminal facilities on the lake front. The financial side of the matter was fully canvassed, and, when the locals had given their assent, contracts were let for the erection of a mammoth elevator at Port Arthur. This terminal, which had a capacity of two million, five hundred thousand bushels, was the first to be built by an organized farmers' company in Canada; it was opened to receive grain in January, 1918, and a boat finished loading at it for the eastern markets on April 22. Subsequently a private hospital elevator with a capacity of six hundred and fifty thousand bushels was completed alongside the terminal in February, 1919, and as business grew a two-million-bushel storage annex constructed to be ready for the crop of 1920.

J. A. Maharg remained at the helm of the Saskatchewan company from 1911 until his acceptance of the portfolio of Agriculture in the provincial government in 1921; he was succeeded in the presidency by Hon. George Langley. In the meantime various men have held the office of managing

---

*The company's profits for 1922-3 amounted to $532,171. During the year it handled nearly 33,000,000 bushels of grain through its country elevators and more than 26,000,000 bushels through its terminals. The sawmill in British Columbia was allowed to resume operations on a moderate scale. On August 31, 1923, the company had 35,880 shareholders and a paid-up capital of $2,821,305; in addition to terminal elevator "H" and plant, it owned 234 country elevators, 237 flour houses, 195 coal sheds and 8 supply sheds. The elevators leased from the government of Manitoba now number 123.

director. Frederick W. Riddell was appointed to that position when C. A. Dunning became Treasurer of the province in 1916. Afterward, in 1918, Riddell went to the Board of Grain Supervisors, and James Robinson was chosen in his stead. Finally Robinson resigned in 1922 to accept a place on the Board of Grain Commissioners and J. B. Musselman, until then secretary of the Saskatchewan Grain Growers' Association, followed him in office.

An amendment made to the company's charter in 1913 fixed the maximum stock dividend it might declare at ten per cent.; stockholders might now hold up to twenty shares rather than only ten shares as heretofore. Each year since the company has paid a dividend of eight per cent. As a rule there have been considerable surplus profits for disposal after sums have been deducted for elevator depreciation, and obsolescence in the case of the terminals. One half of any surplus, it has been observed, must be put in an elevator reserve account, which on July 31, 1923, amounted to $1,765,975. A shareholder on joining the company has only to pay down fifteen per cent. on a fifty-dollar share, or seven dollars and fifty cents, and it has been customary to distribute the other half of the surplus profits as a stock bonus to help liquidate the eighty-five per cent. unpaid. Under this plan, as the result of annual accretions, shares originally allotted before April 1, 1912, were rated in 1923 as worth thirty-seven dollars and fifty cents.

The Saskatchewan Co-operative Elevator Company's objection to entering into a union with the other western companies in 1916 was that it did not approve of their proposal to have one central selling agency in Winnipeg, but thought that each provincial concern, retaining part of its individuality, should market its own grain through the Exchange. In 1920 it expanded its activities by seeking incorporation for a subsidiary, the Saskatchewan Co-operative Export Company, which was given control of its public terminals at Port Arthur. Later, two additional export companies, the Stewart subsidiaries, were formed, one with supervision of the hospital elevator at Port Arthur, the other operating under an American charter with headquarters in New York City. In 1923 a second large storage annex was completed on the lake front, and public terminal elevator "B" leased from the Canadian National Railways. The total storage capacity under the company's control at the head of the lakes was thus brought to over fifteen million bushels. The question of declaring a patronage dividend was taken up at the annual meeting in November, 1923, but action withheld.*

In order that its numerous locals might be given an opportunity to enjoy the benefits of co-operative merchandizing, the Saskatchewan Grain Growers' Association set up a trading department in 1914 to carry on a supply business in lumber and other building materials, coal, binder twine, wire fencing, machinery, groceries, etc. The original intention was that the locals should buy in car lots, allocating their purchases immediately among the members; but many locals adopted the custom of keeping stocks of goods on hand, and some even opened retail stores. At the outset, the department was capitalized on the Rochdale plan and dividends distributed on a patronage basis. However, it was thought advisable to set aside a sum each year to build up a contingency reserve. As prices soared during the war, it became necessary to secure more working capital for the department through the sale of debenture stock with a prior claim on the assets. The Saskatchewan crop failure of 1918 gave the department a severe setback, and as a result it had to draw upon its reserve to meet losses arising from a carry-over of binder twine in a falling market. For the time being things had a serious aspect, but those in charge rose to the occasion. Retrenchment was then practised, and the department ran on an even keel until 1922, when it again suffered through a depreciation in the value of its stock of tractors and other machinery which led to a considerable impairment of capital; a small profit was recorded in 1923.

Saskatchewan has other important co-operative organizations with which the Provincial Grain Growers' Association has maintained close fraternal relations. These include: the Saskatchewan Co-operative Creameries, Limited, which has an array of cream-receiving branches, egg and poultry plants and cold storage warehouses throughout the province; the Saskatchewan Stock Growers' Association, formed for the marketing of live stock; and the Saskatchewan Municipal Hail Insurance Association, whose activities have been described.

*During its business year ending on July 31, 1923, the Saskatchewan Co-operative Elevator Company, Limited, had consigned to it 42,880,425 bushels of grain. Its profits amounted to $442,212, and those of its subsidiary companies to over $200,000; its shareholders numbered 23,286. The company was operating 388 initial elevators.

THE PROBLEM OF THE WHEAT POOL.

The sale of the Canadian wheat crop of 1919 through the instrumentality of a government board taught the farmers of the country a lesson in the potentialities of centralized wheat marketing which has been the occasion for no end of agitation since that date. A résumé of the steps leading up to this venture on the part of the government may be given. In the winter of 1916-17 the Royal Commission on Wheat Supplies in Great Britain made overtures to Canada for the purchase outright of her 1917 crop, but as there was a forty cent. difference between the price asked and the price offered negotiations fell through in March. Shortly afterward the Canadian government, much to the delight of the organized grain growers, took the import duty off wheat and thereby gained for that commodity free entry into the United States, which meant an immediate equalization of prices between the two countries. British buyers were now bidding for wheat in the competitive market so that prices went up by leaps and bounds. By May, quotations for cash wheat at Fort William were ranging as high as three dollars, and the government, foreseeing that regulation of the situation was imperative, authorized the appointment of a Board of Grain Supervisors on June 11, with wide powers of control over the disposition of grain, including the right to fix the maximum prices at which it might be sold. This board brought about a cessation of all trading in futures on the Canadian exchanges, and set the maximum Fort William price at which No. 1 Northern and Alberta Red Winter wheat might be sold from September 12, 1917 to August 31, 1918, at two dollars and twenty-one cents a bushel; proportionate prices were arranged for the other grades. Again, the following year maximum prices for the 1918 crop were fixed from two dollars and twenty-four and one-half cents a bushel downward.

A price-fixing commission had also been at work in the United States and continued to function with respect to the 1919 crop. But the Canadian government decided on another plan for 1919. Authority was given on July 31 for the erection of the Canada Wheat Board which, in addition to its other duties, was intrusted, through its chairman, with the task of selling the year's crop at the highest available world prices. James Stewart was gazetted chairman of the board and Frederick W. Riddell, vice-chairman, while included in its personnel were H. W. Wood, and Col. J. Z. Fraser. A plan was devised by which the farmers were to receive a cash payment on account for their wheat of one dollar and twenty-five cents a bushel, and at the same time were guaranteed a minimum Fort William price of two dollars and fifteen cents a bushel for the season's yield. In exchange for their deliveries the farmers had issued to them participation certificates by means of which they might collect the balance due to them after the grain had been finally marketed by the board. In this way a compulsory pool was created for all wheat grown in Canada during the year. The pool return for No. 1 Northern wheat was two dollars and fifty cents a bushel to each farmer who had delivered that grade; this was estimated to be considerably higher than the average price obtained by farmers in the United States.

In January, 1920, the Canadian Council of Agriculture put forward the plea that the coming season's crop should be handled by the same national marketing agency, as the grain trade of the world was still in an abnormal state and de-control had not taken place in Europe. Though the government held out little hope that it would accede to this request, it assumed the power on June 24 of continuing the board by proclamation "if circumstances made it advisable." However, no sooner had Hon. Arthur Meighen been elevated to the premiership than announcement was made, on the sixteenth of the month, that, owing to the fact that trading in December options was being allowed in the markets of the United States and that control in Europe had already become isolated in its character, the government intended to finally dissolve the Canada Wheat Board. Meanwhile, prices were tumbling on the exchanges, and the grain growers kept clamoring for government action. The Toronto *Globe* lent support to the government's policy on September 22, stating that "the market should be left to find its natural level," and that to raise wheat prices artificially would be "class legislation and bad economics." Again, in October, the Council of Agriculture made another appeal for a national board, and about the same time the Saskatchewan legislature, at the instigation of Hon. George Langley, who said that wheat prices had fallen seventy-five cents a bushel, indicated its desire that the government should market the residue of the crop.

Then, sensing the hopelessness of its endeavor to secure a re-establishment of national control, the Council of Agriculture decided to appoint a small wheat markets committee to investigate the possibilities of building up a centralized marketing system upon the basis of the co-operative agencies existing in the West. H. W. Wood, who acted as chairman of this committee, had made an intensive study of co-operative marketing as practised by the raisin and citrus fruit growers of California. The committee reported that for a selling agency of wider scope to operate successfully it must require that the farmers should "sign a legally enforceable contract to turn over to it all their wheat for a period of five years;" that "contracts must be secured covering at least sixty per cent. of the wheat acreage"; and that "adequate financial arrangements" must be made. This plan was referred to the grain growers' associations, where it excited a good deal of interest, but was dropped by the Council in 1921 as under the circumstances impracticable. In March, 1920, Premier W. M. Martin, of Saskatchewan, put a series of questions to James Stewart and F. W. Riddell on wheat marketing problems, which drew from them a joint reply that was published in May. In elaborating their opinions, these two experts, while not condemning the long-term contract pool, hesitated to recommend it, pointing out that it would fail unless scientifically and carefully managed and well backed financially. If an experiment were made in co-operative marketing, they would advise that it should be in the way of a voluntary pool. Their own personal conviction was that the most effective form of centralized agency would be one controlled and financed under government auspices.

A great diversity of views on the wheat marketing issue had now grown up in western Canada. Sentiment among the rank and file of the grain growers, it would appear, was preponderatingly in favor of a compulsory pool with national control. But those especially interested in the larger co-operative ventures were less inclined to welcome governmental intervention or were even hostile to the idea. Hon. T. A. Crerar, leader of the Progressive group in parliament, said that he did not believe in national marketing as a permanent policy, although his followers were not all like-minded. During the summer of 1921 the prices of high-grade wheat ranged from one dollar and seventy-five cents to one dollar and ninety-five cents, but when the new crop had been harvested they began to sag, and by the end of October were only a few cents above the dollar. It was at this juncture that the little prairie community of Sintaluta became once again the cynosure of western eyes. On September 8 its local grain growers' association held an emergency meeting at which a campaign was launched for a reconstruction of the wheat board "with no diminution of the ample powers conferred upon it" as the only remedy for the untoward situation. The adjoining rural municipality of Indian Head lent its aid, funds were collected, E. A. Partridge plied his facile pen, and a widespread appeal was made to enlist the sympathetic support of the West. A month later the country was in the throes of a general election in the midst of which Partridge crossed swords with Premier Meighen, who had come out as an advocate of a voluntary pool which the farmers might use, if they were so disposed, in preference to the regular selling agencies. Partridge averred that the Premier's scheme had "fatal weaknesses," while Meighen retorted that it was the only "concrete and understandable" proposition before the farmers.

When parliament opened in January, 1922, with the King administration in office, an insistent demand for another wheat board came from the Progressive benches during the debate on the speech from the throne. The government sought legal advice regarding the constitutionality of a board that it might create, only to discover that its field of action in the matter was delimited by the powers that had been assigned exclusively to the provinces. Nevertheless, it sponsored a bill in the House of Commons in March authorizing the formation of a Canadian Wheat Board of ten members as soon as two or more of the provinces would endow it with the faculties necessary to its existence. What the government really did was to pass accessory legislation, leaving it to the provinces to add the feature of compulsion and shoulder the financial responsibility. Ex-Premier Meighen's criticism of this measure as a "jumble of jargon" and a "famished, deformed monstrosity," was rather far-fetched, but another reference to it as an "emasculated" bit of legislation was more or less to the point. The bill became law in June, and a few weeks later special sessions of the legislatures of Saskatchewan and Alberta were called to make the board an actuality; the United Farmers' government in Manitoba, fresh from the polls, remained inactive. But when the Premiers of Saskatchewan and Alberta endeavored to procure the services of a man qualified to head the board, one after another declined in quick succession. Apparently those to whom the position was offered were fearful of the undisguised hostility of the Winnipeg Exchange and of the grain trade generally, the facilities of which they knew they would require, and were also aware that difficulties might be encountered in making proper financial arrangements. The Premiers accordingly had to report failure to Ottawa and the project was abandoned.

THE ALBERTA CONTRACT POOL.

Nevertheless the three grain growers' associations refused to give up their fight for a compulsory wheat board, each of them in turn repeating the demand for it at their annual conventions of 1923. The Manitoba body, however, influenced by Premier Bracken, recorded its opinion that a wheat board could at best be only a temporary expedient, and that the final solution of the problem lay in the realm of co-operative marketing. Bracken said that he was prepared to advise the formation of a compulsory board for one year only, after which a voluntary co-operative system must be inaugurated. Expecting concurrence to this extent from the government of Manitoba, the Houses of Assembly of Alberta and Saskatchewan for the second time put through legislation to enable a board to function. But when Premier Bracken fathered a non-government bill in the Manitoba legislature, embodying the conditions that he had set forth, to the dismay of wheat board advocates it met with defeat on April 27, by twenty-four votes to twenty-one. The unenviable ordeal, therefore, again faced Premiers Dunning and Greenfield of having to seek to establish a two-province board, and, as in 1922, they found it impossible to secure a suitable chairman. They abandoned their efforts on June 22 with the statement that Manitoba's unwillingness to acquiesce would leave trading in futures on the Winnipeg Grain Exchange as usual, and make the operation of a compulsory board very hazardous.

Despite the propinquity of the harvest season, organized grain growers of Alberta and Saskatchewan still hoped that a large volume of the 1923 crop might be marketed on a co-operative basis. On July 4 the U.F.A. directorate in special session resolved to launch a voluntary contract wheat pool, and shortly afterward responsible officials of the Saskatchewan body decided to do likewise in their province. A general committee was appointed in each province to canvass the situation and as a result Saskatchewan dropped out of the race for the year, when it was discovered that an insufficient number of its grain growers were ready to sign contracts. On August 18 the Alberta Co-operative Wheat Producers, Limited, was incorporated under the Co-operative Associations Act of Alberta, and after coping with a great array of difficulties had its pool fully operative by the end of October. It had fallen somewhat short of its objective in gaining signatories, but, nevertheless, had gone on. Wheat growers who signed an agreement with this association covenanted to deliver all their marketable wheat to it for a period of five years. The association became the growers' sole agent to receive, handle and dispose of their wheat which they might mix, condition, blend, etc., and upon which they might borrow money. If an amount equal to fifty per cent. of the wheat acreage under crop in 1922 were not signed up by September 5, the individual growers could withdraw from the terms of the contract or the association itself might decline to proceed. Subscribing growers were assessed three dollars apiece when signing up, of which two dollars went to organization and other expenses, and one dollar to purchase a share of stock in the association. One per cent. might be deducted from the selling price of the wheat by the association to build up a reserve, and two cents a bushel from it for the institution of a company to acquire grain elevators. H. W. Wood, who has headed the wheat pool organization in Alberta, told the U.F.A. convention on January 15, 1924, that the enterprise had encountered opposition, but that this had "acted as a stimulant." If the contract signers at local shipping points were loyal, he said, permanent success was assured.

During its first year of operation the Alberta pool marketed thirty-four million bushels of wheat at prices which brought a substantial gain to the growers. Administration costs amounted to one half a cent a bushel. On January 9, 1924, the United Farmers of Manitoba decided to organize a pool to handle the season's wheat crop; the Alberta model was taken, except that in Manitoba only forty per cent. of the acreage need be signed up. The co-operative association formed in Saskatchewan began in 1924 where it had left off the previous year, and by July 1 had exceeded its fifty per cent. acreage requirement when it had contracted to handle the wheat from six and one-half million acres. A central selling agency has been incorporated at Ottawa for the three provincial pools under the title of the Canadian Co-operative Wheat Producers, Limited. Marketing by pool bids fair to become general in Canada as a result of the experiments made in connection with cattle and wheat. At its 1924 convention the U.F.A. appointed a committee to inquire into the feasibility of marketing other farm products than wheat on this plan, and in Ontario the United Farmers' Co-operative Company, Limited, set up an egg pool on April 1, 1924, for the immediate or future sale of eggs consigned to it by individual farmers or circles, and a seed pool four months later.

CHAPTER XXVII

Entrance into Provincial Politics

THE DOMINION government's nonchalant repulse of the huge farmers' delegation that had visited Ottawa in May, 1918, gave rise to an attitude of mind in rural Ontario which is scarcely susceptible to analysis. Grimly and silently, at one moment, the farmers seemed to brood over the indignities heaped upon them or their representatives on that memorable occasion. The next moment, they became loudly protestant. In the past, to be sure, they had quite often met with courteous refusal from a government in power, had even been mildly insulted by ministers of the Crown, but never had the door been slammed so vigorously in their faces. Had they no part whatever in the political life of the nation other than to cast their ballots for men who straightway forgot their existence? Why should there be such a wide gulf yawning between producers on the farm lands of Canada and the administrators of its affairs? These and similar questions began to aggravate the deliberations of farmers' clubs throughout the province, and the call went up for a repudiation of the partyism which in their opinion had left the agricultural toiler politically without hands or feet.

Revolt was imminent: its standard was raised in a little-to-be-expected quarter. Among several provincial bye-elections scheduled for the early autumn of 1918 was one in the constituency of Manitoulin Island, for many years a Conservative stronghold. Already a number of farmers' clubs had been formed on Manitoulin Island, which acting solely on their own initiative now took counsel together and decided to bring out an independent candidate in the person of Beniah Bowman, an old-time settler. Bowman went at his campaign with a will, advocating among other things: direct legislation, civil service reform, abolition of patronage, and the public ownership and operation of all utilities. The government led by Sir William H. Hearst, scenting the determination of these island farmers, dispatched several of its most talented speakers across the waters of Georgian Bay to save the riding, but to no avail.   Election day, October 24, found Beniah Bowman a victor at the polls by a majority of two hundred and forty.

About the time that Bowman was breaking new ground on Manitoulin Island, organized farmers in the western section of Middlesex County, meeting at Adelaide village, propounded regulations which they thought should govern the entry of the U.F.O. into politics; these they sent out to the clubs for their consideration.   Candidates brought out by the clubs, they advised, should adhere closely to the United Farmers' pro- gramme, and, having waged a campaign "without regard to the convenience of other political parties," should be prepared, if elected, to sit in opposition.   On February 5, 1919, J. J. Morrison, speaking at Mount Albert, pointed back to the day when three-fourths of the members of the Ontario legislature were farmers—a day when the debt of the province had been insignificant; but the farmers had lost control of the governing power, and it had passed "into the hands of other people, who were more used to spending money."   On February 18, J. W. Widdifield was put in the field as a non-partisan, United Farmers' candidate during a bye-election in North Ontario, and won by four hundred and eighteen votes.   The Canadian Council of Agriculture, having observed these happenings in Ontario with interest, resolved, on April 1, that the several associations grouped under it might have full freedom of action with respect to political matters of a provincial nature.

The fact must be emphasized that responsibility for pro- pelling the U.F.O. into politics in this wise had lain, not with the head office which had only given assistance upon request, but with the individual clubs.   As no general election had been fought in Ontario since 1914, and it was common knowl- edge that one would be held shortly, the farmers were on the *qui vive* to have as many candidates ready as possible.   Their leaders professed that the organization would be an entirely independent factor in the contest, looking neither to right nor left.   E. C. Drury in this connection specifically stated on June 26 that no amalgamation was contemplated with "the defunct Liberal Party."   "Go into politics, or go out of farm- ing" was the attitude of mind among the rank and file of the membership.   J. J. Morrison's services were in constant requisition, and, as he flitted from place to place, the unhappy effects of rural depopulation on the state of agriculture was the burden of his oft-sung jeremiad. "Where are the girls and boys who should be here?" he exclaimed at Walkerton on July 31. "Gone to the city! (Under the policy pursued by the old parties the concession lines have been bled white." A provisional platform, written for U.F.O. candidates by W. C. Good, E. C. Drury and Manning W. Doherty, was issued on August 31. In addition to stressing the evils of rural depopulation and the burden of increasing public debt, it advocated: the banishment of party patronage; improved facilities for rural education; the construction of good roads; a scientific policy with reference to the provincial forests; effective control over hydro-electric development; and the introduction of the principles of direct legislation and proportional representation. Nominating conventions were held by the U.F.O. clubs in sixty-four ridings. Premier Hearst and his colleagues, living in fancied security, held that the political uprising among the farmers constituted no menace to their rule. They were immeasurably astonished therefore, as was the province generally, when, on October 20, forty-four U.F.O. candidates were elected to the government's twenty-six.)

The Farmers in Power.

(The Conservatives forthwith resigned, and the organized farmers, having the largest group in the legislature, were asked if they could form a government. As a working alliance with either of the old-line parties was precluded, the farmers had to decide whether they would sit as an independent body in opposition or attempt to govern by a temporary coalition with another occupational group, the members-elect of the Labor Party. Traditionally, certain bonds of friendship had existed between farmer and labor organizations in the province; each were avowedly in favor of the principles of co-operation and of the governmental control and operation of public utilities; accordingly it was thought that a loose alliance between them might be practicable. The outcome was the establishment of a Farmer-Labor government on October 29 with Ernest C. Drury as Premier. The personnel of the cabinet, announced on November 14, had been arranged on a *pro rata* basis to consist of: two labor members and eight U.F.O. representatives, one of whom, Hon. W. E. Raney, a practising lawyer, had been brought in to serve as Attorney-General. The question of appointing an outsider to the post of Minister of Education was mooted for a time but abandoned.

Into the Farmer-Labor government's term of office, destined to last but three years and eight months, were crowded an array of legislative and administrative changes of which only a brief survey may be given. Ontario, at the time, was woefully behind several of the other Canadian provinces in the enactment of social laws, a matter which the new government at once took in hand. Acts were passed in 1920 to provide for the payment of adequate allowances to mothers with dependent children, and to authorize the formation of a board with power to ascertain the working conditions and to fix the minimum wages of women and girls in Ontario employments. Measures of 1921 and 1922 gave protection to children born out of wedlock, guaranteed the maintenance of deserted wives and children, and insured support for dependent parents. Moreover, a reorganization of the Provincial Department of Health was effected in 1920, by which its functions were expanded so that it might accomplish work of a scientific nature in respect to maternal and child hygiene, public-health nursing, and venereal and occupational diseases.

The government's policies were largely shaped by the findings of specially-appointed commissions or committees of investigation. In 1920 a commission headed by Judge T. F. Sutherland, of the Ontario Supreme Court, was empowered to make an exhaustive inquiry into all the problems relating to the suggested construction of electric radial lines in the province. In the hope of ultimately gridironing Ontario with radials the Hydro-Electric Power Commission had already authorized about three thousand miles of proposed track to be surveyed, at a cost of three hundred thousand dollars. A majority report of the Sutherland commission presented in July, 1921, declared that these lines would not be self-supporting, and since they would run parallel to and compete with the Canadian National Railways, to proceed with them would not only be "unwise and economically unsound," but a blow to government ownership. The administration at once refused to guarantee the bonds necessary to go ahead with the project. A committee of the legislature appointed, with J. G. Lethbridge (West Middlesex) as chairman, to "devise a more equitable system of distribution of Hydro-Electric power and a more uniform price," completed its report to the government in November, 1920.

It stated that though a flat rate for power was inadvisable, by a system of zoning and by other methods the high rates charged in rural districts and small urban centres might be lowered. It advised the creation of a Department of Power under a minister, and a rental of two dollars a horse-power per year on all power generated from waterways in the province. The government was unwilling to go the length of these proposals, but by legislation passed in 1921 agreed to pay up to fifty per cent. of the cost of rural transmission lines and cables upon the recommendation of the power commission.

At the request of Hon. Manning W. Doherty, Minister of Agriculture, a special committee was selected in 1920, composed of Professor W. T. Jackman, of Toronto University, Thomas McMillan and M. H. Staples, to inquire into the question of establishing a system of agricultural credits. As a sequel to its lengthy report a savings institution was authorized in the province under government guarantee with the privilege of opening branch offices where money would be taken on deposit at four per cent. interest, and of lending its funds for agricultural purposes.*   Supervision of all loans made was to rest with an Agricultural Development Board. Long-term credits were to be handled directly by the board, whereas for the negotiation of short-term credits farm loan associations might be set up in the rural districts, financed in part by the government and in part by the farmers themselves. Another commission, whose members were Hon. F. R. Latchford and Hon. W. R. Riddell, two justices of the Ontario High Court, was appointed to investigate the administration of the Crown lands of the province during the Hearst government's regime. This inquiry, termed by Hon. G. H. Ferguson, Conservative leader in the legislature, an "infernal farce," brought to light various malpractices and frauds in the administration of the provincial forests which had led to the sale of much valuable timber in Northern Ontario at sacrifice prices.   Litigation was instituted by the Drury government and as a result over one million dollars recovered for the provincial treasury.

---

*Figures for the fiscal year ending in 1923 show that the board had lent $3,729,350 during the year on the long-term plan to 953 applicants.   The security offered was considerably more than double the amount lent.   About one-third of the loans were made in New Ontario.   Sixteen local associations were in operation in the province for the negotiation of short-term loans; these had lent $310,975.   The provincial savings institution has proven very popular, especially since certain of the chartered banks of Canada have been in difficulties.

Hon W. E. Raney proved a very energetic law officer: his department became a storm centre owing to his attempt to vigorously enforce the Ontario Temperance Act, his five per cent. tax on the pari mutuel betting system, and the restrictions which he otherwise sought to place on race-track gambling. The Minister of Agriculture distinguished himself by his furtherance of co-operative activities among farm producers, his efforts to secure suitable immigrants for Ontario's farm lands, and his personal interest in having the British embargo against Canadian cattle removed. The Department of Education's most noteworthy achievement lay in its decentralization of university education in the province; attempts, however, which it made to grapple with the problem of rural education were disappointing. An ambitious programme of road building throughout Ontario was undertaken by the Department of Highways under the direction of Hon. F. C. Biggs. A plan was formulated whereby responsibility for road construction and upkeep was so distributed that the township councils looked after the lightly-travelled roads, the county councils after the chief routes to local markets and the province after those highways where the heaviest volume of traffic might be expected. The government subsidized all work on the roads by varying payments. It contributed twenty per cent. of the cost of the township roads, forty per cent. of the cost of those under county supervision, and assumed sixty per cent. of the financial outlay necessary to construct the provincial highways. The cities had to bear a share of the cost of the provincial highways and of suburban roads. When the government went out of power considerably more than one-half the roads of Ontario had been surfaced in an up-to-date manner.

DISCORD AND DEFEAT.

Reference has already been made to the friction which arose between the U.F.O. executive and the government in May, 1920, over the government's bill for the superannuation of public servants. Objections raised to this measure by J. J. Morrison were branded by the Toronto *Globe* as an unwarranted attempt at dictation. The U.F.O. directorate, coming to Morrison's rescue, stated that his actions had been "thoroughly democratic and in keeping with" their organization's policy to allow a free rein to discussion on all public issues.   Hardly had this dispute died down when another of weightier consequence sprang up, revolving round the question: what principles should determine the further evolution of the political movement that the U.F.O. had gotten under way?   Premier Drury, speaking on June 15 at Orillia, declared that the existing Farmer-Labor alliance must emerge into a distinct party based upon a "broadening out" idea. Eleven days later J. J. Morrison affirmed at Hespeler that this would serve the ends of "a Liberal plan to steal the U.F.O. party." On December 3 the Premier addressed a throng of banqueters at Chatham, reiterating his view that the party which he led must "broaden out" from its agrarian channels. "If I were asked," he said, "to name the new party which will ultimately develop, I would call it the People's Progressive Party and take in everyone." A delicate situation had arisen, and in order to insure outward calm at the U.F.O. annual convention which opened on December 15 a private meeting of reconciliation was held beforehand. But mid-January found Premier Drury again outlining his conception of a new party, and Morrison, in a strongly-worded reply at Wilton Grove, reviewing the circumstances under which Beniah Bowman had been sent to the legislature, asserting that the farmers had gone into politics "for equal rights and a fair representation," and asking whether the Premier was "ashamed of the people who made him."

Premier Drury's attitude in the controversy was that there were many in the towns and cities who accepted the ideals of the organized farmers, but who could not be included in their party unless it abandoned its class appeal.   A "broadened out" party might rule, he argued, through controlling the legislature, and translate its policies into reforms; an occupational group would suffer the disabilities of a minority body.   Morrison's contention on the other hand was that the farmers had revolted against the shackles of a partyism that cut vertically through the classes, with one class always holding power; that they were seeking justice for their industry and economy in administration by means of agricultural representation, and that they should keep to their original course.   Nevertheless, he was ready to admit those in other walks of life who would endorse the farmers' principles. On July 13, 1922, the Premier wrote a letter to his legislative followers suggesting that a conference be summoned at which the proposed party might be formed, and "broadening out" defined. The majority of the house members were agreeable, but the U.F.O. directorate and *Farmers' Sun* hostile. Secretary Morrison once again took the warpath. "We are not seeking domination," he exclaimed at Delta on August 17, "—we are seeking fair representation for the basic industry of this country." A truce was then patched up lasting until the annual convention of 1923. The convention when it met reaffirmed its adherence to the policy of constitutional autonomy, and resolved that it would not sanction the creation of a new political party.

The "broadening out" controversy, though occasioning some bitterness, had been in the main a domestic problem for the U.F.O. and had hardly gone beyond the pale of the academic. But early in 1923 symptoms of disharmony upon another issue became observable among United Farmer members of the legislature, which as they headed out brought on a parliamentary crisis. The government had all along won a measure of support from Liberals in the house and from certain Liberal journals in the province. The gravamen of the dissentients who now appeared in the government's ranks was that Premier Drury had in mind a fusion of their group with that of the Liberal Party. In March, W. H. Casselman (Dundas) left the government benches, to be followed by Andrew Hicks (South Huron), U.F.O. whip, who on April 14, amid the excitement incident to such an event, delivered a long address in which he renounced the leadership of Premier Drury, charging him with having plans for a fusion with the Liberals under advisement and with being "in the open market." The Premier and F. Wellington Hay, Liberal leader, both categorically denied that any such negotiations had ever been conducted. The government, however, under the circumstances, decided on an immediate dissolution and an appeal to the electorate on June 25.

The downfall which awaited the Drury government at the polls had several major causes. Uncompromising variance on the "broadening out" issue, and internal strife among the legislative group leading to public accusations with respect to a fusion with the Liberals, must each have taken its toll of votes from the U.F.O. harvest. More especially did farmers who had been one-time Conservatives in their political faith go back to the old allegiance. Then there was the unmistakable, though to an extent defensible, fact that costs of government had been mounting in Ontario in a day of agricultural depression. Everywhere the farmers spoke of the eighty-six foot wide, provincial highways which had been built as a tourists' luxury and an intolerable burden on the taxpayer. The manner also in which prohibition was voted out in Manitoba on the eve of the Ontario election no doubt influenced the results to the advantage of the Conservative Party who were apparently the hope of the liquor interests in the province. Only seventeen U.F.O. candidates survived on polling day, which brought a Conservative triumph of magnitude.

It was thought that a heavy battle would be waged over the question of "broadening out" at the tenth annual convention of the U.F.O. in December, 1923, but, instead, the organization took refuge in the statement that it would henceforward confine its attention to social, economic and educational matters and abandon political action. But it would not oppose the formation of a political party that embodied its ideals. Just before the Ontario legislature opened in February, 1924, Hon. Manning W. Doherty was selected as house leader of the U.F.O. group. As the result of disclosures made before the Public Accounts Committee of the legislature in the spring of 1924 Hon. Peter Smith, Provincial Treasurer during the Drury regime, was on May 22 committed for trial before the Court of Assize charged with conspiracy to defraud the province in connection with the sale of succession-duty-free bonds, and with breaches of the Secret Commissions Act.

Alberta in the Van.

The western trail toward independent political action was first worn smooth by the organized farmers of Alberta. The U.F.A. from its inception had had the idea that it might finally enter politics, but had remained aloof while the war was on. Nevertheless mention may be made of the fact that when the Sifton administration placed its record before the electorate in October, 1917, Louise C. McKinney, a member of the Non-Partisan League, contesting Claresholme, and James Weir, a second vice-president of the U.F.A., running in Nanton as an independent farmer candidate, were both elected with substantial majorities. The former, who was the first woman returned to a governing body in Canada, had left her signed resignation with the League in order that she might be subject to "recall" in case there

22—F.M.

should be objection to her policies. Largely through the public utterances of these two members and sympathetic aid lent by H. W. Wood, interest among the farmers of the province grew so rapidly in favor of taking independent action that the matter was thrust into the forefront at the eleventh convention of the U.F.A. at Calgary in January, 1919. The assembled delegates passed a resolution stating that such action was now necessary to their continued progress; the local unions in each federal district were urged to hold regular conventions where ways and means of carrying out their political purposes might be discussed; and candidates for office were to be nominated wherever possible.

Beginning at Medicine Hat in March, 1919, conventions were successively held in all the twelve federal ridings of Alberta before midsummer. On July 25th a separate Political Association was formed at Calgary with the avowed intention of giving cohesion to this side of U.F.A. activities. As a provincial bye-election was pending in Cochrane, the Political Association bent its energies towards the election of Alexander W. Moore, whom the local unions in the riding had brought out as their candidate. Moore, after a stiff fight, won by a one hundred and twenty-seven plurality. During the contest Hon. Duncan Marshall had appeared as a leading apologist of the Liberal government in which he held the rank of Minister of Agriculture, while H. W. Wood had matched wits with him on behalf of Moore. On October 21, speaking at Crossfield, Wood had set forth the articles of his political faith in a clear-cut speech which attracted attention all over Canada. He believed, he said, that the farmers should seek admission as a class into the legislative halls of the country just as soon as they developed leaders who were capable of representing them intelligently. Labor and other occupational groups should also have membership, in each case commensurate with their individual strength. Economic justice could only be obtained by an equilibrium of interests. Should the farmers desire anything through the medium of legislation to which they were not entitled, they would then meet with resistance from the other classes, and "a common level" would eventually be reached on that particular issue. The Political Association took umbrage at Wood's bold expression of opinion, and when the U.F.A. convention of 1920 met it was packed with nearly fourteen hundred delegates, as it had been noised abroad that an onslaught would be made upon his position in the organization. When Wood declined to preside at the meeting, Herbert Greenfield, of Westlock, was appointed to the chair. Balloting for the presidency occurred on the third day of the convention and Wood received five votes to his opponent's one. He explained that in no wise did he favor class domination or legislation, but at the same time contended that economic class organization was the greatest discovery made in relation to social progress. A resolution, by the Carstairs local, was accepted, pledging the convention to "the policy of group economic class organization as the only sound basis upon which to build a democratic form of political action." An immediate result was the dissolution of the Political Association.

The economic group idea was strenuously denounced by such newspapers as the *Edmonton Journal* and *Calgary Herald*, but was just as staunchly upheld by the *Alberta Labor News*. Labor in Alberta preferred to consider itself as a homogenous, occupational group committed to its own policy, though prepared to co-operate with the U.F.A. in either provincial or federal elections. As the Stewart government's term of office would run out in 1921, the U.F.A., at its annual convention of that year, decided to gird itself fully for the fray, and on nomination day in July had forty-eight candidates in the field. The government's record had been on the whole satisfactory so far as the United Farmers were concerned and they made little attempt to assail it, resting their appeal rather upon the need for a new viewpoint with respect to the principle of representation. Under the party system, they argued, an ever-widening breach was becoming manifest between the rulers and the ruled. Their representatives, on the other hand, dare not isolate themselves since they would be "at all times answerable directly to the organization." The U.F.A. went into the contest without a titular leader, yet, acting through its fifteen hundred clubs, had better election machinery than the government. Over three-fourths of its candidates were returned, with the result that when the parliamentary session opened in January, 1922, it had a voting strength of forty-two in the House. Herbert Greenfield, an Englishman by birth, with thirty years of farming experience in Canada, was chosen premier. Among those in the cabinet formed were: Mrs. Walter Parlby, a representative of Labor, and Hon. J. E. Brownlee, a member of the legal profession, as Attorney-General.

POLITICS IN SASKATCHEWAN.

Due to a somewhat unique situation in Saskatchewan the attitude of its organized grain growers towards participation in provincial politics has evolved otherwise than in Alberta. The presence of both Hon. W. R. Motherwell and Hon. George Langley in the Liberal Cabinet of Premier Walter Scott had tended to inspire good relations between the Grain Growers' Association and the government. Subsequently when Premier W. M. Martin assumed office in 1916, he had placed two more members of the organization in his Cabinet and had assiduously cultivated its friendship. Under these circumstances little thought of openly combating the government was entertained, and the association may be said to have adopted a policy of benevolent though watchful neutrality. Still this had no bearing on its action with reference to entering federal politics. The annual convention of 1919 resolved that facilities should be provided to enable the farmers in each federal riding to organize, if they so desired, to select candidates for the House of Commons in the next Dominion election who would subscribe to the national platform of the Canadian Council of Agriculture. Constituency committees were at once formed, and these, meeting at Regina on July 31, created a Provincial Executive which established its own office and set about collecting funds for campaign purposes. The Saskatchewan Grain Growers' sweeping victory in the federal elections will be chronicled elsewhere.

The Saskatchewan association has never taken a stand in favor of the economic class idea of representation so popular in Alberta; in fact, Secretary J. B. Musselman evinced a firm opposition to this principle in a speech delivered at the 1920 convention. Delay was counselled in determining the association's policy with respect to engaging in provincial politics at the same meeting and the question referred to the locals for judgment. However, there was a poor response to the queries sent out, and the issue was again left in abeyance after a heated debate in the annual convention of 1921. In April of that year J. A. Maharg, president for a decade of the Grain Growers' Association, resigned his seat in the House of Commons and was appointed Minister of Agriculture in the provincial government. J. B. Musselman gave out the information that Maharg was not going into the Cabinet as a Liberal; in fact, he endeavored to point out that there was a distinct line of demarcation between the brand of Liberalism at Ottawa and at Regina. Premier Martin, having his Cabinet already well filled with grain growers, appealed to the electors in June, and was returned to power a few weeks before the United Farmers captured Alberta. A miscellaneous throng of independents had run in the Saskatchewan election, including four representatives of the Non-Partisan League.

A situation had thus been created which lacked permanency. In September a dispute, which had arisen between Premier Martin and Hon. George Langley over a detail connected with the administration of justice in the province, reached an acute stage and led to Langley's retirement. Meanwhile the Progressive Party had grown active in the Saskatchewan ridings in view of the forthcoming Dominion election. Premier Martin agreed that his legislative supporters might take sides for the federal Liberal Party or the Progressives as they saw fit. This arrangement worked well until Martin himself delivered an address on behalf of Hon. W. R. Motherwell, who was running in Regina as a Liberal. Bitterly incensed at the Premier's participation in the campaign, Hon. J. A. Maharg announced his resignation from the Cabinet on December 5. In consequence the Saskatchewan association in 1922 decided to organize for provincial election purposes, and during the 1923 session of the legislature Maharg became the leader of a group of sixteen members in opposition to the government of Hon. C. A. Dunning, Martin's successor in the premiership. But, when again the issue was raised for discussion at the 1924 convention in Moosejaw, the association, in order to keep peace in the family, resolved to go out of provincial politics. However, there is still a farmer group in the Saskatchewan House in opposition to the Dunning administration, led now by Harris Turner, member for Saskatoon.

ACHIEVEMENTS IN MANITOBA.

After the fashion of its sister organizations in the more westerly Prairie Provinces, the Manitoba Grain Growers' Association had also made bold to tempt fortune in the federal arena during 1919. When preliminary steps toward the organization of the fifteen federal constituencies of the province had been completed, a representative gathering was held at Winnipeg on October 17, where a Political Executive was formed and arrangements made for a campaign of education among the electorate. But as yet, so far as provincial politics were concerned, the inclination of organized grain growers in Manitoba had been to lend support to the government headed by Hon. T. C. Norris, himself a farmer from near Griswold. Events, however, occurring in the adjoining province of Ontario could not escape the observation of Manitoba farmers. Their political morale was visibly strengthened as they saw the United Farmers of Ontario ensconced in power at Toronto during the autumn of 1919, with the result that when they met in convention in January, 1920, their attitude on the provincial situation had changed considerably. Though the Manitoba association hesitated to wade in as deeply as had the U.F.O., it was now willing "that the question of taking provincial action be left entirely to the initiative of each local constituency." Furthermore the convention resolved that, if a majority of the Manitoba constituencies should give evidence of a desire for concerted action, a meeting would be summoned to formulate a provincial platform. A few delegates, eager for a more aggressive policy, thought that their organization was feeling its way too slowly and was still hewing wood and drawing water for the Liberals.

A provincial election was set for the end of June, 1920, and for it twenty-six independent farmer candidates were brought out in an unsystematized and desultory fashion. They were minus a uniform platform, being dependent mainly on local issues and the fact of their agrarian status. Some had only the official backing of a section of the grain growers in their constituencies. But in spite of these and other handicaps fourteen independent farmers were elected, making their group the strongest of four in the house. Having co-ordinated their policies, they chose William Robson (Glenwood) as their leader. Though the Liberals found themselves without a clear majority over all possible opposition, Premier Norris was able to carry on during the session of 1921 owing to the decision of the farmers not to embarrass his administration. Then came the federal election campaign, in the course of which the farmers' desire to support the Liberals was alienated and the result of which in the Manitoba ridings had given them a new vision of their organized strength. The session of 1922 accordingly developed into a nightmare for Premier Norris while the groups manœuvred for his downfall. Eventually, on February 14, the government was defeated on a want of confidence motion by twenty-seven votes to twenty-three, and

Norris offered his resignation.   Upon urging he struggled through until the close of the session.

A general election was arranged to fall in July, and in preparation for this the United Farmers of Manitoba issued an elaborate platform, and perfected their organization. Official candidates to the number of forty were brought out in the rural constituencies, while eight Progressives, so-called, who had adopted the U.F.M. platform, ran in the city of Winnipeg.   Labor also had a conglomerate array of economic class candidates in Winnipeg where proportional representation was given a trial in the voting.   The returns indicated the election of twenty-nine U.F.M. candidates and one Progressive, insuring them a working majority in the House. Various names were mentioned in connection with the premiership, but choice finally settled on President John Bracken of the Provincial College of Agriculture.   Of the Cabinet sworn in only one member had ever had any political experience.

Action in Other Provinces.

Organized farmers in the Maritime Provinces made their first entry into politics when, on July 27, 1920, the Liberal government, headed by Hon. George H. Murray, made its sixth appeal to the Nova Scotia electorate.   The United Farmers of Nova Scotia had only been in existence a few months prior to this date, and consequently felt themselves too unpractised to go into the contest officially.   However, a tentative platform was drawn up, and the local branches given freedom to participate in the election or not according to their own choosing.   The platform called for: a more advanced agricultural policy and an extension of agricultural education in the province; improved highways; an equalized system of taxation; conservation of the province's natural resources, including a scientific policy of reforestation; more acceptable co-operative legislation; abolition of the Legislative Council of Nova Scotia; higher salaries for school teachers; and a sixty days' notice of the date of provincial elections.   Of the fifteen United Farmers' candidates nominated seven were returned as follows: two each for the counties of Colchester and Cumberland; and one each for Cape Breton, Hants and Antigonish.   The party appointed Daniel G. McKenzie, of Malagash, as its leader, and forms, together with four Labor members with whom it co-operates, one-quarter of the legislature.   Largely through its instrumentality an exposure has occurred in connection with the outlay on provincial roads, widely known as the St. Margaret's Bay Scandal. A great sum of money is alleged to have been wasted or grafted in the construction of certain roads, but owing to lack of evidence no one has yet been incriminated. In 1922 Henry L. Taggart, United Farmer member for Colchester, introduced a resolution in the House, which carried, demanding the abolition of the Legislative Council. A committee of five was named, of which D. G. McKenzie was a member, to take the matter up with the Council, but the latter declined to recognize its disutility. As vacancies since occurring in the Council have not been filled it may be inferred that the policy will be to allow it to die through attrition.

A provincial election was also brought on in New Brunswick during 1920. The United Farmers of New Brunswick, though they abstained from forming a centralized political organization, ran a number of candidates who appealed for rural representation and employed the platforms and resolutions approved of in the annual conventions of the association. When the polls closed on October 9, it was found that seven of these had been successful, with distribution in the counties as follows: Carleton, three; Victoria, two; Westmoreland, one. A. Chase Fawcett, belonging to a family of Patrons of Industry fame, was selected as party leader. The farmers' group has been striving for greater economy in public expenditures and reduced taxation; Fawcett has declared that the movement which he represents is a protest against "extravagant ways of government by party machines, headed to a large extent by political adventurers."

CHAPTER XXVIII

THE ORIGIN AND ACHIEVEMENTS OF THE NATIONAL PROGRESSIVE PARTY

SUBSEQUENT to its formation in 1909 the Canadian Council of Agriculture was for eight or nine years the leading interpreter of the organized farmers' collective mind on national issues. This office it discharged faithfully, enunciating the farmers' demands at Ottawa, and offering leadership to the several provincial associations on questions of legislative import. Nevertheless it skilfully avoided the exercise of any agitative influence among the rank and file who belonged to the associations. Such a *modus operandi* had distinct advantages and might have been continued indefinitely had not the farmers themselves declared for a change. The outburst of fervor for independent political action which, as already noted, was so characteristic of the farmers' movements in Canada during 1919, sprang from within those movements and was in no sense dictated by the Council of Agriculture. However, by the issuance of well-constructed platforms on matters of Dominion-wide concern in 1916 and 1918 it gave guidance to the farmer's thinking, and to a certain extent motivated his desire to enter the federal political arena.

An enlargement of the Council took place in 1916 through the admission to it of representatives from each of the western Grain Growers' Companies, the *Grain Growers' Guide* and the United Farmers' Co-operative Company, Limited, of Ontario. Hitherto, the Council had enjoyed no revenues beyond the slender grants made it from the treasuries of the federated associations. Now its finances were put on an entirely different basis by the provision that the commercial organizations would be assessed a fixed charge per shareholder for its upkeep. At once, on August 1, a permanent office was opened at Winnipeg, with Roderick McKenzie as secretary in charge. On December 6 of the same year the Council promulgated a Farmers' Platform which was indorsed by each of the member associations in convention during 1917. This platform was a codification of numerous resolutions and recommendations accepted over a period of many years at the annual meetings of the farmers' organizations and by the Council itself. The major part of it was devoted to a statement of the need for a reform in the tariff laws of Canada, and was strikingly like a pronouncement made by the Council on tariff issues at Regina on October 24, 1913. The Farmers' Platform called for: a reduction of the British preferential schedule to a point where it would be fifty per cent. of the general schedule, followed by a uniform lowering of rates until there would be free trade with Great Britain in five years; the acceptance by Canada of the reciprocity agreement of 1911; a placing on the free list of foodstuffs not included in the reciprocity agreement of 1911, agricultural implements, farm machinery, fertilizers, coal, cement, lumber, vehicles, illuminating, fuel and lubricating oils; a material reduction in the tariff rates on the necessaries of life; and an extension to Great Britain of all tariff concessions granted to other countries. As these changes were expected to cut down the government's revenue, it was urged that additional funds should be acquired by: a direct tax on unimproved land values and natural resources; and by graduated taxes on income, inheritance, and excess profits. Besides the platform favored: the nationalization of all railway, telegraph and express companies in Canada; short-term leasing of natural resources by public auction rather than their alienation from the Crown; the initiative, referendum and recall; abolition of the patronage system; provincial autonomy in liquor legislation; and the federal enfranchisement of women already accorded the franchise in any province.

During the next two years several items in the Farmers' Platform were eliminated by having received legislative enactment. Then, the termination of the war brought problems of reconstruction upon which the Canadian Council of Agriculture deemed it imperative that the organized farmers should state their views. Accordingly the platform of 1916 was remodelled and made more comprehensive in its scope by the inclusion of a number of extra clauses in November, 1918. This revision, some sixteen hundred words in length, was dignified by the title of the New National Policy in contradistinction to the National Policy of protection of a former generation. The tariff proposals of the platform of 1916 were expanded or subjected to changes in phraseology. "An immediate and substantial all-round reduction of the customs tariff" was now demanded, and "unrestricted reciprocal trade in natural products with the United States along the lines of the Reciprocity Agreement of 1911." Household machinery at the solicitation of the organized farm women had been placed among the list of articles for which freedom of entry into Canada was sought. The platform also advocated that corporations protected by the customs tariff should be forced to state their earnings, and that all claims made by industries for protection should be publicly heard before a committee of parliament.

Upon the subject of inter-Empire relations the New National Policy was very explicit: it stressed the view that the dominions should form a "partnership between nations free and equal." It favored the establishment of a league of nations as an international organization for the maintenance of peace. Particular sections in the platform were devoted to recommendations concerning the demobilization and repatriation of returned soldiers, and the measures that should be taken to relieve unemployment in the urban centres. Other clauses urged: "a land settlement scheme based on a regulating influence in the selling price of land"; and "extension of co-operative agencies in agriculture to cover the whole field of marketing"; a check upon government by orders-in-council; a reform of the Federal Senate; a discontinuance of conferring titles upon Canadian citizens; a removal of press censorship and a restoration of the rights of free speech; publication of the facts of the ownership of newspapers and periodicals; proportional representation; the "opening of seats in parliament to women on the same terms as men"; and a "prohibition of the manufacture, importation and sale of intoxicating liquors as beverages in Canada."

THE BREAK ON THE TARIFF.

Another generation of agrarian leaders had come upon the scene since the demolition of the Patrons of Industry at the turn of the century, and in the meantime that organization's political exploits had been reduced to a vague memory. For almost two decades the question of securing independent farmer representation in the legislative bodies of Canada had lurked far in the background. Indeed, upon two occasions only, during the interval, does the matter appear to have reached the stage of public discussion. When the Farmers' Association of Ontario was formed in 1902, as has been pointed out, Alfred Gifford and others had pled for a renewal of political action. Again, in 1910, Frederick Kirkham, of Saltcoats, Saskatchewan, in letters to the *Grain Growers' Guide*, argued for the creation of a farmers' party, a suggestion very unpalatable to certain members of the Saskatchewan association who were in the provincial Cabinet. Kirkham's contention was that the two historic parties, though engaged in factional strife, were quite happy when making common cause against the organized farmers, who, therefore, must not confine themselves to industrial activities. "We have," he wrote, "too long sacrificed our interests to the Moloch of factions, and verily we have paid dearly for it." It may be presumed that the advanced complexion of the Canadian Council of Agriculture's tariff proposals of 1913 was disturbing to both the government of Sir Robert Borden and the Liberal opposition. In April, 1914, a slight reduction in rates to the advantage of the farmer was effected by the government, but this was only a tittle of what was demanded and, had not the war interposed, a political revolt might shortly have eventuated.

In 1915 the Canadian government, requiring increased funds for war purposes, imposed a surtax of five per cent. *ad valorem* on all goods entering under the British preferential schedule, and of seven and one-half per cent. on those coming in under the intermediate and general schedules. The farmers, who made up one-half of the consuming public, bore these additional levies with scarcely audible remonstrance. In the general election of December 17, 1917, a group of Westerners attached to the grain growers' movements were returned to parliament as supporters of the Union government. During the strain and stress of the final year of warfare this little coterie kept absolutely mum on tariff matters. Hon. T. A. Crerar, their unappointed leader, had, on October 28 previous to the election, been taken into the Cabinet as Minister of Agriculture. However, even had they so desired, these grain growers in the House of Commons could with difficulty have forgotten their pre-election views on the tariff. The New National Policy was published just eighteen days after the signing of the Armistice, a fitting reminder that the organized farmers of Canada had intensified rather than modified their views on the tariff issue, and were prepared to act upon them at the earliest opportunity.

The Western farmers' group at Ottawa discovered themselves in an awkward situation during the winter of 1918-19. The government held the claim over them that they ought to assist it in its work of reconstruction.   Yet, on the other hand, they could ill afford to ignore the growing dissatisfaction of their constituents who, as the drought-afflicted season's crop brought in its sorry yield, began to cry aloud against the exactions of the profiteer, the reckless extravagance of the federal government, and the burdens laid upon them by the highest tariff in force since Confederation.   This carking unrest, indeed, was being quickly superseded by indubitable signs of a political upheaval, as the United Farmers of Ontario, cheered by the success of their skirmish in Manitoulin Island, made ready to storm the citadel of Conservatism in their province, and each of the Western associations early in 1919 cleared the way for action on the part of their local bodies. The grain growers, if they hoped to remain in the Union government's fold, were faced with the necessity of repudiating the entrance of their organized brethren into politics, and moreover, unless the government diligently bestirred itself, of abjuring the terms of the New National Policy.   Under the circumstances the majority of them decided to recommit themselves to the social and economic creed which had been dear to them before the election and to await events.   The breaking point came when Sir Thomas White, Minister of Finance, introduced his first after-war budget into the House of Commons on June 5, 1919.

It had been currently reported that the Borden government purposed making enough tariff concessions to hold its Western following intact, but such were not in evidence. The Minister of Finance announced that the surtax on the British preferential rates would be entirely abrogated and that on the other schedules removed in part.   Aside from these steps towards fiscal "normalcy" little was done to meet the agrarian demands with respect to the tariff as set forth in the New National Policy.   Reductions amounting to two and one-half per cent. were made in the duties on certain agricultural implements and of five per cent. in the case of others.   The rate on cement was lowered two cents per hundred pounds in all schedules.   But mowers, binders, threshers and reapers remained dutiable at the old uniform rate of twelve and one-half per cent.   In order to palliate eastern manufacturers for these alterations the freight rates on goods shipped from Toronto to the west were equalized with those from Chicago into the same territory. Low tariff advocates resentfully declared that the government had only trifled with the question of fiscal reform and had offered insignificant relief to the consumer. "High protectionism," remarked the Ottawa *Citizen*, "is still maintained as the finance policy of Canada."

Hon. T. A. Crerar, having foreknowledge of the terms and tenor of the White budget, had transmitted his unconditional resignation to Premier Borden as a Minister of the Crown on June 4. "I am not in accord with it," he wrote concerning the budget, "and therefore cannot support it, either in the House or in the country." J. A. Maharg (Maple Creek), and J. F. Reid (Mackenzie), at once cast in their lot with Crerar, and when A. R. McMaster (Brome), a "free trade" Liberal, moved a tariff amendment during the budget debate, these three and other Western Unionists rallied to his support. On June 11 Crerar spoke at length in the House explaining his reasons for severing his connection with the government. How was it, he asked, that the implement makers of Canada were able to compete in foreign markets, sending out goods to the value of eight million dollars in one year, and at the same time required protection at home? The resolute band of independent agrarians, with Crerar as their putative leader, now shifted to the cross benches of the House of Commons and began to engage in sniping operations on any proposal which was not to their liking.

Meanwhile organization for political purposes went forward apace in Ontario and the West during the summer of 1919. As there were a number of vacant seats in the Dominion House, bye-elections were brought on in seven ridings during October. Independent farmer candidates contested three of these, and by achieving overwhelming victories in each case, gave irrefutable evidence that the new political movement which they represented had become a power in the land. Oliver R. Gould, a member of the Saskatchewan Grain Growers' Association, did battle against Hon. W. R. Motherwell, running as an independent Liberal in the constituency of Assiniboia, and on October 27 won by 5,224 majority. Herein lay the first exemplification of the fact that the prairie West was ready for a complete political metamorphosis. H. W. Wood, John Kennedy and E. A. Partridge were among those who had come to Gould's assistance, whereas ex-

Premier Walter Scott and Hon. Frank Oliver had spoken for Motherwell. In Ontario on the same day John Wilfred Kennedy, as a nominee of the U.F.O. clubs in the riding, carried Glengarry-Stormont against an Independent-Conservative candidate, and Thomas W. Caldwell, president of the United Farmers of New Brunswick, defeated a straight Union government candidate in Victoria-Carleton.

Meeting at Winnipeg on November 11 the Canadian Council of Agriculture gave full sanction to these efforts that had been put forth to elect members of parliament pledged to support the New National Policy, which it described as "based upon the broad, national, economic interest of Canada without respect to any class or occupation." It was decided to summon a conference representative of the various provincial associations at which the question of co-ordinating their political activities would be the main matter up for consideration. As December 9 was set as the date of a deferred bye-election in Ontario North, Robert H. Halbert, president of the U.F.O., was asked to contest that riding in the organized farmers' behalf. Halbert consented, though his home farm was in Dufferin County, and after a spectacular, nip and tuck fight worsted his Union government antagonist by one hundred and eighty-five votes.

The National Progressive Party.

The year 1920 witnessed the formation in Canada, under the auspices of the various farmers' organizations, of a separate political party for action in the federal arena. That this should be entitled a party in the ordinarily-accepted, constitutional sense has sometimes been disputed; yet owing to the fact that it has employed its voting power as a political unit to carry out its policies and has shown a desire to gain control of the government, the designation may stand uncorrected. On January 6 the conference proposed by the Canadian Council of Agriculture met at Winnipeg with one hundred delegates in attendance from the Western associations, the United Farmers' organizations of Ontario and New Brunswick and the Council itself, and gave birth to what it chose to call the National Progressive Party. No light task confronted the delegates when they sought to reconcile the sectional divergencies of opinion apparent among them. Representatives from Manitoba and Saskatchewan, where the Grain Growers' bodies were amicably disposed toward provincial governments of Liberal stripe, were much less independent in their viewpoint than those from Ontario and Alberta. The delegates from Alberta, headed by H. W. Wood, who presided at the conference, were strong for the economic group idea of representation, as were many from Ontario. After lengthy disputation a majority took the view of Hon. T. A. Crerar that the party must not stay too rigidly agrarian; Wood, therefore, and his following were put temporarily *hors de combat.* However, the conference's pronouncement on this issue was diplomatically moderate in tone. "We . . . do declare our intention," it ran, "of electing as many representatives as possible to the House of Commons at the next general election, who will endeavor to bring the farmers' platform into effect; and to this end invite the support and assistance of all citizens who believe in the principles enunciated in this platform." It was further stated that the New National Policy constituted "in no sense a vocational class platform," nor did the Progressive Party purpose making any "demand for special legislation to benefit the few at the expense of the many." So far as party organization was concerned it was agreed that it should "continue for the present to be conducted on the provincial basis" in accordance with the plans of the existing associations.

Upon diverse occasions within the next few months Crerar denied repeated accusations that the Progressive Party had been established to serve a class purpose, alluding to the breadth of its policies. "I challenge any member," he cried defiantly in the House of Commons on March 4, "to go through the new national platform and find any word or line in it which means class legislation." Meanwhile Wood, back among his unyielding Albertans, was talking in another strain. "We are now an economic group," he told the U.F.A. in convention at Calgary on January 22, "preparing to take action." Again, in an interview given to the Victoria *Times* on February 24, he said that the problems of economic class readjustment could only be solved by the classes themselves "with each class represented by expert representatives."

The fourth session of the thirteenth parliament of Canada opened on February 26, and six days later at a caucus of the independent agrarian members the National Progressive Party was organized as a distinct group in the House of Commons. Eleven cross-benchers attended, as follows: Hon. T. A. Crerar (Marquette); J. A. Maharg (Red Deer);

J. F. Reid (Mackenzie); Dr. Michael Clark (Red Deer); J. W. Kennedy (Glengarry-Stormont); Thomas MacNutt (Saltcoats); R. H. Halbert (Ontario North); O. R. Gould (Assiniboia); T. W. Caldwell (Victoria-Carleton); Levi Thomson (Qu'Appelle); and J. F. Johnson (Last Mountain). Having selected Hon. T. A. Crerar as their parliamentary leader, the group decided to follow an absolutely independent course, supporting or opposing the administration as circumstances should dictate. The party's first action was to marshall its strength in favor of a motion calling for an immediate general election. Sir Henry Drayton, now Minister of Finance, when he brought down his budget in May, stated that the tariff of customs would remain unaltered, but to supplement the revenues special luxury and sales taxes would be introduced and the excises increased. The Progressives at once flew to arms. "The government's policy," said Crerar on May 31, "has finally emerged from the clouds of doubt and suspicion and mistrust that enveloped it, and it stands revealed before the country. What is it? It is the old National Policy of protection." Drayton's so-called luxury tax, he said, was wrongly named, since it was "as much, and even more, a tax upon the necessaries of life." On July 10 Hon. Arthur Meighen replaced Borden as Premier and the term National Liberal and Conservative Party was now applied to the government's House supporters.

Through contesting bye-elections the Progressive Party added three to its number in the House during the first sixteen months of its existence. On April 9, 1920, Angus McDonald captured Temiskaming as a U.F.O.-Labor candidate. In November of the same year Sidney S. McDermand won an uphill fight in East Elgin against representatives of both the older parties, being unwittingly assisted in his campaign by Sir George Foster who, in an address at Aylmer on September 10, accused the organized farmers of allying themselves with ultra-radicals who would smash responsible government. Then in consequence of the death of Hon. A. L. Sifton, sitting member for Medicine Hat, the Progressives were given an opportunity to demonstrate their strength in Alberta. On June 27, 1921, Robert Gardiner, of Excel, who combined an advocacy of the New National Policy with the doctrines of the U.F.A., swept to victory in Medicine Hat on the crest of a mighty wave, receiving 13,133 votes to his opponent's 3,369.

Again, in 1921, Sir Henry Drayton, arguing that international trade conditions still lacked stability, left the tariff untouched, and centred his fiscal changes on an increase in the sales tax and a total abolition of the business profits tax; the luxury tax had gone by the board in December, 1920. Government members, mindful of the Progressives' growing strength, had begun to flay them unmercifully in the House, referring to them as a strategic wing of the Liberal opposition. On May 13 Premier Meighen described their leaders as "servile tools and minions" of the Liberal Party, "ready to do whatever they are bid to do;" indeed, they were merely a "delapidated annex" of that party. One Progressive member after another arose to deny these charges and to declare their unwavering independence. During the debate on the budget on May 17, Crerar made his third successive annual assault on the government's high tariff policies, this time adducing a mass of data relative to the mergers that had been formed in Canada, "under the alchemy of the stock promoter's wand," by manufacturers of shoes, glassware and paints. T. W. Caldwell (Victoria-Carleton), whose home in New Brunswick was six miles from the American border, gave the House an interesting sidelight on the crude outworkings of the tariff in his native province. A certain brand of fertilizer, he said, upon which the import tax was ten per cent. *ad valorem*, had been sold during the previous season from the mixing plant in New Brunswick at seventy-seven dollars and fifty cents a ton, whereas the quotation for the same brand in the adjoining state of Maine had been sixty-two dollars and fifty cents a ton. The chemical ingredients employed in mixing the fertilizer, however, enter Canada duty-free. Aware of this fact the organized farmers of New Brunswick, where fertilizer is in constant demand for the potato crop, had proceeded to import the necessary chemicals and do their own mixing. They had discovered that they could make fertilizer of the same quality at a cost of forty-six dollars and eighteen cents a ton, thereby saving thirty-one dollars and thirty-two cents on each ton.

On April 11 the government had announced the appointment of a royal commission to inquire into the Canadian grain trade. The Progressives acknowledged that beneficial results might flow from a properly-conducted investigation of grain-trade matters, but wondered whether the government was not seeking a means of discrediting the grain growers' commercial organizations, especially the company of which Hon. T. A. Crerar was president. Judge J. D. Hyndman, chairman of the commission, denied any ulterior motive, but the *Grain Growers' Guide* thought otherwise, and the Canadian Council of Agriculture on May 9, voicing its distrust, declared that only by "a prostitution of governmental authority" could such a design be carried out. The government press forecast was that the inquiry would lead to "revelations that would split asunder the organized farmers of the West." Having toured the prairies without anything sensational occurring, the commission suddenly appeared at Fort William on June 4, where it held what the grain growers later characterized as a private "hole in the corner" sitting. Former employees of United Grain Growers, Limited, called to give evidence, deposed that the company had been guilty of serious irregularities and wrong-doing in the conduct of its business affairs, had even used false bottoms in the weighing in of grain.

The fat was on the fire with a vengeance. Crerar hurried at once to Winnipeg whence he issued a statement, condemning the proceedings at Fort William as arbitrary, impugning the evidence taken, and affirming that his company had nothing to conceal from an impartial tribunal. Confirmation, he asserted, was lent to his suspicions that the commission had been selected "purely for political purposes" in order to do harm to himself and the grain growers' movements. United Grain Growers, Limited, which had willingly submitted its books for examination to the Federal Cost of Living Committee in 1919 and to the Price, Waterhouse audit of terminal elevators, now complained that in both these instances the information afforded had been "falsified into material for public attack." With an election in sight and great issues at stake the company resolved to protect itself against the danger of further, more virulent attack by taking legal action. Accordingly it applied to the Manitoba courts for an injunction to halt the proceedings of the commission on the ground that the order-in-council appointing it had been illegal. On June 22, after a wordy battle in the Supreme Court of the province, an injunction was temporarily granted and made permanent a few weeks later. The Hyndman commission abandoned its sittings and the matter expired in the Court of Appeal.

THE 1921 ELECTION AND ITS AFTERMATH.

The Canadian populace was now restlessly waiting for the Meighen government to go to the country. During the summer of 1921 the Premier crossed the Atlantic in order to attend an Imperial Conference. On September 1, on the eve of his departure from the British capital, he gave out the information that the parliament of Canada would be dissolved in the near future. The main election issue, according to his forecast, would arise from a divergence of views on the tariff, and in this connection he referred to the Progressives, to whom "free trade" was the breath of life, as the only genuine opponents his government must face. The sincerity of the Liberal's challenge on the tariff he doubted, since it was being made "with muffled drums and uncertain chorus." The announcement of an election was a signal for all parties to spring at once into action. Crerar began his campaign at Brandon on October 5 with a reaffirmation of his unalterable opposition to the principle of protection. He stood four-square for the system of government-owned railways, asserting that a plot was afoot to restore the lines already acquired into private hands. On October 15 he submitted a manifesto to the Canadian people in which he carefully outlined his party's attitude on tariff, immigration and transportation problems, and called for rigid economy in the administration of the public services and a co-ordination of the fiscal policies of federal, provincial and municipal bodies. As the campaign developed the Progressives emphasized the 1918 platform of the Council of Agriculture; they demanded a revaluation and recapitalization of the national railways, and cheaper freight rates; scornfully they alluded to the fact that twelve lawyers sat in the Dominion cabinet but not one farmer.

In anticipation of an early post-war election the Liberals had drawn up a comprehensive platform in convention at Ottawa during August, 1919. A tariff resolution had been accepted which declared that in the best interests of Canada it had become necessary (1) that duty reductions should be made to lower the cost of living and the cost of those instruments of production that were used in industries based on the natural resources; (2) that, more explicitly, nineteen classes of articles subject to duty should be placed on the free list, including agricultural implements and machinery, farm tractors, fertilizers and lumber; (3) that a downward revision of rates should occur on boots and shoes, wearing apparel,

August 1919
promises

and other necessary articles of consumption; and (4) that the British preferential schedule should be fixed at one-half the general schedule. Pledges were given that legislation would be enacted making these proposed changes effective. It may be noted, however, that Hon. W. L. M. King, in his election tour, confined his remarks in the main to the first point in the resolution, and said little or nothing about the other three. In fact, while in Prince Edward Island, he frankly admitted that the resolution was merely "a chart to guide" him on tariff matters. The Liberal leader's policy was to assail the government boldly but to treat the Progressives in a conciliatory manner, urging them to help him defeat a common enemy. For any form of group rule he had no sympathy. "The greatest danger which this country faces to-day," he said at Calgary on November 15, "is group control according to district, or by geography."

An incident of the campaign was the defection of Dr. Michael Clark, of Red Deer, who wrote Crerar that he could no longer follow him because of the class doctrines taught by the U.F.A. This fact was seized upon with avidity for electioneering purposes by the old-line party press. Crerar, moreover, had constantly to answer insinuations that United Grain Growers, Limited, had feared an investigation by the Hyndman commission. The government and Liberals each put over two hundred candidates in the field, the Progressives around one hundred and fifty. The Progressive total is harder to reckon on account of local arrangements often made with Labor and the semi-independence of various nominees. The election, held on December 6, marked the government's utter downfall, as only fifty of its candidates were successful. The Liberals who had made a clean sweep of Quebec and Nova Scotia obtained one hundred and eighteen seats, and were able to assume office. The Progressives were considered to have elected sixty-five members, distributed as follows: prairie provinces, thirty-nine; Ontario, twenty-four; British Columbia, three; New Brunswick, one. Agnes McPhail who ran as a Progressive in South-east Grey was the first woman returned as a member of the Canadian House of Commons.

Hon. W. L. M. King, when duly sworn in as Premier, sought to obtain representation from among the Progressives in forming his cabinet. While he did not suggest a coalition of parties, he intimated that the elevation of several Progressives to cabinet rank would materially assist the government in its conduct of affairs. However, a section of the Liberals with Sir Lomer Gouin as their guide and mentor drew together to checkmate this proposal, and the U.F.O. in convention on December 14 announced itself as firmly opposed to the Progressive Party losing its identity. The *Farmers' Sun*, waxing belligerent, stated that any alliance with the "anti-public ownership, high protectionist Liberal Party" was out of the question. By December 25 the Premier's negotiations had fallen through, and the Progressives made it clear that they would follow an independent course in the House, leaving the rôle of official opposition to the Conservatives.

The possibility of a working agreement being effected between Liberals and Progressives was again mooted during the summer of 1922. On August 5 the *Manitoba Free Press* pointed out that, while a fusion of the two parliamentary groups could hardly be expected, there was nothing to prevent them from pursuing certain specified objects in common. But for a second time the Gouin faction bared its teeth to the government, and a clamor of remonstrance came from the direction of the organized farmers. Crerar, who had favored a *rapprochement* with the Liberals, was now placed in an embarrassing position, and the rumor spread that he was on the point of retiring from the Progressive leadership, particularly as United Grain Growers, Limited, needed his undivided attention. At a conference of Progressive members of parliament held at Winnipeg on November 11 a letter was read in which he submitted his resignation and declared that he had only sought "honorable co-operation" with the Liberals, but had been impeded by those farmers "who from honest but mistaken motives" had thought rather of their class than the national welfare. Robert Forke (Brandon), a Scotsman who had landed in Canada as a steerage passenger in 1882, was then chosen as the party's House leader. In addition to having been a successful grain grower Forke had served a long apprenticeship in the municipal life of his province. The conference decided to accept into the Progressive Party any citizen of Canada irrespective of occupation who adhered to its principles. Nevertheless, when it came to the problem of organizing on a nation-wide basis, those who believed in the economic class idea waged a grim struggle and organization was left to the provincial associations.

THE TARIFF "COCKPIT" 1922-24.

To what extent by means of legislative action would the King administration implement its 1919 commitments on the tariff? This question gave rise to a highly-engrossing issue as the parliamentary session of 1922 advanced and the government's purposes were unfolded. The budget for the year was brought down by Hon. W. S. Fielding, Minister of Finance, on May 23. From its terms it became apparent at once that the influence of the Gouin bloc had been uppermost in the government's councils. Farmers were to be slightly benefited by reductions of two and one-half per cent. in the general schedule rates on the more important agricultural implements and of five per cent. in the preferential rates on tools. Some relief would be afforded consumers by a lowering of the duties on sugar, gasoline, woollen and cotton fabrics, rubber goods, and boots and shoes, but at the same time the sales tax was to be increased by fifty per cent. A tariff amendment moved by the Conservatives proved unacceptable to the Progressives, and Crerar, bluntly condemning the budget as protectionist, adduced a sub-amendment which the Speaker ruled out of order. On June 2 W. C. Good (Brant) dealt at length in the House with what he designated as the Liberal Party's unkept tariff policies since 1893. Had that party been insincere? he questioned. Or was it under the sway of tariff beneficiaries? Or had it honestly changed its convictions? A tense atmosphere pervaded Ottawa, and there were indications that the government might be defeated and forced to the country. On June 8, amid Conservative applause, Sir Lomer Gouin uttered a staunch defence of the protective principle. Fielding, in a last-minute attempt to save the situation, renounced the Gouin attitude on June 13, and presaged a further downward revision in the tariff rates. As a result, with the help of nine Ontario and British Columbia Progressives, the budget carried by eighteen votes when a division was taken on the following day.

The Liberals' protectionist wing was even more firmly ensconsed in power during the session of 1923. Beyond the fact that the British preferential duties which ranged above fifteen per cent. were lowered one-tenth on most goods imported by way of Canadian sea and river ports, and that a permanent offer of reciprocity with the United States in natural products was written into the tariff, the fiscal changes of the year were both few and insignificant. Tariff stability, said Fielding in presenting the budget, was the need of the hour for Canada. While the Conservatives satisfied themselves by picking flaws in the government's programme, the Progressives drew up in battle array. Robert Forke moved an amendment on May 14 which castigated the budget as "a repudiation of the tariff planks in the Liberal platform of 1919," and called for "an immediate and substantial reduction in the tariff, particularly on the necessaries of life and the implements of production." An increase in the British preference to fifty per cent. was demanded and a reciprocity agreement like that of 1911. A long list of Progressives projected themselves ardently into the debate. T. W. Bird (Nelson) thought that the only difference between a Liberal and Conservative budget was in "literary style." Forke's amendment was lost by one hundred and sixty-two votes to sixty-one. But, as the Conservatives refused to accept the budget it was passed by a margin of only eight votes.

Slowly the government began to realize that by sojourning in the protectionist camp and abjuring its 1919 tariff resolution it had forfeited a measure of its strength. The Conservative party had yielded no ground in consequence. As a matter of fact, the Conservative party was shaking off its lethargy during 1923, and, when in December bye-elections were brought on in Halifax, Nova Scotia, and Kent County, New Brunswick, entered into them with zeal untempered. To the government's chagrin both of these constituencies elected Conservatives, and it found itself with a technical minority of four in the House. Within a few weeks a startling metamorphosis occurred in the government's ranks. Early in January, 1924, Sir Lomer Gouin resigned his post as Minister of Justice, and in the absence of Hon. W. S. Fielding through illness Hon. J. A. Robb took charge of the government's fiscal policies. The way to tariff reform appeared open. Hon. T. A. Crerar and Premier Dunning, of Saskatchewan, summoned to Ottawa by Premier King for consultation, gave him an abstract of the Western farmers' views on national problems. The government was apparently facing in another direction. Would it redeem its pledges on the tariff?

As acting-Minister of Finance, Robb delivered his budget address on April 10. Of special interest to Canadian agriculturists were the substantial reductions which he said the government proposed to make in the rates of duty on implements of production used in the farming, fruit-growing, poultry-raising and dairying industries.   The general schedule rates on farm implements were to be lowered as follows: on mowers, harvesters, binders and reapers from ten to six per cent.; on cultivators, harrows, horse-rakes, seed drills, manure spreaders and weeders from twelve and one-half to seven and one-half per cent.; on plows and threshers from fifteen to ten per cent.; on farm wagons, from seventeen and one-half to ten per cent ; on field rollers, post-hole diggers, hay loaders, stumping machines, etc., from fifteen to ten per cent.; on axes, scythes, reaping hooks, hoes, rakes, etc., from twenty-two and one-half to twenty per cent.; and on spades and shovels, from thirty-two and one-half to twenty per cent.   Dairy machines, fruit growers' implements and incubators were to be taxed one-third less under both general and preferential schedules; fertilizers were to be put on the free list.   All these articles, in order that makers of them might be reimbursed, were to be exempted from the sales tax.   The Progressives welcomed the changes involved as a tangible step toward a relief from tariff burdens, although coming far short of their own objective.   Accordingly, as it received their almost unanimous support, the budget obtained a record majority of one hundred and twelve on May 16.   However, fourteen Progressives voted for an amendment moved by J. S. Woodsworth, Labor member for Centre Winnipeg, demanding tariff reductions of a more sweeping character.

PARTY RECORD ON OTHER ISSUES.

In 1922 the Progressives put forth unremitting efforts to secure a restoration of the Crow's Nest Pass Agreement which for years had regulated the more important Western freight rates.   By the terms of this agreement, framed originally in 1897, the C.P.R. had bound itself to accept a maximum schedule of rates on certain products originating in the West and on certain manufactured commodities shipped from the East in return for subsidies and concessions granted by the Dominion government.   Other railways, as constructed, had taken the same schedule as their norm.   But in 1919, owing to economic conditions, the government upon issuing a new Railway Act had suspended the agreement and allowed the Board of Railway Commissioners to fix rates on the commodities in question for a period of three years.   Under this plan rates had risen to a point fifty to seventy per cent. above the agreement level when the suspension was about to expire.

On May 4, 1922, the government appointed a select House committee to inquire into the feasibility of a reversion to the statutory schedule. Progressive members of the committee fought strenuously for a restoration of the agreement in *statu quo;* Conservative members urged that rate-fixing be left with the commission. By sheer obduracy the Progressives wrung from the committee a solution pleasing to the farmers of the West. Parliament concurring in the committee's report decided upon an immediate return to the agreement rates on grain and flour. Other commodities formerly subject to the agreement were to be freed from the suspension in at least two years, and meanwhile were to be awarded lower rates.

When, through the investigations of a royal commission in 1923, it was discovered that a monopoly existed in the fixation of lake freight rates on grain, Progressive members of parliament resolutely supported a bill compelling all ship-owners to file their tariff of rates and changes proposed thereto with the Board of Grain Commissioners,* and giving that body the right to prescribe maximum rates wherever discriminatory or excessive charges were noted. Alberta and British Columbia Progressives have also made strong pleas in the House for a reduction in the differential between the "mountain scale" and "prairie scale" of rates which has had the effect of lessening the profit on shipping grain westward to the Pacific. In keeping with its views on the question of public ownership the party at Ottawa has steadfastly defended the cause of the Canadian National Railways, arguing that without unnecessary governmental interference the system should be allowed to put itself on a basis of economy and efficiency. It has upheld the C.N.R.'s programme of branch-line construction, only to find that programme blocked by the Senate in 1923, and cut in two by the same body in 1924.

The presence of twenty-two Progressives on the Standing Committee on Banking and Commerce of the House of Commons has given that body a new fulcrum in parliamentary affairs. The work of the committee was widened in 1923 to include a general investigation of the basis, function and control of financial credit, and when important witnesses were brought before it they were questioned closely by the Progressives with a view to discovering upon what terms the

---

*By an alteration made in 1924 ship-owners were compelled to file their contracts with the board rather than their tariffs.

Canadian credit system might be remodelled. Backed by resolutions from the Canadian Council of Agriculture and the legislatures of Alberta and Saskatchewan, Progressive members of the committee fought strenuously to secure a revision of the Bank Act more to their liking. Their effort, however, to have bank charters granted for one year only met with failure, as did their attempt to have the maximum interest rate fixed at seven per cent. per annum. In 1923 W. C. Good (Brant) and J. L. Brown (Lisgar) endeavored to obtain amendments to Criminal Code which would make commercialized gambling on the race tracks of Canada illegal, but their motion was negatived in the House by ninety-six votes to seventy-six. W. C. Good has repeatedly sponsored resolutions in favor of the transferable vote in single member constituencies, and of a trial of proportional representation in multi-member constituencies, The government has promised that legislation authorizing the transferable vote will be brought down in the session of 1925.

Insistent demands have arisen from the Progressive benches that the completion of the Hudson Bay Railway be given priority over other transportation works undertaken by the government. Andrew Knox (Prince Albert), T. W. Bird (Nelson), D. W. Warner (Strathcona), C. W. Stewart (Humboldt), and C. C. Davies (North Battleford), have been especially assiduous in bringing the merits of the Hudson Bay route to the attention of the House. In 1922 Progressives voted to pare down the country's naval and military expenditures, and the same year were almost alone in supporting a resolution fathered by A. R. McMaster, Liberal (Brome), to the effect that Cabinet ministers should be debarred from holding directorships in private corporations. The government put through a new combines investigation act in 1923 with Progressive assistance, although Robert Forke was sceptical as to the efficacy of such a measure while Canada retained the protective features in her tariff. The Progressive Party as a whole have favored investigation under federal authority of the subject of agricultural credits with a view to possible legislation in that field. A section of the party has in each case voted for resolutions introduced into the House by members of the Labor group calling for: a restriction of the activities of the Royal North-West Mounted Police to the unorganized territories; and the abolition in Canada of capital punishment.

On May 14, 1924, a Conservative member of parliament told the House of Commons that the Progressives were the actual rulers of the country, and that the executive of government was "simply a Cabinet in custody." This pronouncement may be open to dispute, but the fact remains that the Progressive Party has obtained a strategic position at Ottawa which it did not occupy when the fourteenth parliament of Canada was convened in 1922. Dissensions, moreover, lurk in the ranks of the two historic parties on matters of policy. While the Conservatives have apparently submerged their differences on fiscal issues, they cannot achieve unanimity on the subject of public ownership. The Liberals are seriously divided both in their tariff policies and on the question of public ownership. The Progressives for their part are encountering difficulties of another sort. During the session of 1924 a few of their number established a separate group in the House complaining that they were being forced to act in too close agreement with the government. Early in July with Joseph T. Shaw (West Calgary), E. J. Garland (Bow River), and G. G. Coote (Macleod), as their leading spokesmen they strove to have the powers of the Committee on Banking and Commerce extended so that it might investigate the workings of a central or reserve bank. The *Grain Growers' Guide* has pointed out that no cleavage has occurred in the party on questions of fundamental policy. "Majority rule in caucus, whip domination, responsibility for leader's statements" and other matters of parliamentary organization and procedure, it said, has caused a divergence of opinion. It is expected that a national convention, when assembled, may heal the breach.

Surely the organized farmers of Canada will glean, some lessons from the past in this volume. It must be borne in upon their minds that the road toward justice for their industry has been long and tortuous, and that only through perseverance have they come so far upon their journey. Possibly they will discover how in days gone by they have frittered away opportunities leading to success, or through lack of vigilance have turned success into failure. They must learn that it is imperative that as individuals they should bury their personal ambitions whenever the common cause is at stake. Above all else, they must resolve to run their race with patience, holding fast under every circumstance to those principles to which they pledged adherence when their movements first came into being.

INDEX